TWEETING TRUTH
TO POWER

TWEETING TRUTH TO POWER

CHRONICLING OUR CAUSTIC
POLITICS, CRAZED TIMES, & THE
GREAT BLACK & WHITE DIVIDE

CYRUS MCQUEEN

Cover Design by Alfred Obare (Behance)

Cover Photo by Susan Ely

Library of Congress Cataloging-in-Publication Data

McQueen, Cyrus.

www.CyrusMcQueen.com

Hardback ISBN: 978-1-7355992-0-5

Paperback ISBN: 978-1-7355992-2-9

Ebook ISBN: 978-1-7355992-1-2

For all the women who made me who I am.

Hey baby, what'cha know good

I'm just gettin' back, but you knew I would

War is hell, when will it end,

When will people start gettin' together again

Are things really gettin' better, like the newspaper said

What else is new my friend, besides what I read

Can't find no work, can't find no job my friend

Money is tighter than it's ever been

Say man, I just don't understand

What's going on across this land

Ah what's happening brother.

— MARVIN GAYE

What's Happening Brother, 1971

Contents

Preface i

Introduction 1

1 Waking Up to a Nightmare 11

2 The Joke's on You 23

3 Big Gloves to Fill 35

4 Turning Back The Clock 49

5 Picking At The Scab 65

6 I Wanna Be, I Wanna Be Like Lebron! 85

7 Base Heads 99

8 Locked And Loaded 113

9 The Brotha From Another Planet 121

10 Black Ice 143

11 Color Struck 163

12 The Living Dead 171

13 Cop Blocked 187

14 Coloring Outside The Lines 201

15 On Pins And Needles 213

16 R-E-S-P-E-C-T 223

17 And Still I Rise 249

18 This Shit Won't Go Down 275

19 Funny Business 295

20 Call In The Plumbers 311

21 The Joke's On Us 335

22 "IT IS WHAT IT IS" 353

23 Black Lives Matter 373

24 Amerriccaaah Will Nevvah Be De Same 413

Acknowledgments 421

Preface

The election of Donald Trump and the coarsening of the national discourse embroiled me and many others in perpetual conflict on social media. Salvos among those entrenched across this landscape became routine and saw me attempting to both cope with this new normal and, simultaneously, to articulate exactly what this American moment *meant*. At the intersection of politics and social media, revanchists and members of "The Resistance" barreled toward one another on a bumpy, often perilous road. Communication lines almost bottlenecked as sites like Twitter documented a dangerous impasse. Black and White, liberals and conservatives, the kind and the combative—we all soon found ourselves on a virtual collision course, the daily pileup slowing progress to a halt.

Tweeting Truth to Power began under these inauspicious circumstances. Two years into a caustic tenure, having chronicled my day-to-day disappointments in a president who is careless at his best and dangerous at his worst, I found that my real-time responses neither sufficiently framed his actions nor provided the greater context that this moment represented. The historical implications of a country at war with itself, a nation polarized to the point that its inhabitants operated with differing interpretations of the truth, sent me spiraling into a prolonged depression. No doubt about it: the news was bringing me down. Though I did my damnedest to keep up with the shenanigans and shamelessness coming out of D.C., it only reinforced this feeling of helplessness, a feeling echoed by virtually all I engaged with. We were on a path we had not chosen.

Employing the serenity prayer almost unconsciously, forced to accept the things I could not change, I somehow located what little courage I had and began seeking to change the things I *could*. Initially, I found that humor alleviated those tensions and aggravations, but, at some point, it became clear that I could no longer sacrifice clarity for levity. Merely reacting to this president's output would never improve matters, *or* America. If social media and social responsibility were to offer any hope, they needed to be braided together. With Wokeness soon entering the American lexicon, those who embodied progressive

i

principles, found they could now tap into this greater potential, augmenting their messages with hashtags, and in the process, turn platforms like Twitter into a tool to undergird an anti-racism movement.

Although this wiser alternative found myself and others using our timelines to teach, the strictures of character limits forced us to leave a lot unsaid. Nuances were unexplored, patterns unrecognized, and, as far as Black America was concerned, there was much to glean from some four centuries of rich lessons and resolve—that which might inform not only our plight but also our eventual triumph.

Because the human struggle is in no way new, because despots have divided people for all of recorded history, because racial tumult *is* America's oldest pastime, this sort of repetition provided its own set of answers. Could the remedy for a sick country be found in a resilient people, having long overcome racist presidents and individuals? Even so, I realized, the concurrent pandemics of discrimination and disease did not easily lend themselves to short inspired bursts of writing.

Though I did not see it at the time, a burden had been placed on me, one that demanded I put down the damn phone. The psychic and spiritual toll turned me into a conduit, humbling and immobilizing me, my ancestors and a truth I was almost afraid to channel *plaguing* me. In my 40th year on this planet, which coincided with the 400th year of black life on this continent, my existence felt of consequence for the first time in my life. Amid the dark implications of contagion and a society at a crossroads, a time that reinforced everyone's sense of mortality, I weirdly felt part of a greater purpose. The powerful dictum of Toni Morrison—"I regard my responsibilities as a Black writer as someone who must bear witness—someone who must record"—spoke directly to my reluctant duty. My personal journey soon led me to look without and within, at America's past and my own—the stress, strain, and sleepless nights to follow the manifest of my desperate attempts to chronicle this trying moment. Through this process, I *unburdened* myself. Bearing witness does not encourage comfort, but I hope that my availing myself to these muses brings a measure of peace to others and, who knows, maybe even myself eventually.

Although Donald Trump is central to our unmooring, this moment is much bigger than him. As such, *Tweeting Truth to Power* neither minimizes those events that have contributed to this defining time nor fosters the notion that America's problems begin and end with Trump. I do not wish to overstate his imprint and, in so doing, mischaracterize an era defined equally by our politicians and those who vote for them—

those in our nation who underpin inequality through their own chronic indifference and hate.

As you progress through these pages, perhaps you will agree that I have progressed as well. In this shared journey, evolving over its chapters, the sophomoric humor endemic to the 2016 election, that which accompanied my early standup, graduates into a more sobering, more necessary account: one that speaks less to the folly of a president and more to *what* it means to be a Black American in the early 21st century.

Given the incessant deluge of news, the endless supply of stories, I could easily keep writing. In the last week alone, the legendary Supreme Court Justice Ruth Bader Ginsburg passed, Louisville indicted a police officer not for the murder of Breonna Taylor but for the shots that *missed* her, and oh yeah, Captain Dipshit intimated that he has no intention of honoring the outcome of the upcoming election. Thirty-six days before Election Day, the obvious question is whether Trump's loss will provide these pages with their logical ending. Well, in so asking, we could infer that this is a book about Donald Trump, but lest we make the mistake, he is a symptom of America's sickness; he is in no way the cause. In that respect, Trump is ultimately immaterial. Though four more years of a benighted president would spell doom, these past four years and all we have witnessed, all we have endured, stand on their own. Though I relish and anticipate his fall, and spy the surgical mask at the end of my table, I believe it is undeniable that analogous pathogens have long interrupted our lives. In the coming month the comorbidities plaguing the American electorate will indeed prove to have a major impact on our outcome.

But no matter what unfolds on or after November 3rd, the nation will be on the road to recovery for some time. I for sure plan to keep documenting it all @CyrusMMcQueen.

My only true solace is in the fact that eyes that have yet to open will, too, bear witness, and that they will one day chronicle their own awakening. May this record serve as a compliment to theirs, as others have been of undeniable benefit to me. Our continuance is indeed predicated on *this* connection. No matter where we find ourselves, the way forward is best divined by looking back.

— Brooklyn, New York

October 2020

INTRODUCTION

How do you begin to make sense of the Trump presidency? How do you begin crafting a comprehensive opprobrium to such a catastrophic administration? If you are a comedian, you start where all comedians do: the truth. And the truth of the matter is Donald Trump is an asshole. The kind of asshole even other assholes cannot stand. A man whose imperious rise was almost epically iniquitous. The sort of superlative scumbag who is a rare mix of off-putting and irredeemable, he a rebel with neither a cause nor a clue. It being impossible to overstate his odiousness, may I also posit that he is boorish, brain dead, dangerous, and devoid of humanity, humility or sophistication? He is a copper Caligula, an adult baby clad in a baggy Brioni suit, the type of base individual who wields the most rudimentary understanding of manhood and leadership: that it is all phallus and physicality, machismo, and misogyny.

But Donald Trump *is* the president of the United States. Though it very much pains me to write those words, it is the sobering reality we have been forced to contend with for the past (gasp) almost four years. Even now, as his scandals compound, his lies multiply, and the roughly 70 percent of Americans who did not vote for him (or did not bother to vote at all) are experiencing a plethora of emotions ranging from denial to disgust, all the way up to an all-consuming and visceral rage, the Commander-in-Thief has proceeded unabated along his corrupt and illogical path. I can only surmise that many have simply resigned themselves to this desultory fate—a fate earned through their own inaction and lack of purpose in the previous election cycle—and are now

1

merely conserving their energy to combat the conservative onslaught that is likely to commence come the fall of 2020.

One thing is certain: it is easy to grow weary with this White House. The man is simply too adept at distracting for the average American to withstand the inevitable torpor that sets in once, having finished moving the cards, he creates the hypnotic diversion that allows him to continue his flotsam flimflam, hustling his susceptible middle American marks in this all-too-consequential game of Three-card Monte. His bait-and-switch tactics, leading the media in a daily dance of shock and awe, have left even the most ardent among what has been dubbed the Resistance battle fatigued. That he continues to generate crowds for the circus he has fabricated out of the respect that once fortified the Oval Office is due in no small part to his crafty, clown-like abilities. However his ability to play ringmaster can be attributed to his deft use of that most powerful megaphone at his disposal: Twitter.

Trump has upended the prevailing paradigm for villainy. He projects, he publicly upbraids, and he *loves* to telegraph his next move. There is little to no nuance by way of expertly thought out or timed actions. And lest we forget, the man developed his base by *being* base. Therefore, if we wish to chart his rise to notoriety, it was from the unabashed, often slipshod manner in which he disseminated information through his Twitter handle. His sophomoric attacks on his predecessor provided this beast with the requisite oxygen to swell and begin gnawing away at our norms bit by bit. That he has grown into this larger-than-life, reptilian creature the likes of Godzilla, his fiery rhetoric causing inexorable destruction and distress to D.C.—in addition to every city, town, and country impacted by his tenure—is due in large part to the fuel that social media has provided this swamp dwelling monster.

It was his impetuous, imprudent attacks on the nation's first African American president that initially brought this reality show has-been to my attention. Like many, I believed that the election of Barack Obama represented a sea change in our politics. Even now, I get misty at the thought of that halcyon time, that salubrious period from late 2008 through the beginning of 2009 when the world very much did change for the better. His presidency offered a panacea for a hobbled nation. Ours, a country that had so often limped toward progress, was suddenly *running*. Like many African Americans and fellow progressives, I had viewed it as a watershed moment, a fortuitous culmination of events where the hopes and aspirations of people of color, those who had long suffered indescribable indignities at the inhuman hands of countrymen who treated our very presence as anathema, finally witnessed the planets align—*this* a sort of celestial conspiracy to, at last, create a healthier, more favorable future for us on this brutal terrestrial plane. And given their otherworldliness, I believed that he, his wife, and family would in many ways come to represent a guiding light: the Obama's would become akin to constellations, their arrival illuminating an otherwise ominous American horizon.

That this hero, this god among us, this most articulate, educated, and downright cool brotha could be so summarily maligned and undermined by a cantankerous entity like Donald Trump was perhaps presentiment, a likely presaging of how low America would eventually degenerate. The notion that "Hater's gonna hate" was one thing. That Haters would go on to *weaponize* their whiteness, using that uniquely American birthright to not only question your birth—the very validity of your existence—but subsequently set out to erase any evidence of it, jettisoning all that you had accomplished, while inexplicably supplanting you in your position as if to nullify your very transcendence, was quite another.

The ascension of Donald Trump, compounded by the vanquishing of any lasting vestige of Barack Obama, created an existential crisis for not only Black America but for this Black comedian who had parlayed an impression of our nation's first Black president into a radio and comedy career. Long before Trump darkened America's doorstep, I had found success as the in-house impersonator of the 44th president for several radio stations based out of New York City. Through trial and error and laborious study, I examined his authoritative yet thoughtful intonations. I practiced his unique cadence for hours in the bathroom, bouncing his most indelible words and phrases like "Change" and "Yes, we can" off the tiles until the acoustics convinced me I had fully captured his zest. Hell, my girlfriend at the time could have changed her name to Michelle, for after ascending the four flights of our walk-up, she would find herself ostensibly opening the door to Barry as I would greet her with a canorous, "How ya duh-in 'Chelle?" I had earnestly, almost embarrassingly, gone full-method in my quest to master my performance. I hadn't approached Daniel Day-Lewis levels of dedication—graying my temples, walking around in a navy-blue suit—but you get the picture. I sought out and perused any video I could find of the junior senator out of Illinois, plumbing the depths of the then-new video-streaming site *YouTube* for any and all output. Here I would pilfer their treasure trove, watching and rewatching what I could find, studying these gems intently, even intensely, as he distanced himself from his pack of fellow Democrats. My homework would soon be rewarded as he went on in triumph to seize the national stage, becoming the new crown jewel of the party, the *future* of a floundering country.

Obama's eventual win became a win for me. For eight glorious years, I got to do what I love: record songs and sketches as the man I loved and admired. Nearly every day I got to settle into a recording booth and channel his essence as I pored over pages and pages of comedic copy. When I finally endeavored to tackle stand-up comedy, I brought Barack with me. Taking to the stage, I possessed a nuanced, spot-on impression of the president in my bag of tricks, it never failing to dazzle or to procure the most coveted response every comedian seeks: sheer, unbridled laughter. Indeed, Obama would provide much-needed oxygen for those early performances, as I could simply erect a premise and proceed to inhabit that most popular and beloved of figures. The jokes may not have been very good, but my Obama *was*. Whether he was searching around the Oval Office for a pack of cigarettes he had hidden or playfully admonishing his daughter "not to use the red phone on daddy's desk to call friends," audiences responded with delight to these inspired act-outs, not least because the man himself was so incredibly infectious but because he was compelling to the point that his very *presence* was actually cathartic. Even an approximation of President Obama was enough to send effusive crowds into titters, this fulsome response somewhat guaranteed because the man was simply *that* adored. My subsequent success on stage became inextricably linked to his success in our greater cultural landscape.

The fastest eight years of my life have given way to the most plodding, ponderous, and *painfully* slow four-year period I have ever experienced. When Donald Trump descended that escalator in Trump Tower to announce his candidacy, little did we realize in that foretelling moment how far, too, our country would soon plummet—from heights of progress and empathy to maddening, disorienting depths of regress and antipathy. America was now experiencing a semblance of the bends. This jarring new reality was due in no small part to the fact that one simply could not design two more different presidents. One a unifier, the other a divider. One, an historic figure, the other, a man who mercilessly attacked and attempted to *destroy* that historic figure.

INTRODUCTION

Comparisons to a car crash were apropos considering the whiplash we experienced by the abruptness with which decency was destroyed, our sense of normalcy totaled; given how fast we went from first-rate to a fool, from the gold standard to *pyrite*. Trump in many ways was akin to a centrifuge, separating our citizenry so fast, and with such damaging force, that his whirlwind threatened to divide Black and white permanently.

Therefore, no one was more dismayed than I when this churlish man-child with the gross orange pallor, the habitual liar operating with limited vocabulary and virtue, remained the last punk standing after a crowded Republican primary. The realization that this peculiar son of a bitch had outmaneuvered an overfull pack of improper and ignorant men essentially by proving to be more improper and more ignorant than them—or any candidate I can recall—was not simply insane; it was *indescribable*.

In my quest to make sense of the nightmare unfolding before our very eyes, I began turning my attention to the microblogging platform that Trump himself had so successfully usurped and weaponized: *Twitter*.

Long before he had discovered the platform's inherent power and used it to sow discord, many comedians had uncovered its awesome potential for conveying our comedic thoughts and premises. Crafting a well-received joke within the then 140-character limit was in many ways a test of jocular dexterity. What was once limited to the literal stage grew to encompass this new, expanded, virtual one. Audiences no longer had to be in the room when you spat your silly asides into a microphone. Microblogging and its untapped potential had supplanted the microphone as a viable way to make *greater* numbers of people laugh. In an instant, your comedy could catapult around the globe like a virtual pinball, creating laughs along with likes and retweets—the map lighting up as those totals went up, the validity of your content spanning continents, its impact certified through its reverberation.

So, as Trump seized upon this nascent medium, the showman in me instantly recognized what was happening. He, too, was playing to a virtual audience in short (somewhat inspired) bursts. Although his often-mordant output typically veered toward the vitriolic, his 140-character drivel, often misspelled, often punctuated incorrectly, had become both a cudgel he could wield against his perceived enemies and an addictive drug he could effortlessly dole out to those within his strung-out base. It would be those junkies, those who began rocking MAGA hats and relinquishing their souls to sip this zealot's intoxicating concoction of xenophobia and sexism, who would send shivers down my spine. I knew all too well what the disastrous implications of this diabolical dance were, this highly problematic and most dangerous courtship, and how such race-based idolatry could portend the worst for a country that had yet to sufficiently address its own hellacious past, despite having twice elected an African American as president.

I wasn't wise or powerful enough to prevent the promised unraveling, but something primal in me, something instinctual, knew it was time to at least *attempt* to combat what was happening. It became time to shelve the dick jokes and begin crafting jokes about a *Dick*.

Cyrus McQueen @CyrusMMcQueen · Jul 16, 2016
How could a voter still be undecided at this point? Seriously. How many laps around the buffet do you need to see the T-Bone is undercooked?

⟲ 23   ♡ 104

When it became clear that Hillary Clinton would be facing off against Trump in the general election, I braced myself for the inevitable onslaught of misogynistic vituperation from the man with the hands and temperament of a toddler. I knew instinctively that Clinton represented a time-tested foil for the Republicans, and given the false alarm already sounded around her emails, I was aware that she posed a most vulnerable opponent.

That Trump would seize on those falsehoods was no surprise. That he himself would prove to be invulnerable after the revelation of his juvenile grandstanding on the set of *Access Hollywood*, *was*. The day that *Access Hollywood* tape dropped, it created a cataclysmic ripple in the 2016 presidential campaign. There it was, audio capturing Trump in all his crude, coarse, and prurient splendor. Seemingly impressed with his own imprudence, and touting his ability to violate members of the opposite sex, he even joked about popping breath mints so as to not offend the very woman waiting outside who was likely to *suffer* his offensiveness. The galling audio sent shockwaves through an already shocked electorate and presented me with some raw, unvarnished truth from which to mount an offense against this most offensive presidential candidate.

INTRODUCTION

Trump's petulance and pomposity would be on full display during the debates. The nation would see, in living color, the bombastic simpleton in all his sophomoric splendor. Seemingly unaware of the way he appeared, the Republican nominee sniffed, pouted, and nervously postured in front of the cameras. I can still recall how unsightly he appeared in his ill-fitting suit and barely constrained belly, the beads of sweat rolling rapidly down his jowls, he looking like a melting creamsicle; even the suspicious manner in which his eyes darted about, never quite fixed on the moderator or the assembled audience.

It was during these debates, after a hot mic in the back of that bus had captured his crudeness, that Trump, a man whose ego is only outmatched by his girth, attempted to loom behind Hillary Clinton on stage. His inability to recognize personal space or respect his female opponent seemed to corroborate the tapes very subtext; it spelling doom for his floundering campaign.

Cyrus McQueen @CyrusMMcQueen · Sep 27, 2016
Now #Trumps trying to say his microphone wasn't working well at #debatenight
? I'm sorry, I could hear him every single time he interrupted.

⟲ 151   ♡ 563

At this point in the fall of 2016, as we stood on the precipice of the election, Trump, perhaps sensing that his campaign was on life support given his plummeting poll numbers and the general sense that his particular brand of racism, rudeness, and misogyny was not playing well outside his base, took special steps to begin undermining the political process itself.

Ratcheting up his claims, he declared that not only was his opponent "crooked"—a descriptor that would prove indelible given the rapacious manner in which his followers gobbled it up—but also that our entire electoral system was, indeed, crooked. He began chumming the political waters with a particular kind of red meat that attracted and consolidated those within his own base most attracted to a skewed, conspiratorial assessment of a government they had vowed to distrust.

It appeared the Republican candidate was trying not only to cast enough doubt to create a plausible defense after his inevitable defeat, but at the same time, seeking to bolster an outsized ego that could barely stomach being bested at every turn by a supremely capable, supremely qualified female. That he would begin to accuse Clinton of benefiting from the system that had ensnarled her in senseless investigations surrounding her computer server sounded very much like the final cries of a baby whose candidacy was in its death throes.

As America rounded the corner into Election 2016 and pulled into the homestretch of an exhaustive campaign season that witnessed the country devolve into a caustic facsimile of itself, I, like many, braced myself for Hillary Clinton's eventual victory. Even though the cacophony created by Trump's sycophants, with calls of "Lock Her Up," never quite lost its momentum, even with the hacking of the Democratic National Committee revealing a party at war with itself, I *never* imagined that the nation would go for the fool's gold this golden-haired glutton offered.

Taking the stage during those final weeks of the election season, I sensed a spirit in every assembled audience. With the energy being so palpably fervent, I did not brace myself for the profound pendulum shift our society was on the precipice of experiencing. At this point, my material dedicated to skewering the orange skunk had proven so grossly successful, I assumed an auspicious electoral outcome. Audiences seemed in consensus about how much Trump stank. I can still recall a woman from Long Island nearly choking on her chicken when I compared Donald Trump to a Disney character.

Cyrus McQueen @CyrusMMcQueen · Jun 9, 2016
Today is #DonaldDucks ⌁ 82nd Birthday... Turns out he's not the only cartoon Donald with easily ruffled feathers and nothing below the waist.

⟲ 28   ♡ 78

I had now begun testing on stage material that succeeded on social media. Whether it was a virtual platform or a literal one, I was beginning to see how germane my assessments of our political discourse were. If the number of likes and comments a tweeted joke generated proved it effective, I could then use the comedy clubs to contribute to the distillation process. By finding the proven punch, I could extract the essence of a bit erected within a concrete character limit, then expand on it, adding call backs and tags given the freedom of an enlarged platform and performance window.

I was beginning to take the temperature of the country. I was getting a reading of how Americans responded to these disparate candidates and, more so, how they were likely to cast their ballots come Election Day. I sensed a hope within the electorate that we were progressing toward a more balanced future, one with a woman finally at the helm of the planet's most powerful country. I recall a bachelorette party in Manhattan chanting "I'm With Her" as I lampooned her offensive opponent. The atmosphere was energized, the rumble within the microcosm of the showroom indicating an even larger rumble taking place within the macrocosm of our country.

I felt the collective disdain diverse audiences held for this most combative and caustic of figures. Mothers from Illinois, old couples from Connecticut, nuclear families from Florida, all eating out of the palm of my hand as I painted a vivid picture of Trump's shortcomings as a person and as a leader. There is nothing like collective laughter to convey the acceptance of unmitigated and discernible truths. The flushed faces and knee slapping I witnessed nightly as I mocked this moronic man fueled not only my performance but my overwhelming belief that our country would not fall for Trump's "okie doke."

Perhaps no one was more optimistic than I come election night. The polling was in our favor, the momentum on our side. The scary prospect of undecided voters swinging this momentous election in Trump's favor appeared to be hyperbole only Fox News was promulgating. I settled in for a night that would witness our promoting a deserving, dynamic woman to the presidency. I opened a bottle of wine and poured two large glasses for my wife Leanne and myself as we sat on the sofa to witness history unfold.

1

Waking Up to a Nightmare

Fuck! Motherfuck! Fuckity fuckin' fuck fuck fuck! No amount of fucks can accurately describe how epically, how incontrovertibly, we are all monumentally fuuuuuuuuuuuuuuuuuuuuuuuuuucked! Waking up that Wednesday morning was perhaps the hardest thing I have ever done. Waking up from a bad dream implies the nightmare is over, but how does one contend with the prospect of a waking nightmare? A nightmare with no end in sight? A nightmare that, by all accounts, was just getting started?

Having lost loved ones, death was no stranger to me. The untimely passing of my father and brother prepared me for the utter hopelessness that now descended on my bedroom and, seemingly, the world. The emotion of that day was very much comparable to the catastrophic loss of a family member—the numbness that travels throughout your body, settling into a tingle inside your limbs and extremities, the way in which your neck stiffens, the way in which your mouth waters as if you are trying to taste the defeat that has befallen you, these physical manifestations all evincing the body's instinctual attempts to make sense of an all-consuming ordeal. The tears soon flow in an almost primal, emotional attempt to extinguish a fire engulfing you from the inside. You eventually raise your head to the heavens helplessly, searching for something, anything, to assure you that what you are experiencing is *not* real and can be erased if only you just think and pray hard enough.

Donald Trump's election to be the 45th president of the United States signaled a profound loss for the family of progress and true brotherhood. As I slowly, incrementally, admitted the blisteringly cold truth, I ventured out of my bedroom long enough to turn on the television and corroborate what had happened. The television was on only long enough to confirm the absolute truth of this nightmare, and that I was absolutely *not* alone in my denial, disdain, and complete pathos.

I turned to Twitter, knowing others shared in my monumental sense of helplessness. Almost instinctively, even before I began scrolling through the rants and outpourings of sorrow and distress, I knew it would be incumbent upon me, not as a humorist but as a sentient member of this wounded cadre, to articulate this pain and what it implied about a racist and irascible segment of our society.

Cyrus McQueen @CyrusMMcQueen · Nov 9, 2016
The Election of #BarackObama was a sign of how far we'd come...

The Election of #DonaldTrump was a sign that we'd gone too far.

#whitelash

⟲ 130   ♡ 307

By noon on the day following that foreboding Tuesday, I had experienced six of the seven stages of grief. Throughout the morning, I ricocheted between shock and denial, depression and bargaining, anguish and stagnation. However, I could not brace myself to grapple with that seventh and most difficult phase, acceptance. Instead, I chose to wallow in that third, therapeutic, and almost cathartic stage: *anger.*

Cyrus McQueen @CyrusMMcQueen · Nov 11, 2016
People won't sacrifice 2 hours to vote but waste the same amount of time watching a bad movie... Well, guess what? Now we're living in one.

⟲ 64   ♡ 289

Oh yes, my rage soon crested, it climbing to an incredible height amidst a hurricane of emotions. I then consciously, deliberately, sent that rancor cascading back down onto our shores of disillusionment. The storm raging within me was not limited to those who shared my righteous indignation but rather encompassed those who had not even bothered to enlist in this epic battle before humanity had lost so much ground.

By the time I finally ventured outside to see if, in fact, the earth was still spinning, the collective dismay in my heterogenous pocket of Brooklyn signaled that humanity was in the throes of something it might never surmount. The sun may have been out, but the pall cast over my borough's busy streets and boulevards belied any unseasonably nice weather we might actually have been experiencing.

Cyrus McQueen @CyrusMMcQueen · Nov 9, 2016
After #Obama was elected, I saw black people crying in the streets...
After #Trump was elected, I saw black people crying in the streets...

⟲ 83   ♡ 284

I walked miles, attempting to clear a head that could not, despite the literal and figurative distance I travelled, be cleared. The distorted faces on all I encountered seemed to mirror my emotional state. I passed West Indians and Africans, African Americans and Jews. No one made eye contact. Everyone, like me, moved without a compass. Though our bodies were present, nary a single person seemed present in their body.

At some point, I'm not sure exactly when during that post-election period of despondency, after I had eaten my feelings and tried in vain to swallow my disappointment, I remembered that I was a comedian. Just the thought of getting onstage and being jocular amidst all this unjustness and awfulness was too much to bear. How could I endeavor to entertain, to be funny, to engage in mirth when, overnight, everything had become so unmistakably *unfunny*? Besides, how could I even do my act when I had been preparing for a different outcome? I had ceremoniously closed that chapter in my jokebook, saying goodbye in my mind to Trump and all the silliness of an innocuous folly, a candidate who would be swept away with the historical dust of the 2016 election. I recall furiously crossing out jokes I had prepared. Jokes contingent on the historical converse that were now moot. Yarns about Hillary

13

blocking Bill from constantly entering the Oval Office to offer unsolicited advice. It was a sad day ripping those pages out of my notebook, this violent act almost emblematic, given the manner in which progress had been deliberately torn to pieces. Though I discovered I did not yet have the legs to climb onto the performing stage, I soon found I had enough gumption and intestinal fortitude to get my fingers to take that walk for me. There was a virtual platform I could mount at any time to begin finding the funny, if there indeed was any funny *to* be found, in this new normal.

Cyrus McQueen @CyrusMMcQueen · Nov 13, 2016
Thank God I got Football to take my mind off Trump. I'd rather see conflict that causes brain damage than brain damage that causes conflict.

120 373

There is an unquestioned rule of comedy: always punch up. As Donald Trump prepared to enter the Office of the President of the United States, and thereby become the world's most powerful person, I resigned myself to the idea that he needed to be the punchline, to be, in fact, *my* punching bag. No one who had so mercilessly attacked the powerless, who had engaged in the dangerous dance of racist, dog-whistle politics, who had so maliciously put a stranglehold on our norms and customs, should be spared from the comedian's crosshairs.

As Trump began assembling a rogue's gallery of enablers and cabinet members, the fight, I concluded, had to expand beyond the demented clown to the insane posse he was now enlisting to carry out his evil plans.

Cyrus McQueen @CyrusMMcQueen · Nov 29, 2016
The #Trump Cabinet picks are like something out of Reservoir Dogs. A gang of misfits assembled for one job. He calls Ben Carson Mr. Brown...

19 101

As I began dissecting Dumb Donald and the dumber men and women he began to ensconce around him, my disdain grew mightily. It was one thing to watch a juvenile man ride roughshod over political norms, to witness the cavalier manner in which he disrespected Gold

Star families and disabled reporters, among many others. But to then have to contend with the scoundrels and miscreants, the skunks and scumbags who enriched him, now being *enriched* as reward for their obsequiousness, was almost *too* much to bear.

Even before the election, I had identified this most disturbing element. Men and women of questionable moral and ethical turpitude had attached themselves to Trump, like the insignificant fish who find purpose riding the back of a whale. He may have been the big catch, but these remoras, these whale suckers who fed off his shit, had a particular way of inspiring my ire.

Cyrus McQueen @CyrusMMcQueen · Aug 4, 2016
#ClintEastwood ↗ said the things #Trump ↗ says weren't considered racist in his day... I'm like, yeah it would've just been considered Thursday.

⟲ 21   ♡ 116

Trump was indeed picking up steam, with no shortage of passengers willing to hop aboard his crazy train. What was most bewildering was not just the individuals supporting this monster but the sheer disparity among them. That diametrically opposed people clamored for space on the same backward, broken-down conveyance could not be ignored. Wealth and Fame can be heavy intoxicants, but recognizing many were steadily drinking his deadly concoction of orange Kool-Aid—and, more disturbing, serving it to others—is when I began to realize just how pervasive this soon-to-be president actually was.

As the inauguration approached, anyone who had yet to come to grips with how truly damaging the Trump presidency promised to be needed look no further than the men and women he began enlisting to fill in the details of this dystopian picture. If the president himself was problematic—his heartless words about immigrants, Muslims, and Mexicans, his ability to indelibly paint people of color with the broadest brush possible—it paled in comparison to the very actions he began taking to *bring* his hellish portrait to life.

They say the devil is in the details, and never before had that notion rung truer, with more potent resonance, than with the scoundrels and sons of bitches he began appointing to prominent positions. To view Black and Brown people as inferior was one thing. To implement policy to realize that sociopolitical objectivization and objective was another.

Cyrus McQueen @CyrusMMcQueen · Nov 23, 2016
There's never been a bigger contrast between two Attorney Generals... We went from Loretta Lynch to a guy who probably participated in one.

⟲ 81   ♡ 252

For men like Jefferson Beauregard Sessions to find employ in this dog-and-pony show of epic proportions made my already weary soul wither and splinter further. As I reflected on his newfound fortune as attorney general, I mused on my own lifelong encounters with bigots as a native of that pressure cooker of racial prejudice, the city of Boston.

Men like Sessions and later John Kelly, a native of the same cold, Northern clime as myself, would prove to be perhaps even more enraging because their appointments enabled them to disempower an already disenfranchised people. Trump's empowering these primitive men triggered my sense of emergency as never before. The alarm bells were ringing!

Cyrus McQueen @CyrusMMcQueen · May 11, 2018
John Kelly said immigrant families who migrate here 'don't integrate well'? Funny, I'd say pasty faced bigots from Boston have proven to be the ones who don't 'integrate well'... #FridayFeeling ⌧

⟲ 249   ♡ 968

By all accounts, the man Trump would pick to be his vice president was no better. Depending on who you asked, Michael Richard Pence's special blend of religious fundamentalism and feverish anti-LGBT indoctrination, not to mention the impression he gave off that he possesses a devilish and impish quality, made him the type of bad guy to be most feared. Pence had made his name as a staunch conservative, unsuited for the more liberal leaning times the country found itself in. He presided mightily and happily over a state that barely attempted to separate the church from the pulpit he had essentially erected in his capitol office.

Pence reminded me of Nurse Ratchet, an antagonist who fully embraced her villainy under the pretense that she was merely following rules and regulations. As a deifier of doctrine, a man who undoubtedly was, himself, a deviant, Pence had an uncanny talent for fucking people over with a wry grin on his face. He may have been milquetoast, but, like Ratchet and many other great villains of literature, his serene disposition belied a truly sinister objective.

Cyrus McQueen @CyrusMMcQueen · Feb 8, 2018
Wait a minute... is Mike Pence an advocate of Gay Conversion Therapy because it 'worked' for him?? #ThursdayThoughts

⟲ 260   ♡ 1066

When D-Day finally arrived, when the despotic Commander-in-Chief Donald J. Trump was officially sworn in, it marked a moment we all knew was coming, yet none of us could truly prepare ourselves for. Whether you were a Bernie Bro, or were "with her" or, unfortunately, could not bring yourself to cast a ballot either way, January 20, 2017, was a day now seared in memory for both what it represented and what it portended.

As I wrestled with a sea of emotions, I could barely contain the virulence of the storm raging within me. An emotional surge throughout my body sent an overflow streaming down my cheeks and onto my sweater, my tears resulting not so much from the horror I was witnessing as much as from the sterling memory of eight years prior that was now being violently, inexorably, erased. I was crying for my former president as much as for a country that seemed to have lost its way. As I choked on my tears, my upheaval represented a visceral acknowledgement of the existential threat this sea change posed to Black progress. I was witnessing Hope drown as I became submerged in sorrow.

Cyrus McQueen @CyrusMMcQueen · Feb 12, 2018
And Trump has the nerve to stoke fears about Mexican immigrants... Wish we had a fuckin Wall around the White House cause, they're not sending the best people there... They're sending harassers, rapists, wife beaters... and some, I assume, are good people... #MondayMotivation

⟲ 314   ♡ 917

I thought back to the day eight years prior when I travelled to D.C. to attend Obama's Inauguration. Braving freezing temperatures that

January morning, I stood for hours immersed in a heterogeneous pool of humanity. It was a pool of warmth, combatting the biting cold as the spirit of camaraderie, fueled by the history we were witnessing, heated all who had assembled for one unifying purpose: to observe this miracle with our own eyes. It would be fodder for future tales told to my own grandchildren as they sat with rapt attention in front of my rocking chair and all the details got rightfully embellished. "I seen him with my own eyes. Had to be negative thirty degrees, and I swear he stood TEN feet tall!"

Now, not far from where Martin Luther King had delivered his seminal speech, and where I had seen his dream realized that day in 2009, I was witnessing the dream come to an abrupt, devastating denouement. This new presidency felt like the beginning of the end in many ways, and the gaggle of war hawks and propaganda peddlers Trump was amassing appeared to ensure that it would be. But almost immediately, amid talks of travel bans and walls, a bulwark of our own rose from the embers of our scorched glory. Trump was being challenged at seemingly every turn, and the men and women who had agreed to do his peddling began finding themselves ensnared in an intricate web of checks and balances that promised to stop a few before they could commence their infestation.

The first of many dominoes to drop would be Michael Flynn, the unfortunate-looking man who resembled the very thing he would become: a rat. Though his tenure in the Trump White House was brief, Flynn's early resignation as National Security Advisor marked a trend that would see many of Trump's assorted henchmen following in his footsteps.

Trump's press secretaries and chiefs of staff now seemed to be caught in a revolving door of dismissals and early exits, suggesting that the ship was already taking on water. The fact that his presidency was in peril this early out of port belied an even more serious development: that his only plan to mend the punctures was to basically use the very staff he'd failed to vet to *stuff* the ever-widening holes his scandals were creating.

It was stunning to behold. The ferocity with which Trump attacked foreigners, females, and a former president was giving way to an even more ferocious defense of his own ineptitude as he fought futilely to prevent the pendulum of justice from swinging back.

Cyrus McQueen @CyrusMMcQueen · May 8, 2017
Obama warned Trump about hiring Flynn and he didn't listen to him... Mind you, he's taken advice from Meatloaf, Gary Busy and Latoya Jackson

↻ 41   ♡ 215

Former Attorney General Jeff Sessions, a vile and ruthless elfin-like man, having recused himself from the Russia inquiry, now attempted to make up for his momentary display of sound judgement by throwing himself on the grenades Trump was so casually tossing into a rabidly partisan Congress. The only problem was that a man as destructive as Trump was constantly tossing more and more explosives into an already bombarded congressional landscape. Sessions was going to die a thousand deaths as it became clear to the battle-weary public that his boss was out to destroy both the rule of law, and the Alabaman himself.

Cyrus McQueen @CyrusMMcQueen · Jun 13, 2017
We've only got a few more minutes till #JeffSessions ⌐ tells Kamala Harris she needs to watch how she talks to white folks... #SessionsHearing ⌐

↻ 469   ♡ 1694

The propaganda machine that fueled Trump's rise through the conservative stratosphere was undoubtedly powered by the disgusting misanthrope Steve Bannon. As Trump's chief strategist, he, along with the professional liars and losers gainfully employed by Fox News, began witnessing their own popularity soar as Trump's political career took off. That outfit of racist, opinion-based journalism presided over by Roger Ailes and popularized by the likes of Sean Hannity and Bill O'Reilly may have been the main megaphone Trump utilized to spread his caustic brand of white nationalism, but it was Bannon's direction, his deft ability to fill the empty vessel that was Trump's head, that provided this Frankenstein monster *with* his crystallized motive.

Like the evil doctor, it was Bannon's maestro-like qualities behind the scenes that set this nightmare in motion. He was indeed the mastermind conducting this populist chorus, his particularly polarizing brand of ethnocentrism evoking a bitter symphony, one in which he would now mesmerize the masses using his biggest instrument: Trump.

Cyrus McQueen @CyrusMMcQueen · Feb 25, 2017
Have you seen Steve Bannons mouth? For someone who cares so much about being white, you'd think it would've translated to his teeth...

⟲ 32   ♡ 258

As the tents were pitched, the freaks assembled, and the games begun, the orange clown and his carnival of misfits and transient opportunists began conducting a daily show out of D.C., that never failed to attract onlookers both curious and skeptical. There was, of course, Bannon barking orders from his perch just behind the curtain. Here, the blowhard, who doubled as the alligator man, a man whose leathery skin was equally blotchy, would compound this unsightliness with a set of yellowish eyes that barely hid the madness unfolding behind them. There was Sessions, a man of dwarfish stature whose neck and pallor were redder than the meat Trump routinely tossed to the ravenous spectators. Then there were Spicer and Scaramucci, Siamese twins who took turns conducting press briefings before their abrasiveness and overwhelming ineptitude, in an administration rife with abrasiveness and ineptitude, saw them replaced with John Kelly and Sarah Sanders, fitting approximations of the lobster man and the bearded lady, respectively.

Kelly was a crustacean out of the Northeast, a salty, scorpion-like bottom feeder who had come into his own sucking up the racist scum that churned out of a segregated city. It undoubtedly contributed to the massive claws he wielded, byproducts of an even more massive sense of racial superiority. But Trump, ever with the eye for spotting and elevating scum, identified a true wanton and wicked attraction when he hired Sarah Huckabee Sanders to stand just outside the big tent and rhapsodize daily for the discerning members of the assembled White House press corps. Daily, these intrepid journalists did their due diligence for a nation that hadn't signed up for this circus, reporters who through their relentless, noble attempts to peek behind the curtain, would come to reveal this shit show for what it was.

Cyrus McQueen @CyrusMMcQueen · May 4, 2018

Boy, the Arkansas really comes out of Sarah Huckabee Sanders every time she calls on April Ryan... Since she already resembles a racist bulldog, if black women continue questioning her, one day I expect her to just start barking...

↻ 215   ♡ 922

Perhaps no member of Trump's team irritated, infuriated, and frustrated more than Sanders. Her remarkable ability to lie as if it were a virtue and turn sideshow into main attraction contributed to the carnival-like atmosphere that would come to define the Trump White House. The ambassador of the freak show seemed to delight in her role as spokesperson for the freaks busy behind the curtain destroying civil and religious freedoms, when they weren't defending the indefensible and obfuscating for a president who was up to his combover in crimes and misdeeds. What in many ways became the face of the Trump White House was a face that perfectly represented and encompassed all its superlative repulsiveness. Something was definitely rotten in this presidency. Though the journalists seated before her, and we men and women at home, could smell the bullshit being bandied about, the press secretary emboldened by Trump came to embody, more than any other, his administration's shameless attempts at pretending the putrid was pulchritude.

2

The Joke's on You

The first time I climbed onstage during the winter of our discontent, I had no clue how live audiences would react to Trump material now. The man had so dominated every news cycle and every waking moment before being sworn in that I was unsure, even now that his presidency had only officially begun, if we hadn't had our fill of this fool. Tweeting daily about his latest lie or attempt at covering up the lie had generated virtual guffaws, but how would a real crowd respond to these jokes?

The answer would come quickly and resoundingly. At a show in Queens, my first since this vampire had begun bleeding the country dry in his official capacity as president, I took to the stage to entertain a packed audience in the back of a cafe. I was raring to tackle the topic as I gripped the mic stand but found myself just standing there as a confluence of adrenaline and nerves rendered me temporarily immobile. As I poised myself to begin pouncing on the new president, I began breathing into the microphone slowly. Before I realized it, I was creating a rhythm that began to entrance the excited crowd. The audience, almost anticipating the direction in which I was heading, began to chuckle, then rumble, as my audible exhales set the beat they'd soon dance to. This hypnotic prologue went on for a good twenty seconds, my face indicating my disdain, its contortions riding a head that shook back and forth, back and forth, until finally the anticipation had risen to the top of the crescendo and I split the tension with two words: Fuck Trump!

Oh, the world was indeed ready to shit on this man who had so mercilessly, so callously, shit all over us. I rattled off one joke after another.

Cyrus McQueen @CyrusMMcQueen · Oct 12, 2016
I imagine #Trump is a terrible chess player... He probably insists on being the white pieces, then tries to use his King to go after Pawns.

�vↄ 29   ♡ 168

I can still feel the energy and hear the whistles that went off like fireworks in many a crowd, their loud hissing along with the pops from the applause exploding throughout the showroom after I lit the initial fuse. There really is nothing on earth like a live stand-up performance. When I was not onstage, I would often try to imagine the smiling, flushed faces behind the likes and retweets a particular post generated as my Twitter account became a virtual comedy club. My mentions came to replace the traditional applause that I had grown accustomed to, dispatches from all over the world clogging my notifications with encouraging comments, along with a myriad of emojis and gifs, that corroborated what I had heard nightly with my own ears.

Increasingly, people throughout the world responded to my funny asides. I had never performed outside the United States, but now, in a sense, I *was*. People followed me from as far away as Australia. I received awesome feedback from folks throughout Europe and Canada. My lampooning of this clownish, buffoonish bastard was making people spit up their coffee in Morocco. I began consolidating an energized, steadfast audience across the globe and through their collective disillusionment, I discovered my muse.

Cyrus McQueen @CyrusMMcQueen · Apr 2, 2018
My Aunt Deborah had, perhaps, the best take yet on Trump... "He a damn crackhead! Up twittering at 2:30 in the morning. That's some crackhead stuff! Obama wasn't up at that time. He was sleep cause he worked hard all day. Trump don't do shit, that's why he be up! Damn crackhead!"

�vↄ 3180   ♡ 10767

If there is more than one way to skin a cat, there is certainly more than one way to carve up a feral pig masquerading as a president. Where does one even start with a clown who offers so much comedic fodder? Be it his looks or his words or his unmasked petulance, I have never struggled to find something worth skewering when it comes to dumb Donald. As a humorist, I recognize now more than ever the awesome responsibility that comes from this role and, moreover, the great importance of providing much-needed levity in these very serious times. I have therefore realized, and accepted my duty as, a jester in the court of public opinion, my duty to bear witness to this man-made atrocity and sieve our collective disdain through a well-intentioned, well-maintained comedic filter.

Which again brings me back to my initial query: how does one begin serving up this wild and hairy razorback? After it has been washed, shaved, and roasted, how can an ugly, ravenous animal be transformed into something fit for consumption? I discovered that the news of the day, which vacillated between the damaging and the catastrophic, could be pored over with my particular set of eyes and cooked until I could apportion and present delicious morsels of wit for the public to ingest and enjoy.

So if we *are* going to commence with digging into this pig, what better place to begin than with his stunning lack of comportment? It was one of the first faults I noticed about the 45th president, the first sign I saw that his ascension could spell doom. Never in my lifetime had such an ill-suited man reached the highest office in the land. Mind you, slave owners, mass murderers, and philanderers of varying degrees had all occupied the West Wing at different points in our nation's history, but none appeared to possess such a shocking absence of maturity like 45.

Cyrus McQueen @CyrusMMcQueen · May 1, 2017
Trump thinks we could've avoided the Civil War if Andrew Jackson was President... I think we could avoid World War 3 if he wasn't President.

⟲ 437   ♡ 1241

Having suffered through eight years of George W. Bush, I was used to a president who left a lot to be desired when it came to communicating intelligently. Compound that with Obama, one of the great orators in American history, and the election of Trump marked a precipitous downturn as the country, once again, found itself on one end of a seesaw as yet another lightweight leader kept us all in the mud. It made me long again for a president whose words actually *lifted* me, whose rhetoric actually elevated the country. And it forced me to lament, more than ever, just how much we had sunk with Trump's election.

Since the year 2001, America has essentially suffered through two ne'er-do-wells in the White House, with Obama providing the only true sustenance between two starchy, stale administrations. Trump has left us hungry for honesty and truth, craving a president who actually craves knowledge, a president who possesses enough intellectual curiosity to open a book or, better yet, *read* an entire briefing.

Cyrus McQueen @CyrusMMcQueen · Jan 12, 2018
BREAKING NEWS: They just released the results from Trumps Walter Reed physical. Turns out his High Cholesterol is Colin Kaepernick's fault... His High Blood Pressure is Hillary's fault... His Hair Loss is Rosie O'Donnell's fault... And his Erectile Dysfunction is Obama's fault...

⟲ 2575   ♡ 6617

As the media, along with most of the nation, began realizing that this president was not the brightest bulb in the chandelier, or the sharpest tool in the shed, or, indeed, was about three fries short of a Happy Meal, Trump began taking painstaking steps to prove that he was not in fact, the complete, utter idiot we all knew he was. I'm not sure exactly where I was when I heard the term "stable genius" for the first time, but I do recall looking up to the skies and mouthing "thank you" for this gift from the comedic gods that appeared to fall right into my lap.

At this point in his presidency, having failed to provide any leadership or inspiration, after his shortcomings and scandals appeared to multiply every day, after he had shot paper towels like basketballs into a crowd in a storm-ravaged Puerto Rico like some adolescent hellion relishing in the hell that had just supplanted that paradise, he now had the unmitigated gall to assert that such actions were a stroke of genius? Since it was becoming more and more apparent the emperor was wearing no clothes, I could not contain my disdain at this hypocrite's hyperbolic assertions.

In observing this president day in and day out, I could easily marvel at the ease with which he lied to the public. However, what truly confounded me was his remarkable ability to lie to *himself*. Within seconds of listening to him speak at a briefing, or even at one of his massive ego-stroking sessions that doubled as campaign rallies, I knew I was listening to a man with the most rudimentary grasp of the English language. Yet the self aggrandizing manner in which he openly relished in his own performance, him often pausing after an utterance that would be in your average tenth-grader's wheelhouse, left me wondering just how a man could project such satisfaction given the sophomoric shit he was spouting.

Making sense of this blowhard became easier when you took his pedigree into account. As a spoiled rich kid whose bone-spurred feet were never held to the fire, you could begin to grasp how an unattractive, balding, thin-skinned tyrant who had coasted through life became the man who felt comfortable insulting his much better-looking opponents with the kind of superficial attacks to which he himself appeared to be vulnerable. That sense of delusion seemed to carry over to matters of intelligence and education as it became clearer and clearer, through his stilted, limited vocabulary, that he did not possess the intellectual heft to be considered "genius" yet had likely acquired this false belief because no one around him, or in his employ, ever dared tell him how stupid he actually *is*.

Perhaps the biggest indicator Trump is anything but a genius is the ready assertion that he is, in his own words, *a* genius. I've typically found that the smartest people are so riddled with self-doubt, and a cognizance of all they actually do not know, that they would not dare utter such preposterous drivel. Our president is no such person.

Cyrus McQueen @CyrusMMcQueen · Jan 7, 2018
Donald Trump says he 'went to the best colleges?' Well, so did the Unibomber... You know what you call a mentally ill man with an Ivy League Degree? Crazy...

⟲ 149   ♡ 562

It was becoming harder and harder to observe this buffoon in his natural habitat, waxing sanctimoniously at his campaign-style rallies. It was there that this celebrated doofus would deliver his basic yet incendiary remarks to an even more basic and fired-up audience. As if to validate his villainy, the homogenous crowds would openly bask in the resplendence of his ignorance, lapping up his racist nonsense, lavishing him with praise.

His sophomoric display in Puerto Rico was essentially a metaphor for what he had been carrying out in rallies throughout middle America. He would toss out words and phrases like "build the wall," and the rabid crowd would readily pick them up and then wipe their minds free of all the disastrous, hateful implications pouring out of that very policy. What was Make America Great Again anyway besides a blanket, basic message, a flagrant, futile attempt at wiping racism clean, disguised as a movement to clean up the country's problems?

Cyrus McQueen @CyrusMMcQueen · May 25, 2018
Sucks that every one of Trumps lies has to be treated seriously. "There was a spy in my campaign!" We convene a panel. "Obama wiretapped me!" We investigate. He's like a child who says the boogeyman is under his bed. You check but, the reality is, the true monster's right on top!

⟲ 1304   ♡ 3826

Trump appeared more exhibitionist than polished politician when he wielded his weaponized words like sabers, but his sloppy, almost cartoonish appearance always had a way of undercutting his performance. How such a dull man could use such piercing rhetoric, and stab with such sharp precision, in what otherwise could be considered an amateurish display was dumbfounding. He was juggling swords, and his sweeping generalizations, by contextualizing minorities with mayhem, meant that *we* were the only ones likely to shed blood from this blade. He may have been a caricature, but his words cut deep.

I simply could not stomach the way he would stand with his head cocked, poised to launch into a diatribe about perceived enemies, often invoking a "they" that could have meant a host of diverse, enlightened, or sensible people who *weren't* buying his lies. You could see him sensing that his senseless crowd was salivating for red meat as he steadied himself to serve it up to them undercooked. His rotund, roly-poly appearance on the podium was almost as off-putting as the bilious soundbites he was vomiting up for their satisfaction. As he stood there sweating, a corpulent man delivering caustic asides, he appeared less like a leader and more like a weeble wobble. And like the children's toy, this man-child, despite his mounting scandals and multiple investigations, simply refused to go down.

Cyrus McQueen @CyrusMMcQueen · Jan 4, 2018
I feel like if you worked in the White House, you could just straight up walk up to Trump and be like, 'I heard Dave was talkin bout you.' And Trump would get all mad and go off, lookin for Dave... But the funniest part would be, there would be no Dave...

⟲ 195   ♡ 959

The viscosity of his pomposity, his words never achieving a fluidity or building to a natural crescendo, yet always managing to ignite his crowd, was the chief indicator that the mass of MAGA hats surrounding him could never be confused for thinking caps. He was definitely laying it on thick for them, and despite the ham-handed way he kept the focus on himself, they always remained mesmerized. Here was a politician who had somehow changed the paradigm from listening to people's problems to having people listen to *his* problems. And when he wasn't martyring himself as being unfairly attacked, he busily attacked the media or any host of adversaries, real or imagined, as long as he could drudge up enough antipathy from the crowd.

By all accounts, Trump was playing with fire; with every hate-filled match he tossed, the hopeless men and women who worshipped at his altar threatened to engulf the country. He had unearthed a sort of crude oil that could easily become an accelerant whenever he set his sights on his prey of the day. It was then that the sea of red caps came more to resemble an inferno; his hatred and bombast proved combustible, those hats nothing more than flames that he could fan from city to city.

In politics, much as in the reality television world that Trump was previously immersed in, appearance means everything. In fact, the brand of politics unique to the conservative agenda feeds almost exclusively on the appearance and promulgation of propriety, while actually subsisting and sustaining itself *on* impropriety. It is a dizzying dichotomy to democratic politics. But perhaps I am still guilty of getting drunk off the Obama example, where one could not help but fall sway to the intoxicating concoction of a good man doing good things for a good reason, and managing to look damn good while doing it. One thing *was* clear: the contrast between them was undeniable. Trump, this disheveled, dumpy no-gooder, was actively sullying the presidency with his unsightly insolence.

Whenever Trump carried out his official presidential duties before the cameras, he looked like he was conforming only reluctantly to the formalities of the office. He operated with the air of selfish, self-absorbed teenage babysitters who only grudgingly leave their phones or televisions in order to actually care for their charges. More and more, he affected the demeanor of someone who had better things to do. It was as if he could not wait to escape to one of his properties to golf, or tweet, or do anything *but* make America great. Every time he boarded his helicopter or Air Force One, he was heading not to conduct official business. Rather, he was utilizing the conveyance to escape his responsibilities as it whisked him away to golf at Bedminster or Mar-a-Lago, where he could then hide behind hedges that would obstruct any view of his acts of obstruction.

At this point, the Trump train was already careening off the rails, and every signpost at every station along the way marked merely another scandal his administration was helplessly barreling toward. Never mind that the conductor himself was a directionless, ineffectual wannabe leader, intoxicated on both his enumerated and his perceived powers, a man ill-prepared for the sobriety the job required. In his first year alone, the nation saw him sadistically roll out, then bungle, his Muslim Ban, mess up a condolence call to a Gold Star Widow, sidestep, then misstep, when called upon to comment on Charlottesville, and, lest we forget, futilely attempt to lay blame, yet again, at his predecessor's feet for a trespass he had not committed when he falsely accused Obama of wiretapping him.

His haplessness was becoming the only comedic fodder I was bothering to feed the hungry crowds I performed for. Whether lashing or lambasting him with words or wit, I was coming to see that my opprobrium of the Trump era provided sustenance for insatiable New York City audiences. I knew that crowds within the five boroughs responded strongly to my jokes about our nation's Joke, but I also recognized that, Russia notwithstanding, this lout got elected somehow. So to get a truly unvarnished view of Trump's America, I would have to leave the cosmopolitan bubble where learned and sensible citizens abound and venture into conservative enclaves, bubbles in their own right, where the virulent, racist undercurrent he surfed so effectively had churned into the pipeline he rode all the way to Washington.

I got my chance when an opportunity to perform in southern New Jersey presented itself, and I could finally plant myself firmly in the soil of what the show's producer stated was "Trump country." I pondered how my material would be received as the exits on the Jersey Turnpike crept lower and lower. As I got farther and farther from the familiar, the Trump/Pence bumper stickers on the cars ahead confirmed that I was indeed inching toward a foreign land, its natives unlikely to speak my language.

I landed on the Moon with less than thirty minutes to study the alien life unfolding around me. The older white men and women in the audience were in their natural habitat, wives swilling wine and Prosecco, their husbands sporting colorful, crisply ironed shirts, the contrast between tanned skin and ivory hair making it appear we were closer to Florida than Philadelphia. As I sized up the audience, the producer, as if sensing the purpose of my reconnaissance, reminded me to have fun and, as if to warn me away from wandering into the cold white abyss, reiterated that it would probably "be best" to stay away from the Trump material. But as a Boston boy who has never shied away from bounties of bigotry, I decided to follow Melania's advice. I surmised it would simply "be best" to rip these motherfuckers a new asshole.

As I prepared to boldly go where no brotha had gone before, I noticed that the natives were inebriated and, to my delight, laughing. Tough audiences are par for the course in comedy, but, in reading a room, seeing what they laugh at and, more important, *if* they are laughing, is typically a good indicator of whether your set will succeed. Sometimes, they just may not be picking up what someone else is putting down, but, if you are observant and capable enough, a comedian waiting in the wings can often figure out what the audience will absorb.

This observation, though sound under normal circumstances, proved to be moot as comedian after comedian launched into material endemic to the region. Jokes about the Philadelphia Eagles and Atlantic City bachelor parties got incredible guffaws, reinforcing a solemn fact: I really did not speak their language. I knew, however, that the hurdle would not be too high, given that they were indeed laughing. When an audience has been proven to provide rolling laughter, big and enthusiastic blasts of approval, half the battle has been won.

I would be remiss if I did not mention that at this point in my comedy career I had also experienced the converse. At times, I had found myself in more accommodating climes, in liberal and heterogenous enclaves in Upper Manhattan where there was a surprising malaise despite the diversity of the audience and the paucity of old people. Popular shows where, a young hip audience notwithstanding, the response was shockingly *anemic*. I have lost count of all the instances where I witnessed witty, well-written, well-executed jokes cause barely a ripple. Comedy, after all, is an art not a science.

I took a big sip from my water bottle and swallowed that sobering, cold truth as I waited for the emcee to introduce me. I then drew a long, deep breath and, with one giant leap, bounded onto the stage, endeavoring to boldly go as far as the art form could carry me that night.

The previous comics had left enough New Jersey-related ammo on stage for me to load my gun with a few Super Bowl bullets. Capitalizing on my home team Patriots' defeat that February, I set myself up to triumph by getting them to drop their guard. Appearing vulnerable, I made jokes at my own expense, innocuous asides that got them engaged and even comfortable before I could lower the hammer. Like the formula employed in the sweet science, I appeared to be on the ropes but, my guard, unlike theirs, had not dropped.

Just when I tired of this folly, I began firing off, deliberately and determinedly, shot after shot. I could sense from their drunken laughter that I had rendered them hopelessly, utterly defenseless. Tom Brady turned out to be the best bridge to take me from the perfunctory to the profound. Once again, comedy proved to be an effective Trojan Horse; jokes about regional bullshit carried me right past the gates of this gated community and into a battle I had been preparing for.

Cyrus McQueen @CyrusMMcQueen · Jun 5, 2018
Trump disinvited the Philadelphia Eagles to the White House? Can we disinvite him from the next Presidential Election? #TuesdayThoughts

⟲ 295   ♡ 1727

The first to go down in a fit of laughter was a retired couple from Montclair. The wife let out a piercing howl as she slumped over, her well-manicured claws digging into her husband's shoulder as she struggled to breathe. The whole left side of the stage soon followed, each table erupting as I began tipping, one after the other, the dominoes I had methodically stacked at the top of my set. A large man in an aubergine dress shirt, his cuffs rolled ever so precisely for panache, the paisley pattern beneath leading to a pair of meaty paws barely clasped over his massive midsection, threw his head back and gasped for air after I contorted every muscle in my face to embellish the imbecile in office. Men returning from smoking all went down in a blaze, their demise precipitated by a rapid succession of insults that saw me taking no prisoners as they dared pass back in front of the firing line to get to their seats.

Cyrus McQueen @CyrusMMcQueen · Aug 25, 2016
Seniors voting for #Trump ⌐ won't even be around to suffer with the rest of us. It's like farting on an elevator right as you're getting off.

⟲ 64   ♡ 227

In the parlance of professional comedians, I killed. My barrage riddled the room with laughter, every clap from the crowd mimicking a shot fired as the satire I spit into the microphone ricocheted throughout the venue. When they were not succumbing to the setups I peeled off, I methodically moved in close until I had them perfectly positioned to receive a punch. Septuagenarian after septuagenarian went down in this manner, their political affiliations no match for the comedic muscle I was utilizing to squeeze every last laugh out of them. By the time the lights came up, the showroom resembled a battlefield, bodies strewn about, the people rising slowly, physically drained by what they had been through. Spilled wine on several tables provided further proof of this slaughter and perfectly evoked the bloody battle just waged.

Cyrus McQueen @CyrusMMcQueen · May 5, 2016
#TheRollingStones ⌐ don't want #DonaldTrump ⌐ using any of their songs at his campaign rallies... Guess they don't have sympathy for the devil.

⟲ 23   ♡ 79

But a funny thing happened that evening (no pun intended). I had discovered that Donald Trump, though the preferred candidate of some, was also an incredibly foolish figure whose unmistakable buffoonery led, within that showroom, to a bipartisan consensus. Though my political objectives had peppered my comedic castigation, by highlighting the childish, churlish ways he made an ass of himself on the world stage and in Washington, I had bridged any partisan divide. He finally *became* the butt of the joke. I had found a concurrence when it came to contempt for this man, even among conservatives. Though I had devoted much time on social media to highlighting the serious repercussions of Trump's racial animus, along with the policies fueled by it, I now identified that the inherent comedy in such a clown-like man was, in and of itself, perfectly suited for skewering on both virtual *and* literal stages.

Cyrus McQueen @CyrusMMcQueen · Jan 12, 2018
They're saying Micro is the new buzzword of 2018... As in: The current President of the United States has a Micro-Penis...

⮂ 39   ♡ 262

Later, I performed an autopsy on my performance, listening to a recording of that evening's set, once again applying science to try to understand my artistic discovery. The evidence revealed that the most basic observations about this basic man had generated *visceral* responses. The hoots and hollers, the whistles and the cackles, all aligned with jokes I had made about his appearance and his physical shortcomings. It convinced me that, despite what seriousness and sadness may come out of the news cycle every day, I should never shy away from picking the abundance of low-hanging fruit this nectarine Nazi provided. The success of my experiment that night was so colossal it even caused me to recalibrate my social media approach.

The laughs I discovered buried in that recording, like diamonds in some dark cavern, suggested that, perhaps, levity *could* be found in these foreboding times without necessarily having to venture that deep into the shadows. If Newton's third law states that every action has an equal and opposite reaction, what *better* reaction could be expected from waiting audiences than infectious, unbridled laughter at the expense of this egomaniac? While a sobering assessment of his high crimes and misdemeanors was necessary, the punchlines provided by pointing out his physical and psychological shortcomings had proven to have a universal appeal. I secretly vowed to never again hesitate about hitting such a superficial man where it hurt. I now saw that even low-hanging fruit could satiate and ultimately satisfy a hungry crowd.

3

Big Gloves to Fill

Cyrus McQueen @CyrusMMcQueen · Jan 30, 2018
Because of his race folks in middle America thought Obama was a bad man
when, in actuality, he was anything but... Because of his race, folks in middle
America think Trump is a great man when, in actuality, he is anything but...
#TuesdayThoughts ↻

↻ 279   ♡ 968

O ver a year into Trump's tenure and my Obama withdrawals
were still keeping me up at night. It was then, with my wife
asleep and the house quiet, that I found myself unable to close
my eyes and escape the nightmare I was experiencing outside of
slumber. Night terrors were actually preferable to this boogieman
tormenting the country, holding us all hostage as he sadistically set fire
to every accomplishment of the previous eight years. As I lay in the
literal darkness attempting to come to grips with the figurative darkness
this demon had cast over America and the world, I shivered at the
revelation that the horror had no apparent end in sight.

Many had already begun the painful process of reverse engineering
the Trump victory, dissecting and dismantling it, traveling back in time
in an attempt to pinpoint exactly how and when this alternate reality had
been forged. Obviously, there cannot be a 45th president without there
having first been a 44th, but in deconstructing the disaster that is Donald
Trump, it becomes painfully obvious, downright irrefutable, that we
would not have this particularly doltish and regressive 45th if America
had not first experienced a certain whimsical and particularly progressive
44th. The two men are inextricably linked, least because of their shared
succession from one to the other and more because Obama's
ascendance in politics gave birth to Trump's rise within what were once
the fringes of our society.

This concurrence has had dark implications. Obama's arrival was like light flooding an unlit room—that moment when the sun pours through the window, the golden truth in his oratory floating through the air like flecks of dust particles dancing in a miraculous glow. Yet that political epoch also suggested, given the reaction it ultimately engendered, that Obama's rise illuminated in other ways as well. Where his presidency was symbolic for some, for others it portended a frightening sign of things to come. It is precisely this portent that would inspire the benighted Birther and Tea Party movements. If Obama were the light, a luminescent, dazzling beacon leading America ashore after a rocky and rough passage with George W. at the helm, then Trump is, in effect, a byproduct *of* that very light. He is the shadow cast by Obama's radiance. He is a void, a backdrop, a curtain audaciously attempting to upstage and envelop the masterful actor's remarkable brilliance on the world's stage with complete and downright darkness. It has all the makings of a children's story, or a *horror* story: the drape that discovered its life purpose was to block out the blazing sunlight, the valance that was so envious, so villainous, it could not wait for the show to end and so set out to sabotage the groundbreaking performance, seeking to obscure and ultimately *overshadow* the main player.

As the election dust settled, one thing became certain: Trump could not wait to close the curtains on the Obama show. But the true horror, the difficult-to-digest truth of what ultimately has unfolded in our society, is the bitter realization that a not-insignificant faction of the American electorate actually *embraced* the shade; they could not bring themselves to bask in Obama's transformative light.

We now all know the history. We can trace the genesis of our societal menace to a time in early 2011, even before the now infamous White House Correspondents' Dinner, when Trump decided the only way to contend with the reality of a Black president—who was objectively beautiful, brilliant, benevolent, and beloved—was to question the very *legitimacy* of his presidency. That the legitimacy of Trump's own tenure would, ironically, be legitimately questioned is yet additional evidence highlighting not only the hypocrisy of a man who had long made a habit of projecting his worst qualities onto others but, of the formidable forces of karma.

Actually, the Birther bullshit had been around years before Trump made it his calling card. The first whispers began in conservative Illinois circles back in 2004 when soon-to-be Senator Obama displayed the promise the world would recognize four short years later. But it was just that, mutterings, insignificant rumblings among irascible Republicans, those who knew that in the postmodern era they must cloak racism for its insidiousness to continue unabated and, for these pernicious purposes, undetected. It was Trump, with the megaphone of reality television stardom, who *amplified* the lie, turning murmurs into his ignoble battle cry.

I can still recall seeing this petulant punk, his combover resembling corn silk as it glowed under the studio lights, where, perched on the edge of his chair on "The View," he resurrected this falsehood despite the decries of the hosts around him. Trump resembled a man ready to take a dump as he sat there, determined to shit all over our president. I balked at the temerity of this tyrant who so blatantly, so callously tried to poison the well that America drinks from. It did not matter that Obama was like water, a combination of elements that rendered him in many ways greater than the disparate forces that had come together to create him. It did not matter that in many ways Obama was the confluence of two rivers that, given his mixed heritage, had converged to create a swell carrying a divided populace forward. It did matter to Trump that he was *not*, and he simply could not accept this. He instinctually knew what Obama represented even if, intellectually, he could not bend his warped mind around this immutable truth. Trump, like the rest of us, realized that the election of Barack Obama was a watershed moment in the history of this American experiment, and it offered, perhaps for the first time, an irrefutable threat to the preexisting paradigm of America and how it is run.

America had seen African American leaders rise since the Revolution. From Crispus Attucks to Frederick Douglass a century later, men and women of color and of mixed ancestry had fought and even died for a nation that in many ways was an unformed, unrealized entanglement of what it would become. But at this country's very core, during its nascency and beyond, an inscrutable truth was bearing out for

its Black and Brown inhabitants. This irrefutable fact, "That All Men Were Created Equal," was proffered as the ethos pulling many to this paradise, but as the transatlantic slave trade bore out, Black and Brown labor, Black and Brown bodies, Black and Brown murder propped up and fortified the very foundation of this new world. To put it plainly: America was living a lie. It was a colossal contradiction, a mighty conundrum, a holy hypocrisy that the country swept under the rug until nearly a century later when it threatened to tear the country apart; the precarious post-Revolutionary decades led to an upheaval that would force it to finally contend with that founding promise.

Civil Wars led to Civil Rights as the promise of full-fledged citizenship began its long, hard slough through decade after decade of Jim Crow and sanctioned violence, reinforcing Black American's second-class citizenship until we secured our rights and substantiated them through legislative means in the mid-1960s. Even then, the tenor of Black leadership, born out in the icy and fiery rhetoric of Martin Luther King and Malcolm X, serviced the movement and helped provide an irresistible formula that Black Americans could follow as we moved enchanted and enraged toward a better tomorrow.

To be Black in post-Civil War America was to be forced to live outside your reality in many ways, or at least in your mind's eye, in order to continue living at all in this land. Accepting the harshness of that reality without allowing it to hamper your resolve, if not your aspirations, was the spiritual work my people had engaged in since the sugarcane, rice, and cotton plantations trapped us in physical work during centuries of treacherous disenfranchisement. It was the temperament required to carry us through the century of sanctioned terror levied on us individually and collectively under the domination of "separate but equal." We could only hope for that day of reckoning, for that new dawn, when we would experience the thrill of basic respect and basic dignity.

Even up and through the sixties, the notion that we could somehow go beyond basic sociopolitical rights, and *become* power players, was something of which only the brightest and bravest dared dream. Even as a child, having been blessed to experience the period before and after Obama, I can recall when just the idea, the audacity to proclaim there could be a Black president was enough to prompt your elders to roll their eyes. In an earlier era, such grandiose pronouncements could even prompt a Black parent to level corporal penalties to prevent their children from harboring the wrong kinds of ambition. In the interest of the children, it was their duty, their job as parents and realists, to curtail such fantasies from getting a foothold in young people's consciousness by delivering a cutting reminder of what their parents had reminded them: you are a Black prisoner in a white paradise; do not get *too* big for your britches.

I can recall constant reminders, until the message was seared into my subconscious, that I am Black in a white man's world. The notion of Black folks existing on equal footing with whites in the world of politics, business, education, or even entertainment was so farfetched, so contrary to what I saw with my own eyes, that, in many ways, I never dared dream that big. It was safer, easier to travel through this maze of contradictions if I could resist pointing them out or challenging them. This was the medicine we fed ourselves and one another so that we could escape the precipitous fall, and subsequent pain, of not achieving a dream. In the post-Civil Rights era, "I Have a Dream" for many simply manifested itself as "Just Dream Enough." Dream of that well-paying city gig. Dream of becoming a teacher, an occupation providing some of the only true stability a Black person could enjoy in a postindustrial economy. Dream of dreaming your dream while you worked in a mundane capacity as a servant or a doorman. Dream while you whittled away the best years of your life in a service industry, waiting on the white folks who were living the dream in front of you, barely aware of your presence as your race and station rendered you invisible. Dream of enough energy to get you through the week until a bottle or a bag of instant happy could get you through the weekend so that you could begin the dispiriting process all over again. *That* was what I had come to define as a Dream—until Barack Hussein Obama came on the scene.

It is difficult to overstate what Obama means to me and to Black America. Attempting to convey his importance to a people who have long suffered the chronic reinforcement that they are incapable of scaling such heights is nearly impossible. If Frederick Douglass crawled so that W.E.B. DuBois could walk, and W.E.B. walked so that Martin Luther King, Jr., could run, then Martin ran so that Barack Obama could fly! For a people grounded for generations on this North American plane, the fact that one of us had ascended to unfathomable heights cannot be fully appreciated by many outside our much-maligned outfit. For a people weighed down by the albatross of race, purposefully depressed and debilitated by society's demand that we were born and would live without wings, it was truly a miracle that a brotha, one of our own, could soar.

For countless years, we had been forced to accept athletic superiority as our only crown in a society which trafficked in the invalid theory of Black mental inferiority. The irony, lost on few, was that for decades the only Black man out of Chicago that we believed could actually fly was Michael Jordan. But his athletic prowess and much publicized superhuman exploits, though inspiring, served mainly as a stimulant, a designer drug providing an exhilarating rush that made you *feel* great while otherwise dulling your senses to the reality of your own rabid devaluation. Being children, heavily inundated with all things Air Jordan during his 1980s and '90s media blitz, many of my contemporaries, consumed by Jordan's palliative effect, accepted without question the disastrous ramifications of the Reagan/Bush era— despite the literal drug epidemic their policies exacerbated all around us.

Growing up during this era, I became aware of this blinding contradiction when witnessing Jordan's own egregious abdication, the moment he supplied his now infamous "Republicans buy sneakers, too" gaffe. Here was a person who was synonymous with flight, but who refused to truly take off despite all his media and cultural power. The irrepressible subtext to this intoxicating and successful advertising slogan was "it's okay to 'Be Like Mike'" because Mike himself had no desire to proselytize or philosophize or do more than dunk balls and sell dumb sneakers. His desultory views on equality were in many ways augmented *by* his impact as a pitchman and the disturbing fact that he proffered materialism at the expense of anything truly meaningful. And we coveted items we did not need, distracted enough to not devote our energies to what we truly *did* need. Jordan proved that he could elevate, at times seemingly levitate, but the ultimate tragedy is that he never endeavored to enlist himself in the cause of elevating the millions around him. He merely exhibited excellence within a designated 94-foot by 50-foot perimeter. A safe space. Though whites and Blacks alike readily embraced him, his popularity soared basically because he never dared fly too high.

Juxtapose that with the junior senator from Illinois, a resident of the same Midwestern metropolis but who turned his Windy City wings into an airfoil supplying enough lift to get his plane off the ground. When Obama stood onstage in Hyde Park with his equally magnanimous wife to celebrate his election victory in 2008, he was not hoisting some simple-ass trophy, earned from triumphing in some inconsequential game. He was celebrating an epic victory, one that a nation of people in every city, town, and county could celebrate with fervor. He had seized the brass ring, a ring that truly mattered, and he did it by dunking all over the establishment that had been hacking and undercutting us for centuries.

Cyrus McQueen @CyrusMMcQueen · Nov 15, 2016
I have a dream, one day Presidents will live in a nation and not be judged by the color of their skin but by the content of their character. https://t.co/rt7iOm8sve

⇄ 83   ♡ 280

Whether he was overhauling our healthcare system, rescuing the auto industry, or even tracking down terrorists, Obama met resistance from the very moment he was sworn in that cold January day in 2009. The coolness from his conservative contemporaries on Capitol Hill seemed to mimic the frost I observed on the trees along the National Mall that day. That is why to me the term "Resistance" is somewhat curious and in many ways ironic when applied to the anti-Trump era. Given the Republican backlash that Obamacare and its namesake triggered amongst conservatives, if there has ever been resistance in our time, it was when Mitch McConnell and John Boehner, along with the myriad of losers and lost souls who launched the Tea Party, decided to resist *every* step that Obama took to make America truly great. They stood in hostile opposition to his presidency and simply refused to accept the change he proffered and eventually provided. Resistance to that form of change was transparent and, in many ways, traditional, given the racial makeup of the man himself and of the country that had only granted its African American population first-class citizenship a mere few years after he was born.

That Trump would coin the phrase "Make America Great Again" after Obama had withstood an obstructionist Republican Congress to enact policies that made him the most progressive president in at least half a century was not only ironic but especially insidious given that the idiot championing the term had made it his business to undermine one of the greatest, truest champions this country has ever known. If Obama was, again, comparable to some beautiful plane, an enchanting jumbo jet that jettisoned every antiquated, disparaging notion of Blackness, making enough room for *all* of Black America to board *Air Force 1* with him, his hopes for change becoming our new reality, then Trump was a saboteur, a stowaway riding his coattails, waiting for his moment to bring down the flight. Trump would come to possess every loathsome quality we apply to terrorists. His play for the spotlight, his covetous nature, ultimately fueled his insatiable desire to destroy Obama by attempting to hijack the flight.

Upon reflection, it is quite unfortunate that we never got to fully experience how high Obama could actually climb. Trump, and his Republican cohorts on Capitol Hill, through obstructionism and barbarousness, saw to it that the president would never fully experience what it was like to fly the friendly skies.

Even Trump's rapaciousness, however, was no match for his overwhelming cowardice, ensuring that he dared not take on the subject of his ire in the 2012 general election. No, his Birther bologna was a non-confrontational masterstroke best employed from afar, its mendacity ill-suited as a platform for running against the magic man himself. Trump would never try to fight his way into the cockpit and take over the controls; ultimately, he was too insecure, too impotent for such an undertaking. So, he set out to hijack the narrative instead.

Cyrus McQueen @CyrusMMcQueen · Jul 11, 2016
People blame #Obama cause things didn't change. But like a good doctor he did make us feel better... America is just sicker than we thought.

🔁 29   ♡ 119

Trump, malignant motherfucker that he is, went about the boorish task of spreading hatred, one pompous tweet at a time. He became a disease that attacked not only Obama, with increasing virulence, but every healthy and positive undertaking the president undertook; even going so far as to tell CNN's Wolf Blitzer that it's "a lotta crap" that Obama even gets credit for signing off on the raid that killed Osama Bin Laden. Never once failing to drop his big lie and mantra about birth certificates, Trump set out to confuse and corrupt the dialog about the healthcare overhaul and America's economic recovery (a ploy he would later employ when it came to the nation's pandemic preparedness, arguing that Obama had "left the cupboards bare") by infecting the core of middle America with his cancerous fabrications. He took blue and purple states, places that had experienced a tangible turnaround under Obama, places that had exhibited a renewed vitality, and he exposed an undercurrent that had merely ebbed during his predecessor's tenure. He then fed the tumor of racial animus and resentment by identifying that there were those who, like him, never sat comfortably with a Black man in the cockpit, despite the fact that Obama had flown them, and us, out of a turbulence that had truly rocked this country. Once the devil had diagnosed the disease, he then facilitated its growth, spreading it in every tweet and rally he could until a country apparently in remission saw its cancer return after nearly fifty years.

The seismic shift this country would experience when Obama's main detractor supplanted the Democrat as chief executive created an unnerving rumble felt from coast to coast. His character assassinations of our beloved president consolidated a conservative base, energizing it to the point of actually voting against their best interests, and we watched them carry his fat ass right into the Oval Office. Among Trump's supporters, their racist predisposition enabled them to reconcile themselves to his multiple extramarital affairs, predation, dalliances with porn stars, financial improprieties, tax manipulations, Twitter twaddle, belligerence, and overall uncouthness—as well as the treasonous implications behind his impassioned run; they just could *not* reconcile themselves to a Black man as president of the United States.

Trump was clearly aware of this, even if he knew instinctively that he could never beat the transcendent Obama straight up. But rarely has a bully shied away from taking on a woman or from relishing an opportunity to assert his dominance over another hamstrung segment of the population. So, with Obama now effectively out of the picture, Hillary, a proven punching bag of Republicans, brought out those pugnacious imbeciles, those aptly described "deplorables" who deeply resented women in power, a resentment that ran concurrent with an inherent disdain for *Black* people in power. At least that much had become apparent in the months of numbness following Election 2016.

When Trump stood, poised to take the Oath of Office the following January, my mind traveled back to that warm pool of humanity in which I had been immersed eight years earlier—what now felt like a lifetime. This was not supposed to happen. This was a fever dream, an ice storm crashing elephant-sized hail upon the heads of the progressive family. In contrast to the undeniable warmth belying the literal cold at

Obama's Inauguration, I was shivering in my heated apartment. Trump's Inauguration produced tremors as I watched it unfold in a flop sweat, the blizzard of emotions it unleashed sending chills down my very spine. Winter was upon us.

Almost immediately, Trump set out to set himself apart from his predecessor with policies that would upend the country and send us into the tailspin that has dizzied us since. His move to ban Muslims from several Middle Eastern and African countries from entering the United States—even before filling crucial cabinet positions—was the first sign this president was intent on translating racist rhetoric into racist policies. After falsely labeling Obama as a Muslim, he went about vilifying the entire religion—before rolling out a travel ban that would do nothing *to* make America safer.

Cyrus McQueen @CyrusMMcQueen · May 6, 2017
It's unfortunate the #ACA was spearheaded by a black man... it appears Republicans would rather watch you die than let a black man save you.

↻ 161   ♡ 416

Trump is undoubtedly a simple man, but he deserves credit for recognizing that the simple-minded minions who drank from his poisoned well needed easy-to-swallow slogans. "Repeal and Replace" would become the latest poison he poured down their gullible gullets, his ignorant catchphrase intoxicating them. Although it did prove to be an effective lubricant, an interesting development had taken hold during the seven years following the Affordable Care Act's passage. The poor and the powerless, the very people whose vulnerability Obama sought to assuage, had seemingly developed good will toward his good deed. Certain Republicans in Congress came to realize this, too, along with the existential threat that repealing the ACA would pose to their political lives. That realization was reflected in the margin, albeit narrow, by which Congress eventually upheld the law, despite the destructive charge that Trump spearheaded. Trump's failure to repeal Obamacare reflected the temperature within many congressional districts. Even if the men and women in Congress vocally hated the act's architect, their constituents embraced the lower premiums and coverage his masterwork had provided. Unfortunately, none of this would completely dissuade Trump as his efforts to create a conservative majority on the Supreme Court betrayed this unyielding objective.

By day, I was taking to Twitter to highlight the inadequacies of our president and the even wider disparities between him and his predecessor. By night, I was taking to the stage, conducting a chorus of appalled and outraged audience members who, in increasing numbers, were singing my tune. I still delighted in devoting a couple of minutes to resurrecting my Obama impression—I had never tired of it—for crowds that never tired of *hearing* it. While he was off enjoying a well-earned respite from the spotlight, parasailing and jet skiing, drinking out of a coconut, and wearing fancy unbuttoned Hawaiian shirts and expensive leather sandals, I decided the world did not need *two* retired Obamas. No, me, we, the family of brotherhood and all that was beautiful in this world, missed his shining example. Hell, we missed the normality! If anything, this proved just how much we indeed cherished Obama, even as his light grew dimmer and Trump's tempestuousness immersed us in gloom. While I could still keep Obama's name afloat on social media by punching out tweets, the performance stage provided an even more entertaining and spacious platform by which to keep Hope alive.

Since the former president had, by most accounts, disappeared into thin air (rightfully so, given that such a brilliant, benevolent man would not, could not, allow himself to be the straw man for Trump's shenanigans), I felt compelled to make him reappear on stage every night. And crowds began to coo the second they again heard their beloved president's voice. Often, I would barely get through the first line or two before the men and women in attendance would begin to whistle and clap, the memory of the man flooding them with positive vibes and setting the vibration my impersonation would then move to. Often this theater of the mind became interactive, a moment of suspended belief convincing them that they were once again in the presence of their president. It would often compel an impromptu Q & A, crowds champing at the bit to ask Obama a question, shouting in rapid succession, "What do you think of Trump?" or "Where have you been?!" It brought me joy to bring the audience joy. It was cathartic, therapeutic, to dwell in that space, be it ever so briefly, where we could forget the villainy coming out of the Trump White House, and I could channel our cherished champion.

Trump's assault on everything Obama—from his attempt to "Repeal and Replace" the ACA to the pernicious claim that Obama had wiretapped him—was undoubtedly forged by the uncontrollable hatred he harbored for Black people. But it was Obama, the majestic, magnetic man himself, who inspired Trump's ire in large part *because* he had captured all that Trump coveted without any of Trump's skullduggery. Because the former president was scandal free, Trump needed to create a scandal in order to lessen the distance between the two and bring Obama down to his level. The pleasure he derived from sullying a person with a clean reputation was the driving force behind these relentless attacks. There simply is no other way to explain the incessant, interminable bombardment of baseless lies that Trump rained down on him. Obama embodies everything that Trump himself is not, infamy and ignominy making certain the reality star can never enjoy the sterling prestige earned by the object of his envy.

Neither could Trump lay claim to having succeeded through honest, hard work. He was a man who, by all accounts, had received every break imaginable, given his privilege and race; it especially rankled him that someone like Obama, who was not supposed to achieve liftoff, did it all on the up and up, surprising the world and taking *us* on the ride of our lives. It is the only way to explain why Trump, the eternal brat and bully, continues to besiege Obama, the overachieving and attractive captain, even after it is no longer expedient. This is not political; this is personal.

That Trump would devote precious time during his own presidency to furthering the deception, to attempting to disgrace his predecessor, is curious on its face, but it becomes incredibly clear once you unpack the motivations of a man who had been conning anyone he could for a lifetime. That he himself was raised to be racist is crucial to this analysis, but, perhaps more important, that he was also raised to be duplicitous contributed even *more* to the campaign of misinformation he launched. If misery loves company, then Trump succeeded in compelling the skewed men and women of middle America to join him in his pity party.

By generating enough distrust and outright disdain for the nation's first Black president he was able to then lob any accusation against him, knowing it would stick. For Trump, populism provided that necessary crack, a shared sense of racial superiority getting his foot in middle Americas door, however, his ability to manipulate those malleable minds is what has *kept* him there.

With Trump in office, I for the first time questioned the nature of his intellect. I had long concluded that Trump was not smart in the traditional sense, but here was a man who did not speak well or, I could surmise, write well, yet he had somehow captivated a dyspeptic portion of our population.

For far too long, I assumed, perhaps wrongly and to my own detriment, that dumb Donald was simply too dense to accept that our former president was born in Hawaii. I assumed that racism, a mental disease that allows foolishness and falsehoods to fester, was behind Birtherism, but perhaps I had underestimated the true motivations behind this mendacity. After his deception had fueled a successful presidential run, when, post-victory, he was still gassing up on this grand fallacy, I had to ask myself a tough question. Was Trump dumb enough to believe the lies he spread or, as was more and more apparent, was he smart enough to know that other people would be dumb enough to believe the lies he spread?

The answer came swiftly and resoundingly after Trump had been in office only a few short months. When he completely fabricated the story that Obama had wiretapped him during the campaign, I knew that Trump posed an even greater danger than I had initially estimated. He was no longer taking someone else's lie and running with it. He was no longer creating falsehoods on the fly to serve his fragile ego—or merely being flippant, as seemed to be his penchant when he was preparing to be pugnacious. He was now *in* the lie-making business. Fabricating 24/7, he had turned the White House into a lie-concocting factory that churned out several fictions a day, the supply always outpacing the demand. With a twitter account, a press secretary, and a gaggle of sycophants operating the echo chamber he had created in the West Wing, their lies would travel halfway around the world before the media's army of truth tellers could even get their boots on.

While the world and the media reeled from the deception emanating from the White House, my disdain rose. The lie launching his political career should have portended the disaster to which we were now subjected. The litany of lies Trump increasingly relied on to survive in a role for which he was ill-prepared and ill-suited can always be traced back to that initial whopper about Obama's birth, it the historical hinge that opened the door to this dark portal we are traveling through. A presidency built on deceit, and sustained on subversion and subterfuge got all the sustenance it needed once that big lie received enough attention and nourishment to starve any semblance of truth.

This chapter therefore begins and ends with Birtherism. We can only frame this facsimile of a presidency, this miserable moment in our life and times, by highlighting how and *why* it came to be. The legacies of these two disparate men, and their disparate administrations, will forever be intertwined. Trump's efforts, and ultimate failure, to eclipse Obama's legacy will render the successes of the former POTUS *that* much more appreciable. The contrast between the two, in an historical context, will therefore be stark and discernible. As Trump has plunged the country into darkness, the man he attempted to diminish glows that much brighter. A small-minded, self-absorbed nincompoop, Trump never stopped to consider how his shortcomings and abject failures would make his presidential counterpart—the bane of his existence— shine even brighter in the public's eyes. Trump's entire run has been fueled by a jejune belief that a Black president could not outdo him, but, to the country's eternal detriment, he never stopped to consider that just perhaps *he* could not outdo a Black president.

4
Turning Back The Clock

Donald Trump is a racist. There is no reason to ponder the probability of that which has been proven over time to be a patent, immutable truth. Though the media has been infatuated with posing this question, rather redundantly, ever since he first voiced racist sentiments—and later exhibited racist behavior in his official capacity as president—I reckon it a sort of rhetorical device, an empty query compelled by those seeking soundbites who, themselves, are *clearly* aware of his malice. At least that is what I would *like* to tell myself.

However, the pithy, pitiful snippets that have worked their way into those chyrons in the lower inches of the television screen evince a failure by the talking heads—epitomizing society's even *greater* failure—as they merely project, and thus reflect, our country's utter lack of commitment with regard to this outstanding issue. Race is yet another aspect of the media's mindless routine, relegated to background noise, buried somewhere between sports and weather, unequivocally reduced to just another *thing*. Whenever news outlets do devote a few measly minutes to this all-encompassing issue, the existential implications evaporate almost as quickly as the text on the screen. In these moments, such empty wording lands with a deafening thud, it ceasing to be inquiry and transforming into more of a declaration. It is not a matter of whether or not racism is a factor with Trump—or in our greater society. For those white journalists, now juxtaposed with the reality of this charged era and what *is* of grave consequence for those like myself, this sort of feigned sincerity tends to infuriate, with their obtuseness far more evocative:

49

given what they now so cavalierly report, racism clearly has never been a factor for *them*.

The fact remains that our press, along with the greater public, knows the apparent and unfortunate answer to the question they so casually posit, even if their disingenuousness still works its way into the news cycle with such frequency. Racism, to put it plainly, is as crucial a component of Donald Trump as his blood type. It is the oxygen he breathes. It fuels and defines him. And it distinguishes him from his distinguished predecessor and the millions of Americans who sought to overcome this societal scourge when they cast ballots for Barack Obama and the progress *he* proffered.

The insidious, brutal implication of Donald Trump's election is that a wounded, criminal cadre of Americans brazenly cast ballots for him specifically *because* his candidacy also represented a form of change. Unfortunately, the change in this instance was less in the traditional sense of the word and more of a restitution, a *return* to a dynamic that had defined the American power structure prior to 2009. Donald Trump did not campaign to make America anew but to reestablish a prior status quo. His election would therefore be revanchist, *white* America's form of reparations, an endeavor to Make America Great Again based on the flawed premise that Caucasian control *is* what makes America great. This was the underlying theme to a presidential run that, roaring out of the gates with ghastly generalizations of Mexicans and minorities, established that it would indeed be a campaign unlike any we were accustomed to.

Whether we accepted it or not, *this* would be a presidential race about race. This would be a referendum on the previous eight years and that unmistakable metamorphosis America underwent. And Donald Trump was going to make it so with every flagrant and furtive move— his descent on that Trump Tower escalator sending this country on a descent into sheer madness.

To ponder whether America has a race problem is incredibly offensive. A rumination so superfluous is perhaps the greatest form of histrionics any member of the media can engage in. Simply put, race *is* America. It is the extraordinary excrescence, the poisonous plant, the canker that has been rotting our multicultural society since Christopher Columbus planted the seed—all before French, British, and Dutch colonizers fertilized it, facilitating its ability *to* flourish. Donald Trump is simply the latest in a corrosive continuum to harvest this European hemlock, this monumental blight, for capital and personal gain. One need only trace his devolution, from petulant adolescent punk in Queens, New York, to petulant septuagenarian punk in Washington, D.C., to discover a spoiled man whose entire life and lineage, whose meteoric climb, was impelled by this poisonous sense of superiority. Whiteness, and all the superciliousness associated with it, *is* paramount to who he is.

That Trump emerged in a pre-Civil Rights America, in a home that trafficked in the disparaging belief that Blacks are inferior, is crucial to understanding both the man and the problem he would perpetuate as an adult. His station not only as a male of European descent but as a wealthy white male in an America that reflected and reinforced the implicit power of such a designation shaped his worldview and ultimately influenced his denigrating opinions of nonwhites. Though the deadly vines of his privilege and racial ideologies intertwine hopelessly, his early experiences dealing with African Americans as subservients likely services this vituperation and continues to influence his poisonous perspective on Black and Brown people—while also informing, one might add, how unlikely he is to view us in positions of power positively.

To be Caucasian is to belong to a race that appears to hold some sort of magical and intrinsic value. It is also, perhaps, the perfect way of explaining the stratification of the American electorate in recent years. Even when poverty befalls you as an American of European descent, you can look down on a person of color, even one who may possess more monetarily. Somewhere, our American covenant has granted a certain munificence to white skin, rendering Black culture, indeed our very own flesh, worthless. *Those* are the rules in America. Though we went from chattel, to Three-Fifths, to Separate But Equal, the Civil Rights Movement, which garnered our legitimacy through legislative means, is immaterial to a man like Trump whose identity, his incredulity with regard to Obama, indeed his entire sense of self-worth, are all predicated on this false sense of superiority that his father and his community uphold.

Compound that with Trump's upper-class upbringing and having been sent away to military school, ostensibly rejected from his home, and it becomes clearer how a man reared in perhaps the world's most diverse city could sleepwalk through this country's most tumultuous times, daydream through a sociopolitical reimagining, and exit the 1960s unaffected—his belief in white supremacy undeterred. Consequently, any attempt to separate the troubled man from his most troubled past, from those discriminatory beliefs he ingested and then went on to widely disseminate, would be impossible.

Make no mistake about it: Donald Trump is damaged goods. Even those with the loosest knowledge of mental illness and the manner in which it manifests in a person's behavior and personality can easily determine that the 45th president, in addition to being unfit to carry out his duties, is certifiably *unwell*. Psychologists could likely make short work of an individual whose whole notion of personal value was so gravely damaged by a brutal father and a loveless childhood that, one could conclude, what we have since witnessed on the world stage is, essentially, a man working through these issues or, better put, these issues working *him*, in real time.

Misogyny and bigotry are hard-wired in Trump's mind, as is the more debilitating notion that he is a reject. But the key to understanding him is that while reinforcing his son's insecurities, his father simultaneously reinforced a fundamental, albeit flawed, sense of gender and racial superiority. Trump as we know him, a man undeniably shaped by these defining, somewhat discordant forces that scourge us all, is thus thoroughly convinced *he* is not good enough. His obvious projections, the mounting evidence of his many failures, along with his constant, crippling need for validation, confirms this. Yet somehow, in that same space, he has, paradoxically, convinced himself that he is mightier than the marginalized.

Thus, his filial inheritance, it would be safe to say, consists of a financial *and* a racial endowment. And when Fred Trump also funneled in excess of $400 million to his ne'er-do-well son, even bailing him out as recently as the 1990s by buying nearly $4 million worth of gambling chips in an effort to save his hemorrhaging Atlantic City casino, it also likely reinforced preexisting dynamics *between* father and son. While the father would reportedly hide much of his money to avoid taxes, one could surmise that the elder Trump probably did little to hide his disdain of Donald, the lifeline of cash likely coming with a lambasting that would reinforce his son's feelings of ineptitude well into adulthood. Trump is in many ways a man trying to live up to certain expectations while also living down a litany of financial and personal disappointments, his low self-esteem cloaked in self-aggrandizement, his perpetual underachievement masked by specious and fulsome press coverage that falsely suggests he has always exceeded those expectations.

Given the identity and ideology Fred Trump fostered in his boy, Trump knew his father *had* to be right about Black people, because he was also right when it came to him—that despite the facade, despite the public pretense, despite all the doctored *Forbes* Lists and magazine covers, deep down he really is a dumbass disappointment. Therefore, his subsequent success, if you wish to call it that, from his business career to his pursuit of political power and legitimacy, is really fueled by a desire to not only court his father's favor in one respect but also to confirm all his ill-conceived, skewed assessments with regard to race as well, however unsound that has rendered both men. Donald's hatred is thus twofold. It is his way of honoring his father's legacy while distracting from that other lasting outcome of this most problematic relationship and past: that deep down, he really hates *himself.*

Therefore, to truly understand Donald Trump, understand that, if only in his own twisted mind, he *needs* to be better than Black people, even the most accomplished Black man this country had ever seen. By tirelessly promoting his superiority, even establishing the verisimilitude of his value, others, even he himself, might eventually come to believe in it. For the more time he spends looking down on people of color, women, etcetera, the less time he has left to look down on himself. This peremptory and self-fulfilling practice *is* his only way of actually elevating himself, of proving he has done his papa proud. Thus, the Trump household, his childhood, his parentage, and even the fate of his own siblings explain, better than anything else, who he became. Though their upbringing undoubtedly left an extreme void in both sons, where that toxicity caused his alcoholic brother to destroy himself, Donald has done the opposite, destroying everything around him. One Trump son imploded, the other *exploded.*

This helps to explain why, in the 1970s, the Justice Department, which he ironically now runs, would sue Donald and his father for their brazen, blatant housing discrimination. If the Fair Housing Act of 1968, a follow-up to the landmark Civil Rights Act of 1964, would guarantee that no one could be discriminated against based on race, religion, or national origin with regard to the sale, rental, or financing of housing, the fact that Trump the son would flippantly skirt this rule suggests that this was a man who was both vying for his vile elder's approval *and* was unwilling to respect what the newly minted legislation suggested about Black equality.

That specific act, signed into law by Lyndon Johnson on the heels of Martin Luther King, Jr.'s assassination, itself a result of the leader's tireless work during the decade's latter part as reflected through both his Poor People's Campaign and his more comprehensive, evolved look into the greater detriment of economic injustice, stands as a definitive testament to King's enduring legacy. But for the newly deceased icon, whose crusade had crystallized amid the tenements and urban penury of the South Side of Chicago, to have a New York real estate magnate notate every African American applicant by the letter "C" for colored, before roundly rejecting their attempts at seeking fair accommodations in one of his buildings, meant that Trump stood in dogged defiance of the definitive change that *multiple* generations of Black leadership had shepherded.

If the past is prologue, his presidential objections and insistence on nullifying everything Obama suggests that Donald Trump is an even greater enemy of Black progress than many may have previously noted. His tempestuous history with Civil Rights would now prove prescient as, some fifty years later, we witness him empowering a host of advisors to enact policies to purposely, *specifically* erode those very advancements.

Given this context, we must not overlook that those very same federal courts, in this instance the Southern District of New York, now provide perhaps the only stopgap in dealing with Trump's myriad of mounting crimes, as well as restraining the mounting list of accomplices he has ensnared despite the insulation of his executive privilege and all the prerogatives that go along with it. In fact, Trump's tenure has proven instrumental in testing, and in many ways revitalizing, our faith in the justice system to halt a racist's efforts, whether it be a Manhattan federal judge ordering him to finally turn his tax returns over to a D.A. or a Hawaiian federal judge putting a hold on his proposed travel ban mere hours before it was set to go into effect.

Yet it was, again, that parental impact, the lessons and legacy of Fred Trump, as well as the full scope of a lifetime of hatred toward minorities, that came painfully into ever tighter focus, as he immediately set to wield his seemingly absolute power as the head of government *to* issue said travel bans. His disregard for DACA, his forceful separation of families at our border, the villainous way he has concomitantly set out to orphan immigrant children provides yet further evidence this president, after a lifetime of inculcating his father's insidious values, is intent on marrying rhetoric with debilitating action—thereby confirming his racism beyond any reasonable doubt.

Years of cheap talk and racially inspired directives formerly carried out on a minuscule scale with respect to his properties are now overshadowed by his actions and expanded purview as chief executive—actions that are bolder and speak louder than any of his prior protracted, bigoted bombast. What started as an unwillingness to allow African Americans to live in his buildings has devolved over his adulthood into a desire, and eventually a plan, to evict as many people of color as possible from this country. Whether it is reducing the number of refugees allowed into the United States to historical lows, or ramping up deportations, he has deemed America to be one of his properties. His acrimonious relationship with Civil Rights and that movement's primary beneficiaries has manifested into an all-out war, where walls and cages win the latest in this, his lifelong series of battles against Black and Brown people.

Cyrus McQueen @CyrusMMcQueen · Dec 8, 2017
Why the fuck would you have Trump at the opening of a Civil Rights Museum any goddamn way?? That's like havin Roy Moore chaperone a Junior Prom...

↻ 4374   ♡ 14605

Donald Trump declared war on Black America, yet many Americans appeared unaware of not only *what* this presidency portended but what it would ultimately reveal about a country that so secretly resents our proximity to power. If this nation begrudged President Obama and every forward step Black Americans had made in the decades since Civil Rights were realized, then Trump, through his flagrant efforts to boost Birtherism, encouraged *that* nation to share its awful secret. Having engaged in such widespread, widely known housing discrimination with his dad (not to mention his brazen, bigoted attempt to vilify the very innocent young men known as the Central Park Five), Trump effectively made a case *for* making prejudice public again.

It is now abundantly clear that throughout his lifetime, he has been willing to fall on his foolish sword when it comes to race. Hell, it has proven to be a hill the motherfucker is more than willing to die on. His landing on Capitol Hill after staking his candidacy on this—and being rewarded with the highest office in the land in spite of it—signals to white Americans that prejudice and racism no longer need operate surreptitiously. By demonstrably voicing his disdain for people of color—unapologetically, almost cravenly, connecting minorities with criminality—he convinces a manipulable public that not only is racism acceptable but, in his twisted logic, that Black and Brown people are thereby *unacceptable*. He implores white Americans to decide, his duplicitous crusade driving a wedge within a populace long guided by the propagation of division. And his loaded slogans ultimately gain traction because ours is a society long divorced from principle: we elect who to live with based on selfish, childish wants, *not* on what is actually best for the entire family.

Not to oversimplify matters, but with Trump having forced a fork in the road, the existential implications behind this selection became binary as well; it is either him or us, you are against him or against *us*. The precursor to this negative outcome is neither nebulous nor difficult to compute. This zero-sum game, this clamorous sprint to seize our country's soul would come at an unambiguous cost; it means that the survival of one must lead to the demise of the *other*.

Make no mistake about it: Make America Great Again is a declaration of war. Minorities, whether they be African Americans, Muslims, or those fleeing unfathomable turmoil and penury, true existential crises, would heretofore be deemed the unequivocal enemy. If you can convince a disaffected portion of the populace that your victory is their victory, and that their problems result from some enemy that, through your pernicious attacks, they come to adopt as their actual adversary, then you will not even need to draft them into your war; they will willingly enlist.

The relentless attacks on Obama are, again, the denouement in a lifetime of disrespect toward Black people. We knew we were engaged in a war with this wimp when he fired his first shots at our impressive president. The enemy combatant had announced himself and his intentions to take this conflict to its logical conclusion, the White House. Winning the general election would place him in a position not just to best Obama but to then rack up the casualties as Brown bodies could be detained at the border or denied medical coverage or deported by the gestapo now going by a chilly acronym that encapsulated their cold bloodedness: ICE.

African Americans recognized Trump's endgame even when some of our liberal neighbors failed to fully grasp the high stakes that were involved. Liberalism can be awfully fickle when you, literally, have no skin in the game. Black folks instinctually feel, given a lifetime of relegation and generations of dehumanization hard-wired into our DNA, that Trump presented a danger unlike any democratic foe before him. His election posed an existential threat that, to us, superseded factions. Those who could not bring themselves to vote for Hillary, who were "Bernie or Bust," who would cast protest votes or convinced themselves that a third party and Jill Stein were the only logical choice, could likely fall back on convenient skin and a cozy societal designation. In this respect, whiteness is like a safety school. The Democratic elite shot for the Ivy Leagues, but their hopes unfulfilled, they settled on a state college. However, it looked as if they would be okay. Even if Trump's election was not what some wanted, even if many held their noses and cried as they contended with a shitty outcome no one had fully envisioned, even if they begrudgingly resigned themselves to the reality of this moribund presidency, their future *still* appeared bright.

People of color, conversely, had *everything* to lose with Trump's election. We had experienced the Ivy Leagues by proxy with our incredible president, and we knew on a cellular level that Trump's election would sound a siren, awakening us from our dream like a police officer at Yale, that privileged place we had only briefly experienced now turning on us, our presence no longer welcome, our expulsion thereby guaranteed. If our upward mobility, or in this particular instance, our immobility, could be seen as a threat to the imbalance that had long benefited the majority of Americans, then it would undoubtedly be used against us now—these power brokers ensuring that our eight-years-long illustrious dream *would* abruptly end.

That was why Trump's overtures to African Americans on the campaign trail and shortly after his election were curious, confounding, and downright infuriating. The boogeyman was attempting to barter his way into our good graces. "Whaddya have to lose" and his carefully curated, if sparsely attended, photo ops in random Black churches were nothing more than instances of the big, bad wolf playing dress up so as to get near the delicious meal he craved. His halfhearted efforts belied the very fact that Birtherism, his racist endeavor to devour a Black president, had revealed his fangs; no amount of rhythmless swaying would be likely to sway this proud voting bloc or conceal the wet snout we could all see he had futilely caked with bronzer. It was unconscionable that this mongrel now tried to satiate himself on a handful of Black voters, attempting to fatten us up with hollow flattery so we would be ripe for the picking. He had plenty of dummies at his disposal, from Ben Carson to Omarosa, who professed his good intentions, who, to take from another fairy tale, did their deft take on Hansel and Gretel, proffering their good fortune under Trump's thumb so we would not notice as he prepared to throw us all in the oven and feast on our reduction.

That was why this pageant of dunces after Election Day was so particularly dispiriting. When notable African Americans lined up in the Trump Tower lobby to kiss the ring after his improbable win, the sickness in my stomach threatened to reveal itself all over my shoes. I literally became ill at the sight of Ray Lewis and Steve Harvey, Kanye West and Jim Brown stepping into the shiny trap of flashbulbs Trump had set up on the ground floor of his eponymous building. These were men who the world had celebrated, and who we, as a people, had championed for not only their successes but for also seemingly taking us with them. Through their collective work, they had spoken to the culture and for the culture—whether it was Kanye's illuminating wordplay and artistry or Steve Harvey's title as one of *The Original Kings of Comedy,* sharing hilarious and salient tidbits on what it meant to grow up Black and, later, to be a loving Black husband and father—or Ray Lewis and Jim Brown, greats on the gridiron who transcended sport to become moral authorities and activists, compiling a body of philanthropic work that rivaled their athletic careers. These men, who had undoubtedly sacrificed to become the best in their respective fields, who clearly possessed a vision and a brilliance that powered their improbable rise from the bottom to the top, now revealed, to the world and to our community's chagrin, a glaring absence of those very qualities that had made them so special in the first place.

Where these Greats would go on to confess that they merely wanted "a seat at the table," they would fail to report that, in so doing, they had struck a Faustian bargain. Their entry had come at a hefty cost, granted because *we* were on the menu. Furthermore, one could surmise, they had been offered a seat primarily because they had not stood up for their brother Barack. In fact, they had a spot in the devil's dining room only because they were *not* standing up for the rest of us either. They were

58

there for *themselves*. And that hurt me deeply. No amount of cheese, no slice of cheddar, was better than being in the corner of your community when a man who had declared war on us was, through his win, equipped to besiege that very community, rolling back the gains his predecessor and our predecessors had secured with every new policy and cabinet appointment he made.

It was Trump's time-tested ability to lure Black celebrities with an alacrity that belied his truly sinister motives that ultimately lulled these men into a sense of comfort and complacency. Their wealth and privilege made them invulnerable to his behind-the-scenes maneuvers to position us, the enemy, on ground precarious enough that he could then begin toppling us one after the other. I can still recall this invidious display inspiring me to scream at my television the way one screams at a movie during a slasher film as the unsuspecting victim wanders into a house of horrors. The killer lies in wait, anticipating the precise moment to strike and chop them to pieces. And I was shouting in my head, "Don't do it! Don't go in there!! NOOOO!!!" But Trump's endless parade of well-wishers and ass-kissers offered undeniable evidence of his maddening ability to mask those aforementioned fangs with a smile, as he readied himself to sink his very teeth into our exposed Brown necks.

This ability of his was a woeful portent betraying his potential for pure heinousness, further conveying that he was working out of a truly diabolical playbook. Unlike the Hall of Famers present for the pageant, Trump was positioning himself for victory in the only game that really mattered; the players were, in fact, the ones getting played.

Trump would not have gotten as far in life—certainly not to the White House—had he not figured out how to step on as many vulnerable and gullible white folks as he felt was warranted along the way. His real estate career in and around New York City was littered with casualties: as if it were sport, the litigious builder and the gaggle of lawyers and fixers in his employ blew away the livelihoods of small businesses, small business owners, and that long list of unfortunate vendors who found themselves on the short end of his high-powered rifle. His avarice made him particularly proficient at ruining people's careers, if not their entire lives, with not simply nefariousness but well-curated malevolence. That a dark and damaging racial ideology influenced his every decision cannot be debated. It was his desire to look down on everyone *else* around him, elevating himself by squashing those unable to stop him, that created the blueprint he would draw from to build his shoddy legacy.

To do business with Trump was to place yourself on the losing end, your profits never amounting to more than those somewhat debatable benefits provided by mere proximity to his power. Trump instinctually knew this. He knew that if he could identify unscrupulous African Americans who would hover perilously close to the fire he possessed, like moths to a flame, then he could also easily find and manipulate those who looked like him, those whose best interests also would not be served, and convince them, too, that his fire would somehow fuel their growth.

Far too many Americans have sadly fallen sway to this spell: the hypnotic, transfixing flame, the only source of heat they feel they might ever experience, luring them closer and closer with promises of progress, even redemption, until it is ultimately too late and that fire, unleashed, reveals its true intention not to warm but to *burn*, using them to feed its own insatiable desire to grow bigger and bigger. These unfortunate men and women throughout middle America will ultimately come to realize this too late, if they even realize it at all, their scorched and singed wings destroyed by a blaze they helped create and, whose capacity for destruction they sadly underestimated. In Donald Trump's fire they see their reflection. But though they may bond through bigotry, they fail to grasp that they possess neither the capital nor the capriciousness that his affluence provides him, the carte blanche that supplied the accelerant to his inferno in the first place, the very class dispensation that contributes to the interminable path of destruction he leaves in his wake.

Having lived a life of unaccountability, Trump's tempestuousness could lead him into fruitless battles against threats both perceived and actual, his indemnity always absorbing the inevitable fallout. These malleable minds have no way of knowing that his enemies are not their enemies, or that he has no real enemies except those he outright earns through his own villainy. Trump manipulates moths into believing they are everything they are not and, though they lack his economic power, with their intentions spelled out for them, and a renewed sense of purpose, he persuades these revitalized pests to swarm and attack Black and Brown people, to eat away at the very fabric of this country, all while losing sight of the raging fire engulfing us all.

They have become convinced that it is their right, indeed their birthright, to look down on people of color, without ever stopping to consider that Trump looks down on us *all.* The red hats in red states across this country, poor and disenfranchised middle Americans, feel a false kinship with this crafty cretin, failing to realize that, as American flotsam, they may share Trump's whiteness, but when push comes to shove, their paucity of resources means that they indeed share *none* of his privilege.

Cyrus McQueen @CyrusMMcQueen · Sep 3, 2016
#TrumpInDetroit wasn't much of a success... As nearly 200 empty seats show: Only a #DonaldTrump could keep black people from goin to church.

♻ 335   ♡ 607

If Barack Obama's election represents a fulfillment of Martin Luther King's Dream, then President Donald Trump is his nightmare incarnate. As America spiraled into regression while its new commander and chief ramped up and capitalized off racial aggression, I could not help but think of the greatest champion for equality this country has ever witnessed as a maelstrom of hatred and incivility was unleashed like a flood upon our shores. Having come of age in post-Civil Rights America, my life testifies to the sacrifices of Dr. King and others in the Movement who had suffered a nearly indescribable toll amid sanctioned violence and the omnipresent threat of it—all while struggling to jackhammer a path through our cemented status as second-class citizens. That there was a time when a Donald Trump plagued virtually every city and municipality, ensconced in business and government on the local and national levels, is frightening now that we gag on Trump's particularly combustible concoction of race-based politics, that mixture he has brewed to blow up our norms and erode a half-century of progress. It makes us appreciate and ponder the fortitude that King and other powerful men and women possessed to withstand such onslaughts, who persevered against those who not only rendered our existence as illegitimate but also, through their station and this arbitrary matrix of social classification, had the power to erase us from the face of the earth. That our great forerunners endured and triumphed in the face of complete, unmistakable evil is in many ways unfathomable. To bombard a peaceful haven on a Sunday and obliterate the lives of four innocent little girls because they dared exist in America with Black skin; to murder three men, one Black and two Jewish, in the dead of night on a lonely Mississippi road for endeavoring to engage others in the

Democratic process; to sic German Shepherds on five-, six-, and seven-year-olds in the streets of Birmingham because they dared assemble in peaceful protest against incivility—all this was evidence that my forefathers and foremothers walked through hell on earth to ensure that a scorched landscape could harvest new growth for a new generation.

That epic movement made America what it is today, a nation that seemed to have moved past dogs siccing dogs on children. We lost countless lives, the continuum of casualties stretching from the middle passage to the middle of the last century, but as a people, through faith and determination, through sacrifices and indefatigable efforts, we weathered the brutal storm.

It was *that* legacy, that inviolable honor, that began informing and motivating me as never before, as storm clouds gathered again, now on my watch. Donald Trump had churned up a mighty wind with his rancor and discriminatory directives. This elephant-sized hail of animus now crashed down on a community of people who, post '65, had barely enjoyed a more equal footing before the heavens and the earth seemed to rumble once again, upending every inch of that newly viable ground.

Cyrus McQueen @CyrusMMcQueen · Nov 27, 2016
#Trump 's just a New York street hustler. He played 3-card-monte on the media and poor white folks... "Follow the spade, follow the spade..."

⟲ 23   ♡ 78

A large part of Trump's danger is due to the manner in which he has deftly transformed social media into a volatile landscape, almost summoning the ghosts of the past, the demons and dragons my people had once vanquished. He has resurrected that once-familiar, and all-too-destructive dominion of deplorables, emboldening them as never before, with the anonymity of social media, to be *openly* racist.

Abhorrent behavior, once associated with the enemies of the 1960s sit-ins and captured in black-and-white footage of documentaries and old newsreels, now incited my Twitter mentions on a daily basis. Make no mistake, I am no hero in the true sense of the word. I am no Freedom Rider or Black Panther, suffering the slings and arrows of a rabid and malevolent white public hell-bent on reinforcing my status as a second-class citizen through the threat and application of violence. I am merely a conscientious, caring objector to the vicissitudes vanquishing the progress my people and my president had achieved before the curtains opened on this shitshow. And what a perfect descriptor *to* encapsulate this putrid administration foisted upon the American public. I had never employed the poop emoji as much as when I found myself embroiled in a day to day tête-à-tête with a cross-section of buffoonish and morally bankrupt bigots who sought to validate this shitshow and all of the excrement flying out of the chief executive.

Early in the Trump presidency, virtually every tweet I fired off in this virtual landscape would attract the attention of an emboldened cadre of villains. They never hesitated to unleash a vitriolic rebuttal to my salient assessments of the swamp-like creature they championed. Whether they were bots or just lost souls whiling away the day asserting some false sense of superiority cloaked in a partisan reproach to the truth I proffered, it seemed I never could shine a light on the lies and misdirection coming out of the White House without the roaches and vermin feeding from this scum scurrying every which way when I dared illuminate the half-truths and shortcomings coming from Trump and his long con. The reactions to my 140-character missives became so caustic, so venomous, that often I found myself engaged in a combative, fruitless back and forth with some unnamed bigot emboldened by the false sense of confidence the thousand miles between us had created.

In such moments, the danger Donald Trump poses becomes especially clear. He so encourages these miscreants, these merciless motherfuckers, that they attack without warning or, at times, even without *prompting*. Donald Trump has taken the legacy of lynching and mob rule and modernized it. He has made his boys *proud*, creating a virtual mob of trolls who, inebriated on his intoxicating mixture of mistruth and racial-identity politics, *seize* upon a Black man asserting his humanity, his self-worth, and the humanity and self-worth of his people. Here, they attempt to extinguish the light, to virtually castrate me by calling me everything *but* a man, by calling me the same thing they had called the men and women who marched from Selma to Montgomery, struggling past gauntlets of racial animus: nigger. Donald Trump has successfully transformed Twitter into the Woolworth's lunch counter. Though hot coffee and fists do not rain down upon my head, my ears ring from that all-too-familiar obscenity, forcing me to again swallow that oldest, most bitter of American pies.

Making this new reality even tougher to contend with is that, unlike his prescient predecessors, men like John F. Kennedy and Lyndon Johnson, this president—with a Justice Department headed in his first years in office by an attorney general and Alabaman who had defiantly stood on the wrong side of history during that consequential decade—has now attempted to *strip* key provisions of the very Voting Rights Act that people like James Chaney, Andrew Goodman, and Michael Schwerner had died on that dark and lonely Mississippi road to secure.

Perhaps here is the most shocking revelation to come out of a Trump White House full of shocking revelations. Here is a president who has not only gone to war against a significant portion of the population, feverishly attempting to annihilate their every advancement, but, beyond that, who makes it abundantly clear, with words and actions, that he intends to not only undo Obama's legacy but, Kennedy's and Johnson's as well.

5

Picking At The Scab

The cacophony created by the cantankerous men and women on platforms like Twitter now threatened to drown out every attempt to address Trump's histrionics. That he appeared prone to using prominent African Americans to confuse, conflate, and connect Black calls for justice with criminality would be dangerous enough on its own. However, what revealed itself on social media was a counter-narrative, chiefly authored by him, as he competed for, and often captured, prominent space within our newsfeeds. Sadly, he usually managed to take attention off the facts just long enough to then slip additional lies in their place.

The call to end police brutality, indeed, the emergence of #BlackLivesMatter, created a sense of emergency among conservatives, and provided Trump with perhaps the most irresistible foil yet of his presidency. Misrepresenting the movement would become his most successful hijack *since* Birtherism. Where those earlier attacks were churlish and childish, they ultimately failed to bring down Obama. Nevertheless, they created enough racket in Trump's echo chamber that many who would have been better served by Obama's words and edifying wisdom never heard him over all the white noise. Colin Kaepernick, the former NFL quarterback and champion for social justice, who similarly caught Trump's attention for being unapologetically Black and endeavoring to ameliorate systemic injustice, now presented the president with yet another prepossessing plane he could attempt to tarnish and take down.

Before Trump began assaulting our customs as commander in chief, long before he entered the White House, Colin Kaepernick had made it known, to his team, the National Football League, and a country that worshipped the religion of football, that he is more than a helmeted, one-dimensional gladiator of the gridiron. In seeking to bring attention to the scourge of police brutality—the unlawful, incessant murders of people like Mike Brown, Eric Garner, Philando Castile, and Alton Sterling, among countless others over the course of our modern and distant history—he decided, righteously so, *not* to stand for the anthem of a country that has chronically failed to live up to those values integral to both its laws and ethos.

An act that had become compulsory, given the NFL's commercial commitments with the armed forces, had devolved into hollow pageantry, perfectly suited for a scoundrel and self-professed Nationalist like Trump to come along and weaponize in his evolving vendetta against Black and Brown people. It did not matter that when Colin Kaepernick knelt, he acted for all the Black men and women who had lost their lives at the hands of the very officers sworn to protect and uphold the sanctity of those lives. It did not matter that Kaepernick himself had evolved, along with his protest, at the suggestion of an Army Green Beret who cosigned his gesture and encouraged him that kneeling, rather than sitting, showed more deference to his cause and those who had sacrificed for the very right to protest in the first place. It did not matter that men and women throughout the military, creating hashtags like #VeteransForKaepernick, supported his righteous gesture and his attempt to ameliorate the corrosive conditions inspiring it. None of that mattered in Trump's America. It was incidental that a Black man, who Trump did not respect, knelt for a people who he did not respect: it was the unambiguous, unavoidable fact that Colin Kaepernick represented Black Pride. And that this signaled to others that they, too, should embrace and exhibit an unwavering cultural pride, belying the glitz, glamor, and empty trappings typically associated with sports celebrity, is what inevitably placed the young man on Trump's radar. It made the 49er the *perfect* fall guy for white conservatives, the kind of rich fodder *befitting* a culture war.

Make no mistake, Trump is a basic man. It is difficult enough to convince a bigot possessing neither nuance nor a rich inner life that there is more to reality than race and remuneration—yet this most certainly contributed to his opprobrium of Kaepernick. Here is an athlete whose basic yield would have greatly satisfied a simple man like himself: namely, football fame and the incredible fortune that comes along with it. Additionally, Kaepernick made his millions in a league that had essentially banned Trump from its ranks in an ownership capacity, likely due to his awful personality and equally awful business reputation. Kaepernick, like Obama, had something Trump *covets*. With laudable leadership qualities, a remarkable sense of duty, and an impeccable moral compass, Kaepernick had taken this mantle and made more of it. This caused Trump, pathetic piece of shit that he is, to absolutely *seethe*. Such an intensely small man, he cannot stand seeing others experience his dream, yet alone the wealthy, winsome Black men who he inherently holds in contempt. Despite the fact that Kaepernick, like Obama, acquired the celebrity that this purposeless simpleton values above all else, Trump was loath to recognize that the recognition these biracial men receive is itself a byproduct of their pursuit of virtue and worthiness—something an unprincipled man like himself neither possesses *nor* seeks.

A hallmark of racism, or a person harboring racist ideology running contrary to common sense, decency, and objective truth, is the belief and subsequent rationalization that people of color cannot exemplify characteristics that contradict any of the abnormal perceptions guiding such primitive thinking. When an athlete, principally an African American athlete, steps beyond the playing field to assert their self-value over and above a basic physical worth, in the process bypassing the comfort zone created and serviced by a strict adherence to that relegated role and estimation, crowds that had celebrated their athletic prowess will instantly downplay their mental acuity. It is incongruous with their unrefined conclusions, challenging the very defenses put in place to impede our forward momentum *outside* of sports.

Prior to Kaepernick's protest, professional football players had been implicated in rapes, robberies, and murders, yet few fans threatened to boycott a league that did little more than suspend those athletes. In fact, a wide range of reprehensible, vile behaviors, often caught on camera, did little to derail the NFL gravy train, it never failing to pull into the station to collect record-breaking ad and tv revenue for the owners. Yet accepting the proposition that the anthem protests *did* cause the NFL to lose bread, a counterargument would be that the league was now suffering because, unlike the aforementioned perpetrators, Kaepernick challenged the skewed and prevailing attitudes associated with African American men. That he in the process highlighted the inherent criminality of many of our nation's police officers, exposing their blueprint for Black destruction—undermining a template long employed to summarily criminalize people of color—

made him, from the perspective of Trump and this questionable fanbase, guilty of a violation *more* egregious than those who victimize women or shoot up strip clubs.

Kaepernick's crime is that he is *not* a criminal. For a people burdened by a public narrative nourished almost exclusively on negative stereotypes, anticipating malevolent and criminal behavior from Black men, including Black NFL players, has become custom. From the nightly news to the movies to sports, mainstream culture makes Black males so synonymous *with* violence that reproachful behavior, on and off the field, now seems beyond reproach for a society of reprobates subsisting on these damaging clichés of us. We have long seen how bad press influences not just America's laws but Americans themselves. These grotesque depictions of us predispose others to behave grotesquely *toward* us—that greater ugliness, a direct result of their fears having been normalized, their recoil *rationalized*.

Trump's own full-page ad in New York newspapers, in the late 1980s, calling for the execution of the Central Park Five was itself a corollary to those late-nineteenth and early-twentieth-century newspaper reports of "cocaine-crazed Negroes" that had helped fuel the campaign of terror carried out by the Ku Klux Klan and its like. From the 1890s to the 1990s, attention-grabbing headlines had helped service our reduction, further cementing our reputations. Widespread image manipulation, cultivated in numerous publications, alluded explicitly to this idea that Black males were inclined to acts of depravity and predation, especially under the influence of drugs. Where it would be sowed that our "sexual desires are increased and perverted," the hyperbole-engendered hysteria led to federal and state laws aimed at curbing the narcotics problem—and those perceived Black threats—through severe regulation and even severer sentencing laws.

From the Harrison Narcotics Tax Act (1914) to New York State's own Rockefeller Drug Laws (1973), Black America's almost ineradicable relegation would precipitate an inexorable decline, our freedom again succumbing to white American's arbitrary dictums, our reputability sullied and buried under these bogus ledes. Such PR impeded progress, influencing the fallout whenever African Americans *did* seek civil rights. These gross distortions would elicit an illogical panic that shielded edicts like Separate but Equal. In the War on Drugs, Richard Nixon, in a diabolical campaign to recycle this fright in white America and roll back change, would wage his own war against Black America, boosting his campaign to destabilize Black political activity and torpedo our newly established rights.

On paper and at the time, the War on Drugs did not appear to violate our Civil Rights, but *The United States v Fred C. Trump, Donald Trump and Trump Management, Inc., did.* However, both ran concurrently, with each representing an undeniable attempt at undermining Black advancement. Citing obvious parallels, I have often remarked on our good fortune that Trump, though certainly as bigoted and ballsy as his counterpart in the White House, otherwise lacks Nixon's long game. Given these stifling times, the progressive community could breathe a sigh of relief that the spoiled rich kid from New York was no match for the scrappy poor kid from California. Nixon, not addled with ADD, was driven enough to follow through with his impediments to justice, focusing ahead decades, all while Trump puttered around, mainly concerned with who he could hurt *today*.

Yet both men's unmasked hatred of minorities motivated their respective wars against us. Disrupting Black leadership was a primary objective, as Trump would soon show; promoting misleading, outright false impressions of African Americans became pivotal *to* his war effort. We now see him regurgitating age-old falsehoods as he clamors to feed his famished base. For his soldiers, prejudice would prove no different than vacuum-sealed pouches of peanut butter, rations of race-based fear helping these men and women to fuel up for the fight they enlisted in. Never forget, to win his war requires that he prevail in promulgating the inherent inhumanity of his opponent while, conversely, inflating his and

a conservative public's fundamental importance. By dehumanizing people of color, deflating their significance, and compounding that with centuries-old stereotypes suggesting that African Americans are bereft of both civility and intelligence, the base notion that physical prowess *is* an entire race's only redeeming quality creates the scale by which Trump, and mainstream America, measure Kaepernick's actions, as well as our overall worth as a community.

Cyrus McQueen @CyrusMMcQueen · Sep 11, 2020
Wow Ryan Clark just broke it down... NFL fans would've clapped if players stood in locked arms for breast cancer... autism... veterans... but that they stood against racial inequality they got booed... Just let that sink in: the profundity of America's evil and its diseased minds

↻ 3481　　♡ 9001

Being that African Americans existed almost exclusively in servile capacities long before there was even a United States, our importance to an agrarian economy—this configuration based on profit motives and our *free* labor—meant that our physical bodies represented what little worth we actually held in this land. Resultantly, once we were sold, what little worth we did retain no longer even belonged to us.

Just imagine that iniquity: your own body does not *belong* to you. The trauma of being Black in America is that what little you have is not really yours, and that which you have retained is so devalued that you are made to not even *want* it. Now consider the converse. For someone like Trump, his value can be attributed to the fact that, over many lifetimes, the citizens of this nation have been indoctrinated to deify wealthy white males, not only to rationalize their inhumanity but to accept a questionable accounting of the past that services a convenient but fallacious narrative. Such portraits have painted these men, and power as we have come to accept it, with the brush of infallibility. We can attribute Trump's own political success to his capitalizing on this paradigm, one prominent in the minds of voters who inflate his viability because it helps verify those inherent notions of who they *think* should inherit power.

Our history has been whitewashed, the contours of our race-based society forged during a thoroughly unaddressed past. Be it the rape, torture, and terror accompanying a hellacious institution, or the sheer dynamics of white wealth and Black oppression remaining both causal and static, we must consider the Founding Fathers and the Black bodies they owned. We must accept that this affects the present dialogue, and how Americans look at both the current president and, in this instance, a Black man who tries to address oppression. That the country would turn on the latter at the adjuring of the former hints at the inarguable fact that Kaepernick and Trump are uniquely American creations—as is the corresponding, almost congenital hatred that whites with power harness to help protect their status and bombard Black advancement. It is the race of both men, the necessities of this dichotomous imbalance, that, beyond informing their positions in the American pecking order, determines the reaction each engenders from a conditioned public.

This bears repeating: having been wired to deify wealthy immoral men throughout history, a populace has been conditioned to the point that the crimes of wealthy immoral men in the present day are similarly accepted and summarily justified. The hand of history in our current understanding of race is indisputable, that imprint indelible, particularly with regard to who we choose to vote for and who we choose to vilify. In seeking to understand Kaepernick's crusade—why, for instance, Black men dying at the hands of police *is* an all-too-common occurrence—we must accept that it is mainly because Black lives have *never* occupied a healthy, sustained place in the white American consciousness, even a century and a half removed from the passage of the 13th Amendment.

Somewhere along the way, given that our malformed country consistently proves itself uninterested in true egalitarianism, the Black body itself *had* to become weaponized, facilitating the version of America that they *want* to flourish. Perhaps because of the gravity of this country's original sin, that unreconcilable cruelty indeed triggered a tangible fright in white people. Fear of our reprisal has permeated the American ether along with the conscience of our tormenters ever since. It is why cops and Klansmen alike would send an unquantifiable number of unarmed Black men to meet their maker over the next century and a half—our fingers, fists, and phalluses fodder to feed a narrative in which our sheer *existence*, merely living openly, became tantamount to carrying a concealed weapon. This distortion, and the reactions it engenders proving expedient, a separate white society has come to be sustained on this foreboding alone.

That overall lack of appreciation has ensured the continued derogation of our intellect, and we have seen comprehensive measures taken to suppress it as well. Yet the very fact that our intelligence has been intentionally starved boosted the inception of pseudoscience, its diabolical ideations and distortions servicing gross ideologies that bigots like Steve Bannon would come to feed on and espouse. What is truly maddening, however, is how eugenics—implausible race-based foolishness, such as that people of color possess smaller brains—has not only encouraged discriminatory practices but also fostered a corrosive narrative that has proven regenerative. Centuries removed from bondage, we watch aghast as a new generation of bigoted politicians, men like Iowa Representative Steve King or White House insider Stephen Miller, informed by this outstanding idiocy, weaponize such misinformation to *further* hamstring progress. This very inanity is what also inspires their fearful leader, a repugnant racist in the truest sense of the word, to hostilely and routinely question Obama's own acuity. Trump's open, repeated derision of his predecessor forecast what would later unfold with the NFL. This has become apparent, especially as he used Twitter to blithely spin Kaepernick's shrewd and lawful protest as somehow *unlawful*. We witness him now propagate not only a centuries-old yarn but, its stifling correlation, conflating African Americans' acquisition of education, equality, and justice *with* illegality.

From the cotton fields to the playing fields, that our comprehensive education has been either discouraged or outright sabotaged shows that the road to empowerment is often bisected into progress and regression—in those moments the road is not completely rerouted toward a dead end. Recognizing how easily America's systems can facilitate white supremacy, as well as our own nullification, we as a people watch helplessly as the color line becomes magnetized, our relegation attracting only the negative. The resultant polarization in our society appears to be by design, considering the embedding of our degradation in the Constitution, before the rule of law would rule us out completely when it came to matters of freedom and fairness.

While subversions have varied over the years, perhaps the most persistent and pernicious form of subterfuge post-Reconstruction has been voter suppression and gerrymandering. Whether it was plantation law or the literacy tests implemented to impede our voting after the Civil War, *Plessy vs Ferguson* and the resultant Jim Crow legal regime, *Brown vs The Board of Education* and the blowback with busing—or the 21st century cry to essentially lynch the likes of Kaepernick in effigy—these disruptions form an intricate, unmissable, web-like pattern that invariably traps us. Thus, the torching of the quarterback's 49ers jersey and later Nike products is emblematic of the Black bodies disemboweled, disembodied, and set ablaze for daring to embody progress in a prior period. It conjures a time when our ears, knuckles, and scrotums were sliced off and absconded with as keepsakes, sinister souvenirs displayed in stores and homes as a testament to this satanic social order. Back then, as now, whites who trophied prejudice diametrically opposed those who challenged it.

Though we are well past legal segregation, Kaepernick has disturbed the status quo. The discomfort he has triggered, the abhorrence he has engendered in middle America feels almost reminiscent as we saw raw emotion transform into a visceral scorn, an animus that, given the combustible formula of race, could easily graduate to violent retribution—as we have witnessed so many times before.

Remember, our ancestors' "crimes," like Kaepernick's, were not so much for attempting to better themselves but rather for daring to influence *others*—for appealing to eyes perhaps yet to open, for seeking to show those in and outside our ranks that this arbitrary cast *can* be broken. Shattering that mold loosens the precarious hold of certain power brokers, calling into question their measures to control the narrative as well as our destinies, obliterating any burgeoning or even lingering sense of omnipotence. *That* is the key to why Kaepernick continues to remain out of the NFL. Black self-actualization is kryptonite to those benefitting from Black folks remaining manqué. Our minds and bodies, already anathema in the prevailing American ethos, will still strike fear in the hearts of oppressors, large and small—yet *nothing* like a spirit that cannot be broken. In a system propped up and protected by panic and propaganda, all crusaders brave enough to dare unlock that door to verity—willing to sacrifice themselves to *keep* it open—invite wrath for threatening to break down the gates that have long kept comprehensive change at a remove.

Cyrus McQueen @CyrusMMcQueen · Jul 18, 2017
Michael Vick says #ColinKaepernick should cut his fro? The problem aint what's on his head. White folks are threatened by what's IN his head

⟲ 68   ♡ 265

Colin Kaepernick's true offense is that the soul brother started to read. And by virtue of his awakening, Donald Trump and the NFL power players who represent his billionaire brethren, benefitting from that paradigm predicated on Brown labor and the exploitation of Brown bodies, saw other Brown men *also* awakening, and this threatened to topple the house of cards erected at our expense. It also goes to explain why Eric Reid, Colin Kaepernick's teammate who had joined him in silent protest, went unsigned until 2018 (and remains again unsigned in 2020) in the aftermath of their season-long demonstration. For NFL owners, operating almost as an extension of Trump himself, Reid's proximity to the nuclear bomb Kaepernick dropped, and the dangerous symbol he represented to ownership by picking up and passing along his message, rendered him radioactive to a league doing its damnedest to minimize any and all fallout. An NFL job would temporarily elude Reid because his transgressions, although not criminal, were deemed so by a league that is fine with players who *have* issues but not those who valiantly *raise* issues.

The seriousness of wealthy white men who work in concert to maintain a socioeconomic status quo, one that continues to benefit them first and foremost, should never be overlooked or underreported. For an NFL that had no desire to get into bed with Trump in a business capacity, it certainly conveys a willingness to hop in the sack, and roll around on those crisp white sheets, when it comes to maintaining a power dynamic that piles on Black men who dare challenge this system of subjugation. Because our country continues to capitalize off this miasma is precisely why the football draft itself always evokes a peculiar feeling. Given its implicit and striking parallels to slave auctions—throw in the twang of the Cowboys' owner—and it is almost *too* easy to close your eyes and be transported back to the Antebellum South. Field production, that outstanding and compelling prospect, makes wealthy old white men drool as they engage in the sport of outmaneuvering and outbidding one another for our physical services. This fervid clamor, telegraphing their avaricious motives and that lucrative potentiality, is but yet another tell-tale sign of a similarly soulless enterprise.

Cyrus McQueen @CyrusMMcQueen · Oct 8, 2017
Jerry Jones now says, any player who 'disrespects' the flag will be benched... oh, but they can keep disrespecting their women all they want

⟲ 140   ♡ 531

This is why Kaepernick's silent protest created perhaps the loudest, most deafening alarm awaking a Black labor force since A. Phillip Randolph rallied the Pullman porters nearly a century earlier. And if Nat Turner, a century before Randolph formed the Brotherhood of Sleeping Car Porters, had also called into question Black oppression and sounded a call for Black equality, then Kaepernick represents further connective tissue, now spanning two hundred years. All have utilized pragmatic, often profound, measures to carry us from our hellish past to a better present, albeit one that still sees white dreams and the fortunes of wealthy white men sustained on the nightmarish exploitation and destruction of Black bodies.

We can easily deduce why general managers and owners still seek out Black players who have been fingered in rapes, murders, and all sorts of mayhem, including many who have missed entire seasons due to their vices and villainy, promptly employing them in a league that for years has frozen out Kaepernick. And given that a president who was himself frozen out of the league has now used the young man to settle old scores is itself too curious to go unmentioned. Being a weasel, Trump never hesitates to drive a wedge between any group of people, especially when such treachery could guarantee his personal gain. But because he had already bribed his base to get back at Obama, securing his eventual triumph through tribalism, he was confident he could bring his invective brand of politics again to the fore and, through that process, get *back* at the NFL. By recasting Kaepernick's gesture, Trump would use Nationalism as a bludgeon to pummel, completely reshaping the quarterback's righteous gesture.

Once again, the president pulled this off by selling white America what it *wanted* to hear. The flag and the 49er comparably misrepresented, this divisive imagery utilized to establish either submission or opposition, the president again bifurcated the road. His jingoism has established that progressive-minded Americans *are* the new enemy. By pushing equality to the margins, the American mainstream—and our corresponding notions of a national Identity—remains an exclusive and viable avenue for only the vile and incorrigible.

Kaepernick's cardinal sin is that he forced white folks to look at themselves. And they are appalled by what they see. It kindles an emotion so raw, so unnerving, it bridles a reaction that mutates to fiery indignation almost *instantly*. Our country's contradictions are so profound, our cancer so concealed, that the hypocrisy Kaepernick has tapped into unearths an odium, which is then rerouted *back* at him. His purport has collapsed under the weight of this conservative rumble— buried as the nation has looked to kill the messenger instead.

Kaepernick's protest captured the public's fascination because Americans have built-in ideas of what the flag represents, but it *became* a source of division because they also have built-in ideas of what *Black* people represent. Much of the consternation Kap caused is due to his breaking a covenant: those who had escaped the majority's peripheral gaze, those Black athletes and entertainers invited into white homes, *knew* to accept the denial that kept the grim reality of our race-based society out of their living rooms and, more important, out of their very *conscience*.

Where Kaepernick forces this introspection, it is, again, those players with off-the-field problems, those with problematic personal lives and lengthy rap sheets, who ultimately do *not*. Even with their aberrant behaviors captured on video and verified through cellphone records, these African American men *have* remained viable in sports in the years Kaepernick has remained in purgatory. It is ultimately more convenient for white Americans to look at them and shake their heads rather than look in the mirror and shake their heads. No matter how you slice the matter, it is easy to root for rapists when they help *your* team win. And considering that the incendiary behavior in question has been, by and large, directed at Black women and other Black men, it neither raises alarms nor inspires the same sort of primal, collective outrage as when whites are the victims.

It seems that by embracing such men, many empowered whites can continue the grand charade while assuaging their own guilty consciences, even going as far as convincing themselves that they can offer these men redemption in the process. But by saving them, *breaking* them, those gross dynamics from slavery again come to the fore as owners and fans satisfy their own god complexes with a fanciful notion that they are somehow merciful. Ultimately, cheering for these repentant athletes has made many of them more capable of lying to themselves, even when the converse is apparent. In providing this disingenuous, conditional embrace, however, they betray a glaring hypocrisy: they do not actually *root* for us at all.

Such lack of verity or virtue became even more obvious when the handy excuse—that Kaepernick is not good enough, or had lost a step, or did not fit with a particular team's schematics—masked the fetid emission surrounding the racist decision to continue keeping him off a roster. This does not even begin to touch on the pernicious, perpetual belief that Black quarterbacks are inherently inferior to their white counterparts, or those dubious metrics often employed to corroborate the lingering stigmas that precede every Black man who endeavors to play the position. These weighted and wild opinions concerning such issues as leadership intangibles, and who might better embody such characteristics, has helped turn the microcosm of football, and its uneven playing field, into a pure attestation of greater America's intrinsic, overall devaluation of Black intellect and progress.

But no matter *who* is selected, the results remain the same. The endgame for owners and fans alike suddenly becomes much less nebulous: it appears many can accept losing meaningless matches if it means white America can continue to triumph where it truly matters the most. Given the 2016 election and our political degeneration in its aftermath, this false narrative only serves to insult those with better sense who also recognize the gross implications behind middle America's decision to go with the worst candidate. Like the myriad of mediocre, overvalued quarterbacks selected every spring over the Super Bowl-caliber Kaepernick, many of these same detractors continue to insist that Trump too is simply the better option. However, virtually none of these men and women can bear to face the uncomfortable truth:

such decisions have nothing to do with Trump or [insert Quarterback's name here] being the better choice, and *everything* to do with the fact that *they* simply are not better people.

Cyrus McQueen @CyrusMMcQueen · Jan 15, 2018
Donald Trump maintains he is 'the least racist person'... He may be the least intelligent, the least articulate, the least kind, the least bright, the least prepared, the least insightful, the least qualified and the least fit but, he is definitely not the least racist... #MLKDay

↻ 414   ♡ 1132

Donald Trump, the glorified dope peddler, recognized that Kaepernick and his sobering indictment directly threatened a conservative public that had zero intention of relinquishing its primacy. He launched a successful business feeding a disgruntled white majority the narcotic of nationalism and, on the surface, Kaepernick appeared bad for it. However, viewed through a different lens, the iconoclastic quarterback, mouthwatering grub for the president's animalistic supporters, has served his overall plans to divide and conquer. Kaepernick and the protest he spearheaded provided an almost bottomless well of antipathy into which Trump could lower his bigoted bucket and quench the thirst of his parched disciples.

Cyrus McQueen @CyrusMMcQueen · Sep 22, 2017
Donald Trump referred to Colin Kaepernick as a 'son of a bitch' at his Alabama rally? He didn't even call the #Charlottesville murderer that

↻ 2200   ♡ 3835

Kaepernick, it now appears, has been *good* for Trump's business. And given the litany of tweets, the countless rallying cries excoriating him, and the oxygen Trump's bloviating pumps into his base, business is booming! However, since he has engaged in the practice of sowing division and discord, perhaps drugs offer a better metaphor to describe Trump's enterprise—unlike H_2O, nothing is natural or redeeming about the product he peddles. Racism, like any heavily trafficked narcotic, is a detriment to society, whereas water, like truth, is indispensable to growth and sustainability. Like other highly addictive drugs, racism encumbers the mind and reduces overall resilience. And, as with all stimulants, the more you take, the more *it* takes. Where racism may provide that initial lift, before long, it saps individuals of resourcefulness and reason, replacing it with a manufactured feeling and a growing, corrupting, unnatural motive; its euphoria depends on a steady supply, and an overwhelming readiness to escape reality and the uncompromising bonds that tether us all to it.

Although the pattern, established in every capitalistic country constructed around a profound imbalance, is the principle that in order for one to prevail another must lose, redressing a disparity tethered to racist doctrine can pose an existential threat to those in power. If that long-sustained imbalance is then remedied through sociopolitical change, the longtime beneficiaries of said imbalance will undoubtedly seek retribution, if not corroboration that the inequality that benefitted them to begin with was, actually, *befitting*. It can create a deficit in principle that the unprincipled—men like Trump and Republican leaders—exploit, filling barren minds with a feeling that gets them to look past their multiethnic reality and toward some *mirage*.

This idea, that power belongs where it always has, resting with a racial majority, speaks specifically to those who, perhaps economically deprived themselves, willingly overlook that immediate reality. Racism, their *addiction*, so distracts them from their own destitution—and its actual causes—that it becomes easier for them to ignore, especially when their energies are being exhausted in a frenzied attempt to get their fix. If race-based politics are comparable to cocaine, then Trump is its Pablo Escobar; white power has proven more profitable and addictive than white powder. Trump's monumental success in peddling this race-based euphoria has merely breathed life into a political career built on cultivating and feeding addicts from sea to shining sea.

Every time his rallies are aired, I marvel at the destitute disciples lined up for hits of his highly addictive brand of hate—the mainstream media never failing to capture this ominous transaction. Like any disaster, Trump rallies are ratings gold as a dismayed public watches the demigod blithely toss out vials of vile, vituperative hate-speech to his strung-out audiences. He stands breathing in the adulation and anticipation as the fiends fawning over him scratch and claw for their dope. He had already seen his banal, basic asides like "Lock Her Up" and "Drain the Swamp" resonate with his customers. With the NFL anthem protests, he gained a new product to peddle and a new stamp to help it sell. For a middle America that distrusts women in power (and the Democratic establishment in general), Kaepernick and the cause

Trump misreported became a new high for this drug-peddling president to push. In referring to the quarterback as a "son of a bitch," his mordant grandstanding would satisfy every junky in attendance and, in the process, turn those arenas into trap houses.

Kaepernick has provided the perfect vessel by which Trump can impose his particularly potent brand of populism. Cooking up a deadly mixture with fiery rhetoric he proceeds to spike the exposed vein running through middle America. It is fuckin sad, the manner in which white Southerners and Midwesterners clamor for the crack, panting, almost *begging* the dopeboy for more. "Son of a bitch" became the biggest rock he put in their pipe after "Build the Wall," and, like the zealotry and xenophobia driving that very policy, the racial component to his denigration of Black men and their mothers would keep turning out the assembled addicts in *droves*.

> **Cyrus McQueen** @CyrusMMcQueen · Sep 21, 2016
> They don't like #Kaepernicks ⟶ protest...
>
> They don't like the #CharlotteProtest ⟶...
>
> Maybe they just don't like us?
> ↻ 383   ♡ 579

Perhaps no athlete offers a greater contrast to Kaepernick than the golfer Tiger Woods. Almost universally heralded, he achieved a bipartisan consensus among white Americans before Trump ultimately rewarded him for his mastery at that most favorite pastime of the moneyed class. That they often played together at the president's many country clubs suggests that Tiger's 2019 Masters victory, his first major tournament win after an eleven-year drought, inspired not only the sport's passive fans but a president who spent 181 days during his first two years in office at one of his plethora of golf properties.

In all likelihood, Woods' supremacy on the links would be almost an afterthought if not for white supremacy. The recognition he enjoys by excelling at an elite, traditionally white sport is bolstered by his willingness to eschew his African American identity in favor of a more palatable descriptor—one that ultimately serves conservative interests more than his own. The almost unnatural affinity certain sports fans have had for Woods from the moment he captured his first title, and the greater public's insatiable fascination with him, certainly confound many African Americans who can point to only a handful of Black athletes who have garnered such nearly universal acceptance. But the rabidity of Woods disciples, their fandom betraying a fanaticism that feels almost foreign given the likes of, for example, Venus and Serena Williams, sisters who dominate another country club sport yet whose unapologetic Blackness almost halts hagiography, suggests that something *other* than mere preeminence plays into the public's fascination.

Trump, who never tweeted congratulations to Serena after she too battled back from injury to capture her 23rd Grand Slam title in Australia (while pregnant no less), and who clearly conveyed his opinion of Kaepernick through pejorative tweets, has not hesitated to heap praise on Woods. But beyond that, Trump has bestowed upon him the Presidential Medal of Freedom, revealing an uncomfortable truth about race, one which most people of color are both familiar, and fed up, with. Operating as an extension of white America, and typifying off-putting perspectives influenced by not only this country's dominant tastes but by a problematic power dynamic that extols certain African Americans at the expense of others, Trump clamors to celebrate Tiger because the golfer, through decades of ups and downs, never failed to maintain that he is closer to them than he is to *us*. Simply put, white America fully embraces Tiger's success because Tiger does not fully embrace his Blackness. This presents an interesting dichotomy, considering that those like Kaepernick and Muhammad Ali, or Tommie Smith and John Carlos, *sacrificed* their careers and prominence in the lucrative stratosphere of public awareness out of deference to an ever-expanding sociopolitical consciousness. Tiger's appeal may be undergirded by political correctness but, by continually ignoring our reality and embracing an almost milquetoast image that merely services brand merchandising and a capitalistic ideal, he therein makes it easier for the greater public *to* buy into solely innocuous images of Blackness.

Cyrus McQueen @CyrusMMcQueen · Sep 7, 2017
Lets be real, Maria Sharapova looks at Serena the same way Trump looks at Obama; intimidated by greatness they got Russians to help em cheat

♻ 620   ♡ 1592

The athletic prowess of African Americans has always captured eyes, but those athletes averse to making waves, preferring instead to wade in placid bipartisan waters, are who truly capture the hearts and fascination of a public typically thrilled by the daring, dazzling physical feats of Black bodies, yet not necessarily by brutally honest and penetrative intellectual truths proffered by Black minds. Because America has a profound problem concerning its racial past, this unresolved history continuing to affect its very present, athletes like Woods or Michael Jordan give that public a reprieve by consciously avoiding race. Their value is therefore tied to *alleviating* feelings of culpability. Sadly, this mollification buttresses the imperiousness that most white Americans assume is their exclusive birthright.

One could argue that this *is* the true value of Woods and Jordan to white America. Beyond their exploits, duly marketed and monetized, the cachet that both have achieved while servicing this end appears to justify their avoidance; both have witnessed their success grow wildly for fulfilling these feeble expectations. By their avoiding race, the greater public, too, can avoid it, along with the white guilt that is its almost inevitable byproduct. This preferred outcome has far-reaching implications: while these athletes' unquestioned merits are admired, a fanciful notion can take root that race and racism do not hold them back and is thus no longer a factor.

"Be like Mike," that famous and loaded tagline, takes on added meaning when weaponized to ameliorate such guilt—while also serving the convenient narrative that nothing stops either you or others in your community from scaling such superlative heights. Generations of young Black men like myself have cultivated hoop dreams, going to bed every night eyeballing Jordan's action-packed posters. My own youthful bedroom walls were shrine-like, covered floor to ceiling with stunning images of him rising over his towering combatants, his arms extended Christ-like, all facilitating the deification. This iconography was all the more ironic given that, though he could seemingly walk on air, Jordan had zero intention of martyring himself. I still recall lying awake nights, the streetlights and the headlights of passing cars conspiring to create my own personalized highlight reel as the light gently swept across my limited horizon, enveloping me in the dream. Having unknowingly inculcated propaganda, I would unconsciously hold firm to a belief that if I could mimic Jordan, I, too, could leap forward as he had, clearing those bewildering margins that firmly kept most African Americans just outside the American mainstream. Shit, I even shaved my head, shearing my blackness to *affect* his likeness.

This heavily trafficked idea, that athletic superiority has been our exclusive domain, it coming at the expense of speaking up, means that Blacks and whites alike have adopted a stereotype that leaves the paradigm of ownership and labor unchanged. It ultimately reveals a self-fulfilling prophecy that further reinforces our relegated roles and the racial forces shaping them. While men like Woods offer palatable diversity, in the process gaining welcome into white homes, their success overshadows the struggles most of us continue to endure. Our lack of otherworldly talent and market value to these power brokers prevents the rest us from penetrating the forcefield that keeps us in the prison of their periphery. White America embraces Tiger and Jordan not simply as exceptions to the rule but as exceptions to *their* rule; by continuing to win on an ultimately insignificant scale, these athletes leave that rule unchallenged.

In no way would this prove more apropos than when Tiger visited the White House to, ironically, receive his Freedom. Given his history with Trump, having not only won tournaments on the latter's golf properties but having also planned to design a course with the Trump Organization as part of a massive luxury project overseas, Woods has reflected, and resurrected, America's most problematic past—his relationship with the president indicating even *broader* racial implications than initially presented. Their business partnership brings to mind the idea of a "house negro," a term reserved for those slaves who blindly adopted the attitudes and values of white ownership and who, through deference and misplaced fealty, helped to fortify the fiefdom of those individuals and their families. House slaves, within this historical context, operated in many ways as ambassadors of their masters' economic success, their obsequiousness often obscuring the utter brutality behind a criminal enterprise sustained through forced labor. They ate better, were treated better, and, as a result, looked to better off than their brethren—their polished appearance almost mirroring their masters' with hand-me-downs *confused* for benevolence. By adopting the mannerisms and trappings of their oppressors, they served as a sort of unofficial advertisement for the benefits of bondage.

Cyrus McQueen @CyrusMMcQueen · Dec 7, 2017
Wow, Lindsey Vonn said she would turn down an invitation from Trump to visit the White House? Well that explains why things didn't work out with Tiger Woods... Turns out she was the black guy in the relationship.

⟲ 145   ♡ 711

Of course, Woods is no slave in the literal sense, but his commercial viability, not to mention that he and Trump share a mentality shaped by

America's unresolved past, reinforced by a dynamic predicated on each man's occupying their defined roles, means that his success is nowhere nearly as important as the president's. That Trump *heads* his own criminal enterprise suggests that his racist nature will always succumb to his equally primal but more pressing desire to incubate and increase his business. That he projects a facade reinforcing this insidious ideology, while rewarding Woods for supporting it, means that Trump ultimately wins despite the appearance of a mutually beneficial relationship. Using Tiger in this way, Trump may be able to profit off the golfer in perpetuity.

One of the biggest mistakes we can make is to presume that only whites can further white supremacy. As Woods illustrates, the door that has opened to him ultimately hangs on an historical hinge. By entering the big house or, in this respect, the White House, a person of color can perpetuate the problem by endorsing racism, by choosing to underwrite it instead of undermine it, by choosing to convey its innocuousness instead of betraying its heinousness. And sadly, for Woods, and the rest of us, he found the *wrong* hat to try to pair with his iconic red shirt.

6

I Wanna Be, I Wanna Be Like Lebron!

In contrast to those hollow men of color golfing with the president or parading before cameras in the Trump Tower lobby after his election, a growing number of shrewd athletes have joined the chorus of resistance, providing epic remediation to the epidemic Trump exacerbates. When LeBron James, NBA champion and philanthropist, discovered that his greatest contribution to society comes from being an architect of change and, moreover, a conscientious objector to the destructive forces eviscerating people of color, he placed himself directly in the crosshairs of a conservative president and a media apparatus that champions that destruction.

Long before the buffoon in the White House singled out LeBron, who's blistering rebuke used a mere three letters to perfectly encapsulate the president, the "bum" had made it known that he views *most* young, innocent, African American males as criminals. Herein lies the great irony: James, a young African American male who is anything *but* a criminal, and who has evolved beyond the confines of sports celebrity, is now bringing attention to the unresolved criminal activity in our nation's police departments. When LeBron upended the prevailing narrative surrounding villainy and virtue, as had Kaepernick, Trump had to *somehow* find a way to turn him into the bad guy.

When James donned a hoodie in deference to Trayvon Martin and wore an "I Can't Breathe" t-shirt during a pregame warmup, Eric

Garner's final words, much like the sweatshirt precipitating Martin's final moments, became transformative. Mere items of clothing now became instruments conveying a larger meaning to unschooled eyes, particularly those accustomed to basketball stars' selling otherwise meaningless sundries. Because LeBron has resolved to be "more than an athlete," Donald, the purposeless simpleton, would once again *smolder*. This truly disturbed, down to his greedy, racist bones, a man who predicates his business model on ripping people off. Trump's avariciousness and viciousness simply cannot reconcile to a beneficent Black man creating a multimillion-dollar enterprise while also displaying incredible levels of altruism.

Trump, who always manages to fail *up* in his lifetime of lies and lawsuits, is eaten alive by the fact that not only has LeBron built an empire but has done it honestly. Considering his inheritance and the tax manipulations that helped secure his solvency—along with a father who in many ways operated as a fulcrum in these financial improprieties—it must be noted that, unlike Trump, LeBron achieved his yield *without* a dad involved in his life. LeBron's success, his pure greatness, cannot be undervalued. The Horatio Alger myth may reduce the rise from poverty to a misleading formula of hard work and determination as sole determinants of achievement, but the truth is that men bereft of financial and other tangible investments from a father rarely ascend to superlative heights. It is telling that James finds himself the source of much of Trump's obsession and envy given that his inauspicious beginnings and eventual successes, like Barack Obama's, were tethered in no way to patrimony or lucrative family trusts. Both have also prevailed while operating under the long shadow of race, their accomplishments only *further* highlighting Trump's abject failures. In an America fortified on our detriment, his nepotistic benefits and routine bailouts are indicative of a bankrupt, enabling society that, despite the prevailing stigma surrounding minorities and government handouts, provides welfare to wealthy men time and time again.

It was when the NBA star took to social media that Trump would seek to hamstring the Black athlete, restraining LeBron in those rusty old handcuffs of generalization, just as he had with Kaepernick. Remember, in an America historically and hostilely opposed to Black education, when it can no longer contain us corporeally, interning our minds becomes *essential*. Because James has utilized Twitter to unite and instruct while the anti-intellectual Trump uses the platform to separate, it has made the champion a target of an entity needing, above all else, to *weaken* such an impact. When LeBron tweeted, "Hate has always existed

86

in America. Yes we know that but Donald Trump just made it fashionable again," the impious Trump, who projects his colossal shortcomings onto others, was left with no resort *but* to call the moralist "dumb."

However, long before Trump took aim at the King, James had helped vanquish another inveterate bigot named Donald. Donald Sterling, then owner of the Los Angeles Clippers, found himself in the headlines in 2014 when various media outlets ran leaked audio of the billionaire espousing especially problematic ideas about African Americans. Sterling, cut from the same tattered fabric as the 45th president, had let slip that he did not want African Americans publicly associated with the Clippers or his girlfriend outside the team's roster. Like his presidential namesake, the man harbors an irrational hatred of another magnetic, transcendent Black player in Magic Johnson. But the owner received one hell of a wake-up call, his hateful and haughty disposition disastrously incompatible with not only the times but a league that is mostly Black. Given that words matter, and actions matter more, Sterling's many problematic displays—his lecherous assessments of these men's naked bodies while visiting the locker room, often boasting of their prowess as pure physical specimens; the fact that he referred to these athletes as *my* players instead of *the* players—suggest that that operative possessive word, along with the uncontested term "owner," carries collateral weight and would need reassessment, as the NBA would soon undertake.

That Sterling deemed "his" athletes as property, reflecting a mentality fortified by the unresolved dynamics emanating from slavery is but one of many eerie parallels between Trump and Sterling. Both men built vast real estate empires while, subsequently, building reputations for often refusing to rent to people of color, a similarity that cemented their objectively repulsive legacies in the eyes of James and the greater community. The emergence of men like Magic and LeBron as league ambassadors threatened Trump and Sterling's timorous sense of masculinity, secured as it was solely through wealth and whiteness. It betrayed a barely contained jealousy and emotional instability rooted in a profound sense of inadequacy.

While men like Trump and Sterling hate the average Black person, nothing incites their palpable disdain, like a proud and successful Black person. As these Hall of Famers have evidenced through their portfolios, acumen, and overall cache, such unrivaled power truly threatens small men who desperately need to stand on somebody Brown in order to feel tall. So when a 6'9" Black man, working behind the scenes, impelled the NBA commissioner to cut ties with the bigoted billionaire, even threatening to spearhead a potential player boycott of the playoffs if Sterling were not ousted, it established, irrefutably, LeBron's reputation as a *true* leader. His real legacy would come not merely from victories on the court but as someone who also sagaciously champions his people, who will use his leverage to help level white supremacy and permanently improve an intransigent sports landscape— while also readying himself to take on any garden-variety bigot moving forward, whether these tanned tyrants build their shoddy legacy on the West Coast or the East.

Cyrus McQueen @CyrusMMcQueen · Sep 23, 2017
LeBron James called Donald Trump 'a bum'... Excellent old school insult! May I also submit:
Dodo
Dipshit
Dumb Dumb
Palooka
Lummox
Butthead

⟲ 103   ♡ 591

Like Kaepernick, James exhibits a worthiness that highlights, by contrast, the utter worthlessness of Trump and a conservative media. He thus becomes a true threat *because* of the edifying model he erects for others to follow. It is this value that almost redefines what we have come to associate with MVP's. Because LeBron embodies the words of Nelson Mandela—"As we let our own light shine, we unconsciously give other people permission to do the same"—Laura Ingraham, a mouthpiece for the state-run media that is Fox News, felt compelled to call him out. Considering James had not hesitated to stump for Hillary Clinton in 2016, (or when it came time to launch his "More Than A Vote" initiative to bolster black turnout in 2020), Ingraham's admonishment, that one of the NBA's greatest humanitarians, should just "shut up and dribble" was more than the utterance of a basic woman; it was indelible, undeniable propaganda that created a massive ripple in the partisan waters in which her viewers chose to immerse themselves.

I WANNA BE, I WANNA BE LIKE LEBRON!

By attempting to silence our salient voices, Ingraham had hoped to reduce one man's inestimable worth, and one people's mammoth impact on this country, down to a pitiful four-word reprimand, a rebuke that encapsulates white conservatives' rough estimate of our overall value. She willingly shills lies and misinformation for a network whose modus operandi is to deceive and disrupt, its bleached blonde talking heads happy to die on this steep hill of abasement. If Santa could not be Black, then, by the same token, she could summarily dismiss a benevolent, bearded Black man who opened the I Promise School in Akron, Ohio, and who provides scholarships to *thousands* of underprivileged and underserved children. For a president who produces nothing but one Ponzi scheme after another, from his fraudulent and moribund Trump University to his shitty steaks, it is not only ironic but fucking *laughable* that a Black man who creates legitimate educational opportunities finds himself so oft maligned by the users and abusers within that toxic conservative bubble.

Here again, the prevailing paradigm of athletic excellence, which someone like Woods has adopted wholesale at the expense of a broader, more meaningful sociopolitical impact, makes a free person like James *persona non grata* to a media outlet that prefers sophistry over any meaningful dialogue. Truly maddening is that, when James would nullify nefarious ideas tethered to our collective manhood—in one instance, attending the basketball game of his teenage son—his very presence on the sidelines, peppered by a palpable love for his progeny, becomes fodder for a corporate media entity that cannot bring itself to celebrate a Black man even *when* he is celebrating his son. "Shut up and dribble" was now augmented by a similarly dismissive admonishment, mouthed by Jason Whitlock, another of Fox's boorish blowhards, he imploring the proud dad to, "Sit yo ass down!"

Because broken homes and absentee fathers form a chronic Fox talking point, fulfilling the network's malicious but well-maintained narrative, a Black man who refutes this stereotype and cultivates an enviable bond with his own son—exemplifying a good father for those in *and* outside the community—must remain the bad guy even though he is objectively *good*. And, as with the overreaction to Kaepernick, because LeBron was ostensibly beyond reproach, we had to watch, frustrated and flabbergasted, as a racist media apparatus clamored to turn the doting dad into something reproachful.

Where a paper tiger would fold before our eyes, true champions were roundly rejecting invitations to eat rubbery fries and room temperature "hamberders" with McDonald. Defying the bad rap long associated with Black athletes—those who move to gated communities, yet metaphorically close the door behind them—LeBron's majesty is attributable to him having never put up those walls. It is what unites more evolved men like himself *with* the greater community. Those like James would come to rightfully recognize, that their personal fortune is no substitute for our collective progress. Even if LeBron had not gone on to suffer the not-so-subtle indignity of having a poisonous pejorative spray-painted on the gate of his California home, he knows that his race—and neither his otherworldly accomplishments, nor the number of commas in his net worth—ultimately precedes him in the hearts and minds of far too many Americans.

However, "heavy is the head that wears the crown," is an adage that fittingly conveys what transpired in the fall of 2019 when King James found himself at the center of an international controversy concerning the NBA, China, and a somewhat supercilious American public that, nearly overnight, began reprimanding the champion. After Houston Rockets General Manager Daryl Morey tweeted support for prodemocracy protesters in Hong Kong, his well-intentioned gesture led to a precipitous fallout that ensnared the league and many of its marquee players, who were *in* China to play an exhibition basketball game when the controversy unfolded.

Antipathy to the Chinese government had been growing rapidly in the months since it introduced legislation to allow the extradition of Hong Kong dissidents to the mainland for trial. Hong Kong police attempted to tamp down the protests these developments inspired, and as violence between police and protesters escalated, with hundreds of thousands now flooding Hong Kong's streets, Chinese President Xi Jinping asserted his government's unwavering and unilateral control over the city. It all took place during a year that marked the 70th anniversary of the Communist Party's coming to power in China. This would serve as the backdrop to a geopolitical conflict that put the NBA in the crosshairs of both the Chinese government and a U.S. government led by an ignominious president who *never* misses his opportunity to impugn an American sports league and its players—especially one comprised primarily of African Americans.

In interest of transparency, when I first viewed LeBron being queried about Morey's tweet, I was underwhelmed. I wished he could have dispensed a pithy response that would have both resonated with my progressive principles *and* satisfied a perfervid public. However, any disappointment would soon dissipate as a deeper assessment of the variables at hand roused me to censure not LeBron, as many in the media were want to do, but those in and outside of politics who rushed to lambaste him while neglecting the stringent double standard and historical precedent that now asphyxiated the young man. My hackles were up not because he had failed to provide the convenient answer, but because assassinating the character of an altruistic Black man appears to be a sport not unlike the death sprints those before him had to endure before being lynched in the public eye. LeBron's words had become enmeshed with a reprimand of Morey, a middle-aged white executive who had spearheaded the controversy in question—and who, it should be noted, had promptly deleted his tweet, tucked his tail, and hid after LeBron factored into the equation. LeBron's admonishment of Morey became fodder for those whose ethical relativism unknowingly inculcates disparaging opinions of wealthy African American males.

That LeBron became a lightning rod for an international discussion on free speech was not only shocking; it possessed ironic implications given the Trump White House would soon weigh in. For a president and vice president to tender judgement on government abuse abroad was fuckin' *laughable*. Having abused their own vested powers to stifle dissent here, this administration has consistently proven they are anything *but* virtuous. At this point the preponderance of bullshit is so incessant, so immense, one does not know where to begin carving up the contradiction. Given that the Trump White House suppresses protests with troops and teargas, persistently threatens free elections, the American postal service and every vestige of a healthy democracy, its heavy authoritarian hand has only helped *this* country wade into autocratic waters. This does not even touch on a matter of unique pertinence: their desperate calls for an NFL boycott when Black men were exercising their freedom of speech on *our* shores.

Mike Pence's words, that NBA players criticize the United States yet "lose their voices" when it comes to China, as with his further reprimand that the mostly Black league acts like "a wholly owned subsidiary" of Beijing, is all the context needed to determine that these players were pawns in a greater game between conservatives. The same can be said even of self-professed progressives, who rarely shy away from matters of freedom around the world yet chronically duck their responsibility, and inherent hypocrisy, here at home. That the actions of police across the Pacific so galvanized Americans is particularly confounding when considering the cycle of sanctioned violence perpetuated by American police—and especially in view of *who* exactly continues to benefit from a paradigm in which a third of the U.S. prison population remains African American and unfree.

Cyrus McQueen @CyrusMMcQueen · Oct 25, 2019
I 💜 #CharlesBarkley ⬛... He echoed the very sentiments I expressed on here yesterday. Pence has an issue when Kaepernick and others express freedom of speech here, yet supports Hong Kong? Furthermore using black men as pawns in a culture war is so gauche. https://t.co/zm0gRl5krZ ⬛

⟲ 562   ♡ 2077

That the Trump Administration had felt so compelled to weigh in on this issue while members of his own family profit from their Chinese business interests—from trademarks and patents, the steel used in their buildings, and even the shitty neckties they manufacture there—is almost as noteworthy as the fact that the white public largely chose, once again, to indulge their unconscious bias and besmirch Black ballplayers. Such belligerence is disconcerting, these developments belying the far more sinister and criminally underreported fact that Trump, who again hates nothing more than wealthy, winsome, successful men of color, has failed to divest himself of his *own* business interests. Those outstanding ties, the Constitution's emoluments clause notwithstanding, are all the more curious in light of intrepid reporting in *Politico* that Chinese state-owned companies were "constructing two luxury Trump developments in United Arab Emirates and Indonesia"—in addition to the fact that in 2012 Trump had struck a refinancing deal involving the Bank of China worth "tens of millions" of dollars; a loan he is still very much on the hook for.

The ironies are unyielding in the Trump Administration. That the president and a jingoist GOP have made anti-China rhetoric central to Trump's reelection campaign provides even greater context to the NBA incident. As we would witness his lugubrious response to coronavirus, prompting his desperate search for a scapegoat in the months to come, China eventually became the ultimate wedge issue for white Conservatives who suddenly found themselves vulnerable. Yet factoring in Trump's primal, almost pathological hatred for men of color, we cannot ignore the implication that a mostly Black league's losing business overseas was probably music to that motherfucker's ears.

The fallout on social media would prove great, with many tweeting their disapproval of an NBA star, on iPhones no less, while not many tweets seemed to clog my timeline admonishing Apple CEO Tim Cook for his removing an app from devices that directly assisted the ability of Hong Kong protesters to track police. Given the fiery front-page fodder to come, it appeared more convenient to denigrate a Black millionaire than those white billionaires whose iniquitous global interests go mostly unscrutinized.

Throughout the media barrage, with newspapers running stunning front-page images of LeBron's jersey being set ablaze, the defaced fence of his LA home and stirring echoes of the past would cut through the smoke, the flames and the vitriol searing an indelible impression in my mind. I think back to Muhammad Ali and perhaps the most powerful and profound sentence uttered by a Black athlete in the 20th Century. "No Vietcong ever called me nigger" takes on added resonance in these newly ignited culture wars. LeBron, by refusing to take on Communists, by refusing to be a political football, by refusing to give a white media apparatus the goddamn pleasure of backing down, would, like Ali, inspire the ire of a bellicose public that never fails to go after the dark meat, even when its banks and multinational corporations—not to mention its very own government—are full of jive turkeys.

Cyrus McQueen @CyrusMMcQueen · Oct 24, 2019
I don't wanna hear any more about the NBA and China till we start talkin about the Presidents daughter and China... You know, the one with White House clearance who magically secured 16 new patents over there... Fuck outta here...

♻ 729   ♡ 2938

As LeBron James has set himself apart, as a champion and, international fallout aside, a man of true substance, some in sports media surprised me. Many of those who had lauded his incredible accomplishments now were ready to address *and* correct the many insipid accusations Trump was making against him, Kaepernick, and the Black community at large. Jemele Hill, the African American former ESPN host and one of the best sports journalists around, would be the next big voice to break through the crude cacophony created by Trump and his crackheads, in the process positioning herself as the next target for him and his emboldened gang of degenerates. Her accurate admonition—that Trump is "a white supremacist"—led to her censure by a network that, profiting from the league Kaepernick had run afoul of, decided it too could not countenance her uncomfortable truths. ESPN's decision to suspend her is not very surprising given the historic lack of welcome for Black dissent in the workplace. Like the very man who had inspired protests throughout the NFL, her veracity made her a villain to those unscrupulous individuals in power who consider this particular brand of fact-based, well-informed, political discourse to be bad for the egos and ignoramuses who contribute to, and thereby constitute, the league's cachet and revenue source.

Cyrus McQueen @CyrusMMcQueen · Sep 13, 2017
#JemeleHill ⌐ callin Trump a White Supremacist is a fireable offense? If it looks like a duck, and it walks like a duck, and it's named Donald

⟲ 394   ♡ 1310

Truly maddening is the discomfiting fact that what has proven bad for everyone else has been good for Trump. Hill, almost by proxy, temporarily replaced Kaepernick as Public Enemy No. 1, her notoriety perfectly suited to feed the desperate need of a president and a public *craving* their Black villain. To her eternal credit, like those NFL players who took on Kaepernick's cause in his absence, Hill refused to be drowned in the virulent waters churned by a churlish Trump and entities within conservative media. Embodying a righteous cool, and pure grace under fire, her stoicism spoke volumes amid the deafening silence that was enveloping her.

To place what happened with Hill in even greater perspective, we need not look very far to find people of color who *are* willing to parrot despicable, deleterious respectability politics, stroking white egos as well as their own outsized ones, while playing the discordant tune of tolerance and "toe the line." Their nearsightedness is nothing novel, bringing to mind a time long ago when some Black leaders all but discouraged resistance to white supremacy, resulting in such disastrous events as the Atlanta compromise—when the reward for not seeking sociopolitical change was seventy more years of disenfranchisement for Black Southerners. Acquiescence had long set a dangerous precedent that the prescient likes of W.E.B. DuBois would rightfully lament, as some 125 years removed this dubious line of thinking *still* shrinks our prospects. As for the accommodating among us, well, they simply see *their* dominion expand. But be they company men, or simply those hooked on the conservative catnip of obedience, what so many Black contemporaries fail to disclose is that the drip drip drip of slow progress is itself a slow death. Like water torture, its damage is gradual and far greater than any purported benefits.

The fact remains that those who take their time with progress only fortify the converse. Anyway, this otiose idea that conservatives can spearhead definitive change ignores that the only way forward comes when those controlling forces finally are forced to loosen their grip. When progress ebbs instead of flows, those preaching patience, those refusing to make waves, would belie that you then have to suck up awfully hard just to get anything. Without hard pressure, without proactive force, the levers of power represent a rusted valve, those passages running dry, unlikely to produce anything likely to quench our thirst for true change.

At the time, you could still find those like Hill, her brilliant and brave cohost Michael Smith, or even a sage, uncompromising truth-teller like Max Kellerman on the network willing to impugn both white supremacy *and* the corporate cultures codifying it. That only Kellerman remains at ESPN corroborates the sad fact that, when given the choice, black pride will always be excised.

Among the handful of prominent African Americans, in and outside sports media, challenging the damning notion of Black "obedience" and corporate obsequiousness, Hill's true legacy was cemented the moment she made the courageous decision to battle this storm head on, willingly launching herself into perilous waters, swimming against the dangerous current carrying us further and further from truth or any true semblance of racial justice. When she tweeted truth to power and remanded Trump as a white supremacist, then boldly refused to delete her salient, sobering, incontrovertible appraisal, she became the next delectable meal for his legion of zombies to feast on. Her erudite, sound assessment so triggered these strung-out, soulless corpses that we would witness those veritable walking dead descend on her via social media, attempting to devour the very woman, and brain, that had roused them.

Cyrus McQueen @CyrusMMcQueen · Sep 13, 2017
Sarah Huckabee Sanders calls for Jemele Hill to be fired for condemning racism?
Isn't firing a black woman for speaking up, I dunno, racist?

⟲ 500   ♡ 1413

As those like the president benefit politically, while those like Hill and her cohost suffer professionally, the rules of engagement for people of color have undoubtedly, almost uniformly, changed. With the country devolving, a great national discord seeps, inexorably, into every aspect of our lives, no segment of society untouched by enmity; seemingly no single person bereft of bad blood. A war has been declared against us and a more equitable society, and increasingly this campaign is carried out on our phones and in our computers. We find ourselves forced to simultaneously defend and attack, in and outside our places of work, as skirmishes once relegated to the streets are now carried out in *tweets*. Here, where the second front has opened and social media is the new battleground, progressive voices—men and women of color, every battalion and regiment in what has come to be known as the Resistance—have laced up and, locked and loaded, prepared for whatever the common enemy unleashes each day.

In this new phase, as political leaders compete for the hearts and minds of moderates, the formerly disaffected, their virtue triggered by our national turpitude, are compelled to serve. This galvanized army, this motley band of individuals escaping the prison of indifference, the old guard and the newly engaged, converge on social media, our pathos, and, in many ways, our sense of patriotism prompting us to engage in vicious salvos in a proxy war. The mighty keypad supplants the sword as we fight to secure ground in this new, vast, virtual terrain.

Here, Trump lobs one bomb after another into the Twittersphere. His prejudice and petulance rain down like shells, the shrapnel piercing and wounding progressives and people of color alike. Often, we can barely seek cover before he fires off another blitz or two or ten, often in rapid succession, he taking no prisoners. This is the theater where I find myself withstanding his morning onslaught, then returning fire with my barrage along with the men and women fighting alongside me.

Though few of us can match his firepower, with his legion of lost souls retweeting and fortifying his attacks, it is clear that this, like most conflicts, is being carried out on the frontlines by an unfortunate few who have much in common with those entrenched opposite them but whose similarities the fog of war forever obscures. I very much want to espouse the oneness of all, but it is easy to lose sight of the beautiful, resplendent forest because of the hollow dead trees blocking our vision. I realize, rather begrudgingly, that the painfully disruptive effect of racism on its victims is somewhat proportional to the pain and disruption it is sourced from. And though it is difficult to address this dichotomy, almost acknowledging the humanity of an enemy that will not reciprocate, I often pause to ponder the unmistakable fact that racial prejudice *is* learned behavior, it a manifest of unresolved pain and almost *debilitating* fear. Even as I find myself in the social media trenches attacking many a #MAGAT, I lament that behind their empty avatars are likely men and women sinking in quicksand, having grabbed for the wrong vine in an attempt to free themselves from the consuming conditions that have destroyed a once-vibrant middle class. I recognize what is perhaps the most difficult thing for a person of color to recognize: there are white Americans who, like me, are rightfully dissatisfied with a country that has disenfranchised them. And in the illuminating power of that discovery a bridge might be found that could carry us both over the morass that traps us. It would often cause me to search for a rope that could pull us both out of the muck. But even in these honest moments, when this spirited back and forth might dissipate into a healthier discourse, their determination would arise to put me in my place, with a reminder that I am just some "liberal loser" who cannot see the good Trump is doing for the country or, worse, just another "nigger" "playing the race card." And with the stranglehold that centuries-old lie had on them, their addiction to it incredibly, almost insurmountably strong, they would take a rope that could free us both and attempt to hang me with it.

After constantly combatting white conservatives on Twitter, I reckon that their race, like ours, appears to be the crux of their problems. Here race and the sheer magnitude of its insidiousness come even more painfully into focus. Where my Blackness in a white world has created my detriment by design, their detriment, by default, emerges from their inability to continue profiting off that dynamic. Because their returns are diminishing, they make the reduced power of their whiteness responsible for the plethora of socioeconomic problems affecting that community. Many will conclude that the absolute power they once enjoyed has been diluted by virtue of a Black president and a Black community incrementally clawing its way out of a void. Thus, for them to continue being white, in every positive connotation of the word, we must continue being Black in every *negative* connotation.

What these terminal Twitter bigots maintain with hyperbolic bombardments is that, though our race has long precluded our standing in the winner's circle, we are still losers in their eyes. Moreover, many feel their occupancy of and return to gilded status should, subsequently, come at *our* expense. Equality would never be part of their endgame. Seeing "nigger" so often in my notifications reveals to me that the real solutions to their problems will never be adopted, especially if it must come at the expense of caste.

The war in which we are embroiled takes on a new profundity as white conservatives cannot seem to find a natural way to secure this peremptory position. As changing demographics, growing wealth disparities, the exacerbating effects of an opioid epidemic (and coronavirus pandemic) level the playing field in this country—many will only bring themselves to stand on equal footing with us just long enough to then eviscerate us through policy or policing. And here, by using our disadvantage to regain their advantage they can ensure that, through our fall, they *can* once more look down on us.

7

Base Heads

Trafficking in the narcotic of white nationalism, which now competes fiercely with opioids and methamphetamines as America's preferred high, Donald Trump has emerged as the country's preeminent Drug Lord after staking his claim, shoring up the competition, and flooding the market with his particularly potent mix of race-based fear, discrimination, and demagoguery. Although it remains to be seen which drug will mar more lives and cause more all-consuming, long-lasting damage in its totality, we can attribute both the nation's racial problem and the opioid epidemic to a dereliction of duty at the highest levels. We've witnessed previous efforts by those in control to profit off pain by establishing, then exacerbating, a problem—before going on to create enough demand for their prescribed remedy to legitimize their entire business model. That racism's systematic destruction has claimed multiple casualties over multiple generations, generating ghastly outcomes, is but one of the many parallels between white power and white powder.

To dig further, employing Karl Marx's astute observation that "religion is . . . the opium of the people," it is not too difficult to deduce further how white supremacy has provided a comparable lift to the American masses by utilizing many shared properties to attract and addict those desperately searching for a sense of purpose just beyond the high. In this regard, we cannot overlook the role of religion in molding a race-based society, especially when considering the role of evangelical Christianity—not just today but in the past as well, when strict interpretations of the gospel were instrumental in furthering the institution of slavery. Ours is a country ultimately shaped through such dogma—this a nation which, as a result, would come to tolerate *and* promulgate bondage.

To separate religion from discussions of race in America would be as futile as attempting to separate eggs or flour from an already baked cake. That those principal ingredients have so bonded to create the country we are today, here, this fourth century into the American experiment, we must accept that race and religion are thus inextricably linked: both are baked deep into the American psyche, equally responsible for forming our lasting tastes. To deconstruct our society by removing race or religion from a recipe written into our very own Constitution is impossible. Both have so infused and informed our politics as well, and so thoroughly permeated every layer of the culture, that we can definitively conclude their culpability in also shaping the tone and tenor of our national identity.

Consider the role of race in crafting a white Christian utopia and the long-held notion that Black and Brown people need God, specifically a white Christian God, and now compound that with the animalistic, primitive qualities routinely ascribed to us. Given these determinants, it is not at all surprising that the nation's newest villains, men and women of the Muslim faith, generate substantial antipathy among white evangelicals, ostensibly replacing African Americans as America's primary source of fear and target for derision. Whereas African Americans practiced the right monotheistic faith but were the wrong color, Muslim immigrants have the misfortune of practicing the wrong religion *and* being the wrong color. Their fate is therefore sealed in a country that hopelessly intertwines race and religion, it utilized as a cudgel to bludgeon those deemed enemies of the people.

With the role religion played in assuaging a slaveowners conscience—not to mention the very fact that slave owners and segregationists worshipped the same white Jesus as did slaves and integrationists, yet the Gospel did not sway the former to live up to the ethos that "All men are created equal"— it suggests that the Muslim faith, though vilified, is but a red herring for the red hats. Their desire for a dominant white society supersedes any differing interpretations of God.

Religion thus appears, on its surface anyway, to be more in service of maintaining a white status quo in America as opposed to any moral or ethical consideration. With conservative politicians pushing religion and religious conservatives pushing politicians, this sort of incestuous relationship has nullified any notion of church and state being separate. It is indeed this very fusion that has helped embolden this political block. Policy and Gospel have so blurred that it has galvanized a segment of the American electorate to consistently vote for impious politicians and, increasingly, against their own best interests.

Immediately post 9/11, we witnessed a widespread devolution, almost mimicking the fearmongering employed for decades to denigrate African Americans. Islamophobia quickly supplanted the sort of classic race-based hate America was known for, as white conservatives, empowered by white evangelical zeal, would author a new, albeit familiar, narrative. Here we would observe the public clamor once more to drink from the poisoned well of prejudice. Considering that many Muslims have neither the benefit of being born here, nor in many cases the ability to attain citizenship, it becomes painfully obvious how Trump has managed to capitalize off their vulnerability during his tenure. Yet that white America buys a godless president's version of what constitutes villainy is an irony too conspicuous to ignore. Despite this glaring and inherent hypocrisy however, he has sadly managed *to* fortify the frightful notion that these God-fearing individuals and their families do not belong here.

Cyrus McQueen @CyrusMMcQueen · Dec 2, 2016
If we're doing a Muslim Registry, can we also do a Registry for all the maladjusted teenage white boys with a predilection for guns and D&D?

⟲ 74   ♡ 288

Perhaps Birtherism should have portended the disaster that later ensued when Trump would ban entry into the United States for those traveling from several Muslim countries. Where the whopper about Obama's birth certificate elicited enough of a reaction amongst fringe Republicans, its patent falseness pretty much prevented the GOP from wielding it against him in the 2012 general election. Though the Tea Party would emerge and promulgate the lie that Obama was born elsewhere or was secretly a Muslim, the reality of his Hawaiian birth and Christian faith ultimately rendered such assertions a tough sell. This was also, of course, partly due to the fact that the party itself, and its previous nominees like John McCain and Mitt Romney, men invariably tied to ideations of virtue, were chary to plumb the depths Trump so loved to frequent. But with the ignoble real estate mogul as president, he was free to resurrect this sales model. Enough Americans had bought his bullshit, empowering him to push it further—to tether hate *to* policy—his travel ban signaling that the businessman could almost *completely* capitalize on white America's fears. Scarily, Trump had been put into a position to punish Black and Brown people for representing on paper the very drastic embellishments he had already misrepresented to his customers about the former president.

When Birtherism failed to derail Obama, it stuck Trump with a warehouse full of merchandise he could not sell. Like those shirts labeling the wrong Super Bowl victor that must be destroyed, Trump found a way to turn a profit on what had become dead stock. The Muslim Ban represented stagnant merch being moved, as he repackaged and repurposed the glaring falsehood embedded within it for a naked white public more than willing to cloak themselves in a lie. The very embellishment emblazoned on Make America Great Again Caps perfectly accompanies shirts declaring the Buffalo Bills as Super Bowl Champions. Trump took racism from wholesale to retail, empowering both border agents and mom and pop stores to buy in. With alternate realities in vogue, he outfitted an outraged, outrageous white public that felt entitled *to* question the validity of those donning turbans and burqas—the very emigres they were convinced had "invaded" America from "shithole countries." Trump operated sinisterly and swiftly, even swooping in to satisfy the cravings of his customers *before* they could become dopesick.

Here, much as the MAGA movement mimics the ingredients of drug addiction, I posit a further assessment: race-based addiction also resembles behaviors typically associated with gambling. How fitting that a former casino owner, having defrauded and depressed a gambling mecca in a once-booming destination, has convinced those who desperately tie their solvency to a big score to let it all ride on white? The flashing lights and bells accelerating the intoxicant's effect, with his finding a pull through prejudice, Trump has created a new nexus to deliver white America from its heterogeneous reality. 1600 Pennsylvania Avenue has now transformed into a classless travel destination, a vulgar spectacle where droves of Pennsylvanians and Ohioans, philistines corrupted by a known libertine, pursue this fading mirage. These pilgrims can be found posing for pictures before its imposing gate, its regality crystallizing in the minds of these men and women who come to prostrate for their king. But having gambled away their future, many come to resemble little more than thrill seekers, chasing a windfall that will never come.

Yet we must acknowledge the greater irony that, while he profits off xenophobia, he simultaneously profits off the very source of that fear. Donald J. Trump possesses levels of duplicitousness and nefariousness that many have overlooked, the business of racism ultimately no match for his bigger business of billion-dollar arms deals and luxury hotels. Trump and his crime family continue to enact overt, and covert, deals with the Saudi Royal family while simultaneously banning those from their neighboring countries from traveling here— thus, he profits while fortifying his business partner's regional power. The centuries-old conflict between Sunni and Shia, for example, gets a hell of a lot more complicated with infusions of advanced weaponry, exacerbating complex relationships while preventing Yemenis and Iranians from fleeing regional calamity.

Given the Trump administration's animus toward Iran, his alliance with Saudi Arabia, and his travel restrictions, the Muslim ban has come to represent less an act of Islamophobia and more a concerted act of terror, the work of an arsonist who starts a fire and then blocks every exit. Equating Muslims with terrorism, the conservative narrative he has helped author, painting the religion's men and women with the broadest possible brush of bigotry, prevents their fleeing humanitarian crises or actual terror in the case of threats from Isis or Al-Qaeda.

For the United States, a nation of immigrants now heavily inundated with the intoxicant of hatred, white conservatives' addiction immunizes them to the reality of any similar or even shared history— this impacting the very idea of *who* can represent America. Moreover, ideas of who could *consider* themselves American or even venture to our shores, see the complexities of our complex over complexion arise once more to addle our society. The ghosts of America's unresolved past have resurfaced to haunt our future. Where African Americans are still very much vilified and systematically victimized, Muslim immigrants, by *not* being native-born, by *not* being bestowed with that indisputable set of inalienable rights, offer a new, irresistible scapegoat for proponents of white power to pounce on—physically and figuratively.

That many detractors of multiculturalism themselves descend from English, German, Irish, Italian, and Polish immigrants, along with ancestors from throughout Eastern Europe, many of whom had sailed into Ellis Island and other ports of entry a mere century ago, and less than that in many cases, makes assertions by those constituting the Alt-Right not only curious but spurious, fallacious, and ultimately spineless.

It becomes all the more quizzical when considering that the ringleader of this circus, the clown prince himself, can not only point to a mother born in another country but to *two* emigrant wives. His own personal history makes Trump and the cause he champions that much more confounding, especially when not too far down the road, we would see these sorts of neuroses lead to conflict.

Yet that many European immigrants had elected to continue this culture of abuse, long after crossing over means that race in America operates as the worst kind of frat. As many stepped off the boat, they stepped right onto the necks of a Black and Brown underclass, their new status afforded for having entered into an unspoken covenant. The hazing rituals unique to the striving downtrodden have merely been replicated as we see America's caste system generating new pledges every generation. The turbulence of U.S. history testifies a willingness to protect this perceived status at all costs—even if through the threat and application of violence.

It is a peculiarity that Noel Ignatiev, author of the groundbreaking academic study and bestselling book *How the Irish Became White,* unearthed through his years of research. In a 2019 *New Yorker* article that asked the author about the genesis of his 1995 magnum opus, Ignatiev responded that he "wanted to understand why the Irish, coming from conditions about as bad as could be imagined and thrown into low positions when they arrived, came to side with the oppressor rather than with the oppressed." These sorts of developments have shaped not only American cities like my hometown of Boston but the greater country itself—while the wondrous converse remained *unrealized.* Ignatiev, and most progressive-minded individuals, have been left to "imagine how history might have been different had the Irish, the unskilled labor force of the north, and the slaves, the unskilled labor force of the South, been unified."

Cyrus McQueen @CyrusMMcQueen · Aug 12, 2017
Trumps comfortable denouncing Obama or the Media but suddenly he gets tongue tied when it's time to denounce the Alt-Right? #Charlottesville

⟲ 406   ♡ 1188

Long before the events in Charlottesville, Virginia, exploded onto the front pages in August of 2017, the incendiary remarks and actions by Trump and his rogues' gallery of irascible right-wingers leaked enough accelerant, enough inflammable, bigoted bombast it made the ensuing blast almost inevitable. That this nation has never healed the gaping wound left by slavery, yet plows ahead, decade after decade through Jim Crow and beyond, makes the events in Charlottesville that much more painful—albeit predictable. Considering how legislation and social restructuring had once declared African American pride and progress anathema to a society created and advanced on the invalid theory of white supremacy, the notion that our nation has incrementally inched backward, as the oft maligned inched forward, makes the disastrous events, culminating in an innocent woman's death, that much more tragic.

That Trump, as the chief author of this narrative, can suggest white America is losing ground belies the overabundance of evidentiary proof—those unmissable ill-gotten gains secured solely through genocide and bondage. Yet what truly sticks out has been the mendacity *behind* the lie, the paucity of historical accuracy, the almost whimsical way in which Trump, Bannon, and the boneheads belaboring their revisionist views pieced together this political platform. With vitriol masquerading as virtue, it promised an inevitable collision with truth and outright resistance. This skewed interpretation of America's past and present would indeed prove *combustible*.

At the core of the argument mounted by the aggrieved is a fallacy: that America and its history are under attack. Since proponents of that view also deem present-day progress under a Black president to be a threat—enough to not only launch the campaign to Make America Great Again but also for it to resonate—makes this need to rehash centuries-old battles that much more curious.

Though Obama had secured America a measure of health care reform and kickstarted a stagnant economy, many in the country would react poorly to the African American president's virtue. Where he may have offered treatment for our centuries-long sickness, the unfortunate fact, proven upon Trump's election, is that far too many Americans suffer from a preexisting condition. In short, the very ascendance of Trump conveys an uncomfortable yet irrefutable fact: this country is not a Black man's to save, it is a white man's to destroy.

With members of the Alt-Right finding purpose in re-litigating the distant *and* recent past, it meant that not only would we have to fight to preserve the ground secured in this era, but in many ways to *regain* ground won in former eras—that which was only obtained through unfathomable carnage.

Cyrus McQueen @CyrusMMcQueen · Aug 12, 2017
Trump has technically had more bad things to say about Meryl Streep than he has about David Duke... Just sayin...

#Charlottesville

235 942

The firmly held belief that the Confederacy was somehow victorious, and that its cause was anything but satanic, has been embellished in far too many monuments. This centuries-old mistake inflicted upon the eyes and minds of the citizenry of the South, succeeds by conflating barbarous individuals with piety. By immortalizing these despots, this sort of immoral iconography provides that evil itself is preserved. It suggests that such hatred has now been thoroughly engrained in those dead *and* alive. Considering that this original sin nearly tore this nation apart, and that the sinful men and women profiting from that evil endeavored to triumph over every concerted attempt to bring an end to this madness, it thus renders those efforts to shield this fiction that much more sinister.

Yet I have come to surmise that white conservatives have been so connived into thinking these men were everything they were not, that the cognitive dissonance employed to defend such glaring guilt has proven no match for judiciousness *or* justice. With generations spoon-fed such gross falsehoods, this mythologized past now rots the present—it is why we see many clamor to now safeguard this strychnine of a lie for future generations.

That Trump's chicanery reflects that same sinister attempt to distort the truth, makes his pitiful assertions that "many fine people" had assembled on both sides of the Charlottesville debacle, in and of itself, erroneous. Let there be no mistake: there is only one bad guy when fascists engage with anti-fascists. This much was crystal despite his bold attempt to mischaracterize modern white supremacists as *innocuous*.

Ultimately revealed in Charlottesville were symptoms of a disease that has long eroded our society's immunity to ignorance. Of utmost pertinence is the immoral iconography I previously cited, the erection of statues celebrating those like Robert E. Lee and Stonewall Jackson. Yet it is important to reiterate how these loathsome characters, true losers, were resurrected decades *after* their historic defeat, becoming weapons to strike fear in the hearts of Black citizens. Over and above allowing these harbingers of hate to look down once more on Black folk, has been the sad way in which they have *literally* cast a pall over all present-day progress.

The Unite the Right March through Charlottesville, emerged out of this dark practice. By extolling evil, it prevented us from fully extinguishing its flames. The tiki torches dotting the midnight landscape on that August evening were lit from a fire that never died, one that enjoyed a sufficient supply of oxygen long before this president provided a mighty wind with his rancor. Hiding a lie in plain sight and normalizing it to the point it is not only readily accessible but also touted, while, conversely, denying truth a similar platform and preventing it from enjoying the same nourishment and attention, it desensitized a significant segment of society. Truth has been starved, to our eternal detriment. Again, a conceit born from widespread deceit corrupts the morally bankrupt. Much like the majority of poor Southerners pulled into the cause of secession a century and a half prior, the high delivered by looking down on people of color finds many willingly sacrificing their lives, souls, and sanity for just *one* more hit of hatred.

Cyrus McQueen @CyrusMMcQueen · Jan 11, 2018
You can't take Trump Supporters seriously because, he'll boast about shit nobody would EVER boast about and, these fuck heads eat it up... He's like, "I walked down the street better than anyone's ever walked down a street!" And they're like, 'That's right! Obama woulda tripped!'

⟲ 217   ♡ 1018

The deep pathos permeating the country after the events in Charlottesville resulted not only from the incredible violence that erupted in its streets but also from the indelible fact that hate had become so emboldened, so enabled to flourish, it had handcuffed our society—exposing our inability to actually escape this gloomy fate. Charlottesville in many ways would represent a watershed moment. With the leading voices in rebuttal to sanctioned violence temporarily overpowered by fascism's latest incarnations, the progressive community found itself stranded on an island. Encamped around the statue of Robert E. Lee in locked arms of solidarity against this rising tide, the physical bulwark created by these brave men and women came to embody the manner in which progress itself was being drowned out. The incendiary incantation "Jews will not replace us" telegraphed a growing trend in America: a swelling sea of hatred threatens to reverse the sea change of progress post-Civil Rights. The flames of their torches mimicking waves in a violent storm now engulfing the country, brought to mind that memorable quote from *The Tempest* when Ferdinand remarks, "Hell is empty and all the devils are here." Here we saw a rabid, enraged phalanx of lost souls, excited by a skewed purpose and energized off their fix, pushed past the brink of sanity, their drug-induced mania leading to acts of incontestable assault and murder.

The crooked objective of their cause—a white America that they can only realize by destroying diverse life—is the theoretical precursor to the criminal acts of vehicular homicide and mob assault that would unfold. But this celebration of sorts, this family reunion of disparate, somewhat splintered hate groups gathered as if for a homecoming, could only have swelled to this crescendo, fulfilling its awesome potential, under *this* most problematic of presidents. He had so polarized the electorate, so popularized racial antipathy, that racial aggression accelerated nearly as quickly as the Dodge that plowed into those peaceful protesters.

White Supremacy, like other forms of drug use, had seemingly been relegated to the shadows, to the domains and domiciles of the seriously addled. To now see it brazenly indulged in public, its users mainlining on Main Street in this day and age, was sobering. That shock of witnessing many succumbing to their addiction, actually *embracing* their disease as if legitimizing it would absolve it of its intrinsic detriment, was *chilling.* These felonious acts in service of even greater wrongdoing, made that midsummer night's nightmare even more horrific than its initial portrayal on the nation's television screens. It revealed that a hell of a lot more people in the United States than we thought were piping up on prejudice.

With the White House, both houses of Congress, and soon the Judiciary all dominated by the impulse of racial primacy, it cloaked under the *guise* of conservatism, this unveiling in Virginia revealed a country deeply addled and on the brink of moral collapse. Where the Right formerly espoused an idea of moral superiority as the anti-drug party of Reagan, the events in Charlottesville show that conservatives have taken a far sharper right turn away from the party that once turned up its nose at moral failings. The GOP has clearly carved out a new lane— unabashedly displaying the hate that shapes its underbelly.

The president shows zero intention of bursting this balloon of bigotry, not when his fascist strain of fentanyl is getting them higher than they have ever been. He now encourages white America to *embrace* this, to throw off the tethers of respectability and remorse and give themselves over to this habit no matter how many bodies pile up.

Cyrus McQueen @CyrusMMcQueen · Jan 12, 2018
Republicans say they don't want uneducated and low skilled people coming to the country... Kinda ironic when you consider it's uneducated and low skilled people who keep them in power... #FridayFeeling

⟲ 191   ♡ 589

When Heather Heyer lost her life the image of that automobile ramming into a diverse crowd of men and women was the first time many Americans witnessed racially motivated actions manifest into outright murder.

Yet it is important to point out that when that white nationalist got behind the wheel, he was under the influence of an intoxicant that had heavily compromised both his mind and his motor skills. After binge drinking bigotry all weekend, consuming hit after hit after hit of pure, potent prejudice, he had ostensibly overdosed. All these factors would facilitate his decision to destroy a manufactured enemy he had been prescribed to hate. When he opened the door to his vehicle that afternoon, he all but closed the door to truth or any idea of racial harmony. OD'd on demagoguery, not only had his vision become clouded by the time he placed his foot on the accelerator, but his mental state had been altered to the point he was, in effect, *hallucinating*. Racism, that mind-altering drug, had robbed him of sound judgment after years of chronic abuse, and off he went on a cataclysmic trip, perceiving peace as problematic, him now discerning a diverse pool of people to be a direct threat.

Despite his deliberate actions, the hard and immutable truth is that he likely never would have stepped on the gas that day if he himself had not first been a victim of gaslighting—his murderous impulse in no small part due to the despot in office and the pathetic brand of grievance politics he pushed. Like those captains and generals, past and present, who have championed racial genocide while proffering problematic solutions, they misdiagnosed his *real* problem. It brings to mind the very doctors who have triggered a similar dependency, and epidemic, through pain medicine.

The analogous aspects of race-based privilege and addiction further abound when considering how, like most drug addicts, proponents of white supremacy cannot point to one way in which their habit has improved their lives. On the contrary, those suffering this awful affliction can only point to families torn apart and to a world that has passed them by as their crippling addiction roils them in a self-destructive spiral. As they chase that ephemeral high, the race to the bottom, the road to dependency, will be paved with enablers like the president and Republican politicians, opportunists who *encourage* this destructive behavior—theirs becoming a codependent relationship that sees one enhanced by the helplessness of the other.

White Supremacy, like most unhealthy addictions, leads to the same inglorious end, yet, sadly, it less often destroys the user than it creates collateral damage: those who come into contact with the seriously addled in the throes of their addiction sometimes pay the ultimate price. Heather Heyer, like Viola Liuzzo a half-century earlier—a mother who was murdered by the Ku Klux Klan in 1965 while transporting activists in Montgomery, Alabama—has become the latest freedom fighter to answer the call to combat hatred and pay with her life for doing nothing more than fight to facilitate progress and further a society painfully hamstrung by this disease. Two Caucasian women, both in their thirties, in the prime of their lives, enlisted in the cause to improve the lives of those of a different race than themselves. That decision would place them on the right side of history yet on the wrong side of a white supremacist's weapon of choice, their sacrifices leaving two families with a gaping void at the moment their unmistakable virtue found itself in the path of pure, pathological violence.

This nation's sadistic relationship with violence against Black, Brown and progressive minded people suggests that none of us should ever feel so comfortable with the semblance of peace that we will not put it past this country to live up to an oft-forgotten yet foreboding verse in its very own anthem: "No refuge could save the hireling and slave, from the terror of flight, or the gloom of the grave." What Francis Scott Key intimated, and the Colin Kaepernicks and others within Black and other progressive communities instinctually know, is that freedom and equality are never *guaranteed* for us and ours. In fact, history has shown that the only guarantee after taxes is some form of death awaiting those who fall on a certain side of the color line in this purported "Land of the Free."

The sad reality is, our own torturous past predicted the torch procession that illuminated that dim Virginia night. This fire, spreading over centuries from the extermination of Native peoples, to the long nightmarish slough through the slavery era, to decades of segregation, institutionalized lynching, and race riots throughout the 19th and 20th centuries, has portended the rekindling *we* have now witnessed in the 21st.

8

Locked And Loaded

Cyrus McQueen @CyrusMMcQueen · Oct 29, 2018
Trump had the unique talent to make Jews AND Muslims less safe. Not to
mention Blacks and Latinos, LGBT and Women... That's what you call two hat
tricks of Hate: anti-Semitism, Islamaphobia, Racism, Xenophobia, Homophobia
and Misogyny... He's the Wayne Gretzky of White Supremacy

⟲ 419   ♡ 1158

Charlottesville tore at this nation's moral core due to the cool manner in which the president stated to the world, in no uncertain terms, that the cause of the Alt-Right was *his* cause. I recall my fitful attempt to digest his crude equivocation, and the sour sensation his piteous explanation left in the pit of my stomach. "Many fine people" has echoed in the dismayed minds of progressives since it first passed Trump's indelicate pie-hole. Most will remember where they were when the President of the United States punched *them* in the stomach. Those who bore witness to a lugubrious leader, failing to walk the fine line before him, were forced to absorb his intentional failure, as his leaning into dereliction would come to *electrify* America's fringes. These actions would be charged to America's conscience, leaving the truly marginalized in a worsening state of shock. Yet sadly, Heather Heyer's murder presaged the even greater violence to come. Those malleable minds, molded by Trump's own stubby fingers, would soon see several compelled to even greater acts of savagery. Our country was quickly putting out a rash of fires—only not nearly as fast as our fucked-up president could set them.

The most indelible audio from that war-like weekend, the most searing sound to come out of Charlottesville, was the concordant chant that those gathered would repeat over and over and over. "Jews will not replace us" penetrated the ears and consciences of anyone truly conscious. This primal scream, bellowed by an assemblage of proud bigots, was echoed by those thoroughly convinced of the "white replacement" theory. For a world not far enough removed from the horrors of the Holocaust, it is dispiriting that the corrosive cause of the Third Reich, has been reenergized. Right-wing extremists not only resurrect the "lost cause" of the Confederacy but similarly dust off devils that our grandfathers dispatched only seventy years ago. These extremists promote a pernicious world view that the rest of the world, through World War, has roundly, resoundingly dismissed. Now, rather disturbingly, Jewish Americans and their African American brethren *both* find themselves facing sleepless nights under this new normal.

Donald Trump, and the hate he harvests, has completely altered our political landscape. He is culpable of coordinating the best efforts of those intent on making America hate again and endangering the lives of not only African Americans but also women, Latinos, Muslims, *and* Jews. As a result, our safety and sense of value is compromised by those he empowers to literally and figuratively undermine our autonomy. Perhaps most perplexing of all, and a testament to his truly diabolical ability to damage the lives of those on diametrically opposite ends of the religious spectrum, is that he somehow makes the lives of both American Muslims *and* Jews less safe. Two short years following Trump's improbable election, Charlottesville revealed that his nefarious brand of nativism has a ground presence beyond the policy level, signaling that there are indeed foot soldiers who have signed up for war.

It stands to reason that those operating without reason or sound judgement would adopt a president's lies when they bolster their own, his eagerness to entertain and embolden their fringe foolishness leading to a symbiotic relationship. Yet if Trump could adopt and promulgate foul falsehoods—that Obama was not born in the United States or that Muslim terrorists were heading to the Mexican border in secret caravans or that it was not parents but *gangs* of Central American traffickers who were bringing children across the border—it becomes even more plausible that this brand of insanity *would* eventually lead to barbarity. This is why America in the year 2018 soon saw an enraged, newly energized phalanx, emboldened to eviscerate Jewish Americans in conjunction with the traditionally darker targets of the far right.

Cyrus McQueen @CyrusMMcQueen · Oct 23, 2018
Ironically, no one needs Jesus more than white evangelicals in this country...
#TuesdayThoughts

⟲ 311   ♡ 1281

In the twelve months after Trump placed his hand on the Bible to take the oath of office, the Anti-Defamation League counted nearly two thousand incidents of harassment and physical assault targeting Jews. As our long national nightmare entered its second year, with the White House a proven incubator of discrimination, we would witness Hate's disciples begin to move on the country. On the heels of a week when over a dozen former presidents, actors, and media figures received pipe bombs in the mail—the common thread their vocal opposition to Trump—a nation still suffering shell shock from Charlottesville saw yet *another* monster emerge from a fire he had set.

The mass shooting at the Tree of Life Synagogue in Pittsburgh's Squirrel Hill neighborhood marked the biggest act of violence against Jewish people on U.S. soil in our country's history. That an irredeemable, ignorant man like Trump had so callously and carelessly fed feeble minds along the fringes with hate speech, fortifying their fears and rationalizing their idiocy, while absolving them of any wrongdoing, makes it less surprising that the pathetic piece of shit had fertilized a plant that subsists on bloodshed.

For a man like Trump, who harvests hate, the Little Shop of Horrors that he runs can succeed only where racism and weapons of war are ubiquitous. Even before he was sworn in, mass shootings in America had only become more omnipresent. Following the Columbine High School murders in 1999, with Virginia Tech, Sandy Hook, and Parkland, among others, tearing at the country's heart and conscience, our nation's dark, disturbing relationship with the sword revealed a society all too familiar with catastrophic violence. While a variety of contributing factors, including their age and susceptibility, had misled the disturbed young men responsible for those tragedies, the nation has since cultivated a growing body of disgruntled adult males whose similar ire they now aim at specific ethnic targets.

Americans have a long, problematic relationship with guns, along with the very Constitutional Amendment many use to rationalize their irrational, violent behavior. Considering many have often brandished a Bible to justify similar behavior, we must remember how guns and religion were used in tandem to cut through the wilderness of North America. The wild men and women wielding these life-altering instruments had carved an inexorable path of destruction, decimating the Native population. While maintaining control over other ethnic people, pioneers carved up land, and doled out *death*. Self-anointed the almighty, they empowered themselves to create a heaven out of a hell or a hell out of a heaven depending on which tool they chose to utilize. It is part of the American identity, the notion of a West that *needed* taming, of John Wayne and Gary Cooper, of white might wreaking unfathomable bloodshed, the Constitution riding shotgun as they blazed a demoniacal trail from sea to shining sea. It is that uniquely American archetype, the gun-toting, God-loving cowboy, that the country now, in the throes of these heinous acts, finally must audit, finally must ascertain as the *antithesis* of anything heroic or godlike.

Cyrus McQueen @CyrusMMcQueen · Jan 17, 2018
Why do racist people always mention how their great-grandfather was Native American but never mention how their other great-grandfather was absolutely, positively, downright racist?

♻ 60   ♡ 439

Quite plainly, this deranged love of advanced weaponry, this unnatural affinity, this convulsing, finally has convinced the country to stand at attention and address not only where we are heading as a society, but *who* we are as a people.

Simply put, guns in the present-day United States would not exist in such sheer volumes, if not for fear. Fear is the antecedent to arms races and arsenals, to assault rifles and stockpiles of sophisticated weaponry. It has helped launch an era where, in the purest sense of irony, gun lovers in our God-fearing country typically hoard enough ammo to take on the army of a small one. Fear undergirds the lie, the high-caliber lie, that the president, the Republican Party, and the bloated, unchecked gun lobby use to brainwash middle Americans—the sort of idiocy that is forged through the insidious falsehood that someone who is *different* is coming after you. It is this scaremongering, this blather of "bad hombres" bombarding our border to rape and pillage, espoused by a president who is himself, ironically and plausibly, guilty of rape and pillage, a true outlaw incarnate, that ultimately triggers these base individuals and shapes an epic showdown in the movies of their minds—ones they are determined to then star in.

One of the president's popular refrains is: "The Democrats are gonna take away your guns!" Dissected and examined further, since white progress is hopelessly tethered to the regression of minorities, hollow, tenuous ideas of masculinity prevail *because* of this problematic dynamic. Thus, what Trump essentially intimates to his zombies is none other than: "The Democrats are gonna take away your penises!" Ironically, gun sales under President Obama went up drastically, the man having become the target of much of this irrationality. "Obama is gonna take away your guns" often operated in concert with this panic, his rise confused with, and inextricably tied to, their impotence.

Herein lies a key to understanding not only Trump's ascent but perhaps the entire pernicious notion of race itself. "Obama is gonna take away your guns" is an unquestionable and unforgettable revelation: the nation's first Black president had indeed taken away their manhood. He successfully challenged their variance of masculinity. Though they desperately tried to resist all he accomplished, they were too indolent, too ineffectual to compete with what he represents. Therefore, they would rely on Trump to get their manhood back for them. Performing an autopsy on Election 2016, we can logically conclude that Trump ultimately did not need the Republican Party to achieve this end. When it came to this destructive and thinly veiled objective, he had nominated *himself.*

Curiously, since Trump himself operates with a dubious idea of masculinity, predicated on predation, misogyny, and racial superiority, he imparts to his followers that they can only correct their parlous position in America, indeed their very own impotence, *through* force. Still, this observation cannot even begin to touch on an allied matter: the militarization of America's police forces, the immutable, decades-long transformation of weapons of war into tools for minimizing Black citizens, confirming the abashing notion that *we* pose a threat to them.

For far too many white men, in and outside law enforcement, guns are phallic, their size and superfluousness often commensurate with a shrunken ego—many sacrificing self-actualization for self-importance and desperately overcompensating for profound feelings of inadequacy. AR-15s become little more than steel appendages, their lead supplanting life as these men's inability to advance their own positions leads them to attack ours, to demote through demolition. Mass murder in this regard is little more than some orgiastic, depraved bacchanal. What Trump and his "Second Amendment people," those idiots ingesting and espousing this racist world view, actually communicate is that the only way to continue profiting off a precarious imbalance is to continue following the lead of the seedy gun lobby—to essentially *lead* with lead.

Consider the implications of such dark idolatry. Where Black masculinity and, more important, Black male prowess have triggered race-based hallucinations for centuries, what are guns, and in this regard specifically assault rifles, besides big Black penises for purchase? Because this notion of protecting your family has become loaded given larger, lingering issues concerning economic vulnerability and overall lack of fulfillment, it also conflates virility and violence. This outcome, ironically, is the only example of how these men actually attempt to own their fear as gun manufacturers go on to reap ungodly profits.

Cyrus McQueen @CyrusMMcQueen · Jun 7, 2018
America has long used crazy white guys with guns to keep the country safe... But my question is: Who's gonna keep the country safe from the crazy white guys with guns? #ThursdayThoughts

↻ 261   ♡ 1095

Additionally, by insisting on erecting steel slats along the Southern border, Trump doubles down on this widespread deceit in service of an illusory sense of safety, his wall a feverish yet futile attempt to fortify a crumbling white castle. Trump knows instinctually that white dominance—specifically, white masculinity as we know it in America, from the hunter to the gunslinger and all the tired tropes generations have adopted without audit—survives on a dying lie. This idea that the only thing that can stop a bad guy with a gun is a good guy with a gun— or the even more insane notion that a gun in every house is sounder logic than no guns in no houses, or the mendacity that a metal barrier along the Mexican border makes Americans safer—has persisted by penetrating the minds of men whose power is derived from controlling the population. A power-in-numbers rubric, which long provided the appearance of omnipotence, now withers with America's fluctuating demographics. The fracture is compounded when that false masculinity, exposed by the perceived threat of diverse peoples not only emigrating here but *demanding* their equal rights, inspires these men to turn their sites on immigrants, their fellow countrymen, and even *themselves* with greater frequency.

Cyrus McQueen @CyrusMMcQueen · May 30, 2018
What I don't get about Roseanne and Conspiracy Theorists at large is, they can believe the most far fetched, fucked up shit, like Pizzagate, yet can't bring themselves to believe black and brown people are their equals...

↻ 660   ♡ 2728

This *last* realization truly flabbergasts me, considering how effective notions of "white genocide" have been in underpinning conservative ideology. Though suicide can be attributed to a host of factors, from economic insecurity to undiagnosed mental health issues, "firearms were the most common method of suicide used by those with and without a known diagnosed mental health condition," according to the Centers for Disease Control and Prevention. For a nation ripped apart at the seams by opioid addiction, the steadily rising suicide rates across the United States should have triggered a moratorium on the proliferation and accessibility *of* guns. So it is utterly confounding to see white Americans increasingly taking their own lives, without it igniting any true national dialogue around suicide itself. Much like the delayed discussions surrounding drug dependency, it is curious that these truly existential crises do not drive the headlines the same way that border walls and manufactured crises do.

Is this obscene obfuscation by design? Perhaps the actual reason is too craven: for those entities who *are* culpable in creating and compounding that unique hurt, it has proven easier, and more advantageous, to simply bury the pain, to suppress it through pills, pistols, and propaganda. Whether it is Pfizer or Johnson and Johnson, the NRA or Smith and Wesson, when Big Pharma, the gun lobby, and now a white Nationalist president work overtime to distract these benighted Americans from the truths governing our world, those who adopt their distorted reality, their myopic vision, can no longer tell where the lies end and the truth begins.

It all comes back to that debilitating fear I previously pointed to. Simply put, I have come to believe that because the truth itself is so frightening, this element of base individuals elect to frighten others. Like their fearful leader, like all bullies really, because they themselves are scared they therein *choose* to scare.

Yet in a country ruled by the catastrophic yet compelling forces of race and domination, the gun drug actually operates in conjunction with the race drug. Even if the actual gun, in this regard, is merely a facilitator for achieving the high, white privilege and power are still very much the dope in the needle, the chipped white rock that provides the lift. It is as if gun manufacturers realize the weapon is a necessary vessel to deliver the charge. Because the instrument itself, this unmistakable conduit catalyzes and facilitates those feelings of euphoria and invincibility they use this very knowledge to buoy their morbid business.

In America, it is increasingly apparent that somewhere along the way Christianity took a backseat and the Glock replaced God. American men of a certain ilk and inclination eventually propounded: what is the point in imagining an ethereal God when *you* can be God and control your destiny, that of your fellow man, and those you view as a threat? When you can easily smite them for their affront to your authority and autonomy? When you can use your perceived power to drive them *from* the physical world? *This* is what motivated a 21-year-old man to murder nine people in a Bible study at Emanuel AME Church in Charleston, South Carolina. It is what motivated a 40-year-old man to murder six people in a Sikh temple in Oak Creek, Wisconsin. And it is what motivated a 46-year-old man to murder eleven people in the Tree of Life Synagogue in Pittsburgh. When he walked into that peaceful haven shouting "All Jews must die," he was not some proud American exercising his Second Amendment right. He was an anti-Semite exercising a right that the Right and their diseased brand of nationalism had convinced him was his and *his* only: to play God against a people whose existence it was his exclusive right to exterminate.

This belief, that a synagogue helping relocate Hebrew immigrants, equates to "racial replacement," and the comparably absurd yet heavily trafficked fallacy that men like Jewish billionaire and philanthropist George Soros operate a global clandestine conspiracy to control world events and further a liberal agenda, pollutes so many minds that by the time these men venture into places like Squirrel Hill, they are nuttier than a fresh jar of Skippy. Seemingly no longer capable of operating on their own behalf, they become operatives of that soulless portion of the populace that Trump and his deities of disaster have implored to make America great again. And that hellish reality can only be realized, that myopic portrait can only be painted, with the blood of non-white believers.

9

The Brotha From Another Planet

In the immediate aftermath of the Tree of Life Synagogue massacre, as the horror reverberated throughout the country and around the globe, I took inventory of my past, beginning with the exacting process of tabulating why this profound present-day event truly gave me such pause. In the ominous attic of memory, both bad and good reside, taking on qualities often incommensurate with whatever initial value they were tagged before being assiduously stashed away. A reappraisal diminishes much of what was once considered important, yet what was thought insignificant would shed its irrelevance, like the very dust it had collected, new breath reconstituting the old. This evocation would force me to stoop as I now grappled with the increased pertinence of certain unearthed emotions.

I was born and raised in Boston, Massachusetts, like Pittsburgh, an Eastern city shaped by a once-booming industry and still very much defined by the blue-collar communities that sustain it as a working-class hub. Although the poison of prejudice has spared no pocket of America, Boston in many ways stands alone as a racial pressure cooker of a city, with its disparate neighborhoods dazzlingly disconnected and defined by its occupants' race and ethnicity almost by design. Therefore, were I to appraise my own life, I would find that the measure of my worth was decided early on by my emergence into a world and, specifically, a city that only a short period prior to my birth had to be dragged forward to

121

honor Civil Rights legislation and legal precedent that had languished unrecognized and unimplemented for over a decade. By the time, I was thrust into the fire, disparities in education had long been determined as possibly the best indicator of how and why America's race problem persisted. This was due, in no small part, to the deliberately criminal manner of enabling this scourge and allowing it to subsist on separation and perpetual ignorance. If the only true antidote to racism is integration, and more specifically, as I have come to discover, interdependence, then it is painfully apparent how this disease, without proper avenues for treatment, without exposure to the cleansing benefits of multiculturalism, has marred multiple generations both inside and just beyond the city limits.

If we examine Boston as a sort of control group in this regard, and contrast it with another American city like Honolulu or even an international one like London, where boundaries predicated on race are less severely cast and where interracial marriages and cross-cultural friendships are more noticeably forged, the results are glaring and gross. Boston, without a doubt, showed telltale signs of infirmity at the time of my birth. Racism, plainly put, was *in* its DNA. Having barely progressed in the post-Civil Rights years, it had the ironic distinction of being a Northern hub that resembled the South in almost relishing its racial resentments and the resultant polarization among the impacted slivers of its incorrigible populace. An otherwise cosmopolitan place—very much the epicenter of education, art, and technology, a place to which some of the greatest minds the world over had flocked for centuries, attracted to its halcyon campuses—it also was a municipality oddly defined by a decidedly anti-progressive, anti-intellectual underbelly that enveloped those microcosms of advancement. Its residents could often delight in their defiance, impervious to any residual progress seeping into its proud, predominantly working-class outer domains.

Boston's configuration around race was indeed by design. As Jim Vrabel, author of *A People's History of the New Boston,* points out, this paradigm "started all the way back in 1910, when John F. Fitzgerald, grandfather of John F. Kennedy, defeated the Yankee banker James Jackson Storrow to become mayor and put the Irish in charge of running the city." As Vrabel goes on to disclose, "Ever since, mayoral candidates had cultivated ethnic and class conflicts in order to appeal to an electorate now made up primarily of not only the poor and the working class but also recent immigrants." Given how the city's racial divisions have merely grown since my great-grandfather and namesake Cyrus McQueen Senior arrived in South Station right around this time, the author's findings hint at the sort of charged discord multiple generations of Black Bostonians would be forced to withstand. The city's unique tribal politics—indeed the enduring success of its entire sociopolitical framework—have been undergirded by its politicians and its people for over a century.

Some aptly call Boston a sleepy town masquerading as a city and, in that regard, it is very much a small town, its patchwork of indelible neighborhoods defining it almost exclusively. As a resident of the predominantly Black neighborhood of Roxbury, nestled in the inner city just beyond Back Bay, I was painfully aware at a very early age, as I shuttled between the blue-blood bastion and my beloved pocket, that Black people would magically appear or disappear depending on which direction I would head as I approached an invisible demarcation line. Captivating images greeted my impressionable young eyes as I travelled home from private school in the Back Bay, walking a perceptible step behind my mother and sister Amber. I noticed punk rockers supplant white businessmen as we made the jump from Commonwealth Street to ritzy Newbury Street. My low vantage like a viewfinder, a resplendent new world washed over me. I snapped up the engrossing intrigue block by block: the shock of neon, the whirlwind of colorful characters, the omnidirectional activity creating the impression of a human coral reef.

I will never forget the pulsating energy of Back Bay's vibrant thoroughfares, the ombre of its human sundry, the Eurythmics and the Talking Heads hollering from the Tower on the corner, before it all dissipated rather abruptly in the mishmash of heavy traffic and homelessness that would greet me at Mass. Ave., the stark contrast of the haves and have nots betrayed by the flood of competing stimuli that attacked my raw young senses. I remember the stagnant smell from the subway, the heavy exhaust from hissing ancient busses assaulting my young nostrils, until it would all fade around Berklee College of Music. As we approached the Christian Science Center and I breathed in the air around its sparkling, sumptuous reflecting pool, the reflection of Boston's racially cast topography would greet us there, too, right on the other side of Symphony Hall. Here, New Edition would drown out New Wave as a turn down Columbus Avenue revealed a distinct change of palette accompanying these new and endemic rhythms, announcing our home was close.

However, in just a couple short years as a Black Bostonian, I would have to accept the inherent perils at hand, innocence in no way a reprieve from irrepressible forces that could easily jeopardize self-preservation.

It was all so confounding to my young mind, forced to process where I was, or conversely was not, accepted, my trepidation intensifying as I traversed this twisted labyrinth of distinct and potentially damning districts. Venture too far north and the residents of Charlestown would remind me of my place. Venture too far south and the residents of Southie would *put* me in my place, reinforcing my position in the pecking order by order of pejorative or likely personal injury. Before I was old enough to ride a bike, I had to find balance amid scattered booby traps, these conflicting but invisible dynamics shaping the physical reality of a place I came to regard as cold in every sense of the word.

Being born to two strong parents, a father native to the city and a transplanted mother, her migration to this metropolis for the sole purpose of capitalizing on the world-class education it offered, my destiny was predetermined by her profound desire to procure those very same unique opportunities for both her children. But Boston, the echoes of *Brown v Board* notwithstanding, remained a city very much reflective of the national pattern in which local property taxes determined public school funding. Despite boasting several of the country's top colleges, the city could not say the same for its severely underfunded, underperforming public schools. Despite a reputation as home to many of the planet's premiere universities, it also alienated the young minds of its working-class citizenry, those whose pedigree mostly kept them out of its Ivy League pipeline. This would, of course, form the backdrop for the busing crisis that erupted in the early 1970s, when school integration was finally enforced, pitting working-class white Bostonians against working-class Black Bostonians. The law finally forced a city mired in intransigence to bypass its arbitrary boundaries erected around bigotry and bullshit; with a better, brighter future fleshed out in a definitive manner, many hoped it would move beyond the superciliousness associated with flesh.

Cyrus McQueen @CyrusMMcQueen · Jun 7, 2018
When he was a young man Malcolm X worked at the Parker House Hotel in Downtown Boston. Just discovered Ho Chi Minh also lived in the city as a young man and, also worked at the same fuckin Hotel... So apparently, nothin turns ya Revolutionary like servin white people in Boston...

♻ 117   ♡ 673

Still, the commonalities of class were ultimately immaterial in a city and in neighborhoods where its Black citizens, residents of its darker domains like Roxbury, felt the suffocating pressure from white Bostonians who seemed to fashion a desire, and in many ways their entire identity and deportment, around an agenda to make Black Bostonians *persona non grata*. Growing up in the city, I would become familiar with this contemptible, combustible element via the dangerous intersection of race and sports. Bostonians' reverence for their sports heroes was almost paradoxical considering their often palpable disdain for any signs of diversity beyond Boston Garden or Fenway Park.

Observing the inebriated output of the citizenry on game day was its own compelling crash course in how to minimize risk. To this day, I associate the mouth-watering smells of sausage and peppers on Yawkey Way with a tightness in my chest as they permanently intermingle after an ominous afternoon in 1992. This was when the home of the last major league team to integrate its roster provided the backdrop for a pitch hurled at my head. On a fateful trip to McDonald's, I was making my way to the other side of Boylston Street from the stadium when I took a fastball high and inside. The car horn augmented the pejorative hurled at me, or, in hindsight, maybe it was the other way around because I remember being immediately startled upon being hit by that old American heap. Left dazed, I could not say if it was Clemens on the mound that day or if the game got delayed, given the clouds had gathered in a figurative *and* literal sense. Despite being a native, with visiting African American athletes providing similar testimonials, one could argue I never really *had* the home-field advantage. Suffice it to say, I learned to steer clear of the area during home games.

Regardless, by the time I reached high school I had been called a nigger on the bus, a nigger on the train, a nigger in the store, and a nigger in the rain. Being accosted on my ride home once, having dared to sit beside one of these dinosaurs, I recall that I just stood up after she gutted me, held inside whatever was left of me, and quietly changed seats. Now, my resignation was in no way due to my accepting this lowly estimation of myself, but rather in having simply accepted that *this* is what folks were like here. That snarl had risen up out of nowhere to snatch me, predisposed entanglements proving I was in no way invulnerable. And though she would soon retract her claws, transferring her grimace to the rapidly changing world outside her window, the damage was done. The old relic staggered off the bus somewhere around Roslindale, but I just sat there for the rest of the ride, chewing the inside of my cheek, anger eroding my enamel as I grit my teeth in an effort to bear it.

I will never forget that feeling, my chattering, panicky desire to get back to Roxbury—the 'bury—so badly, wishing the bus would make it to the Forest Hills stop *faster*. I was almost willing those wheels to turn, that engine to churn, so I could transfer to the Orange Line and shuttle quickly to Roxbury Crossing, where my fear and frustration would dissipate, the chill subsiding in the blanket of Black Boston, regenerating me in its warm, comforting embrace. Though I was the tender age of thirteen, that neighborhood meant *everything* to those like me, no matter our age. It was all we had, a safe place, our only lifeline in that cruel mass, the only treatment available in an often-malignant town, its rejuvenating properties *invaluable*. Though by design crime became concentrated within its inner-city borders, as a clearing in the wilds, despite the discernible, prescribed pitfalls, I knew I could move a bit more freely in this urban jungle. Be it ever so humble, there was no place like home.

But as the neighborhoods and attitudes of white Boston encircled and asphyxiated us, Roxbury would become a district almost always on the defensive, besieged by city and state power brokers and their incessant attempts to bisect it with highways, to erode its boundaries, to eat away at its precious real estate due to its proximity to downtown. City planners had ushered in an era of gentrification that could come to fruition only *with* the displacement of its Black residents. As Karilyn Crockett, points out, "The state's proposed Inner Belt and Southwest Expressway would have a devastating impact on Boston neighborhoods with significant black populations." The author of *People Before Highways: Boston Activists, Urban Planners, and a New Movement for City Making* states how these proposed highways "promised yet another barrier to black constituencies' political and economic self-determination."

All this is why the negativity associated with "illegal aliens" is as familiar as it is fallacious. Having spent my formative years in a city that made me feel as if I were some alien life form, even if I could venture down to City Hall at any time and procure a copy of my birth certificate validating my belonging, the atmosphere in and around Boston ensured that I would almost always struggle for air. Though John F. Kennedy, our 35th president born and raised in the same Northeastern hub, had so eloquently posited that "Our most basic common link is that we all inhabit this planet. We all breathe the same air. We all cherish our children's future. And we are all mortal," the unmistakable message impressed upon a sensitive little Black boy was the converse. Where we may have resided on the same physical plane as white folks, attitudes and denigrating actions reinforcing and upholding our societal designation slowly made clear to me that we definitely did *not* inhabit the same planet.

Cyrus McQueen @CyrusMMcQueen · Feb 6, 2018
Welcome to America... Where you stand for the Anthem and, when your team wins, you get to trash the fuckin city... But kneel for the Anthem and March peacefully through that same city and watch, the Police will make it clear: You're not on the winning team... #TuesdayThoughts

⟲ 243   ♡ 697

The process of my alienation began when, shortly after my eyes had opened wide enough to begin adjusting to the stark Black and white projections playing out in this coastal labyrinth, I entered a new school and my puzzled existence became more abstruse. Now old enough to benefit from educational opportunities located far from the city itself, my mother, who deeply cherished her children's future, lathered on the cocoa butter, slipped me into my long johns, stuffed me in my snow suit and snow boots, and sent me out on a rocket ship resembling a school bus. It carried me beyond the confines of my neighborhood, and even the city, to a far off, distant planet. The Metropolitan Council for Educational Opportunity, or METCO, was the scholastic program responsible for busing bright young people of color to the Boston suburbs to attend better-funded public schools in a strategic effort to promote the virtues of voluntary school desegregation. As a post-Civil Rights diversity initiative, it would serve as a first-rate model for a country that, on a national level, had stagnated in its efforts to bring comprehensive reform to an education system that disastrously correlated household income with opportunity—it continuing to limit one's advancement, particularly if they were a person of color.

Thus, my mission had been articulated for me when I finally touched down in this stony white space, makeshift map in hand, to locate Ms. Rybolt's first-grade classroom. Upon reflection, I might as well have been Neil Armstrong as I stepped off that spaceship to survey the sumptuous expanse unfurling before me. As I set foot in the town of Weston for the first time, I remember murmuring my teacher's name over and over between shallow breaths as I firmly gripped my Smurfs lunchbox like a life preserver and soon found myself absorbed by a school of children. The voice that soon popped into my head proved that I was determined to follow the unambiguous directives out of mission control, even if it was merely me talking myself through every little step I took.

The excesses of white wealth in the 1980s were on full display here, the conspicuous consumption of trickle-down economics creating a dazzling, dizzying picture that contrasted distinctly with the one I had come to know as normal. Here were homes with swimming pools, tennis courts, and even superfluous supplements such as giftwrapping rooms reflecting the largess of unregulated capitalism, the luxury vehicles parked beside them the same vessels that often shuttled my classmates to and from school—the exact same ones at which I would often sneak a quick, covetous glimpse when I embarked and disembarked my rusted bus.

By day, I touched down on a planet where the flush side of Reaganomics reached the intended beneficiaries of his tax cuts on income and capital gains, while back home, come evening, I witnessed the negative effects of that very same voodoo and the spell it cast over Black and Brown Americans who did anything *but* gain. As Reagan proceeded to pulverize unions and shutter mental institutions, ramping up the morbid, moribund War on Drugs as the influx of crack cocaine and its corresponding prison sentences compounded matters, creating a rich tapestry of tragedy in Roxbury, I watched with alarm as the lifeless men and women of color delivered by these deleterious decisions, those who had been discarded and deemed American flotsam, wandered about this dystopian backdrop muttering to themselves. As crumbling infrastructure embellished this hellish picture, shuttered businesses replaced once-teeming buildings, their hollowed shells mirroring the void within the women and men who claimed them for shelter and shooting up, this gallery of ghouls searching for life, or any facsimile of it, and periodically putting themselves on display, for a bit of change, for any compensation, in order to continue this living exhibition.

As a six- and seven-year-old standing beneath the Orange Line's newly defunct el train, holding the hand of a mother who quickly shuttled me beyond the discernible blight, I watched men who were cloaked in its darkness eventually emerge from the shadows to plead their cases and, upon receiving their settlements, immediately transfer these greenbacks into the waiting hands of hustlers, their solvency slipping right away in this secret and ritualistic shake. This was a time of simplistic, dismissive slogans, when addiction was blithely addressed through admonishment, when those who succumbed to the needle (long before it would poke middle America and be deemed a public health crisis) were the true forgotten ones, their pain palpable yet unregistered, noticeable yet *null*. It was a time when men would shout four-letter words at passersby, their sunken cheeks signaling an unforeseen consequence, this erosion telegraphing that a growing four-letter monster, exacerbated by a president's indifference, was fast approaching to level this area for good and wipe most of them from the face of the earth.

I vividly recall seeing my cousin Butch shortly before the storm would claim him, when he was bowed and barely keeping afloat. It was a beautiful summer day but, upon realizing that the gaunt man emerging from a similarly gaunt and indistinct hovel on Northampton Street and wading ahead of me was my once mighty cousin, it created a cloud blocking out any radiance emanating from the August sun. This pall engulfed us both on this late summer afternoon in the South End as mesmerized, I began following him for no discernible reason.

I trailed him fearfully at first, scared he would see me but terrified that he would notice that I had seen him, a mere reflection of the man who could once claim to have muscles the size of bowling balls, something we younger cousins exclaimed gleefully as we gripped his bulging biceps, jumping and swinging on his solid frame as if he were a human jungle gym. I watched now as, rudderless and reduced to a hull, he bobbed along the sidewalk. The Charles River appeared to have moved inland as the Mass Ave. I observed transformed into a busy waterway almost instantly, its current appearing to carry him, at times threatening to capsize what was left of him. He almost resembled a pirate flag now. Every block or so, you could tell that another wave had crashed into him, his Black skull and bones, thoroughly baked by exposure, absorbing the impact as he curved forward, briefly overcome, slowly stooping over for what seemed like an eternity. Watching raptly, perched on the steps of any number of stoops along the way, I waited patiently for each particular tide to ebb before he finally, fitfully, resumed his wayward passage.

I continued following him, appalled yet transfixed, the excitement I felt that of a child sneakily watching a forbidden horror movie. I was spooked yet exhilarated, disturbed yet determined to finish what I had started. And the long and the short of it is, I simply could not turn away. But though I fancied myself some sort of storm chaser, I was way too young, my vision and conscience too unformed, too unschooled, to understand what I was watching. I was neither capable of grasping this grotesqueness nor able to process the sheer magnitude of his impending destruction. But mostly I was simply too naive to fathom either the virulence of these uncharted waters or the depths of my cousin's abyss. It would take several more blocks before I realized Butch was heading nowhere. I do not quite recall exactly when I decided to call off my maritime pursuit, but I eventually did somewhere around Columbus Avenue, where he turned right and, dodging several cars, disappeared on the other side of the intersection into the vortex of Back Bay.

I will never forget floating after my cousin that summer afternoon—or the denouement to this American horror story when, shortly thereafter, I found myself staring down at him, his heavy lids from that afternoon now closed completely, permanently, his near skeletal remains and the cheap suit blanketing him a reflection of what had become a global pandemic. "God-DAMMIT!" I recall my father exclaiming, his anger gathering momentum as it ramped up to a host of colorful words. "He had to follow in ya FUCKIN uncle's footsteps," he loudly upbraided, unbothered by the bowed heads that popped up inside the funeral home upon his rendered verdict.

Later, I learned that my father, like his brother and his first cousin who now lay before us in permanent repose, had all battled this squall, yet he had been the only one to emerge victorious, the only one to lock himself below deck in a basement apartment for days and days before finally, fatefully, steering out of it. His audible frustration was an odd puzzle piece that I held onto for years, until much later, when it helped me fill in a picture of my father, and of a family that reflected the great promise and eventually the greater pain that awaited so many Black Americans upon migrating north in the early 20th century. Fortunately for my father, and for the life that he would live to create, he escaped it all well before addiction and disease conspired to create the perfect storm in the inner city, his palpable anger that day perhaps a sign of survivor's remorse, yet also, undeniably, a blistering, visceral lesson to the young son standing beside him not to follow this same frightful course.

Cyrus McQueen @CyrusMMcQueen · May 22, 2018
For those who don't know, I'm Cyrus McQueen the 3rd. Cyrus McQueen the 1st was born in 1875 in Rocky Mount, NC. His father named his first son after the Cyrus McQueen who freed him years before the Civil War ended. He lived until 1949... 1949!!That's how close we are to slavery!!

⇄ 416   ♡ 1642

THE BROTHA FROM ANOTHER PLANET

As I began charting these new waters, processing the indelible lessons now rounding out my comprehensive education, my eyes opened wider and wider as, on a daily basis, it became apparent that I was being plucked from one extreme and placed directly in another. Though Roxbury clearly had plenty to perplex me, up to this point, after only a handful of years on this earth, I really had not experienced the angst, isolation, and fear that came upon me now in a new school, surrounded by students who neither looked the way I did nor regarded my arrival with warmth sufficient to melt the iceberg between us.

I was made aware, for the first time, that my visage differed, my epidermis engendering a different response from those around me, my broad nose, kinky hair, and overall deportment in no way reflecting what this cruel new world perceived as normal or in any way desirable. This marked the beginning of a twelve-year journey that would carry me all the way into my eighteenth year, a journey that paralleled the physical round trip I endured as I orbited between Blackness and a white world that was perfunctory in its attitudes and actions with regard to accepting me. Though this trajectory provided a world-class education, I also underwent a metamorphosis, a revolution informed and influenced by my perpetual status as an outsider. Though I revolved around these confounding circles, I eventually learned the painful truth: the world very much revolved around them.

My real education, then, came from being an alien in another world, learning to navigate spaces that only proved tolerant in short bursts or for prescribed six-and-a-half hour increments, my isolation determined by a willingness—or unwillingness—to adjust to these confusing conditions. I learned early on to leave Roxbury on the bus: for me to assimilate, to thaw this frost, my success in a cold white space was predicated on my ability to warm to these new circumstances, to pack away most of who I was, to slowly disappear into this whiteout, losing parts of myself in hope of thereby *finding* acceptance.

Despite my best efforts, my alien status was compounded when, shortly after I took on this mission, my mother left my father and moved us to the neighboring neighborhood of Dorchester, then and now a predominantly Irish Catholic enclave that, in tandem with South Boston, provides a viable environ for blue-collar white Bostonians to achieve home ownership. Thus was created a homogenous network that fortified their dominance over a nearly impenetrable dominion within the city's limits.

Entering into a pact with her best friend, who had also left a problematic marriage, my mother took a tandem step with her toward the future. Bringing along her three children—along with my sister Amber and I—we all moved into a Victorian-style home, braving this new world together, in the process becoming not just one big happy family but also *the* only Black family to rent in this particular pocket of the neighborhood.

That house on Wellesley Park became an island unto itself, as I shuttled between two hostile environments: the more easily endured micro aggressions of well-intentioned whites in the suburbs flanking the macro aggressions that soon bubbled up in the city, with both operating as oppressive bookends to a young life squeezed by slightly different yet similarly crushing forces. I could never completely warm to my daily ten-hour round trip, despite earnest attempts. Given not just the coldness of the climes, but having moved to a predominantly Irish Catholic neighborhood, I now returned every day to a house that felt less like a home base and more like a space station on a neighboring white planet, the atmosphere posing danger due to one's prolonged exposure to its elements.

Cyrus McQueen @CyrusMMcQueen · Jun 2, 2018
I'm tired of people saying we have to be better, we have to be civil... Fuck dat. Obama was better, Obama was civil, and they took his kindness and called it a Kenyan... This country shows little respect to black men, yet alone erudite ones... So some times you gotta fuckin roar!

⟲ 2694   ♡ 13662

The first sign of trouble came on an otherwise mundane morning as the daughters of my mother's friend, space cadets themselves, squeezed into her car with my sister and me to make the five-minute trek to our launch pads, our respective bus stops being diagonally across the street from one another. The moment would sear itself into my subconscious for it was the first time in my young life I witnessed that palpable tension I desperately tried to process actually *flare* up. Though it was freezing that day, the Cold War in which we had all been unwitting participants would instantly turn hot.

As we sat buckled in the back in our pink and blue space suits, we passed a garbage truck idling at the end of our street. One of my co-passengers pointed to the man perched on the back and revealed that he had relieved himself on our side lawn. What happened next remains vivid despite my bestrewing it for the better part of thirty years in the opaque corners of my mind's attic. Upon corroboration from two more of my co-passengers that he was, indeed, the one who had delivered an indelible message in the form of urine along the side of our house, like some junkyard dog unleashed upon the sole Black household for blocks and blocks, the demeanor of my mother's friend transformed in an instant from placid to *apoplectic*. Suddenly, the canorous vocals of Phil Collins on the radio competed with her righteous indignation. "WHAT?! WHAAAAT?!" The genesis of his actions were clear to her, if not to our unschooled minds. It was undebatable that, given our noticeable presence, he had felt compelled to mark his territory and communicate in no uncertain terms what he deemed a trespass. That we were also smack dab in the middle of a decade, and a Reagan presidency, when respect, like so much purported wealth, had *zero* intention of trickling down, this disgusting act was apropos. Upon later reflection, the irony was not lost on me that this had, indeed, been *the* only kind of dribble we could have expected to gross in the mid-1980s, as Black America proceeded to get pissed on, in one form or another.

That man's blatant disrespect invited her wrath, this one vile gesture creating a volcanic eruption that vaulted us all forward as she slammed on the brakes, the safety belts, like his racist actions, briefly halting our forward momentum. That it was the year 1985 and we had been thrust into an alternate dimension, an implausible journey reminiscent of the highest grossing film of that year, would become apparent many years later when, upon dusting off this dark recollection, its irony would be rendered clear to me. But alas, those obvious parallels were lost in the charged moment when her Pontiac became a DeLorean. Before I could begin processing what was happening, I was pulled backward as the car, now speeding in reverse, caught up with this truck carrying all kinds of garbage. With the uneasiness of a sentient six-year-old, I watched as she rapidly rolled down the driver's-side window, as if cranking an old-fashioned engine, an action betraying the notion that we had, undoubtedly, traveled back in time. When she extended a well-manicured finger, its blood-red tip beckoning him, this garbage-man sauntered over with the misplaced swagger common amongst commoners. I remember the hair cascaded down his neck like a mane, the mullet of curls beneath his cap somewhat resembling the hood of a cobra, the danger this wild animal posed perceptible even through an iced windshield.

More than three decades later, I recall the disgust written all over his disgusting mug when he leaned down to face her, his venom at the ready. But she had charmed the snake right into her trap. Before any of us could realize what was happening, she reached out and grabbed his arm, throwing him completely off balance and pulling him halfway into the car. I had not seen her reach for the blade, but there it was, suddenly appearing in her right hand. In one swift motion, she pressed it against the exposed veins along his wrist. He was now on our level as the fear registered in his face nearly rivaled the fear plastered all over ours. In that split moment, his hostility and machismo drained out of him faster than the stream of piss that had prompted this entire conflict. I can still hear his high-pitched caterwaul as he pleaded with her, saying, "Lady, please! Lady, please don't!" She had not turned down the radio so by this time our pleas, and Phil's, contributed to the cacophony. I remember the whites of her bulging, unblinking eyes glowing in the dark cockpit, shooting additional daggers into this wimp. Her clenched jaw and the indelible creases along her forehead telegraphed the force with which she had wrangled the feral sanitation worker.

It was all over almost before it began really, her finishing what one man's haughtiness had started. She had brought him down to earth alright. As the words "MOTHERFUCKER!" and "NEVER AGAIN!" rang in my ears, she had released him, thrown the car back into drive, and we took off, barreling toward our destination.

Although never spoken of again, this provided an unforgettable lesson, gleaned through the power of observation and verified by the visceral reactions it elicited from all involved. I learned that nothing can stop white folks from looking at us differently, but that it is incumbent upon us and us alone to stop them from *treating* us differently—be that with a deliberate show of force or, in a more figurative sense, by using a mind that, due to our daily slough to the suburbs, would become sharp as a blade and provide the best weapon any of us could wield against white trash attempting to abscond with our humanity. And upon rewind, this showdown retains an almost cinematic quality, and the aforementioned parallels have also proven apposite, as quashing a bully has proven to be the best predicate for a brighter future.

The legacies of Malcolm and Martin had helped provide the litmus test for a young Black body navigating this new world in post-Civil rights America. Though the beauty and benefits of integration would eventually be realized, I discovered that the ugly flip side of that coin would almost always be ambivalence or outright animus. I realized then that we may have secured our rights, but it will always fall upon us to secure our respect. One of the most important lessons of my life crept up on me this seemingly inconsequential day in the first grade as I entered into the conveyance that would carry me away. I recall the cold had created a frost on all of the windows, but due to the fortuitous events of that early morning, I could now see clearer than just about anybody on that fuckin 'bus.

Cyrus McQueen @CyrusMMcQueen · Jun 11, 2018
Many well off white folks don't think their success was determined by race, and many poor white folks think their race should determine their success...
#MondayMotivation

t⏀ 139   ♡ 566

Though I quelled it for many years, the memory of that morning would inform my bewildering back and forth volley between worlds. As I helplessly ping-ponged between white spaces proven potentially hostile, that overt, definitive display of prejudice was soon supplanted by a steady stream of subtle indignities that began emerging out of my day-to-day minutiae. For the first time in my life, I seemed to struggle to breathe, this desultory journey to another world confirmed by the anoxia of the white suburbs, the absence of atmospheric pressure replaced by another kind of mounting pressure as I found myself untethered and lost in the vast void of outer Boston.

I recall that tightness in my young chest, feeling lightheaded and lethargic as I navigated this disorienting maze of offhand hallways and profound highs and lows, my spirit slowly succumbing to the elements in my new elementary school—while my peers perplexingly, astonishingly, appeared almost to float. As I traversed those corridors of confusion, eyes rarely met mine, their sole role seemingly to find their own reflections in me; our different carriages, mine laden with burden, meant I could neither provide that mirror nor, as a result, receive full acceptance. My albatross meant that *they* were the ones moving with momentum.

Hindsight suggests that this was my introduction to crippling anxiety and bouts of debilitating depression, but such things, I came to learn, were another prerogative of privilege. Those within the majority, ironically, the same ones looking past me yet managing to be looked *at,* accrued acknowledgement of their own disquietude, along with ample resources devoted to ameliorating whatever plagued them. As a poor Black boy, I *was* the plague and could neither claim to be experiencing social anxiety nor reach out to a ground control invested in validating me or guiding me through these daily duties.

As a result, I turned inward, focused on drawing and writing more and more as paper and pencil increasingly supplied my only real sense of refuge. My notebook provided the only control I had in a world and among circumstances where I appeared to have none. I practiced penmanship persistently and became proficient at illustrating monsters. I identified with Frankenstein and the Wolfman, their perennial outsider status suggesting these drawings were less illustrations of monsters and more examples of self-portraiture, created by a little boy discerning that he had more in common with marauding mutants than with his actual peers. As I desperately searched for belonging my little Black ass even took to howling at the moon like some preteen wolf. Convinced I must be a monster, I decided to *embrace* it. True story.

Here, I languidly moved through this confounding space, ironically detached, my spirit almost independent of my anatomy, the only interactions I engendered based on the oddity of my appearance. I was not even a mascot, which Malcolm intimated in his magnificent memoir. Mascots are celebrated. I was no mascot, I was a mannequin. I felt like window dressing. A prop positioned to paint a convincing yet inauthentic scene. For those looking in, I was engaged, even embraced, by my peers and teachers. By all appearances, I reflected the liberal leanings of this adopted community, even coming to embody the very idea of diversity itself, an idea that the presence of a busload of Black students suggested was tangible. I was someone they could tout, actually reach out and touch, if just long enough to snap a class photo or discern that my hair felt "like a sweater." In fact, the longest I managed to hold interest typically depended on my haircut of the moment, the epic construction of my high-top fade one Monday transfixing all onlookers, their desire to investigate its texture and flocculence the only time eyes remained on my person longer than a perfunctory glance. The classroom and the playground would turn into a virtual petting zoo.

This very outcome, and the backdrop of a very busy barbershop, eventually led to one of the handful of spankings I received as a child. My mother, who one Saturday insisted that the barber shave a part into my head, triggered an epic, unmitigated meltdown not that long after I entered the Weston Country School. Hearing her directive, I began murmuring under my breath, my childish protestations of "Nooo-wah... Nooo-wah," soon coupled with fervid gesticulation beneath the cape, these sudden rapids indicating that simmering anger had reached a rolling boil. This prompted the barber to reach around me with a meaty claw and clamp down on the back of my neck, halting my ferment. As the clippers' edge chiseled into me, my heart raced. My mother's desire to maximize her little boy's cuteness had filliped this arbitrary yet innocuous decision. Yet as he finished carving the indelible flourish into my scalp, I could almost feel my white classmates' subsequent attempts to trace it with a finger. And I . . . fuckin' . . . lost it!

As the barber made it snow with talcum powder, doffing the cape with an audible snap, my feet hit the floor before the loose hairs could. I scampered over to my mother, wailing and raising a fist—a petulant move I had no doubt observed and imprudently adopted from those very same classmates. Of course, it was a fool's errand, this sort of behavior achieving the opposite with a hardworking Black mother who indulged no foolishness on a good day, yet alone such arrant displays of disrespect. Though she said nothing at first, the shock and awe registered amongst the barbershop's sea of Black faces, with nearly every patron nearby rendered slack-jawed and speechless, corroborated that I had crossed a fine line. I had touched a tripwire, and they were bracing for the boom to follow.

As I faced impending doom, a corporeal reminder for this oh so grave trespass, as she grabbed my arm to march me to the gallows she had no way of knowing that my protests, and the subsequent fallout, were predicated on my deep desire to blend in—to *not* stand out, to not give the white kids one more goddamn thing to point out. And though my physical trauma would produce effects similar to my emotional anguish, as I cried and convulsed I was overwhelmed by an agony that now threatened to truly suffocate me. Once again, I struggled to breathe. As she laid into me it was as if I were being waterboarded by my own tears. But even drowning would have been a more welcome outcome for a sensitive seven-year-old suffering through a pain even more acute than that produced by her lashes.

As this event evinces, though my presence in these Massachusetts towns made for quite the compelling picture, a deeper meaning can be inferred. Because I had decided to don a disguise to mask what was unfolding beneath the surface, my plastic and placid facade belying turbulence, it suggests that to play this game required a similar lack of emotional availability from me in order to withstand the empty trappings and even emptier gestures of suburban Boston. Disillusioned, struggling to find an equilibrium in this elite setting, I was stifled in my ability to truly express myself. I learned the piteous truth of being Black in white spaces: if we want to exist at all, we have to exist as figments of their imaginations. We *have* to operate within the limited perimeters of their hearts and minds. I found that whatever it is that made us who we are, that verified our realness beyond any relegation—or that, God forbid, actually betrayed our true inner value—was immaterial in a community that was incurious when it came to determining, let alone truly appreciating, our authenticity.

Recognizing early on the futility of such a task, I *chose* to wear the mask. That demoralizing tactic, that dispiriting ploy, sadly proved most effective when bold haircuts and definitive cultural statements did not undercut it.

Adapting meant adopting your irrelevance. These are the crippling conditions often unconsciously administered and unwittingly accepted by us. It is the unspoken price of admission that people of color have to pay to enter into predominantly white and even self-described progressive places. Whether their reactions are callous or simply off key, whatever they project onto us is the identity we must adopt. I can be passive as long as it is preferred, animated so long as it is encouraged— this discovery inspiring my earliest comedic forays, after I learned that particles of approval were to be found by operating as the class clown. But long before discovering the power of comedy for riposte purposes, I learned that playing the fool works in my favor, laughter providing a facsimile of acceptance even when the joke was on me.

Aside from these earnest efforts at comedy, the sad and overwhelming truth is that I was rendered mostly inanimate, paralyzed by the mounting sense of alienation that was articulating my bifurcated reality and influencing my increasing isolation. It was my first experience with a recurring theme that followed me all the way through college: being looked past, not looked at. Blackness, I discovered, is actually an *absence* of whiteness, a condition that precludes us from being seen as more than the sum total of our parts, any wonder or intrigue never surpassing a passive interest in the compelling contrasts of our cultures, phenotypes, and physiognomy. That solemn lesson, gleaned through the unforgiving gaze of preference, was drilled into me as it had been for strivers long since departed: in America, *what* you are is nowhere nearly as important as what you are *not*.

It is a haunting feeling, a hollow feeling, of being present yet remarkably absent at the same time. Of suffering through the wrong kind of attention. Of being Black in a white space. Of being squeezed. Of being breathless from the pressuring weight of antipathy. That singular sensation, of your spirit being asphyxiated, *you* merely gasping to somehow adapt to this atmosphere and those skewed expectations. It even manifests at times into desperate, sporadic attempts at being someone you are not, moments when you find yourself flailing, rather futilely, like a chameleon mimicking the most popular white kids, trying to signal that you *do* exist, your true self smuggled in like a stowaway, ensconced safely in this echo.

It was a feeling only alleviated, albeit slightly, when, older, after an adolescence of mostly looking inward, surviving on one lung, my life expanded outward, and I was finally, fatefully, gifted a second one. I was able to draw a much-needed deep breath of fresh air from the literature of thinkers and prophets who had themselves experienced this same crushing pressure. Due to their insight, instinct, and great prescience, I managed to locate a map—one they had purposely left so myself and others could find our way out of this dead end.

It was then that the words of Malcolm X and Maya Angelou, housed in a home that doubled as a library, began to aerate what was, by many accounts, a lifeless body. My bibliophile mother having curated an impressive and meaningful collection, her affinity for the architecture of truth now provided me with ample blueprints. I started reading voraciously, devouring the gorged bookshelves, unconsciously constructing a political perspective unmolested by the brutal constraints of racial stigma. This development found me reveling in the resultant discoveries only such an authentic liberation can engender. The salient messages embedded within these volumes formed the basis of the aggregate lesson I took away, one pivotal in the life of a young Black boy in Boston: *never* internalize white supremacy. It was almost *too* easy to hate yourself, given the amalgamated effects of chronic negative reinforcement, it particularly rife in a society and an American city that can make you uncomfortable in your own skin, and incidentally, so comfortable with your insignificance that you can lean into it—this oppressive endgame fully realized when you eventually take the reins, undercutting yourself and those around you, because growth ironically comes to *feel* unnatural.

No, I learned the most revolutionary lesson that I or any Black person could: to cultivate a worth independent of their spiritual frugality, to communicate to those like me that it is okay to throw off those tethers and live unapologetically, incontinent in your pride, infectious with your sedition. To do differently would be to cosign the lie, to exchange your inherent wealth for their moral bankruptcy. Accept that and you *are* broke.

Cyrus McQueen @CyrusMMcQueen · Jun 12, 2018
55 years ago today, Medgar Evers was murdered in his driveway in Jackson, Mississippi... His life and ultimate sacrifice is a testament to the power of education, organization, and mobilization in changing this world... "You can kill a man but you can't kill an idea"... 🙏🕊️

🔁 597   ♡ 1383

These didactics breathed life into a slowly suffocating spirit, providing the oxygen necessary to finish the mission. Also, prior to this, I was fortunate to change schools to one in a town and planet closer to my own. In the predominately Jewish town of Brookline, two neighborhoods removed from Roxbury, I forged the friendships that had eluded me earlier. I began mixing with Jewish classmates in this more cosmopolitan setting where my *otherness* was far less polarizing, my cultural awareness and personal awakening paralleling those of my new classmates. I was invited into homes and to events where my maturation and quest for growth were mirrored by blossoming young men and women in the Jewish community who, like me, were coming into their own and forging a deeper appreciation for the struggles of their forbearers. That high-top fade soon found a yarmulke atop it, as Bar and Bat Mitzvahs elicited my first fruitful invitations to the otherwise frosty suburbs. I fondly recall the first time I was referred to—and later came humbly to accept—that I am "a *mensch*."

Social acceptance miraculously bred even greater learning opportunities, for around this time, with Alex Haley and James Baldwin having laid the groundwork, the impassioned, penetrating words of Elie Wiesel and Anne Frank informed my deeper understanding of the human struggle. Their first-hand accounts of how systematic racism had so eroded a society, inspiring unfathomable acts of terror, supplemented my education and overall assessment of race-based crimes, while highlighting undeniable parallels between their plights and those of my own people. Bearing witness to man's inhumanity toward man, the lessons of how indifference ultimately fortifies forces of ill will, *illuminated* my young mind with its beacon of blinding, unassailable truth. Books like *Night* had a profound impact as they articulated with painful honesty what I was struggling to ascertain. Though I may not have been the subject of hate, my experience up to that point had suggested I most certainly was not loved in many Massachusetts circles. The crippling weight of indifference that rendered me a perpetual outsider in Boston's white suburbs, despite spending hours there every day, was in ways comparable to the lack of acknowledgement and acceptance felt by many others with whom I was coming to identify. They had also become immersed in American spaces, yet, puzzlingly, anti-Semitism kept them separated.

This fact most resonated within me after the Tree of Life Synagogue massacre. Having spent significant time in Jewish communities in and around Boston and New York City, having felt unconditional acceptance and kinship there, it troubled me deeply that our similar disregard by a diseased sociopolitical movement—one grown not out of love but mostly indifference—pulled Americans apart, and all because apathy had been allowed to supplant love, facilitating the proliferation of hate.

10

Black Ice

Right around the age of twelve or thirteen, I encountered a new dynamic, one that I soon deemed as a personal affront. For the first time in my school career, I was compared and contrasted with a Black classmate who looked like me but who lived in the white suburbs both physically *and* mentally. On the surface, we both appeared to be aliens, but by actually residing in a space station on this seemingly liberal planet, he had come to identify less as an outsider, and instead began adopting the hollow, hubristic tendencies of the natives. Though we looked the same, he acted and sounded like *them*. Where we were the only two Black boys in the entire grade, he had, somehow, managed to overcome a hurdle that I consistently tripped over. I remember listening with envy, my self-worth withering, as he relayed news of attending sleepovers and get togethers, my invitation seeming to be perpetually lost in the mail. Later, arriving at school on mid-winter Mondays, I was confronted with evidence of ski trips I had also missed out on, the lift tickets stuck to the zippers of their North Face and Columbia parkas, conspicuously jutting out like affluent badges. It augmented my unhappiness, especially given that I was on year two of a hand-me-down, its once crimson hue fittingly diluted to an embarrassing blush, its down feathers seeking escape through various pinholes as I extracted them slowly and surreptitiously before they could attract attention.

Almost inevitably, we were one day pitted against each other, Black conflict that eventual outgrowth from the pressure of seeking validation on the verge of a white world. What eventually compounded matters, and led to conflict between us, was when, not a week into the new school year, he seized on my otherness with delicious aplomb, singling me out—or, more specifically, singling out those less-than-sumptuous sartorial stylings my single mother had outfitted me in: my TJ Maxx collection was definitely not something a wealthy kid would piece together amid frequent forays to the ritzy Chestnut Hill Malls. It was the first time a Black peer replaced a white one in this respect, exemplifying a haughty disdain fueled almost exclusively by privilege, his lawyer father indulging his superficial and material wants, keeping him outfitted in the latest Air Jordans, which provided ample ammo when he decided to zero in on me and my scruffy Reeboks.

The delineation between the haves and the have nots was never more pronounced than during that first week of September. Back-to-school, this parade for the privileged, was the backdrop to our meeting on the blacktop. Expensive basketball sneakers notwithstanding, word of my budding talent at the sport signaled to him that I posed an existential threat to his status as the prized token in town; in his muted mind, I *had* to be challenged. In retrospect, the encounter had all the ingredients of an enthralling nature documentary rife with mellifluous narration, me representing a wayward lion wandering through an inhospitable wilderness, unknowingly encroaching on his territory, threatening his supremacy among his prized pack of pussies. He was an unchallenged, untested, *wannabe* king. His ego belying a lack of true grit, his suburban softness signaled that he did not stand a chance in this epic *tête-à-tête*. He had no way of knowing his perfidious Pride was pieced together by a false sense of pride sustained solely through stereotype—his superficiality belying the fact that his race had limited his estimation to mere surface, his power parlous at best, and likely perilously close to disintegration having been forged by his false sense of bravado along with their fickle expectations. My success on the court, and at subsequently courting the acceptance of my white peers within the strict parameters of this specific cliché, directly endangered his fleeting sense of value in a community that undervalued us both.

And so, the game was on. This modern-day Battle royal would later bring to mind Ralph Ellison's tale of Black boys pitted against one another for white delight.

It was nearly high noon when me met for our recess showdown, our classmates thrilled that I had accepted his challenge to a duel. If anything, I knew that my body as well as my Blackness were on the line as I competed for inconstant white acceptance predicated solely on my success at fulfilling this tired, deeply entrenched stereotype. The late summer heat created an oven on the asphalt, the bright sun baking our bodies as we hacked at each other in a hackneyed display of Black worth. Given the high stakes, the epic conditions behind this epic matchup of one on one, we elbowed and even tripped each other as we raced to score points with our white peers. I still hear the cheering section imploring him to "kick his butt" as I used my more sizable body to push him out of his comfort zone. Sadly, he had grown too comfortable going to his right—and going up against white boys who would not lean their bodies into him and force him to his left. At this point, I had become so proficient at playing the game, both outside and inside of school, that basketball, much like my socialization in the white suburbs, had made me ambidextrous. My survival in urban and suburban Boston had so depended on code-switching and the ability to adapt to the language, leanings, and life forces of contrasting communities that going left was as easy for me as going right. He had grown comfortable playing white kids half his size, on pristine courts; I had made my bones aiming at a milk crate nailed to a tree, my shot honed by mastering angles and going up against bigger lions who would not hesitate to embarrass you with a show of force, or freakish athleticism, often sending you home, defeated and deflated, your tail tucked between your legs.

Failing to score after several attempts, and down 4-1, he attempted to even the score with an errant elbow. His sharp limbs, comparable to the branches behind the backboard on which I played in the inner city, opened up a bloody tributary between my nose and mouth. He then managed to make a bunch of buckets in rapid succession on fluke shots that tied it up and forced me, flustered and now furious, to regroup. I called time. Channeling my inner Charles Oakley, I retrieved the Roxbury I had left on the school bus. Recommencing the match, I promptly knocked his ass right to the ground. His knee now resembled my nose. As he pleaded "FOUL!" to no avail, I tasted *blood*. I quickly began indulging in my other talent: trash talking—a foreign language to an adopted alien like himself, letting him know in no uncertain terms that I would *never* lose to a "white boy." He may have had a silver spoon, but I possessed a silver tongue and, with lessons newly gleaned from Malcolm, turned this match into a lambasting, the court becoming an approximation of the field and the game a referendum on house niggaz everywhere. I was doing it for beloved Roxbury, that mighty hamlet where I still lived with my father on the weekends and where I and my magnificent idol had both come into our own.

I was also doing it for fickle acceptance no matter which way the ball bounced. I was ignorant of this as my self-righteousness sent him packing. I cannot recall the final score, but, though I eventually would win the match, we *both* lost. Our lunchtime entertainment for the white kids was ultimately pointless and utterly superfluous, as we fought only to fulfill their antiquated and questionable perceptions of us. And though we appeared to be headed in opposite directions, him running from his Blackness while I was running toward mine, our exhaustion that day was undeniable. I wanted to win so badly, he *needed* to win so badly, that I recall a fatigue unlike anything I had likely experienced up to that point in my young life. The beads of sweat pouring down my head and back, the soaked shirt clinging to his, betraying that our bodies were indeed on fire. They had overheated from the pressure we placed on them to matter.

This inscrutable outcome disguised itself as validation in the moment. His noticeable disappointment and even my triumphant boasting belied the fact that neither of us could claim victory. We hated ourselves so much we were willing to take their shitty high fives and back pats and convert those into a love that it was not, these tokens of affection they now gladly tossed at us amounting to little more than chump change. Whatever we felt, or convinced ourselves we felt, be it a remedial sense of Black pride or a greater sense of acceptance, our thirst for approval only left us worse off. Like drinking salt water, this silly exercise left us more dehydrated. Two young Black boys tried to kill each other because there was room for only one. Instead of turning our backs on this peanut gallery, we turned on each other. The ball was in their court after all. And as it bounced away, rolling onto the field after I had slammed it in victory, I recall his standing there taciturn, the gulf between us and the humid air thickened by a deafening silence, interspersed only by our audible pants. We both felt the enervation in that moment, hands on our hips, attempting to guzzle air in our efforts to cool two souls on fire. The memory of that day is vivid and visceral; twenty-five years on, I am still trying to catch my fuckin' breath.

Cyrus McQueen @CyrusMMcQueen · Mar 4, 2019
I was a fat lil black boy growing up in the inner city of Boston and even I'd be lying if I said I didn't wanna grow up to be Dylan McKay... The Porsche, the pompadour, the poetic sensitivity... He personified cool perhaps better than anyone in our generation... RIP Luke Perry...

⟲ 329   ♡ 3403

My basketball Battle presaged what I would endure decades later in my many attempts to gain acceptance, via manufactured diversity initiatives, into the entertainment world. The open calls for Black performers would provide chilling flashbacks to that day on the Black court. Often these network talent searches for Black comics and writers, cloaked within the stark stifling confines of competition, became Battles royal in their own right as young, bright, beautiful, and gifted Black entertainers lined up like prized cows in cattle calls to be observed by a gaggle of gatekeepers in a comparable game of impressing your oppressors. With our abilities again being auctioned off, this centuries-long manifestation would tie what was left of your soul into tight knots, your stomach betraying the forces swallowing you up. Sometimes you would beat out literally thousands of competitors, your performing acumen or writing packet setting you apart from the pack, before the diversity initiative would disappear, mysteriously, bafflingly. The futility of your fight for recognition would later be confirmed when you discovered that white writers and comics outside the confines of said competitions landed coveted positions—positions that had not been advertised but rather simply passed through word of mouth or friends' referrals, signaling beyond any shadow of a doubt that we could never truly vie with them for the opportunities privilege could procure.

I have come to learn that cronyism is a chronic condition likely to continue limiting my ascension; the entertainment industry, like so many others, reflects ensconced relationship patterns predicated on race and proximity as opposed to axiomatic merit or ability. And when you consider that far too many white Americans, including comedic writers, neither forged friendships with a diverse array of people, nor reached outside their limited social circles, it is painfully obvious who shares, and thus receives, opportunities. It is a stirring reminder of what I experienced throughout adolescence and young adulthood, when, despite rubbing elbows with my white peers, and despite the appearance I was appreciated, I still could not secure an invitation to the party.

The impetus behind the "diversity" initiatives held by these television networks, and the training centers supplying said talent, would later be revealed: they had been rolled out after the stunning lack of representation, long unaddressed, inspired these half-baked, halfhearted attempts to diversify the pool of talent. For both entities, it would help to establish an *appearance* of acceptance, one that could at least pass a sniff test. But where these places desperately clamor to catch up with progress, the deafening roar created by progressive-minded, pissed-off young people of color banging the drum of diversity in the ears of gatekeepers and decision makers who long ignored the problem is often the decisive factor *in* facilitating this long-gestating change. Whether it is this pounding or the one they receive in the press, they suddenly convene panels and procure scholarship money earmarked for the most earnest among us. And we flood these gates, now opened however temporarily, in hopes of becoming the handful of drops scooped up in these disingenuous white hands.

Our desire to be seen almost always succumbs to that deeper, far more pressing desire by people with privilege to *not* see you, our exclusion all but guaranteed despite this much publicized illusion of inclusion. I vividly recall going before one of these panels of complacency, smugness, and self-adulation at a Manhattan improv comedy school. The event would prove to be downright dispiriting, the paucity of diversity on full display, a glaring signal that despite my having been recommended for, of all things, a diversity scholarship, my real competition would be their palpable, profound disinterest. In hindsight, perhaps I was foolish to assume the cold climate of the school's halls and its common areas would suddenly warm upon receiving my teacher's endorsement. Perhaps I should have anticipated, instinctually, the insidiousness of indifference, that slick poison so often administered to us in predominantly white spaces; even self-professed progressive ones. Perhaps I should have remembered what most people of color can corroborate: whether it be a school, office, or social gathering, when you integrate a space, your arrival can feel tantamount to having dropped onto a glacier, the frigid reception reflecting something similar to a cold war, no one making the smallest effort to even acknowledge your presence, let alone break the ice, verifying, once more, the often stifling effects of these climes.

Proof of concerted efforts to freeze us out came on *this* particular day. Though my undeniable purpose was to prove I belonged at the school, every step I took through its hallways of homogeneity, even into the interview itself, substantiated the opposite: I was unquestionably, unequivocally, an *outsider*. Their utter lack of attention, a disdain both fueling and influencing their apathetic posture, cast such an all-encompassing pall over the proceedings that a glowing recommendation could not shine through it. How they managed to suck their own dicks without kneeing themselves in the face is beyond me. My enthusiasm and grasp of game, a hallmark of their comedy curriculum, was no match for the game these gatekeepers played on me.

That awful recurring theme, of being played, revisited me as one of the two interviewers did not look up from a laptop even once to address me over the course of the meeting. It was as if they had discovered something unusual in an earnest Black student, and then set about conveying, in earnest, that I did not belong. Once they established a pattern of perfunctory engagement, they went further by asking not a single follow-up question—despite my foolish, vain attempt to fill the void by coupling my answers with questions to them about their teams and improv background. This fulsome exercise was ineffective—they were wholly impervious to my presence—and simply *heightened* this folly to its maximum. The interview ended abruptly after six or seven minutes.

Though I will go to almost any length to establish my merit, on this afternoon it was clear that they were just going through the motions. While I had left it all out there in performance after performance, class after class, year after year, I found myself again jockeying to prove my jocular talents, my *worthiness* in the eyes of these egotistical, mediocre, white male thirty-somethings. Their fraud began to filch an emotional accrual. I continued grasping for a grin, a nod, even a slight wrinkle at the corner of one mouth that would somehow signal I had lessened the distance between us. Alas, my ardor was for naught. I rose, picked up pieces of myself off the floor, and glumly exited.

I remember stumbling out as you often do after these things, dizzy, disoriented, and nauseous, as though I had been climbing a mountain I could never summit. My inability to scale this icy, daunting monolith meant I had also likely plateaued during my career ascent in spite of my feverish, active striving for greater progress. Given the torrent inside me, fighting for an acknowledgement that, in my heart, I was now aware would likely never come, it was almost a miracle I remained upright long enough to make it back down to the lobby. Recognizing the sheer futility of this fucking shit meant that, despite opting for the stairs, I plummeted quickly. The anger soon came, too, no doubt, my mind's eye indulging images of violent, delicious, satisfying retribution, a compelling desire to hurt others cresting—but not before inevitably transforming into that equally visceral, yet far more dangerous, desire to hurt myself.

In the numb immediate aftermath, the solitude of the staircase shielded me from the plethora of slowly blending emotions, although neither it nor a studio apartment ultimately protected me from the impending gales. Frozen visages of fellow mountaineers, would-be comics, flashed before me as I made my harrowing descent, their Black bodies likewise not built for this kind of atmosphere, their futile attempts to make it to the top signaling their dreams also likely died in the same dark, foreboding stairwell. Passing ghosts, the flickering bulbs mirroring the light wavering in me, I somehow made it to the street and finally home, back to base camp, where I crumbled, the heavy blows to my ego, psyche, and soul, along with the good news I never did get completing the devastation laying waste to my insides.

The indelible lesson is that to be Black in the latter part of the 20th century and into the 21st is to stomach a new incarnation of discrimination. Pejorative has given way to repudiation, a far more acceptable form of denigration, and for me and a new generation of Black folks, the N-word has been supplanted by a more palatable yet similarly damaging one: No. Where youthful innocence gave me access to suburban spaces, where the undeniable nobility of some in the aftermath of the Civil Rights Movement in many ways helped me secure a visa, I have learned as a grown Black man that I can no longer expect to benefit from such altruism or even hope to be granted entry at all. The sting these pricks created would only intensify when, as an adult, I realized that the more we seek out opportunities, the more opportunities we give them to *cut* us down with a No.

Exacerbating this revolving door of rejection are those instances when the brotha who looks like you, who by all accounts shares your alien status but who dons the disguise—in some cases, even *embodies* it— is slipped a golden ticket to much fuss and fanfare. By embracing a narrow, unchallenged vision of us, thereby gaining entrance into these circles, their willingness to reflect back an anemic, otherwise bullshit interpretation of Blackness proves gainful. Their invitation to the masquerade secured, Blackness becomes nothing more than a façade. Those who gain a pass when this version proves palatable always have a funny way of compounding already confounding dynamics.

Auctioning our abilities, our talents tethered to this feigned benevolence like a chain, sublimates our struggle in service to this sanitized display—these immutable dynamics even molding our own questionable desires—this, a selection which is ultimately accepted by all parties due to the *guise* of exception. Waiting to be asked to dance like demoralized debutantes, this quest to be the favorite, posing and preening to attract their charitable gaze, clinging to the wall and every telegraphed intention, while the decisionmakers make their picks leaves us excitedly deciphering their Morse code of fickle, fleeting interest as if our lives depended on it. Given that our futures appear to improve with each promising gesture, we thrive in this distorted, misleading moment of before, happily allowing that hopeful outcome to comfort us, like a warm embrace, the other side of this encounter not nearly as important as what *we* convince ourselves of in this minute where hope still resides.

For many, this delusion is so complete it compels them to indulge conceit, shrewdly relaying their skewed interpretations to the others, employing ploy in an unabashed attempt at upstaging one another. As we stand there, shoulder to shoulder, waiting with the gravest anticipation for just the right jingle to call us to the floor, we hear those canorous keys to opportunity, and are oh so happy to dance—so happy, in fact, that we silently vow not to step on any toes. But there can be only *one* Cinderella. That unconscious willingness to fulfill the white world's expectations of Blackness shoehorns our spirit to fit a too-tight sole, contorting us into positions that can become otherwise *numbing*.

To be absorbed in a world of entertainment that is lukewarm at best is all the more problematic when considering that, for most African Americans, recalcitrant diversity panels continue to be a necessary evil often standing between us and opportunity. It is an assault on my conscience to know that affirmative action, born out of necessity, does not register as such when my presence and the presence of my fellow Black performers, much like my fellow Black students granted temporary passes into suburban circles, are tolerated only in order to fulfill quotas that are more questionable than quixotic. Though the benefits of representation cannot be overstated, when you are simply filling a slot, one among a finite few selected to enter into enclaves of economic privilege, the merits behind your placement, your aptitude, or even your preeminence are likely overshadowed by the pall your dark skin casts over your actual proficiency—your race ultimately informing your *true* value in America beyond any consideration of your overall caliber. With your Blackness constantly compared and contrasted with whiteness—or even some twisted preconception of what it means to be Black—existing on your own merits, itself a worthy idea considering the inherent worth of your humanity, is impossible. The breadth of your importance, indeed the full estimate of your significance, is only ever being measured by a white ruler. Though you look to be an equal player, you can never win this game, especially when the scorekeepers, these conspicuous gatekeepers we consciously and unconsciously vow to wow, are not actually counting our buckets to begin with.

Cyrus McQueen @CyrusMMcQueen · Apr 27, 2018
Funny how no one on #FOXNews ⌐ is telling Kanye to 'Shut up and make beats'... #FridayFeeling ⌐

⟲ 88   ♡ 441

The lie sold to me my entire life was revealed when I realized that it is not enough to go to school with white folks or be loosely ingratiated into their worlds. Their acknowledgement of Black people, however minimal, always convinces them that they do enough to alleviate the race problem even if those like us, who share neither their pigment nor their privilege, likely continue *to* lose, our true worth never quantified. Though they are not active racists, their passive participation in integrated spaces and even sluggish acceptance of a Black person, any Black person, in their minds and in the collective conscience of their communities absolves them of any accusations of impropriety or prejudice—all while they conveniently overlook the factors that *keep* them privileged, those very same factors that, by the same token, keep *us* punished.

This brings to mind that most penetrating quote from Dr. King: "In the end, we will remember not the words of our enemies but the silence of our friends." I long ago learned, in that bivouac of the suburbs, that implied acceptance is a fleeting setup, the premium placed on appearances often leaving us exposed and painfully aware of the paucity of legitimate warmth. As a Black child, you oftentimes bear witness to the way in which the sheer implication of growth is maddeningly, almost readily sacrificed for the real thing, these inauthentic impressions gaining precedence over any valuable impression you can make.

Later, witnessing the failure to launch of diversity initiatives—with many purported allies putting forth only a modicum of effort, unwilling to go the distance, to shepherd in change through time, dedication, and personal sacrifice—signals that people of color are usually left with no recourse *but* to fend for ourselves, their tiny efforts no match for the institutional juggernaut put in place *to* jettison parity. The true colors of many a so-called ally are revealed because, when push comes to shove, they have no actual skin in the game. For African Americans, this surprise will come sooner than later as you barely enjoy adolescence before learning altruism extends but so far, you suffering a staggering fall from expectation—this world you have inherited making short shrift of your naiveté.

You know that at every interval in American life, your fate and future hinge on a barrier barely open wide enough to get your foot in the door, while neighbors, classmates, and coworkers freely move along unimpeded paths of upward mobility, enjoying the power these designations produce. Your fate, like your father's and grandfather's before you continues to, ultimately, depressingly, rest in their hands. As an African American, you are restricted to one lane in any field, whether it be education or even entertainment, anywhere the dynamics of ownership, stewardship, and power, upheld by historical traditions that have remained static for generations, place you on the *outside* looking in for opportunities. While your white contemporaries occupy the inside track, your predetermined fate keeps you at a competitive disadvantage, your success in this race far less assured than an eventual loss.

After spending my lifetime with a foot firmly planted in both worlds, surfing this dual reality, what is even more debilitating, is the supplemental realization that the head start many of my contemporaries enjoyed during childhood has generated by adulthood an insurmountable distance between us. It is one thing to not enjoy fidelity and fellowship during youth, to be omitted from plans and parties; it is quite another to bear witness as they catch wave after wave, the fruits of financial planning and beneficial business relationships, having been forged by families and members of the fortunate class, while you spent your evenings and weekends an ocean away from these incubators of economic privilege. Here the benefits of diversity, indeed our very own potential, will succumb to the suburbs' potential for propagating privilege—our race in this regard no match for established patterns that betray the inner workings of power and those whose proximity always sets them up to inherit it.

By the time I realized that I had been in the towns of Weston, Chesnut Hill and Brookline during the wrong hours of the day, it was too late. By all accounts, spending my youth in predominantly white schools had provided the beneficial foundation of a fabulous education, yet plans for my peers had been set in motion the minute they were born, through trusts or inheritances, through the properties and stocks that would constitute their eventual windfall. My Black ass was behind the eight ball, prey to defeat as the whims of white will, whether arbitrary or by accident, were all it would take to cue my perilous plummet. Being Black in America means that I have not been set up to succeed, which only leads to a logical conclusion: I have been set up to fail.

Cyrus McQueen @CyrusMMcQueen · Mar 8, 2019
My wife being from the UK and me being from Boston definitely has an affect on our household. Like, when I'm home before her and the apartments a mess, I rush around straightening up... I'll shout 'The British are coming! The British are coming!' as I'm washing all the dishes...

⟳ 1225   ♡ 10311

This corrosive theme was confirmed in March of 2019 when the Department of Justice charged nearly fifty individuals with taking part in a college acceptance scandal, ensnaring Felicity Huffman, Lori Loughlin, and other well-known individuals, as well as several high-profile corporate executives. All had shelled out small fortunes to get their children into some of the nation's top universities, including Georgetown, Yale, and Stanford, in the biggest college cheating plot the country has ever seen. The company at the center of it, established by a shady businessman to act as intermediary, offered hefty bribes to these colleges on behalf of their unscrupulous parents, all to secure their ne'er-do-well's enrollment at these competitive schools.

Working-class and marginalized people almost tacitly understand that the wealthy can procure and capitalize on educational opportunities for their children, given vast resources for tutoring, test prep, and tuition. The prevalence of my more privileged peers in Massachusetts bypassing Brookline High to attend prep and private schools like Phillips Andover Academy and Beaver Country Day, before matriculating to Harvard and Dartmouth, reveals to me an entire network dedicated to achieving a clear-cut aim, even if my lower-middle-class reality meant I was unlikely to ever travel that path.

Still, this inferred notion that the fruits of labor are no match for the fruits of wealth is no more apparent than now, after it has been unearthed that some of these parents literally paid others to take the SAT and ACT for their sons and daughters. The level of subterfuge employed to subvert the system, this masquerade that would undermine academic institutions and our faith in them—even purporting in some cases that some of these children were accomplished athletes regardless of whether they displayed any actual ability or even *participated* in the sport in question—is absolutely enraging. It is a toxic theme and part of a problematic history that includes quotas on Jewish enrollees at elite schools a century ago—in addition to a "pay-to-play" paradigm that is predicated primarily on big money donations and dubious legacy enrollments.

A recent Duke University study, *Legacy and Athlete Preferences at Harvard,* confirms this damaging, albeit well-known trend. Some 43 percent of the white students enrolled in the school were admitted not on merit but rather as athletes, or because they were children of faculty members, or because they were tied to major donors, or "legacies." We observe these entrenched patterns not only negatively impacting diversity but our greater society as well, as stagnation and mediocrity routinely supplant true progress and innovation.

For years, I knew intrinsically that I could never compete with the well-connected, that the disastrous vestiges of segregation would likely undervalue my own talents and intellect. I, along with my brethren, would have to settle for the scraps of second best—state schools or even community colleges—as we navigated the virulent waters churned by these intergenerational deficits. But here had come ocular proof of that which was basically staring us in the face all along: the inherently corrupt nature of the wealthy simply promulgating privilege by selling it to the rest of us as pedigree. Considering the debilitating debt most young Americans will incur to acquire a higher education, these events not only highlight our country's wealth gaps but, in many ways, how such disparities only become further entrenched. For far too many, financial and family circumstances will keep them fettered for decades, preventing them from experiencing any semblance of class mobility. Previously, I had posited that we could not win a game when they did not even count our buckets. As this scandal demonstrates, those on the margins, irrespective of race, have cause to now question the futile motions we go through, the toil and the toll when it comes to achieving this so-called American Dream. Our ability to even get *in* the game has proven equally as daunting: especially since these gatekeepers, those we are driven to impress, have actually called game before we lace 'em up.

What the admissions scandal suggests is an absence of true competition. Given the sharp practice employed by those seeking to maintain status, this duplicitousness leads me to question those who can only thrive in a rigged system. Now living in New York after decades in the academic hub of New England, I find myself recalling countless encounters with those attending the Ivy's that left me scratching my head. To say that I found myself unimpressed with many preppies is an understatement. I remember muttering "what a dumb motherfucker" under my breath after engaging with one slack-jawed, self-possessed bastard while attending an event in Cambridge. He made sure to tell me he went to Harvard. (I had not inquired.) In hindsight, I wish I had had a wittier comeback, riposte worthy of a Matt Damon/Ben Affleck script, but both my mind and negritude would be neutralized by anger. Being nineteen, less tactful than now, and possessing *copious* amounts of could-not-give-a-fuck, I soon mentioned to someone else, and more audibly—since he was within earshot—"Wow, I didn't think they let *dumb* motherfuckers into Harvard!"

Encountering a handful of conceited preppies is not nearly as off-putting as those attitudes we encounter while performing an autopsy on privilege. Frankly, we often harbor the naive expectation that we can help, through methodical dissection, the very discourse that has long fueled our disconnect. Most people of color can recall fruitless conversations with white Americans about race and class—moments when their inherent blind spots were revealed during our earnest attempts to see eye to eye with them.

Consider, for example, the election of Trump and the splintering of the Democratic base. Recall the myriad of ways in which the Democratic Party takes for granted the working-class and minority vote, while highlighting the comfortable position of many middle-class Americans, the preservation of their socioeconomic status determining their vote more so than any other factor. Conversations about this would naturally go deeper to reach a logical conclusion, but, as I have discovered in many cases, the denial of privilege is so primal, so *instinctual* in those we seek to engage with that this natural defense mechanism tends to morph into outright contempt almost instantly. Incredibly telling is the compulsion of many to tout their inherent merit, doubling down on both the otiose belief they are colorblind and on the ironic, supplemental assertion that they *too* worked hard for everything they have. Yet most will conveniently neglect not only their unconscious contributions to racial inequality but also the fruits of their forefathers' acquisitive nature. Additionally, by offering up the explanation of hard work, such a declaration, in that very same breath, negates the reality of most marginalized persons who *themselves* work hard.

This bigger point always succumbs to that disconnect I previously pointed out. In America working hard is quite often inconsequential, yet many continue to avoid this fact since tropes provide a handy shield from accusations and greater accountability. Many simply elect to ignore that our great and justifiable pother is predicated on *who* is routinely rewarded with opportunity—and ultimately compensated better *for* their hard work. Given that race and gender still correlate disastrously with whose time is considered more valuable, that "hard work" defense, digested by the descendants of slaves and suffragettes still earning less on the dollar, usually meets with an eye roll, if not an "Oh, shut the fuck up!"

I can only qualify their protest as a manifestation of guilt, a feeling stemming from the sobering realities of systemic oppression, our relegated roles, and their undeniable advancement due to this fact. But herein lies an interesting dynamic. We often must withstand a weighted dialogue related to affirmative action and welfare: the widely held notion that we are benighted and thus undeserving, emboldening a public to openly question our gains—despite their undeniably benefitting from the intergenerational deficits we have suffered due to slavery, segregation, and their aftermath. Yet calling out privilege similarly enrages many who grow indignant the second you dare to count up their receipts when pointing out our purposeful depression. Highlighting how many benefited from generational wealth generated through multiple revenue streams—think profit, dividend income, capital gains—while conveying how their inheritances, both filial *and* racial, not simply their earned income, play a more crucial role in cementing their caste than their own merits in many cases, and this evaluation tends to produce a deafening silence. Factoring in the loopholes and tax manipulations that also enable those with privilege and property to protect and grow their wealth—such as Trump's penchant for deflating the value of his real estate come tax time and later inflating that value when it was time to divest—we cannot help but draw certain inferences. Witnessing this rigged game, I conclude that racial inequality can only have stemmed from such profound insecurities, such a timorous sense of self that, as with Trump, one not only supplants their diminished inner value with adventitious material but subsequently it compels one to cheat in service of maintaining that artificial ideal. This often appears their only recourse given the primal fear that an even playing field can lead to their eventual loss and, potentially, our revenge.

We discover the cold sobering truth of being Black in America the day we realize it really is about who you know. Yet, as our relegated roles and lack of fruitful connections come to reveal, it is more about who you do *not* know.

As if to contextualize what you have felt instinctually from the moment you landed in the suburbs and struggled to breath, you recall that profound lesson: Blackness is an *absence* of whiteness. It confirms how exactly we have managed to lose this race. Feeling as if you are anathema is tantamount to having asthma; debilitating when you do not secure that much-coveted inside track.

Cyrus McQueen @CyrusMMcQueen · Mar 12, 2019
Fred Trump... Felicity Huffman... Lori Loughlin... Rich parents are like having a fuckin genie... Their kids can sleep their way through high school and get into Yale... Black kids gotta bust their ass in high school and, if they do get into Yale well, we know they can't sleep...

⟲ 335   ♡ 1817

While traveling in privileged circles, people of color find ourselves presented with another kind of hurdle. In such settings, you likely elicit backhanded compliments—"you are so articulate;" "you speak so well"—posited as ointments to assuage the irritation triggered by your sagacity. However, the intention behind such bromides is not to make a Black person feel better as much as the converse: such a comment makes *them* feel better about themselves and their illusions, those latent feelings of superiority revealed when this low valuation of your people suddenly yields a higher return than expected.

The ability to seemingly relinquish one stereotype is offset by their inability to disabuse themselves of another. As a person of color, you find yourself in a curious position: confirming a great opinion of you confirms the worst opinions that have prevailed about your people, this indulgence of your own exceptionalism coming at the expense of your brethren. That you have sidestepped those boobytraps of which they will not speak—those centuries of intentional, perpetual starvation—and come to possess not only a full mind but one that can readily decipher their hollow plaudits inspires genuine shock. As you proceed to devour and promptly eschew this insipid flattery, as if it is an undercooked entree, your dissatisfaction engenders an almost reflexive repentance. As they find themselves tasked with whisking their bland assessments away, they proffer inauthentic penance with great speed, trying to distract from the bad taste they left in your mouth in the hopes of salvaging a measure of good will.

That moment they register their dubious surprise is the very instant the insidiousness of race can be realized. You had been expected to relish in their surprise—a move that would bely the very intellect you supposedly wield. Choosing to wallow in such hollow flattery would mean you invalidate this accurate impression of you while validating that inaccurate tally they accrue of themselves. I never cease to be amazed by those who readily assume we would willingly corroborate this subtext, these cloaked impressions, these crafty attempts to have us devour empty praise, mistakenly assuming that such disingenuous acknowledgments would satiate us or make us whole. Perhaps even more bewildering is their expectation that you would in no way betray that the very opposite has occurred, that they have basically plunged a dagger into your heart.

On these occasions, with so much left unsaid, our collective discomfort finds a way of lingering in the ether. In this moment, African Americans often find themselves compelled to challenge their inquisitors as we grapple with an overwhelming impulse that has thrown our gut, heart, and mind into a spin cycle. With resignation, we take up the task of demolition and go about strapping dynamite to their clinical distortions. The wiring job is delicate, your heart races and you do your damnedest not to blow up first—all your work would be ruined then. So you set out to edify methodically, highlighting how the very contours of supremacy have taken shape, and thus shaped them. This is not an improvised device—no, you present in painstaking detail exactly how they have inherited this incendiary construct and come to live in this lie of whiteness, the views of their Black neighbors ill-formed and inaccurate, rendered as they are from a distorted height and the inauthentic perch of imperiousness.

By this point, if you have done your work correctly, you trigger another level of surprise, albeit something you yourself can enjoy. As they backpedal, almost tripping over themselves to try to diffuse the situation, you derive a modicum of satisfaction in having moved the dialogue forward. But, having also detonated their belief system, you are saddled with a burdensome choice: either drag them through the rubble toward the light or allow them to remain in that hovel, where once the smoke has cleared, they will dust themselves off and likely begin rebuilding this long-standing construct to the exact same ruinous specifications.

In examining both cheating scandals and election scandals, a president whose pedigree set him up to take the office as if it were his birthright, his underhanded power grab buttressed by his Black predecessor who, operating aboveboard, still pulled off the impossible, the contrast between Trump and Obama provides more than a sliver of insight into the entire notion of privilege. The former perpetually underachieved while the latter overachieved yet finds his merits and his transcripts, Ivy League placement, and position as head of the *Harvard*

Law Review routinely called into question, his brilliance *habitually* besmirched. Nothing threatens white mediocrity like Black excellence, so much so that this pernicious pull to protect privilege and, again, that precarious sense of true inner value witnesses the Trumps and Loughlins, the Huffmans and Kushners stack the decks in their favor out of a primal fear that privilege will evaporate the second, to paraphrase Dr. King, justice rolls down like waters and righteousness like a mighty stream.

The corruption of Trump and countless others of wealth and influence, in their business practices and beyond, shows as much as anything that these members of the white firmament have never fully shared King's dream. It is one thing for Black children and white children to hold hands. It is quite another for Blacks and whites to compete fairly for coveted slots at elite schools and corporations; on movie screens and comedy teams.

Our race is stigmatized in yet another way: those traveling in these elite circles summarily paint affirmative action improperly as an unfair advantage, while asserting that their legacy admissions and easily procured internships, hefty donations, and even doctored test scores do not. In the end, it is easier to question our perceived advantages than to question their litany of literal ones. But perhaps most distressing, we can easily posit that it is the prime, purposeful reason we remain unseen. By being invisible, we cannot compete and, as a result, *advance*. It is why, whether it be the Negro Leagues or Motown, HBCU's or Klutch Sports, the paradigm for Black progress has had to exist and operate independent of the spiritual frugality and economic parsimony of white America. Necessity being the mother of invention, our abilities so undeniable, we *have* to create our own avenues.

It is abundantly clear that the only way the privileged in our society can save face is by continuing to turn their backs on us. Such measures ultimately ensure their merits can never be challenged. Meanwhile, by challenging our merits, their viability remains unencumbered, and *we* can never gain the competitive advantage.

This tool for self-preservation, however petty and pointless, however transparent, still damages. What further depresses my spirit, aside from interactions with some dumb student leaving me dumbfounded, is the realization that while places like Harvard occupy the rarefied air of scholastic preeminence, its institutional history as incubator of leadership, as the gold standard of academia worldwide, perpetuates not merely where power is learned but, more important, how power *looks:* it and its Ivy brethren have helped codify a system of racial and wealth imbalance that has gone unchanged for centuries. 1636, the year of Harvard's establishment, is less important than that it is a mere seventeen years after slaves set foot in Jamestown, Virginia, the educational institution itself subsequently corollary to that other institution in which unpaid labor was essential in establishing and facilitating white wealth. With exhaustive research revealing that many of the school's presidents brought slaves to live with them on campus, such labor likely helped shape the perspectives of countless students who would pass through its gated grounds.

Even more revealing is that for a university so steeped in tradition, which so relishes its haughty history and dominion that it deliberately and thoroughly hid for so many centuries its particularly problematic past, its statues and portraits of past presidents thus present an incomplete image. The bedrock of this country, like that underlying the very buildings on Harvard Yard, continue to be obscured by the excrescence blanketing it. That socioeconomic climb, that uncontested quest for upward mobility, like the poisoned ivy inching up its enclosures, masks that such institutions have come about at a price few are willing to acknowledge—or pay.

11

Color Struck

Cyrus McQueen @CyrusMMcQueen · Apr 28, 2018
They told LeBron to shut up...
They told Kaepernick to stand up...
They told Kanye to keep it up...
#SaturdayMorning

⟲ 265   ♡ 738

I t is a sad commentary on the state of race relations today, having born witness to the vicissitudes occurring in America upon the election of Trump, to know that the theme of tokenism, the willingness of certain African Americans to accept a brutal paradigm of power, has not only been resuscitated but, now appears more popular than ever. In the history of Black people struggling and striving in America, at every juncture throughout our tempestuous history we find people of color who, like my eighth-grade rival, grow so adept at deferring to privilege it fortifies their subsequent willingness to allow said privilege to exploit them.

Long before Kanye West confused and conflated Black calls for freedom with "free thinking," certain African Americans would disseminate disinformation routinely to the rank and file. These unabashed attempts at consolidating power, transparent ploys at enhancing their own status by swindling credulous subjects through their discursive spell, found some of those targets openly embracing ideas and conventions that ran contrary to our community's best interests. Many, at times, would regurgitate this antithetical poison for even *greater* consumption. Thus the history of Black America is littered with prominent people of color who compromise sonorous, seditious calls for justice with self-serving appeals for placidity and moderation.

This recurrent bane to Black advancement often exacts its subterfuge from close proximity. Be it the pulpit or the schoolhouse—

witness how deferential authority often capitalizes on its cloth and letters, fleecing those members of our flock who earnestly buy in, convinced that the road to salvation has a payment plan, even as this slow crawl usually accrues an inestimable toll. Slick preachers beget the bourgeoisie, these Black-owned businesses now staffed with a modern incarnation: the company man. Quizzically, many herald those who witness the drip drip drip of progress flowering their garden as if it were a sign that their very own fortunes could suddenly pivot, this brand of conservatism notable only in highlighting by contrast the surrounding blight, exposing the prospects of those Black neighbors on either side that go statically unfulfilled, their plots equidistant yet *fruitless*.

Sweeping, comprehensive change often threatens not only the status quo of white power brokers, but also those Black proxies who fight fervently to preserve their own preferred status. From Southern plantations to the turn of the last two centuries, African Americans who have enjoyed status present a perfect foil for the progressively inclined, eagerly parroting the politics of the privileged class given their own approximation of advantage at the apex of Black society. Though America has cemented the immutability of race, deferring equality indefinitely, by preserving a position just above their Black counterparts, many experience the ostensible joy of being as close to white as possible. This shared entitlement even places them in a somewhat parallel position directly across our great divide. By spreading that conservative catnip of obedience, buttressing a social construct with a pernicious stratagem, we find these somewhat comparable forces consistently interring progress. Whether one is white or Black is ultimately tertiary, for these saboteurs, by all appearances, can be said to enjoy a mutually beneficial relationship, one that reinforces *both* of their envied positions. Thus, the color line is *conserved*. If race is predicated on a hierarchy, then those who identify with whites—who covet their color and internalize this theory of supremacy with zeal, yet by biology can never be white—go to the mat to secure those approximations. Wrestling with their true identity is nowhere near as important as maintaining a position atop a pecking order—or any social order in which they can haughtily look down on those who, in their view, are less wily.

In the Black community, this damaging dynamic has at times revealed itself through colorism and incendiary connotations suggesting that lighter skin and "good hair" are preferable. In this yearning for those Eurocentric effigies of validation, blindly coveting these cross-cultural representations, they actually become no different than trojan horses; for our self-hatred is easily smuggled inside this idolatry. Proof of this treachery can be found in the evolution of that "Black Bourgeoisie," a problematic ripple emerging out of plantation life that would serve as the prototype for social advancement well into the current era. That these inextricable subsets serve as a flawed measure of influence and prestige among people of color even to this day is a painful reminder of how the tentacles of racism and "shade-ism," and the corresponding values of this matrix of classification, entangle us generations later. Oppressors *and* the oppressed alike have ingested the insidious pull of race-based ideologies, devices used to absolve power grabs, while certain persons of color unscrupulously seeking prominence buy wholesale the historical revisionism frequently employed to reframe the reality shaping our society. Yet ultimately, their belief that they can pull off this bait and switch depends on the pride of their brethren. Their ability to unload their knockoffs remains wholly contingent on those who are *willing* to barter their Blackness.

For Kanye West to develop an affinity for Trump despite Donald's open hostility to his Black predecessor—not to mention his subsequent acts of hostility against people of color in his official capacity as president—means that the jackass rapper either chooses to ignore Trump's questionable motives, and gross misuse of power, *or* he foolishly believes he can obscure those motives while aligning himself with that power source. Much like those moths throughout middle America wearing MAGA hats, transfixed by Trump's flame, Kanye, too, is drawn to Trump's fire without realizing that their commonality carries only so much weight. His skin color offers a true estimate of his tarnished value in Trump's biased eyes, much like those who don red caps yet lack capital. Yet despite his own wealth, Kanye's success in a field that does not challenge Trump's ego, is what *actually* enables the bromance between the two narcissists. The rapper can adopt the same hubristic tendencies, but by thriving within the strict parameters of stereotype, he ultimately poses less of a threat to powerful white people than *true* iconoclasts.

The week that West went off the rails will not be soon forgotten by anyone with even the loosest understanding of the intersection of race and politics. By donning the Make America Great Again cap, Trump's modern equivalent of the white hood, the unambiguous sartorial choice of bigots, and popularized as the *pièce de résistance* within that irascible body, it soon became crystal: Kanye West *embraces* ignorance in the name of popularity.

Although neither of these mercurial men has a good grasp on reality, the questionable mental health of both West and Trump is not nearly as pertinent as their haughty disdain for those who challenge their ego-fueled cries for attention—that which is so often confused for authority. Sadly, like those who blindly cosign their exploits, they have proven themselves to be little more than followers themselves—chasing the sanctified grail of celebrity while, maddeningly, mistaking materialism *for* virtue. If it is true that "those who stand for nothing fall for anything," then Alexander Hamilton would be apoplectic upon seeing the presidency reduced to a kleptocracy while sycophants shout through the megaphone of celebrity, adopting and promoting a despots falsehoods.

Cyrus McQueen @CyrusMMcQueen · Apr 26, 2018
What's fucked up is, George W. Bush could technically get on tv right now and say, 'Kanye West doesn't care about black people'... #ThursdayThoughts

ti 195　　♡ 905

Perhaps West's greatest threat to our collective sanity would come when, having captured the zeitgeist, he then doubled down on his right-wing belief, flippantly remarking that slavery was, somehow, "a choice." Even had the country not witnessed the atrocities of Charlottesville, his insouciance and casual rendering of the greatest blight on the history of mankind would be a bridge too far. That this misinformation continues to fester, that generations of Southerners openly overstate the importance of slave owners while disastrously understating the horrors of bondage, means that we are still fighting an uphill battle even *without* West's misstep.

That conservatives minimize the Confederates' culpability in the institution of slavery is not nearly as disturbing as what West did in that instant to misrepresent the struggle of our ancestors—those who endured the unmitigated hell they *inherited*. By confusing this crucial fact, while failing to assert that yesteryear's conservatives were the architects of not only slavery but also the corrosive social restructuring that manifested post emancipation, Kanye essentially absolves those entities of any blame for what was for them, and them only, a *choice*. It is unfathomable that he allows his own power and privilege to cloud his mind and thereby render judgement on the hallowed men, women and children whose entire existence was enveloped in *unutterable* pain. As his

166

so-called "love" for Trump puts this pitiful backslider on the front pages of news outlets everywhere, he strikes a particular blow to not only people of color but *every* member of the progressive family aware of the falsehoods underpinning his opprobrious assessment.

We must not overlook that Kanye's dumb display comes on the heels of the completion of the National Memorial for Peace and Justice in Montgomery, Alabama, it now unofficially competing with the hundreds of conspicuous Confederate memorials dotting the South— memorials, it must be reiterated, that *augmented* the terror of the Jim Crow era. In the very same week that this long-awaited, long-anticipated Lynching Memorial opened, the world watched in bemusement as a heralded Black performer, who once possessed the intestinal fortitude to declare, "George Bush doesn't care about black people," aligned himself with the new face of bigotry in the United States.

Witnessing his ricochet between problematic public appearances and events of private personal turmoil, I cannot help but ponder: Is this some form of performance art? A ruse to engender a reaction? Another example of his flouting convention while exorcising, albeit with great acuity, his own personal demons for the purpose of even *greater* publicity? No matter which way you slice it, though, whether his intentions are honest or duplicitous, given the conviction with which he expresses himself, and the unmistakable outcome, it leaves most Black Americans with the immutable impression that, by parroting these lies and communicating this mendaciousness, Kanye ultimately *helps* to legitimize hate. His support of this president only lends validation to his lethal venom. But perhaps most distressing of all, upon contextualizing this, his most damaging of diatribes, is that, by willfully replacing our oppressors, by electing to *join* the mob, we witness one of our own lynching himself.

Without delving too deeply into the Kardashian vortex of malignant self-aggrandizement, something remains to be said regarding such a sybaritic engagement, those particularly vexatious individuals profiteering egregiously, ignobly from fame and indignity. Certainly, shameless self-promotion, coveting notoriety despite the costs, is not a foreign concept to a public figure of Kanye's renown. Being that the family in question occupies a lucrative and envied, albeit perplexing, position in the public consciousness is, one can argue, what certainly inspired that marriage to begin with. The fact that both had attained a certain status, and could compound it through coupling, is, yes, one obvious takeaway.

However, the genesis of that union points to broader implications. Upon deeper analysis, the whale Kanye feeds off betrays the far more discomfiting fact that, as a remora in American waters, he is tortured by the fact that his race prevents him from being the big fish. Comparable to his dalliance with Trump, his joining the Kardashian school suggests that his unarticulated reward would be attaining some semblance of whiteness or *greater* acceptance. He could somehow satisfy this insatiable desire by *being* Kardashian, adjacent to that very privilege across our great cultural divide. This goes a long way toward explaining those capricious, often caustic public displays he seems to unleash with greater and greater frequency. Whether superstardom has its prerogatives or the prerogatives of white privilege inspire this mirroring exercise, Kanye appears to be attempting to doff his Blackness, and the reality that keeps us all tethered, with each blast of hot air his adoptive family and their caustic media bubble pump into his overinflated ego.

Cyrus McQueen @CyrusMMcQueen · Apr 25, 2018
Shit, you know it's bad when Kim Kardashian is the Woke one in the relationship...

⟲ 107   ♡ 671

I am certainly no mental health professional, but mental illness of some kind seems to be a factor with West. What I am qualified to diagnose, however, is the off-putting and peculiar condition that seems to befall all Black people who exhaustively pursue whiteness. As aliens, we have seen this moonwalk with others who, factoring in their fame and deep desire to transcend race, seem to lose their minds, their inherent genius sublimated in a covetous clamor to catch up with that white whale. Placing Black brilliance on par with white mediocrity is enough to drive one crazy to begin with, without this added business suggesting that such humdrum—here a coterie of vacuous reality tv stars—can somehow underscore and cosign that brilliance.

Toni Morrison eloquently elucidated on this tragic, pyrrhic pursuit in *The Bluest Eye*. Like the character of Pecola, West's behavior seems to be symptomatic of something far graver. And while those displays alienate characters in the novel like Claudia, we as a community come to recognize, and grow disenchanted with what similarly unfolds with West. Morrison almost diagnoses our own malaise upon being inundated with Kanye's mercurial displays when she says of Pecola,

"She, however, stepped over into madness, a madness which protected her from us simply because it bored us in the end." And here West, a man devoid of intellectual honesty, more consumed with being regarded as a genius across all lanes than with laying the actual groundwork, fails to recognize this cultural touchstone, littered throughout literature and our history, a convention that has served as a cautionary tale for generations. Like much of his music, everyone knows Kanye simply samples things that have come before, his sick tune a knockoff of a taboo we have long witnessed; he affecting the same silhouette that Michael Jackson had cast against an unsparing white background. Coming from Chicago, and moonlighting by selling sneakers to Republicans and kids who could not afford them, perhaps he seeks to out-Jordan Michael too, following the same invidious path in hopes of transcending Blackness.

Cyrus McQueen @CyrusMMcQueen · Oct 14, 2018
The same people who hate Kaepernick are now embracing Kanye? So, they hate a black man who kneels but, they love a black man who doesn't stand for anything...

⟲ 3726   ♡ 12932

Given rumblings that Kanye wanted to run for president in 2020 (even weaseling his way onto several state ballots), one wonders whether he will simply be satisfied being the *Black* Donald? Just another inexperienced egomaniac using the presidency to pack his profound emptiness? Merely one more tortured soul conniving the purposeless for political and personal gain? Would this mark his racial transformation, an unqualified Black man finally advancing in America, signifying that, at long last, he can walk in his torturer's shoes? Would such a farcical development thereby complete him? Or perhaps this moral disintegration alludes to something more sinister: the obvious, frightening correlation to O.J., yet another Black figure who consciously, criminally avoided race until he could not any longer.

The obvious parallels to his adoptive family and the Shakespearean tragedy that played out in the mid-'90s suggests that irony is not dead after all. For in this clamor for white acceptance—and the inability to accept white rejection—we cannot help but wonder whether Kanye would also chase *it* right over a cliff. He drives toward a position at which he can never arrive, his quest to outrun our collective reality and his own personal tragedy, like Pecola's and O.J.'s, also producing a staggering scene, it a spectacle where all onlookers would merely gawk to glimpse this slow roll toward self-immolation.

12

The Living Dead

To be Black in America is to die a thousand deaths before your actual one. The inevitability of your literal demise, matched by the inevitability of your figurative one, produces a sort of spiritual deterioration long before any physical disintegration—with both competing in a race to see which of these concordant forces claims your soul first. This eroding energy, along with the practical impediments blocking you from the mitigating effects of affordable care and treatment, contributes to your compromised life expectancy.

For a Black American, life expectancy itself takes on ironic dimensions when you consider the cold, brutal implications behind your dearth of opportunities, your resultant lack of prosperity, and your peripheral station. You are thus forced to surmise: under these corrosive conditions, what kind of life are we really expected *to* have? Managing to survive to adulthood is no small feat in an America at war with you from the moment you open your big brown eyes to take in all this calamity and confusion. But, with our transparency forcing me to be transparent, I can fully disclose that though I made it through childhood and adolescence surrounded by physical death, I never completely overcame the discomfiture, the greater torment, that likely commenced the moment I realized I was unseen. This haunting feeling from childhood that I am invisible, like some Universal monster, revisits me in adulthood like a recurring nightmare. Painful memories, long submerged, float to the surface as the daily deluge of racially motivated incidents, corroborated by personal experiences, compound my anger and contribute to my growing sense of disillusionment. As the macro aggressions of the Trump presidency from its first days gave birth to an epidemic of micro aggressions, this flood of racially fueled encounters, engulfing a new era in American life, could be considered none other than a direct corollary of the torrent that Trump himself so consciously sowed.

Being that America has historically had a race problem, the rising tide of intolerance trickling down throughout the country cannot be viewed as an abstraction. Despite the almost tedious obtuseness of the news media, racism does not occur in a vacuum. Though oft spoken of in surprised terms, such news reports fail to impart that this outstanding plague is neither anomalous nor sporadic but rather pervasive and *perpetual.* Racism's surreptitious presence in the present era, often hidden through indifference, first advanced through the dark layers of subtext—before eventually transforming into the terminal cancer that would eat away at the country. Racism can well be considered an epidemic, and this societal malady, like most pathogens, can only proliferate by passing from person to person. That the psychological scars it produces often go unnoticed, is a testament to the causal relation between hate and its targets' isolation. By reinforcing its victims' insignificance, racism renders their perpetual wounds undetectable. Individuals suffer in the open, yet because they have been so stigmatized, their degradation outshining and outpacing their persecution, eventually no one can *hear* their scream. And that deafening silence has allowed Trump to amplify an attitude, creating an echo chamber that drowns out any hope of harmony with a discordant and thunderous chorus.

The unfortunate truth, evinced through my life and the lives of countless people of color in this country, is that Donald Trump could not have capitalized on the forces of animus and ambivalence had they not already existed. He could not have exacerbated America's race problem this egregiously if America did not already have a horrendous race problem *to* exacerbate. His conducting such a bitter symphony, orchestrating public displays of prejudice, echoes a sick tune that most Black Americans are all too familiar with. This malignancy is likely first visited upon each of us at an early age and remains there, lurking just over our shoulders, for the remainder of our lives—its potential to flare up at any time, like a dormant volcano that suddenly spreads ash and fire, presenting an omnipresent threat to our well being.

To perceive a human being with Black skin as a danger to be redressed—because her or his mere existence poses an existential threat to another person's parlous sense of power—signifies a profound sickness that might almost be humorous if it were not so unbelievably sad. When a white Starbucks worker called the police on Rashon Nelson and Donte Robinson, two Black men waiting in the coffeeshop for a friend, she set in motion a series of events that had the unmistakable potential to end in tragedy.

This incident, ironically occurring in the City of Brotherly Love, is not an isolated one in respect that African Americans, specifically African American men, continue to endure an abusive relationship with police—arbiters who often bridle at our mere *presence*. Still, the premise that Black skin correlates with criminality, despite the absence of any activity or evidence to determine such, only partly explains the motivations of a society that looks to solve problems that do not actually exist. What the pathology of prejudice reveals is that this barista's disease had so robbed her of sight, she began seeing things that were not there. By indulging the verisimilitude of their villainy, she projected unfounded fears onto two innocent men. The painful conclusion is that, when it comes to those enforcing the arbitrary, unwritten rules of white spaces, our image is always at the mercy of their imagination. Because two Black men remained in her sight for too long, their noticeable appearance challenging her desire to see us disappear, her only option was to seek to erase us *through* force. Her hallucination ultimately hid their humanity. It is discomfiting to realize that neither the police force nor any mitigating forces in her world would at any point disabuse her of her skewed beliefs, as all signs point to the likelihood that, on the converse, they only reinforced them.

Having had this monster mask affixed to me throughout a lifetime in such spaces, where in a split second I could be perceived as some werewolf—in those moments when I was not imperceptible, or an invisible man—the irony was not lost on me and many others that those two brothas were not only the real victims but also, perhaps, the most vulnerable ones in Starbucks that day. This was confirmed within moments when the real monsters, the *erasers*, showed up to remove them, helping crystallize a truly horrific vision. Often, invisible men are visible only long enough to be deemed a threat—enough time for police to come along and make them disappear completely. Thus, to be Black is to vacillate between figurative and literal absence. The illness of racism, the absurdity of suffering as a person of color for an activity as innocuous as sitting down, makes this malady only that much more confounding. Racism proves to be a disease disproportionately affecting Americans, but, whether it comes as contagion or addiction, it is Black Americans who *receive* the deadly treatment.

The nation, in never coming to grips with its original sin and sickness, was instead prescribed a system of legal segregation, immediately followed by an intense regimen of white flight. America is not only a country ill-prepared to address the root cause of its illness, but, a country that, by all appearances, is more than fine with continuing to mask its symptoms through separation, indifference, and inaction. Throughout the history of the United States, hallucinations of race have been the accepted reality, forcing Black people, more often than not, to conform to every unrealistic, ignoble portrait of us so long as it either confirms white fear or services white comfort. Our humanity invariably suffers, its disregard reinforced by the lack of true interdependence. Exacerbated by the dynamics of exclusion, we see this feeding a self-fulfilling agenda that *keeps* us perpetually askance.

When humanity is malnourished in homogenous bubbles, heterogeneous spaces cannot thrive. Far too many Americans are raised in virtual quarantine, their communities and opinions closed off from the veracity only found by venturing beyond these confines. These hermetically sealed enclaves incubate the bacteria of bigotry, passing along the undiagnosed illness from parent to child, neighbor to neighbor. This overwhelming lack of culture turns these places into Petri dishes; those shared views and, most important, shared fears are normalized and legitimized while outsiders are delegitimized and, unsurprisingly, regarded as abnormal and even *scary*.

Cyrus McQueen @CyrusMMcQueen · Apr 23, 2018
I'm willing to admit Democrats were racist in the past if Republicans are willing to admit they're racist now...
#MondayMotivation ⌁ https://t.co/BAlyGHM1nW ⌁

⟲ 178   ♡ 718

Looking back to Ancient Greece and Plato's Republic, we can recognize and appreciate the greater context of this complex elucidation, its striking relevance straddling two millennia. The allegory of the cave, Socrates's edification on the freedom of thought, it over two thousand years removed from our current manifestations of mental slavery, provides great insight into the construct of race and the resultant ignorance that has chained generations of Americans in a tomb of torpor. Though I just posited how most suburban and rural communities resemble bubbles, what more apt descriptor is there than that allegorical cave that Socrates and his brother Glaucon dissect through their dialectic of prisoners chained in a cave? Since no Black American can be seen without passing before the twisting fire of race, our true selves become deliberately obscured. With our reputations proceeding us at all intervals, many come to embrace those misrepresentations—responding to our objectification or to the convenient stereotypical image we cast. For what else was that Starbucks worker's 911 call other than the desperate plea of a woman tethered to a distortion, a woman who would rather kill, or see them killed, than be dragged out of her cave, forced beyond the limited perimeters of her heart and mind?

The great philosophers' rumination appears all the more prescient when considering the implications of infotainment in this day and age and those deliberately misleading media apparatuses orchestrating furtively behind people's backs. For a Fox News feeding the fire, with its monomaniacal focus on border walls, the low-hanging walls in the allegory prove apt, representing not simply cover from reality but a barrier to facilitate manipulation and further block those bigots like our barista from the verity that can only be found beyond this artifice. Yet many are quick to dismiss any notion that a puppeteer, or, in our nation's case, a president's chicanery, was behind it all, when most knew that Trump and Fox were projecting lies on a screen.

All this suggests that the concept of "fake news" has been around a lot longer than we may think, along with, those individuals imprisoned from childhood—a condition the ancient philosopher himself would ponder. In a community bereft of diversity—one neither structured around nor striving for the antidote of interdependence—far too many white folks grow up witnessing only *other* white folks carrying out normal everyday behavior, fulfilling specific roles and receiving certain treatment. Because they have, in effect, been chained in the cave, their eyes never observing the contrary, they erroneously conflate young African American males *with* criminality. Given the only dispatches penetrating these bubbles come from media that effectively fan those flames, it only helps to corroborate those unsound fears. Sadly, by adulthood, it affects not only their perceptions of African Americans but also their attitudes, actions, and treatment toward us, and mainly to our detriment.

This problematic dynamic extends beyond closed-off communities, or even the confines of a coffeeshop, to impact virtually every fragment of our broken socioeconomic framework. Only witnessing white people fulfilling specific roles leads to the confused, equally damaging belief that only white people *can* fulfill certain roles; this brutal falsification is integral to marring Black advancement across a wide spectrum, while marshaling in mediocrity and impugning progress from the business world to the world of sports. Only seeing white CEOs or white head coaches is misconstrued to mean that only white people are qualified to be CEOs or head coaches, or, applying such clinical perplexity, are *more* qualified for these positions. The whole notion of "quality" has hence become synonymous *with* white skin. Where those attempts to redress discrimination will almost immediately inspire ballyhoo about *reverse* discrimination—or the belief that more qualified persons will thereby lose out—it suggests that diverse hires will always suffer from those fires of deformation. It is *this* intrinsic stigma that subjects us to perpetual setback in the supercilious eyes of the majority.

Conjecture that quality, not race, should solely determine opportunity hints at something even more revealing than any babble that Black folks must therefore be inferior. It lets on that those entities enjoying unfettered opportunity cannot bear the thought of standing in the shoes of those whose race *has* impacted their opportunities or lack thereof. By all accounts, such an exercise, contemplating the idea that, due to unfairness, one *could* suffer a staggering reversal of fortune, is scary to the point of panic, a prospect that most individuals find truly foreboding.

By expressing pique at the idea their own person could be devalued due to such a superfluous matrix as race indicates that the answer staring them right in the face, that *true* lightbulb moment, need not be unplugged through indignation—as such umbrage comes at the expense of *enlightenment*. Primacy always has a funny way of tripping up progress in these moments, with hubris lapping humility in mere seconds. Yet such a flagrant lack of logical thinking is to me, and most marginalized people, incomprehensible. It means the resultant lack of representation in American spaces is nothing *but* illogical yet, given their unabashed petulance, likely to *persist*.

What this really means is that even an overqualified African American cannot contend with such chronic unconscious bias and widespread resentment. We could set ourselves on fire and *still* not be able to compete with these contortions—try as we might, we still cannot actually be seen, or rather accepted for both who *and* what we are. Because our world, rife with imbalance, continues to reflect a particular, even peculiar reality, many boldly choose to accept that outcome, ignoring iniquity because of its personal benefits, preferring instead to view this warp as happenstance not habit, or inconsequential when it is all too encouraged

Cyrus McQueen @CyrusMMcQueen · Apr 20, 2018
Think about the decades and decades of shady dealings it took for Michael Cohen to get in trouble with the law... Two black guys just had to sit in a Starbucks...
#FridayFeeling

⟲ 379   ♡ 1136

Given this greater context, we can conclude that what took place in Starbucks that day was tantamount to an ill person invading what should have been an aseptic space. However, considering what the cafe has come to represent for many, this sort of snubbing was almost fated.

The atmosphere inside the ubiquitous coffee shop reflects a certain *chill*. Despite the company owner's self-professed liberal leanings, that a cross-section of well-heeled white America sits for hours at its wooden tables, without arbitrary time limits, while light jazz manufactures a facsimile of sophistication, means that this so-called safe haven is defined by a particularly misleading tenor. The chain has since multiplied exponentially, but in years past I considered it a secret club that did not welcome people like myself. It felt like a spot where white folks paid for overpriced coffee and typed noisily on their Macs, a place where they could affect a posture saying, "I'm better than you and I'm only *granting* you brief access." It a spot where guys in horn-rimmed glasses and pilly sweaters read Jonathan Franzen while sitting next to stylish yet sour young women with severe bangs feverishly texting on their iPhones. The distance it created between us and its regulars felt eerily familiar. Shit, in many ways, it *was* America.

What unfolded that afternoon in Philadelphia is strangely suggestive of the fate awaiting Black people bold enough to seek comfort in certain spaces. Having spent most of my life as a Martian, I am familiar with the cool indifference that greeted me at every turn as I toured this expansive panorama of privilege throughout adolescence and adulthood. Thus, what this incident further indicates is that, while divcrsity initiatives may have opened doors for me and a prescribed number of Black people, without this pass, we would *cease* to be able to move subsequent generations forward. Hell, even with the visa of affirmative action, the attitudes, evidenced by my scholastic history, were not guaranteed to always be accommodating.

Much like the garbage man on my street that ominous day in Dorchester, the scandal at Starbucks suggests that integration, at least as far as some white folks are concerned, remains a matter of *limited* exposure. When you as a Black person take it upon yourself to integrate self-segregated spaces, risking prolonged exposure, you stand a great chance of meeting with rejection or, as played out in this instance, *ejection*.

White supremacy is so thoroughly cloaked behind the veil of privilege, its diseased nature obscured by this mask of respectability. Yet as our political climate has heated up, many have opted to finally shed this uncomfortable guise. Here that look of tolerance would soon betray the horrible intolerance long festering beneath the surface. Racism in all regards has always plagued the suburbs, schools, and places like Starbucks. Only now, the overblown reactions of a militarized police force, dispatched by a seemingly endless supply of instigators, looks to eradicate us with revitalized force, as if it were oddly *us* possessing the virulence.

Cyrus McQueen @CyrusMMcQueen · Apr 19, 2018
I'm amazed Starbucks has to "train" its employees to see black people as human beings. Let that sink in. Your company has to train you because your parents didn't. THAT'S what it comes down to. People have been failed by their families. Seems many Americans are absolute failures.

⟲ 1186   ♡ 3475

Although the coffeeshop itself, attempting to ameliorate fallout from this bigoted blunder, closed its stores for an afternoon of racial sensitivity training—deliberately dragging its workers from their segregated caves, moving incrementally toward the light—its efforts are ultimately tantamount to giving a cancer patient a cough drop. Many white Americans, given their once-comfortable majority, had shown little interest in comprehensive reform, but the malignancy having gone unaddressed in their communities for so long, it has since become, in many ways, terminal. The company now attempted to address centuries of supremacy, solidified in a society that perpetuated the problem despite decades of squandered opportunities to promote solutions on a macro or micro level. Their effort, though to a degree laudable, is too little, too late. We might even call it disingenuous: if it takes diversity initiatives or diversity training to ensure our entry and subsequent respect, we must ponder whether, if left to their own devices, they would ever grant us as a people *complete* entry or *full* respect?

The answer appears to be a resounding no. When Howard Schultz, the company's former CEO, later announced his candidacy for the presidency, he revealed his own sickness through the banal assertion that he did not "see color." Asked to comment about the racial profiling incident and whether it would be an issue for voters, he squandered the opportunity to eloquently establish his opposition to racial injustice, instead offering up a hackneyed and hollow response. "Colorblindness" would turn out to be a colossal blind spot for the candidate.

Yet people of color often wonder aloud why men such as Schultz even attempt to don the mask of respectability, to reach for that handy "colorblind" disguise, as predictable and off-putting as the oft-uttered supplemental assertion, "It doesn't matter if you're green or purple." We well know who he feels *should* fulfill certain roles, given that his rise to prominence bears witness to a patent paucity of diversity in boardrooms and shareholders meetings—in direct contrast to the diverse multicultural world blooming just beyond the threshold of his corporate headquarters.

Schultz's ineffectual statement was nothing *but* a slap in the face, a sting that would linger and then intensify upon the announcement that Mike Bloomberg, another tone-deaf billionaire, was entering the 2020 race. Perhaps Shultz's contention that he did not see color is a literal account of life in wealthy circles where he is unlikely to see color—or to borrow again from Plato—it indicative of eyes accustomed to *another* form of darkness. But, again, it is likely an admission more revelatory than romantic. Having long ago discovered that, in America, Blackness is just an absence of whiteness—meaning when they cannot see *themselves* they cannot see you—what Schultz has revealed is that a company catering to such entitlement is merely an extension of the man who ran it. Howard Schultz does not see color because he does not need to.

Moreover, we can easily posit that Howard Schultz does not *want* to see color. *Seeing* us takes work. Recognizing us means recognizing those forces responsible for fashioning our disparate realities—those that are most culpable for perpetuating our problems. For Black people, our existential crusade to be seen in our totality—to be acknowledged and embraced because of our Blackness *and* our individuality—his dubious statement would leave a taste as bad as his burnt coffee. His moribund campaign, his insistence on proffering quixotic platitudes, signals that the wealthy have zero intention of amending the power imbalance in our society, even *when* running as third-party candidates.

When members of the majority do attempt to minimize the impact of race, we cannot help but wonder whether it is a shrewd attempt at minimizing those lingering feelings of culpability. It reminds me of those clumsy moments when, as the only African American in a particular setting, I often encountered one or several problematic persons who seemed to delight in drawing attention to this very fact by marking my arrival with an off-color remark like, "Yay, the Black guy's here!" In that instant, they made clear the apparent lack of any clarity. Alcohol consumption tends to compound these situations, of course, as this form of truth serum lowers their inhibitions and raises the probability that their biases will emerge, your tightness thus triggered by their loose lips.

In these moments, forlornness sets in long before any sense of belonging or brotherhood. Your heart grows heavy—not out of any fear *per se* but because they now force you into an inner monologue. Your mind races as you lament the fact you must deal with this bullshit, thrust into the out-of-body experience of contending with what you are in the room before you have an opportunity to establish *who* you are in this room. Thus, your work is cut out for you as you navigate social settings and conventions as the sole person of color; you feel like it is a job, the *opposite* of relaxation. Granted, such juvenility is likely, in their minds, an off-key attempt to reduce their tension—like those who are so conscious of your race they will guiltily, repeatedly, tell you it does not matter—yet it almost always achieves the exact opposite effect, confirming, incontrovertibly, that for them, your race indeed *does* matter.

Black folks so often find ourselves battling contemporaries who do not hesitate to point out race when it *should not* be a factor that we marvel at those who find a way to dismiss it roundly when it actually *is* a factor. The entire notion of "colorblindness" has a way of annexing insult to your injury, its insidiousness cutting like a scythe, especially when the supplemental inanity—that these interlocutors think they are doing *you* a favor through their arbitrary declaration that race is not germane to a certain conversation—often feels like they are squeezing lemons over your fresh laceration. This motion to remove race from their defense, this otiose idea that one can even provide this sort of magical absolution anyway—it not being an issue simply because *they* had so determined—

is nothing *but* a clear indication, given such unabashed hubris, that many members of the majority have *already* ruled you out. Their blinders prove to be blindfolds, whether we consider this pointlessness a matter of sheer defensiveness or not; by trumpeting their uninformed feelings, these arrogant displays amount to nothing more than slipshod attempts to exonerate themselves and others from further warranted scrutiny. Their arguments thus represent an act of self-preservation, their inability to see the whole picture, or you, more in service to brand than anything egalitarian or even virtuous.

Given the growing fallout from incidents of discrimination in the public sphere—perhaps the reason Meghan Markle and Prince Harry had to move from the UK or the reason the Academy of Motion Picture Arts and Sciences fails to nominate persons of color for Oscars—honest discussions about racism in the media and beyond often succumb to those whose attempts to diffuse these bombs neglect the very fact that, in most of these purported instances, they have *already* detonated. It becomes akin to watching soldiers throwing themselves on already exploded grenades. These pitiable displays make zero fuckin' sense. This sort of defensiveness is not selfless at all but rather an act of sheer futility. You cannot bring anyone back *after* the explosion. Ignoring the damage wrought by this destructive incendiary device, this savage social construct, cannot heal *any* of the actual wounds it produces.

Such subjective assertions are ultimately as disrespectful as they are dishonest. And being that we are now embroiled emphatically in the Trump era, there is no shortage of people of color to be found strewn about our bombarded landscape, their lives and legacies maimed by this literal and figurative onslaught. Whenever white Americans insist that race is not a factor, given the evidence to the contrary, given the cages and carnage and loss, given the horrendous reality of this American moment, it amounts to nothing more than a staggering misuse of energy at a time when we desperately need to stop the bleeding, not simply overlook this bloodletting by declaring anyone's trauma to be superficial.

Cyrus McQueen @CyrusMMcQueen · May 14, 2018
What's lost in this conversation about the white lady callin the cops on the Barbecue in Oakland is... if she had just chilled the fuck out and played her cards right, they probably woulda made her a plate... 💯

🔁 1021　　♡ 7737

The Philadelphia Starbucks incident represented an ominous precursor as more events would soon signal that the country's temperature was indeed climbing. These race-based run-ins—evincing how truly stagnated our society is, how shockingly pitiful many have become—run the gamut from the asinine to the atrocious. Some are all but legendary, given not just the ignorance of the individuals involved, but for the sheer *lunacy* that ensues when the disease of racism erodes the human mind. Whether it is Barbecue Becky, Golf Cart Gail, Target Teresa, Permit Patty, or Corner Store Caroline, alliterative monikers bestowed upon monsters who attack people of color for any host of perceived horrors, the media never seem to exhaust their supply of incidents *or* incendiaries. The stimulus may be as superficial as grilling in a public park, playing soccer in a field, shopping in a department store, selling water, or making the grave mistake of bumping into a white person in a store. Though their latent absurdity keeps these incidents on the front pages for days, even weeks, the comorbidity of having an avowed Nationalist at the helm, makes these nationwide outbreaks that much more grave. And that profiling incidents pepper our sick country, from the Bay Area to New York City, signifies that a red-state problem is actually an *every*-state problem. It does not matter that people of color have long been over-policed, punished more severely for the same crimes committed by others—now merely *existing* as a person of color in Trump's America is ostensibly a criminal act. To be Black is to be born with an open warrant. We need not even commit an infraction, for our sheer presence is now enough to be deemed a violation, the dialogue long unfolding in a host of diseased minds given plausibility by a president who himself hears voices.

Where a generation of moderates had been willing to indulge us, stomaching us in limited quantities so long as we did not upset the appetites and tastes with which they governed diverse spaces, many Americans under Trump are no longer even interested in the charade of toleration. The attempt to see our humanity, even if we reflect back an innocuous image, has been replaced by a profound desire to, again, not see us at all. By 2018, the America we knew for fifty years had given up the ghost. The innocent, inoffensive image of Blackness that gained a foothold in our world post-Civil Rights has been cast out; in its stead, a parade of Black people engaging in basic, mundane activities is now viewed hostilely.

Cyrus McQueen @CyrusMMcQueen · May 15, 2018
Barbecues are one of life's great pleasures... If you see a buncha black folks grillin, and your first thought is to grab your phone instead of grabbin a rib, something is seriously wrong with you... But, I guess you probably need a soul to enjoy soul food... #TuesdayThoughts

⟲ 650   ♡ 2884

Perhaps the most troubling incident among a series of troubling incidents occurred when Lolade Siyonbola, an African American graduate student at Yale University, fast asleep in her dorm's common room, was awakened by an army tasked with protecting these spaces. When it comes to patrolling and upholding privilege, few spaces are protected with more vehemence and vigilance than America's colleges and universities.

Again, having traversed a scholastic landscape littered with booby traps throughout my years in New England, I was well aware that many campuses resemble a battleground. They might appear to respect diverse opinions, but aside from HBCUs, they don't often exhibit a sustained commitment to diverse peoples. Campus society, as I experienced it, is in many ways a microcosm of greater American society, accurately reflecting those entrenched patterns of privilege and legacy that truly impact inequality.

When a college dormitory became a bivouac for a Black woman, the unconscious fears of a white woman led to a conscious decision to cast her out of a what *should* be a safe environment. That this self-professed place of tolerance and higher learning became the setting for an ambush, symbolizes the degree to which the disease of racism often defeats even "educated" thinking. It is a scary proposition to know that your race can obscure your actions, or in this instance, *inaction.* The irony of being Black in America is that you are considered a threat even when asleep, while it is your disparagers who walk around never opening their fuckin' eyes.

It usually places us on the defensive, troubleshooting and minimizing risk. Throughout adolescence and young adulthood, our elders hand down lessons in self-preservation, attempting to mitigate the actions of a white public empowered to determine our worth and, consequently, our fate. Still, what gave me and fellow people of color pause in this instance is the discomfiting notion that, even when we excel, even when our merits are *magnified,* this American tangle can still ensnarl us, our defenses no match for a societal designation there to trip us up whether we are running or at rest.

It sends chills down my spine to know that the cold-blooded reactions we often engender in many Americans cannot be warmed or even dissuaded, especially in a moment when our defenses are down—when even somnolence, a state where we easily reflect back an image of calm, uninfluenced by any misperceived or misinterpreted words or gestures, is not enough to short-circuit the hardwiring that leads to these race-based hallucinations. This almost unquenchable desire to rid themselves of Black and Brown people suggests something even more disastrous than an addiction to race-based primacy. Given its potential to wreak illogical, inexorable destruction, it more closely reflects the rules associated with combat. Unarmed African Americans were falling victim to those who had completely surrendered to their hateful impulses. It was now inescapable: white America was at war with us. Whether the battlefields are Starbucks or Yale, golf courses or apartment complexes, the variety of incidents and even greater variety of basic, harmless behaviors at the center of these controversies suggest we will never be inoculated by the innocuous—the trifle can easily be blown out of proportion and *used* to bombard us.

Trump's America would now supply a seemingly endless barrage of baseless attacks. Sitting in your car, in your yard, on the sofa in your *own* goddamn apartment, it takes little to fillip an offensive against us as we come, more and more, to resemble enemy combatants. Much like men at war programmed to regard the enemy as less than human, political expediency fuels their aggressive batteries, stripping away our worth to justify any and all dehumanizing behavior toward us. If the hallowed grounds of a college campus can present grounds for reversing racial progress, then it portends the worst for Black America whose guiding lodestar, from Mary McLeod Bethune to Barack and Michelle Obama, has been the beneficence of education. If a young Black Yale student's nightmarish nap suggests anything, it is that we are not safe anywhere.

If my previous assessment holds, that we have been set up to fail, this influx of racially excited incidents raises an even more depressing proposition: that ours is a reality where we have not been set up to live, we have actually been set up to *die*. With opportunities whizzing past faster than the bullets on our block, marginalization ensuring that misfortune will likely visit us way before good fortune ever does, this primal desire *to* erase us is herein realized via the overblown reactions of an obstinate public whose only prerequisite for passing that threshold is to press three numbers on a phone

13

Cop Blocked

Cyrus McQueen @CyrusMMcQueen · May 11, 2018
Seriously, white folks should have a limit on the number of times they're allowed to call the cops on black people in one lifetime... "Miss, I know you find them suspicious but, you already exceeded your allotment when you called to complain about your neighbors rap music"...

⟲ 377   ♡ 1764

Before the incident at Yale, a far more disastrous event had unfolded at the University of Cincinnati: a campus cop shot and killed Sam DuBose, a Black motorist, after pulling him over for a missing front license plate. Nearly a year to the day later, a police officer murdered Philando Castile, a Minneapolis, Minnesota, motorist in another routine traffic stop. One can hereby argue that driving while Black is more treacherous than the myriad dangers already inherent to road travel, our fate an *unavoidable* crash, with violent encounters between Black motorists and police seemingly the rule instead of the exception. But while the two cases bear similarities—the race of each man and the fatal outcomes of both—of critical importance is the fact that in one case it was a campus police officer, in his capacity as a school safety officer, who felt *empowered* to exact deadly force within the perimeter of a campus.

Often lost in the discussion surrounding police misconduct, and the need for sweeping, comprehensive police reform, is the similar need to redress the actions of campus police and security guards, who are held to lesser standards than officers of the law yet are often emboldened to bend the law to their will. Ascribed powers within a private jurisdiction, those possessing a maladjusted disposition, along with an inferred license to deploy their issued weapons, typically contribute to the danger. As many people of color can disclose, it is this verisimilitude—with wannabe officers taking matters into their own hands—that easily transforms inconsequential moments into critical ones. As we observe in nature, the smaller, seemingly insignificant snakes are often the most potent. And as has been routinely evinced with American policing, those deemed otherwise unfit, who carry a complex over their own relegation, those toiling away in the insignificant underbrush, will be the ones often looking to strike.

Although the murder of Trayvon Martin at the hands of a demented coward masquerading as a neighborhood watchman would spark the Black Lives Matter movement, his murderer, like the officer in Cincinnati, was not maintaining the public safety as much as policing private property in service of our country's resident ideology. Where the deaths of Eric Garner, Alton Sterling, Freddie Gray, and Walter Scott (among countless others) bring up severe questions concerning restraint and the character flaws plaguing police forces throughout America, a further perplexing question compounds matters in the deaths of DuBose and Martin: How do we even begin to address rent-a-cops? Those armed individuals who are relatively unseasoned yet *emboldened* to exact deadly force?

The 2012 murder of Trayvon Martin represents in many ways a watershed moment. For the first time in a 21st century climate, after the advent and proliferation of social media, a centuries-old problem garnered substantial attention in the public arena. Yet Martin's murder is in many ways a corollary to that of Emmett Till nearly sixty years prior, an image of Till's decomposed corpse on the cover of *Jet Magazine* an historical bookend to the now-iconic image of Martin in his hooded sweatshirt. Where Trayvon's image would now be broadcast across the social media landscape, the killings of both, and the subsequent acquittals of those responsible for their deaths, both influenced *and* framed the justified movements triggered by these unjustifiable acts.

The deaths of African American men at the hands of law enforcement have long been publicized, from lynchings at the turn of the 20th century to the murder of Amadou Diallo at the turn of the 21st. The ghastly details of Black men hanging from light poles and trees in town squares, like the blood splattered concrete betraying the bullet-riddled Black bodies piling up in cities across the country, have remained newsworthy as the eleven o'clock news telegraphs these horrors nightly. But the rising significance of social media, precipitating the gradual erosion of our traditional forms of media and transmuting the manner in which these horrors are shared, has now transformed a country *and* the dialogue surrounding the ongoing war against Black and Brown people.

#BlackLivesMatter, the movement and hashtag created by Alicia Garza, Patrisse Cullors, and Opal Tometi, defines the new Jim Crow era. It brings attention to the blight of racial violence mainly *because* it brings our long-suppressed voices to the forefront. African Americans have screamed for justice since we were screened at slave auctions, and yet the cacophony of our plaintive cries, exemplifying our existential dread almost always fell on deaf ears. If America has been anything, it has been consistent: in a nation of over three hundred million people, no one seemed to hear our appeals some four hundred years into our harsh sentence. Yet a centuries-old problem now inveterately seeps into a new century. This new highway of communication, created by sites like Facebook and Twitter, bypasses the traditional forms of media that traditionally blocked out our cries. The marriage of social media and social responsibility sees us managing to now *amplify* what has always been there, while also breaking through the sound barrier encasing many Americans.

What would likely have been a one-and-done story in a previous era now generates the traction these homicides warrant. That many of these horrors are captured and broadcast in real time adds impact, making smartphone technology itself the best weapon any of us can possibly carry in this new era. With camera phones supplanting random camcorders, ubiquitous abuses are now matched by the ubiquitous devices readily available to document them. Stories can no longer be buried faster than the bodies at the center of these crimes. "Cop-aganda" is now being dealt a significant blow as video evidence contradicts the stock excuse offered up that police involved shootings are always warranted and beyond reproach. The tales of these young men, and the corrosive forces culpable in their premature deaths, have spread and spread as a nation that once turned a blind eye to such misdeeds now has its very lids pried open by a persistent cadre of progressive, young

Black people, forcing an apathetic white America to ingest and digest these egregious killings like a scene out of a Kubrick film.

As the nation was implored to #RememberHisName, I found myself immersed in a swell of likeminded individuals keeping afloat the memories of the tragedies behind this torrent. But I kept coming back to Trayvon Martin, the young man whose 21st-century lynching was, indeed, the lynchpin for a movement.

To be a teenager on the precipice of adulthood is confounding enough without the added ingredient of race and a bourgeoning masculinity, both of which directly threaten a society—one helping to cultivate this negative image that precedes young African American men at all intervals. That a mundane activity like walking to and from a store holds an element of danger for a young Black male makes the process of coming of age potentially catastrophic, that dormant volcano likely to blow at any moment, the sickness of supremacy erupting to place your life in imminent peril. Although your age or ignorance can make you oblivious to these crippling conditions, your youth and stigma are often the actual accelerant that leads a paranoid white public to paint you with the broad brush of criminality. In a split second, you can embody their worst fears, while they, emboldened to be judge, jury, and executioner, will come to embody yours.

Although the murder of Martin and what unfolded with the young sista at Yale are rarely spoken of in the same breath, the connectivity of the crimes against them is at the forefront of my mind. Having achieved my college education in Boston, higher learning enveloped me in an irradiating glow, yet I, too, can bear witness to the shadow of suspicion that seems to follow us around grounds where even scholastic preeminence cannot shake the preexisting condition of being Black in America or the sharp silhouette that that image projects against a severe white background.

Cyrus McQueen @CyrusMMcQueen · May 11, 2018
An African American man named Richard Overton celebrated his 112th Birthday today, making him the oldest living World War II Veteran in the United States...
But given he's survived more than a Century as a black man in America, doctors have actually placed his age closer to 220.

⟲ 376   ♡ 1343

My childhood and adolescence in and around Boston prepared me for more discreet displays of discrimination. Though I had experienced a few flareups, my disrespect often came in the furtive form of suburban disregard. I was not fully primed for the open disdain visited upon me, and a host of Black male college students, as our presence in a privileged urban setting seemed to elicit unwanted attention. A young Black boy in a predominately white town simply does not engender the same sensations and reactions as a slightly older, Black, 6'5" 240-pound man on a predominately white campus. As my growing sense of self slowly developed, unfortunately too slowly for me to process the ever-present dangers percolating just beyond my scope of awareness, I soon faced a vestigial of racial animus harvested in the incubator of a hate-filled heart. A demonic entity made itself known to me in the form of a police officer who, for the better part of my years there, would be a chronic source of conflict and torment. To this day, his funk clings to my memory, it lingering like the stench from a thousand cigarettes.

To find myself on a college campus as a freshman was to experience a wholly new freedom. To also find myself within the city itself, in a more cosmopolitan setting than the horribly homogeneous suburbs, was cause alone to rejoice. Not many words can describe those deliciously intoxicating days of young adulthood, to find a tribe of likeminded individuals in that ephemeral period before the ravages of time impress upon you the unforgiving rapidity with which life advances, these fleeting moments barely lived before languishing forevermore as memories. The intensity of this pulchritudinous period of life, matched only by an extreme yet futile desire to recapture it, soon precipitates the clarity that complements this passage—when you realize that, what was once ahead of you is, with the fateful snap of a finger, now *behind* you.

I can still sense that undeniable energy along the Fenway bordering the college. And as I now paw and pore over this palpable souvenir, I am transported back to the transformative stretch of time when I not only discovered the city had a heartbeat but that *I* was actually vital, me and thousands like me indispensable to its vibrant function. Brother, I can still taste that crisp late autumn air, my visible breath like smoke corroborating that after an adolescence of anoxia, I could finally breathe fully. I almost guzzled the air as I crossed the street, the red lights and the brake lights, like big bright cocktail cherries, embroidering the early darkness blanketing all of this bustle and creating a warmth despite the cold as I journeyed these few now-familiar blocks buzzing with all the excitement of juvenescence. It was dizzying to be a part of it all. To belong. To be finding myself as I got lost in the stimulating abundance on offer.

I found spring, an actual *bounce* to my step after being tightly wound for so long amid the confounding conditions in suburban Boston—not to mention the calamitous conditions of its urban core that wound me even *more* tightly. I now felt as if I were floating, reflecting the buoyancy I had long associated with my white peers as I almost hovered from one end of this universe to the next. Immersion in university life proffered a sort of cleansing, this period an undoubted chrysalis. Untethered from parents and pasts, we were all placed on the same level, if just for these brief few years.

Yet this backdrop became the setting for the first of many baleful encounters with the man who would be the bane of my Boston existence. The revenant descended out of the December darkness enveloping these streets, killing my buzz, this woeful portent betraying the darkness that soon enveloped me.

It is funny how you can detect a menacing presence even when it is not immediately decipherable, when normality appears omnipresent yet a feeling of danger looms. Perhaps being Black had programmed me with a rear-view mirror, triggering the very hairs on the back of my neck to stand up. I had this weird sensation that I was being stalked, like some bright-eyed doe being trailed by some ravenous lone wolf, when after traversing the quad and the student center, I snaked onto Huntington Avenue, the main artery bisecting my campus and pumping it with life. Here, I would soon make what turned out to be an imprudent decision, turning down an alley to take a shortcut to one of the dorms.

When this ominous feeling compelled me to look over my shoulder, danger announced itself in an indelible Boston accent: "Whaddya doin heyaah?" His words were acid in my ears. Though I was an undergrad, I was also an 18-year-old Bostonian with a Doctorate in Race. I instinctively knew that what appeared a simple query was undeniable evidence of an underlying wickedness, proof of a poison generations had swallowed. His words were indeed formed by the toxicity that had formed him—his esoteric intonations, like his racist intentions, part of a *dreadful* legacy. As I *slowly* turned, the beam from his flashlight nearly blinded me. I can still make out that spectral silhouette, slinking toward me as he cut the distance between us in half almost instantaneously. In that moment, he resembled less a police officer and more a phantasm creeping out of my spine-chilling nightmares, turning this dark alley and the danger on full display into a potential torture chamber.

As we locked eyes, we came to rely on our separate years of training. With his hand inching toward his holster, my own instincts quickly kicked in. Hearing my mother's voice, the residual admonishments from "The Talk" she and I had had at least semiannually, the directive to remain *still* overrode the concurrent order coming directly from him.

That coming-of-age discussion took place for the first time when she recognized that I was big for my age—occurring when I was about thirteen, right around the time my friends were Bar Mitzvah'd. This lesson, a rite of passage, would prove pivotal to my maturation because she knew my very survival was contingent on it. Like all Black mothers, she was cognizant of the moment when her son would pass that invisible threshold into threat; that, like every little Black boy, I would rapidly transition from emergent to emerging danger. And whatever was left of my innocence was pretty much jettisoned as she coupled this drill with a blistering rebuke of white Boston, her castigation replete with the injunction: "You can't do whatcha little white friends do! Cause the police *will* not hesitate to *kill* your Black ass, ya hear me?!"

This sentence having concluded our session, its lasting impact would boil down to that impressive dictum, which she applied with absolutely *zero* saccharine. Her indescribable love for me, her only son, demanded that her words land hard. And as difficult as it was for me to hear them, it must have been even harder for her to have to *say* them, to have to disabuse me of any fairy tales my childlike mind still clung to. And though she had indeed forced that bitter pill down, her method proved its merits for I retain that astringent truth to this day. She knew I would not receive this meaningful lesson, perhaps the most important of my young life, from any of my teachers, yet she knew I desperately needed to learn it *now,* especially as neither of us knew when I would be tested.

My mother knew the wolves were lying in wait, her lecture soon proving sibyllic. As I stood immobilized in this dim alleyway, the future had now caught up with her vision. But though the cop *was* quizzing me, I had yet to return to my body, so I actually remained still, per her tutorial—absent, of course, a racing heartbeat. With his hand nestled next to the handle of his eraser, he repeated his query, *much* louder this time. "Ima ask ya again, WHAT THE FUCK ARE YOU DOIN HERE?!" I remember attempting to speak, yet, in the heat of the moment, my senses went haywire; my mouth ran dry, and I could no longer taste the crisp air, or anything for that matter, as the lump in my throat—much like the prejudice blocking my way—prevented my voice from being heard. Though I quickly processed the variables at play, the sight of his weapon, and more important, his hand hovering over it, temporarily paralyzed me. He had indeed caused a panic considering the time it took my cognitive functions to reboot. Suddenly, though, I remembered the answer to his loaded question and muttered that I was a student. The words had barely left my mouth before he unloaded a barrage of "HOW LONG YA BEEN GOIN HEYAAH?!" and "WHERE'S YAH FUCKIN I.D.?!"

As I oh so carefully proffered the requested material, he shined his torch on it, then back to me, then back to it, and finally back to me, where it lingered, the blinding brightness of his Maglite incapable of outshining the blinding bigotry powering this whole disgusting display. His beady eyes remained on mine for several more seconds. I was locked in the eternity of his creepy prolonged glance, his dead-cold expression unnerving, effectively signaling that I had not yet been exculpated. Those few seconds became the longest minutes of my life until he tired of this folly and finally, reluctantly, relinquished the I.D. back to me. As he turned to leave, this dark cloud having created a tempest of emotions within me, he snaked back out of the alley the same way he had entered, his eager hand ready to draw, his earnest gaze trained on me. As he retreated into the shadows, not one to let this moment evaporate without a final, foretelling thunderclap, he cautioned, "You be careful around heyaah."

That storm forecast would prove accurate. As the weeks and months unfolded, the Terminator—as I came to describe him, given his resemblance to the liquid metal villain in the second film, along with his serpentine ability to slither up behind the brothas on campus—would never fail to make his menacing presence known. He remained furtively, perpetually, over all of our shoulders in this colored game of cat and mouse. Sometimes we would be congressed with a group of coeds in the quadrangle and, in a quick flash, there he was. Other times, as we emerged from the library after hours of customary drudgery, BOOM, he instantly appeared, planted directly opposite us, his short stature, crew cut, and ever-present mirrored sunglasses evoking images of the T-1000 as he deliberately stared us down. In other moments, with his wide gait, youthful appearance, and the manner in which his hand seemed to hover over his eraser, he more resembled Billy the Kid, always primed for an eventual showdown with any host of young Black males whose only misstep was daring to exist on equal footing with our white counterparts—the true trespass in his eyes—and, given the nature of collegiate life, placing us constantly in his crosshairs.

The winter of my discontent eventually gave way to a literal and figurative thaw; campus life warmed yet again amid the glorious New England spring. A frigid quarter spent mostly indoors gave way to resurgent activity bubbling up all around me after months of bitter Boston cold as I and thousands of coeds emerged from hibernation and clamored to claim our much-needed moments in the sun. If university life had ebbed during the winter, it flowed again in the months of April and May as all the attributes associated with spring, and youthful vitality, converged in a festival for the senses. My bloom was now mirroring those of the trees and flowers, the life evidenced in them reflecting the life surging within me. The cross-pollination occurring in horticulture was no match for that which was occurring in campus culture, with ideas and intentions planted in fertile minds during the winter months blossoming into real and exciting possibilities. We all now found ourselves shedding coats and cocoons, fleeing the dorms to flourish outdoors.

This was to be my narrative, too, as I headed outside after class one afternoon in late April. Recently introduced to classical music through the epic springboard that is Vivaldi's *Four Seasons*, it felt as if his masterpiece were providing a suitable soundtrack to my own movements. His indelible sound had since taken up permanent residence in my head—and not any inferior renditions that almost feel hurried, as if trying to hurry up and get the shit over with; I mean, Vivaldi interpreted by virtuosos like Itzhak Perlman, where the strings almost seem to *jump*. *Those* heavy violins toward the end of the spring concerto were devouring me as I chewed up the sweet scenery. Making my way to the student center, almost levitating, these compelling notes articulating my traverse, I happened to glance behind me and there, to my surprise, my crush stood in front of the adjacent building talking to her friend. Ciao bella! After months of swallowing my nerve, with the impetus of romantic pursuits and the confidence the sun seemed to imbue in me, I decided to backtrack, my body nearly on autopilot for an almost 180 degree turn. My plan: to smoothly cruise up next to them and strike up conversation.

Now, as any young lad can attest, those moments before you announce your interest in a young lady are uniquely terrifying, almost prompting neurological attacks, this unharnessed energy causing your body to tremble as the electricity taking your senses on a rollercoaster ride prompts you to silently pray that what is unfolding within you will not be telegraphed by any noticeable nervousness or, God forbid, *tumescence*. Thankfully, on this day, I overcame this hormonal turbulence.

My pulse steadied and my stomach, after taking up temporary residence somewhere between my chest and my throat, returned to my abdomen. Settling into a cruising attitude after turning around, I even managed to insert a dollop of swagger into my determined stroll, moving deliberately yet *suavely* toward her.

She was now a mere fifty yards away, half a football field, a distance that I could breach most effectively by crossing an actual field of grass. As I bounded across it and neared the apex of its incline, her back to me, I spotted the dark sea of curls beneath her baseball cap undulating in the breeze. I could hear every beat my heart made in these fifteen seconds as the wind seemed to carry me down the knoll toward her, her stunning silhouette, her most compelling contours, coming into focus. The only thing now separating us was the brick walkway I had triumphantly bypassed.

My tunnel vision had obscured the danger encroaching upon my path. With only a few feet of grass remaining, my nemesis materialized out of thin air and now hovered between me and my beauty. I guess I could not hear the killer robots' haunting and imposing theme over the music in my mind. Though I had bestowed upon him many nicknames, from the Terminator to the Wolf, on this day he again affected the posture of Billy the Kid—hands on hips, wide stance, almost willing me toward him and a crash. I was headed for a showdown alright, the midday sun beating down, a campus newspaper blowing past like tumbleweed, all contributing to this surreal scene, a heightened moment reminiscent of the Wild West.

"What makes ya think ya can waah-k on the grass?" I was literally being cop-blocked. I was dumbstruck by his sudden appearance and further dumbfounded by his dumb-ass question. As he sized me up, his mirrored gaze obscuring that beady set of eyes, the sun reflected a quick flash of light, betraying that they were clearly burning holes into me. I made a futile, albeit foolish attempt to explain that I was doing what everyone else does. But it did not matter that all sorts of bullshit went down on this grass, from hippies playing hacky-sack, to impromptu frisbee tosses between frat boys. *Their* recreational habits were beyond reproach. This became apparent as his furrowed brow indicated his consternation at this young Black male not only dismissing his concerns but, in the same breath, asserting permission to mimic the behavior of his white classmates. He took a weighty step in my direction, anchoring the hectoring that followed. "Whatcha say guy? Wanna say that again?"

I intrinsically knew my success at diffusing the situation was contingent on not taking this bait, so, wisely, I left it dangling there. "Yeah, ya gotta smaah-t mouth on ya. Get the fuck off and waah-k on the path!"

As I digested his challenge, a surge of fear and frustration instantly supplanted the excited emotions I had been experiencing. It was hard to stomach the fact that I had been intentionally, inimically stopped dead in my tracks, this myriad of conflicting feelings swirling to create a sour sensation in the pit of my belly. Turns out the route I had attempted to create, was impossible to carve out in a city and a country that wanted me to stay in my lane. My shortcut had drawn the unforgettable wrath of a white cop whose whole deportment seemed influenced by a deep desire to prevent young men, and indeed an entire people, from making up *too* much ground too fast. Our presence, and, more important, our progress was more than enough to make *him* uncomfortable, so he profiled me, policing the *idea* of what I represented.

A Black honors student on academic scholarship with no criminal record being beyond his realm of comprehension, meant he needed to disabuse me of my self-pride. My prestige signaled that he needed to *break* me. So, he set about *following* my shadow, that dark blot affixed to dark men from all walks of life that, despite better circumstances, we can never circumvent. Having been introduced to philosophy around this time, Plato's *Republic* providing a comparable springboard into the classics, those previously cited parallels would provide further insight into a man and a subject that were both highly misunderstood. Any of the towns in or around Boston, Worcester, Western Massachusetts, or even New Hampshire could provide fitting facsimiles of Plato's allegorical cave, suggesting that the malformed mind of a man molded in such impenetrable darkness would regard only the aforementioned shadow *as* reality. We were both shackled to the prison of his mind: he likely wanted, for his own sake, to keep me there or, better put, to bend *my* reality to fit *his* distortion—where seeing me or any brotha in handcuffs would thereby validate those inviolable but false impressions. Notwithstanding his mirrored shades, his eyes could adjust to neither the sun nor my light as he looked to pull me back, inexorably, toward the murk.

That dark potential likely influenced my fear in this moment, though, bizarrely, it manifested itself only in the form of a nervous laugh. I finally muttered something to the effect of "Ya gotta be kidding me, right?" The officer, seeing I was hooked, seized on my anxiety, ratcheting up the implicit absurdity by laughing right back in my face. His mordant impulse now heightened the morbid implications of this moment's unspoken subtext. He was having *fun* at my expense, delighting in the discomfort his hijack had created—especially now that he could see that his terroristic act had thrown me off course. Through a devilish rictus, he then delivered a series of sinister lines, made all the more chilling by the juxtaposition of jocularity with the serious undertone he was imparting through crooked front teeth. "What? What's the matt-ah, ya deaf? Ya haah-d a hearin? You betta TURN the fuck around and waah-k on the FUCKIN path!"

This frightening reiteration finally struck me down. I was grounded. The violent violins from winter had returned, replacing the airy season of hope, that crescendo in Vivaldi's final concerto now reflecting the piercing intensity of our impasse. I must have stood there immobile for several moments, though, as humiliation has the tendency to do, it seemed to stop time, those few seconds lasting forever. But despite the apparent levity, this was no pregnant pause, I was not trying to play up this moment, I was desperately seeking delivery from it and the evil that had engulfed me. Though we grinned at each other, the silence between us was disquieting. Lessons of standing up and securing respect melted away faster than my half-smile; my face soon broadcast an undeniable look of despondency, generated by the gravity of the situation and my mounting feelings of cowardice. As an 18-year-old any confidence I wielded was completely manufactured anyway. Not yet comfortable in my own skin, my young bravado quickly crumbled right there on the spot, my countenance betraying that I had been *exposed*. Like a truffle pig he sniffed out what little value I contained, that precious dignity buried deep beneath the artifice, and snatched it right up.

Though I had been through such encounters before, and had ingested the hard-earned lessons, this incident would hollow me out in record time. I had to reconcile this all right then and there, knowing that knives of the figurative or literal sort would be meaningless in a gunfight. The Kid had driven this point home as he kept his right hand nestled right next to his eraser, while I had to contend with everything happening outside and inside of me. I processed this mighty confluence in real time—all while observing the object of my affection slowly disappear from my periphery. As I took inventory of the wreckage, cognizant that one false move could down my craft forever, I swallowed hard, my pride racing to the pit of my stomach, and wallowed in the chagrin. It pains me to have to relay this, even some two decades later, but I then turned, dejected and defeated, back the way I had come, exactly as he commanded, the memory and promise from two minutes prior submerged in a maelstrom of emotions articulating my protracted and profound embarrassment. By the time I skulked back over the hill, she was gone, he was gone, and a tiny piece of me was gone, never to be recaptured.

To be Black in America is to suffer the indignity of being intimidated, emasculated, followed, flanked, stalked, tailed, trailed, hunted, or violated at one time or another. Whether this horror unfolds on the road, in a store, or on a college campus, the shape of harassment often resembles the contours of coursing, the sight of your contrasting Black skin providing the motivation for your murder or capture. For people of color, sadly, this dark, stark potentiality becomes something you have to learn to live with

.

14

Coloring Outside The Lines

The baffling and far-fetched fallacy that young Black men are inherently criminal—and their white counterparts inherently virtuous—was upended in the month of March in 2018. When the city of Austin, Texas, found itself besieged by a serial bomber, the capitol region waited with bated breath as five package bombs detonated, killing two and injuring five. The reign of terror—an eerie precursor to events months later when over a dozen pipe bombs were mailed to East Coast media outlets and individuals who had publicly rebuked Trump—stood out not solely because the acts themselves were so heinous but also because they seemed to reflect the ravages of war. The unmistakable evidence of embroilment, given our polarized populace, suggested that this magnitude of conflict may be the new normal. For a nation negotiating a Muslim travel ban, whose president was doing all he could, rhetorically and legislatively, to identify men and women of a certain faith as terrorists, that homegrown terror had evolved in this manner meant America would now be forced to contend with a disaster of its own making.

When the serial bomber, a homeschooled 23-year-old white male who harbored strict conservative and religious views, blew himself up as police closed in, it reverberated throughout Black America, less because his victims were African American and more because strict religious views were often all it took to label a person of color a terrorist. In our post-9/11 world, that monster mask was routinely affixed to us—despite a growing list of maladjusted young white males carrying out systematic and violent attacks. With these perpetrators operating with a sense of impunity, their race was now pushing America to look inward: increasingly, the face of terror came to resemble the boy next door.

Yet any hopes that America had begun to digest these difficult truths were immediately vanquished. Following the bomber's suicide, the Austin police chief, upon reviewing the young man's recorded confession, declared that it was "the outcry of a very challenged young man talking about challenges in his life that led him to this point." That anemic assessment of a brutal individual whose actions irreparably damaged countless lives was troubling enough, but the officer of the law went *further*, declaring that he would *not* label him a terrorist since the confession did not "mention anything about terrorism." It is important to note that, at this point, the nation was less than a year removed from the catastrophic events in Charlottesville, where Trump, too, offered up a feeble, bullshit response to premeditated murder. Here the president's abdication would come thundering to mind as yet another figure of authority callously downplayed the scorched earth a violent man had left in his wake.

In this haunted world we were now white-knuckling through, a frightening pattern was taking form: one that brazenly validated white anger while virtually vindicating all who acted on it. Trump had uncovered a fault line in our country and was *dancing* on it. We were now feeling the aftershocks of that initial rumble when all this raw, unchecked animus was unleashed. That those who followed the president, incontinent in their xenophobia, now felt warranted to carry out physical attacks, it would come to shatter any lasting variance of normality.

This war for the soul of the country, this existential conflict, became evident after the events in Charlottesville, Las Vegas, Austin, and Pittsburgh—yet many Americans seemed oblivious to the overpowering evidence. In the era of Trump, with good and bad so irrevocably blurred, many sadly still viewed evil in black and white, neglecting the fact that, with this particular president and the hate he gave voice too, it was pretty clear we all were operating under gray skies.

Cyrus McQueen @CyrusMMcQueen · Feb 27, 2019
Jim Jordan repeatedly tried to stop Cummings... Why wasn't he so earnest to stop it when he was a wrestling coach??? 😂 #CohenTestimony 🔗

⟲ 549   ♡ 2246

That murderers could be "fine people" and a domestic terrorist a "challenged young man" leaves little doubt as to which color our society prefers to paint as the enemy. Yet in March of 2019, the world watched in horror as this phenomenon proved to not only be plaguing the United States. Terrorism erupted on the other side of the globe with a 28-year-old white Australian entering two mosques in Christchurch, New Zealand, and taking the lives of fifty people. That this event occurred exactly one year after the Austin bombings is but one of several eerie parallels between two disparate countries' now experiencing an all-too-common threat. The thread of white nationalism would now connect our distant nations, the hatred sowed in both forcing us all to contend with this new iteration of terror. But that a manifesto written by the perpetrator would reveal much of the same denigrating language Trump himself had uttered about "allowing" Muslims to flow into the country, before going on to mention Trump himself by name, was, by this point in our lowly era, not all that shocking. It was certainly nowhere as notable as Trump's own response when asked pointedly if he agreed that White Nationalism was on the rise. His remark, "I don't really," before insisting that it was just "a small group of people" after initially attempting to deflect with the now redundant "I don't know enough about it yet" betrayed his ability to simultaneously contradict himself and *telegraph* his true feelings. That he followed up his insipid remarks about the Christchurch massacre by defending his very own hateful record on immigration, saying "people hate the word invasion, but that's what it is," would leave little doubt as to *who* he was really aligned with.

This unfortunate fact was reinforced in El Paso, Texas, in August of 2019, the symbiosis between Trump's rhetoric and those domestic terrorists now following his lead *unmissable*. When one of his supporters drove across the state, culminating in the cold-blooded murders of twenty-two people at a Walmart, the rain of bullets he unloaded was an undeniable and axiomatic consequence of the very climate Trump had created.

As Americans absorbed this latest mass shooting, these occurrences now repeating themselves every few months—even within hours in the cases of El Paso and a rampage that would take place in Dayton, Ohio—

the plausible deniability proffered by gun advocates and the president belied the fact that Trump's infernal imprint was all over these events. Like the Christchurch shooter, the vicious young male from Texas issued a manifesto, and he, too, employed incendiary terminology like "invasion" and "ethnic replacement." Though he authored the script in question, his doggerel suggested he likely had plagiarized Trump and others on the far-right—mongrels who continued to get by on the whole "Great Replacement" fallacy. The remedial president's propensity to play coy all while cozying up to white supremacists was now his signature move. Yet the unwillingness to disavow David Duke, the Alt-Right in Charlottesville, or even a White Nationalist a world away in New Zealand, though insulting to people of color, became even *more* infuriating when you stopped to consider that Trump was now intent on insulting everyone *else's* intelligence. Tossing red meat and blowing dog whistles is only going to attract *one* thing. Yet truly disturbing is that he would continue to play dog whisperer, much to the chagrin of a public who knew such disgusting dalliances portended disaster.

Perhaps nothing highlights what a lowlife Trump is more than Jacinda Ardern and her swift, substantive response to the Christchurch shootings. The New Zealand prime minister, within 24 hours of the tragedy, had moved to change that nation's gun laws and ordered flags lowered to half-mast nationwide, all while helping raise over two million dollars for the victims. She then met with Islamic leaders throughout the country, making sure to assure these men and women that *all* mosques would now be patrolled. Her thoughtful actions reverberated around a world that had witnessed a deficit in decisive American leadership in response to tragedies of this magnitude. A mere ten days following the shootings, she helped facilitate a ban on assault and military grade rifles, never once failing to call the calamitous event an act of terror, while displaying a dynamism and compassion that helped her country heal. Her true caliber suggests that, in many ways, Ardern *could* lay claim to being the actual leader of the free world.

Where Trump and many in the conservative West left a profound void, especially in summarily diminishing gun deaths as matters of "mental illness," Ardern's actions are a poignant lesson for the global community about the profound benefits of no longer allowing boys to do a woman's job. Where Trump and his spineless Republican coterie roll around with dogs, a woman commanded authority in the face of their gutless attempts at authoritarianism, muzzling the very mongrels who followed their lead. Moreover, Ardern has now sent an indelible signal from the bottom of the world that hate *can* be leashed.

Still, the Christchurch terrorist, like those in Charleston, Charlottesville, and El Paso, lived to be handcuffed by police, while African American men nationwide continue to succumb to the mere specter of criminality. More often than not, men of color are left lying in pools of blood despite the dearth of any actual blood on their hands. That the murders of Stephon Clark, a 22-year-old Sacramento man who was fired upon twenty times in his grandmother's backyard after police confused his cell phone for a weapon, and 26-year-old Diante Yarber, fired upon more than *thirty* times as he sat in his vehicle in a Walmart parking lot, both occurred within a month of the Austin bombings illustrates our diabolical double standard when it comes to criminalizing only certain young men.

Because of the flawed matrix of race, every Black man in America who reaches the age of 22 or 26 can, like me, recount moments when only the grace of God has stood between them, an overzealous cop, and a tragic ending. Yet the revelation that bona fide terrorists did not die at the hands of police—or, as in Austin, could be eulogized in a manner that reduced their murderous rampage to the sort of generalized drivel you might hear from a high school guidance counselor—was *disturbing*. In America we now contend with a reality where 21-year-old white men are arrested without incident after leaving twenty-two dead bodies in their wake, while Black men selling cigarettes are strangled and *left* for dead.

By now, the right-wing response to homegrown terrorism had proven incommensurate with the gravity of the crimes. It leads me to conclude that, America is yours to destroy if you are white. Given the rabid resistance to the often-gallant attempts of Obama and other progressive minded people to actually *save* lives in this country, that a bloated gun lobby and the GOP preach the politics of destruction has all but ensured America's worst impulses will only continue to prevail. Criminality being cemented to us—like a pair of boots that almost guarantees we are likely to go down—it suggests that white perpetrators could continue carrying out ghastly premeditated murders and, never be considered any more than "challenged." It leaves me fully convinced that to be Black in America is to star in, yet hope to survive, your very own slasher film. With white rage overindulged, whether you are a survivalist stockpiling guns and building pipe bombs, or a police officer, the criterion of 'Us versus Them' would see those vindicated, and those victimized, continue to be delineated by the color line. With their vexation validated, maladjusted men in America will keep carrying out vendettas. Thus, it is no mystery *which* of us is more likely to get out alive.

Cyrus McQueen @CyrusMMcQueen · Dec 19, 2018

So, Trump puts troops along the Border but, he withdraws troops from Syria...
That's like taking the smoke alarm outta your kitchen and puttin it on your
swimming pool... Fuckin fool... #WednesdayWisdom

⟲ 1129   ♡ 3743

The demonic plan to separate families along the southern border is not an aberration or an unfortunate abstraction, either historically or within the brutal context of Trump's presidency. It is an inevitability due to the incendiary rhetoric, articulated by Trump and his senior policy advisors—think Stephen Miller and former Attorney General Jeff Sessions—whose irrational hatred of dark people betrays their even darker hearts and minds. In fact, we now know this very outcome can be attributed to explicit directives, given by Sessions himself, at the behest of Trump. A *New York Times* article, detailing a spring 2018 phone conversation between the former Attorney General and several U.S. attorneys, reveals that Sessions declared in no uncertain terms, "We need to take away children."

The article goes on to state that despite the concerns expressed by federal prosecutors, Sessions and then deputy attorney general Rod Rosenstein would go on to admonish all five, stating that cases involving undocumented immigrants should never have been declined and that it ultimately did not matter how young the children were. With the Justice department now "a driving force" behind the separation policy, thousands of migrant families fleeing cataclysmic conditions in Central America and Mexico were soon met with the modern equivalent of slave catchers—federal courts having been weaponized to obliterate these nuclear families with an atomic force from which many may never recover.

Yet these human rights abuses were set in motion the minute the president and his followers casually tossed out the idea of ending Hillary Clinton's freedom during the 2016 campaign. With such scatological scourge bandied about and imbibed, this audible excrement exciting those in these expletive-laden pep rallies, we saw her perceived crimes garner enough belief that the truth could not overpower the stigma they attached to her. Perhaps the public should have braced itself for horrors now being unleashed on the immigrant population after "Lock Her Up" took hold. If a white woman of differing political leanings could inspire such bloodlust, it portended the ease with which this president could ascribe criminality to Brown immigrants. We would soon learn that in the era of Donald Trump, law and order is little more than a plaything in a wealthy white man's hands.

That this nation had already displayed a tenacity for destroying the lives of young Black people is of particular note. The murder of Tamir Rice, a 12-year-old Cleveland boy shot dead by police on a playground, should have foretold the horrors that would eventually unfold when, once elected, Trump could begin targeting the vulnerable in earnest. Even innocent children, it seems, are in no way immune to the whims of an immoral man, one who appears to check off the boxes of those whose religious and racial differences confirm their lack of value in his incarnation of America.

Forced family separations along the southern border becoming widely known, migrants fleeing unfathomable horrors in Central and South America are now finding themselves embroiled in a whole new one—a netherworld of the Trump administration's making. The ghastly dispatches from places like McAllen, Texas, are almost *too* much to bear. Living through this unfortunate era in American history has felt tantamount to riding a rollercoaster without a safety bar. The twists and plummets presented by a president devoid of empathy would leave most sentient Americans with whiplash. But because there appears to be no bottom, no leveling off, no seeming end to each and every dip, we are left to ponder, how much further will he, and we as a society, fall?

Cyrus McQueen @CyrusMMcQueen · Jan 28, 2019
My neighborhood in NYC is a hodgepodge of humanity. Yemenis run my bodega, Koreans run my dry cleaners, Hasidic Jews run my coffee shop, Puerto Rican's run my diner, Jamaicans run my barbershop. But I've never thought: I wish they'd speak English. Such thinking is deeply flawed.

⟲ 2920   ♡ 13537

It was undeniable: the Trump administration was now responsible for the greatest human rights violation on American soil since Jim Crow. And like the sanctioned terror that marred generations of African Americans, when brothers, fathers, and sons would suddenly *disappear*, their families divided and irreparably damaged, for migrants, too, it is their race, their disposability in the minds of white supremacists, that provides the motive and permission for such retribution. It is impossible to overstate the singular pain inflicted by Donald Trump on thousands of migrant families in the name of "zero tolerance." The sheer meanness, the cold, brutal, and unconscionable callousness of the policy, suggests, more than any of his egregious trespasses, that our president is a bona fide sociopath. It is no surprise that he would identify with and develop an affinity for Andrew Jackson: we have to go *that* far back to find such an *unfeeling* president, one whose pathology saw to it that he inflicted unadulterated pain on innocent people of color.

To forcibly separate crying children from their mothers, requires a level of heartlessness that is difficult to describe. By literally prying families apart, Trump and the Department of Homeland Security under former DHS Secretary Kirstjen Nielsen—who brazenly covered for the White House with misdirection in the Senate and the public arena—came to personify the living face of evil. In many ways, their criminal directives resemble the systematic separations carried out during the middle passage as well. It again speaks to the contradiction at the very core of our nation with regards to people of color: the danger we apparently pose, can *never* square the actual danger being posed to *us*.

Sadly, not only would this historic tradition persist but, so too would those efforts to reduce the scope of these abuses. Of the roughly 5,000 children deliberately separated from their parents, Trump would only cop to half that amount all in an effort to minimize these grievous acts. Notwithstanding the 545 migrant children it would later be reported could not be reunited with their parents and were, in effect, permanently orphaned, no amount of spin could erase the fact that these children were not being "well taken care of." Yet that two young migrant children eventually succumbed to illness was itself a likely consequence *of* this depraved operation; one in which human beings were treated like animals. These incidents, we now know, were exacerbated by a lack of medical attention, in addition to the children's being forced to sleep on mats on the ground inside steel mesh cages—fenced in areas that were callously dubbed "dog kennels."

It is heartbreaking, and given Trump's culpability and subsequent denial, utterly heartless, to learn that seven-year-old Jakelin Caal Maquin died while in detention after being detained at the border. That some three weeks later, eight-year-old Felipe Gomez Alonzo succumbed to illness—after being released from a hospital—marked the horrific culmination of events Trump and the GOP had boldly *set* into motion. Trump's further denial that border agents bore any responsibility, as well as his brazen attempt to blame everyone from the child's father in one instance to the Democrats and Obama in another, represented a despicable low, even for a president who was perpetually plumbing the depths.

Yet young immigrants still live in corrosive conditions, lacking basic necessities like diapers in some instances, with some detained children tasked with actually caring for infants in their parents' absence. The hellishness of their plight is paradoxical when one considers the self-professed Christian faith of their Republican perpetrators. That Felipe Gomez Alonzo perished on Christmas Eve would resonate with me more than anything—especially considering how much this president and his party love to tout their religiosity. Yet despite their hagiography of Jesus Christ, despite citing the virtues of the gospel, that they inflict such unconscionable pain on innocent souls leaves one *recoiling* at the blinding hypocrisy. Autographing Bibles symbolizes Trump's willing and callous desecration of not only a sacred text but also the guiding principles inscribed within it. And this devolution of the country from virtue, from true Christian values, into one that openly debases them, has his imbecilic handwriting all over it.

Cyrus McQueen @CyrusMMcQueen · Jan 28, 2019
Assimilation is a thinly veiled distraction masking the immorality lurking beneath the surface of our society. They ultimately don't care if you speak the same language cause they ultimately don't care about people of color. Eric Garner said 'I can't breathe' in perfect English.

↻ 269   ♡ 862

The fate awaiting people of color emigrating to America is like that which met most native-born Black and Brown people. In many ways, the immigration discussion *is* a ruse, a glaring distraction to woo conservative voters, given the fact that jails are *already* overflowing and the industry of privatized prisons needs Black and Brown bodies to fill its cells. Yet too often, the dialogue centers around the idea of "assimilation," a loaded word within the wider context of demographic shifts and the fear of a darkening populace. What gets lost in the discussion is that the extreme measures being taken, the detention of migrant families and children, can only be viewed as a manifestation of *that* fright. The inevitable changes occurring within the U.S. population is how many appear to justify these injustices, yet for a Republican-led government that broadcasts doomsday scenarios about caravans of terrorists, it is all an attempt to mask their practical concern: they can only continue controlling the population *if* a white majority is preserved indefinitely. The sorts of draconian punishments we observe being carried out in customs *and* corrections are directly attributable to this unabashed desire; the creation and maintenance of a racial underclass.

Though chattel slavery is a thing of the past, given the exploitative dynamic at hand, the countless going uninsured and without a living wage, it is hard to argue that working under the table or for the bare minimum, is *not* the modern equivalent. It is difficult to deny that, if left to conservatives, people of color, whether newly arrived or native born, would be faced with a reduced set of options—the best case scenario, serving *them*.

Race is so married to politics, and the prevailing status quo, that those writing and altering the laws do everything from gerrymandering congressional districts to deporting Latino parents. It is a devil's bargain that many in middle America appear all too willing to strike. The fact remains, it is impossible to engage in the political process, or to ultimately put down roots in America, from a concrete cell. Encaging people indefinitely—the sheer fucking cruelty of taking children from mothers or fathers—appears a small price to pay for those fighting to preserve *their* American way of life.

Cyrus McQueen @CyrusMMcQueen · Jan 27, 2019
Tom Brokaw said Hispanics need to work harder at assimilation? Interesting... I think old white men need to work harder at not being unconscionably racist... What in the actual fuck...

⟲ 2763   ♡ 12051

When Immigration and Customs Enforcement (ICE) agents began hunting Latinos around the country, conducting stings and entrapping hardworking domestics, cooks, day laborers, and a host of others (many employed off the books by rich, unscrupulous men like the president himself, who has hired, and chronically underpaid, such workers in his hotels and golf clubs in order to maximize his company's profits), it sent shockwaves throughout the country. Even for a nation that has employed a similar stratagem with people of color, whether it was to detain, deport, or dispatch, the searing efficiency of this governmental agency in carrying out these aims leaves people of color bristling, experiencing an historical déjà vu. The coldly clinical malpractice of a white America once again on the hunt gives me chilling flashbacks to my own experiences of being tracked by my Boston boogeyman, where the legality of my presence ultimately proved immaterial to forces empowered to *facilitate* my absence. But that the law could be utilized to defend the indefensible, where a mere 300 miles down the Northeastern corridor, an Ecuadorian pizza deliveryman and father of two, a man in the process of changing his immigration status, could be lured to a military base in Brooklyn under false pretenses and arrested, is a telltale sign that *assimilation* has never been the objective.

Amid this ruination, that you had legendary news anchor Tom Brokaw remarking that most American's didn't want "brown grand-babies," it brought to bear the cold, brutal bigotry *critical* to preserving American culture as we know it. Because conservative ideology was enjoying mainstream exposure, these opinions now perpetuated by the most trusted names in news, it meant our country was likely to continue overlooking its deep moral failings.

With his dispiriting words, Brokaw also confirmed my deepest concern about many power brokers—those who espouse and posit the fallacious idea that the country can only continue to thrive *by* failing its Black and Brown citizens. By unconsciously validating not only white Americans' feelings of precedence but by concurrently suggesting that such thinking is *beyond* reproach, the roots of racism would remain firmly embedded in American soil. Resultantly, that poisonous outgrowth of primacy, that unique excrescence personified by an obdurate public, would only burgeon, blocking out the radiant light of truth.

15

On Pins And Needles

The political fight to prevent a darkening America was soon augmented by disturbing developments within the world of entertainment. Long before leaving the den at Fox News, Megyn Kelly had displayed a predilection for sharing prejudiced opinions in her capacity as an infotainment television personality. Her declaration: "Santa just is white" is what first brought her to my attention. But despite the negative reaction those comments engendered on social media, Kelly, surprisingly, experienced minimal corporate fallout after her particularly heartless soliloquy.

However, after moving on to *The Today Show*, the host inevitably shot herself in the foot when she maintained that dressing up in blackface "was okay" when she was younger. The fact that it has never been okay is beside the point. A regressive political climate is what made the newly viable Kelly comfortable with sharing this errant perspective on network television. But between her morning TV colleagues like Al Roker dispensing *eclipse*-level shade and the Resistance flooding Twitter to issue righteous rebuttals, it was soon clear that she had failed to read the room. The almost immediate fallout from her remarks reflected a surprising trend where white tastemakers and power players were finding themselves increasingly out of touch with a more sentient public. Those recoiling from this charged era evinced that a level of heightened sensitivity was slowly developing despite the sort of routine callousness coming from the White House.

Kelly's punishment was swift and severe, with the host losing her morning show gig—it, a pattern we would soon see replicated with Roseanne Barr and "Papa" John Schnatter, household names also forced to step away from their eponymous brands for relaying racist sentiments. By the year 2018, though such unabashed malignancy had rent our citizenry, I was encouraged to find the fed-up among us *galvanized* and utterly determined to reduce its spread—no matter how appetizing it appeared.

Yet these lessons were not universally learned, as the fashion community could be observed tripping over this stumbling block every few weeks. Here, the disturbing origins of a range of products would go on to elicit a collective gasp. A dismayed public again bristled when those seemingly impervious to progress—here, iconic houses like Gucci and Prada—produced a string of garments steeped in the deep tradition of minstrelsy. It was as if we were witnessing threads of racial resentment being stitched *back* together, these trendy developments belying those gaping wounds already left exposed by this vicious past. Where issues of cultural appropriation in fashion had already become a point of contention, these latest attempts to monetize on such ignorance typify the sort of ersatz plaguing the industry—one that finds itself consumed with supplanting one unhealthy trend with another. And like Fox News, that it too promotes a flawed, fucked-up Eurocentric beauty standard betrays nothing but a lingering disdain *for* diversity. Yet even the absence of Black models on runways and in ad campaigns cannot explain *this* particular kind of harshness—choosing to depict Blackness as caricature—one that sees an industry resurrecting long-dead, centuries-old fabrications in an attempt to bring it back into style.

Cyrus McQueen @CyrusMMcQueen · Jan 25, 2019
Trump's trying to save face in the Rose Garden saying ICE has arrested 'volumes' of criminals who've come here illegally... I'm like, yeah, well the FBI has arrested volumes of criminals associated with your fuckin campaign too... #FridayFeeling

↻ 1640   ♡ 6092

For centuries, blackface was an effective tool for promoting our second-class status. As a wide range of products propagated racial propaganda, our subservient role would be cemented in these likenesses. Nutcrackers and bottle openers adorned with sambos and zip coons cast our debasement, the heated cauldron of hate cooking our image before hammering home these gross mischaracterizations. Thus, Black Americans were forced to observe our objectification *and* our hurt rendered indelibly in a bevy of objects.

With our dehumanization experiencing a mass-appeal, these items helped underpin the race problem as stereotypes, now working in tandem with our literal abuse, forced a depressed people to contend with wounds both physical and psychic in nature. That nearly two decades into the 21st century piggy banks and salt and pepper shakers of mammies have merely morphed into Gucci turtlenecks and Prada monkey charms proves that we are still on a dangerous trajectory. When H&M rolled out an advertisement depicting a young Black boy sporting a t-shirt reading, "Coolest Monkey in the Jungle," it reflected the horrors that naturally ensue when Blackness is left to white interpretation. Yet the fact these products even saw the light of day is far less troubling than the clear indication that no people of color were involved during any stages of development to prevent such insidious merchandise *from* hitting the shelves.

From concept to rollout, given the attention, the sheer number of eyes that likely pored over these disturbing images with *none* registering a problem, it points to the larger dangers created by our absence. When Black people are voided, our voices disregarded, our presence abrogated, most businesses come to resemble a vacuum. The filthiest notions, permitted to pervade these spaces, leave little to no room for real growth since regression *fills* the void. Here, not only does veracity suffer but we see authentic perspectives sacrificed. An insular, intransigent corporate culture, more interested in aggrandizing than diversity *always* ends up settling for convenient fabrications. Since our true selves can never compete when distortions are prioritized, even if one were to accept the plausible deniability proffered by these fashion houses—that these outcomes are not deliberate but rather incidents of absent mindedness—the pain these pricks cause would still be felt. Comparable to the very pins piecing these fabrics together, it is undeniable that racial bias is instrumental to churning out such gross output.

Shrinking Blackness to the size of a sweater, something that slips on and off after an immersion in the cold waters of abasement, these companies expect customers to *accept* a standard in which we are diminished. Since we are already operating from a great deficit, shit like this merely appends unnecessary insult to injury. A black turtleneck in lieu of burned cork or makeup, fulfills the same flagrant objective—one which ensures that our pain remains. Recalling the legacy of minstrelsy, of which this modern output *is* a direct corollary, our humanity has no place to dwell, let alone thrive, in this theater of the absurd. That Burberry, less than a month removed from Gucci's blunder, would send a model down the runway in a sweatshirt with drawstrings resembling a noose signals that the world of fashion, much like the world of the South, is *intent* on pushing a more palatable, revisionist history. Much like Trump's MAGA hats, it too dusts the dirt off a painful past in order to make falsehoods, and even fearmongering, *fashionable.*

Considering these fashion *faux pas,* my mind cannot help but connect the legacy of lynching in this country with the troubling image of that young Black boy in the H&M campaign. As a child of color, his image and eventually his life are at the mercy of an unfeeling, often ferocious public so comfortable diminishing his worth it ensures that he will grow up in a world that is indifferent to whether or not he lives or dies. Once again, the memory of Tamir Rice and a life cut short thunders to mind. Just as he was murdered while simply trying to live, given the unhealthy disposition of white authority in this country, we will continue seeing the growth of Black America stopped dead in its tracks.

But be the perpetrators cops or Ad Execs, I keep coming back to fashion specifically, that veritable playground for the well-heeled. Here, our desire to be regarded betrays an equally conspicuous irregularity, somewhat mirroring those indelible European forms into which we still, by and large, try to fit. I often ponder the hold that "high fashion" holds over our community, considering our earnest attempts to swath ourselves in pricey and coveted sundries bely circumstances that are typically not reflective of such privilege.

Yet African Americans come from a tradition where we *do* prioritize dressing well, even in times of economic uncertainty, mirroring a refrain popular in my own family that, even when we had little money, "we were never poor." With so much wrested from us, that small area we *can* control will inspire the most creative among us to defy our socioeconomic reality. Potent minimization sees us maximize our sartorial proclivities. That people of color possess great panache and indelible flair—bringing to mind men like my father who "dressed their asses off" and my grandmother, who could not afford an entire wardrobe of expensive department store wares yet created sumptuous garments on the home sewing machine for herself and her children— reveals a culture that routinely overcomes the most debilitating strictures. Very often, that strong sense of pride has helped *refute* our relegation, our forced improvisation seeding great innovation.

For myself, as I came of age during an era when Black haberdashers could not fail and footwear, from loafers to tennis shoes, reflected a young man's cache in our community, I would grapple with the fact that, at a time of Reaganomics and when mortgage rates reached more than 15 percent, sneakers seemed to be all a young person of color *could* endeavor to own. It was the beginning of an awareness that such imagery—not simply of Black tastemakers in the worlds of music and sports who drive these superficial distractions but also that deeper, more damaging desire to reflect the trappings of white wealth—belied the inarguable fact that white wealth *keeps* us trapped. My genuine attempts to understand why Eurocentric designs and products hold a stranglehold over us collectively, us invariably tying our self-worth to an aesthetic that excludes healthy notions of ethnicity, *still* leaves me distressed.

As a Black man, it becomes harder and harder to accept this stark reality, especially as those among and above us clamor for these aspirational symbols, conveniently avoiding the fact that for far too long, far too many of us have never dared to *truly* aspire. We live in a socioeconomic cavity, no doubt, and things like sneakers are merely a filling. Whether it is an expensive pair of Jordan's or Adidas, their rubber and leather represent a barely affordable bridge over our morass. Dwelling in a deprived community, we clamor for *any* form of status possible. Impoverished yet surrounded by sybarites, unbridled covetousness produces a flood of envy, unleashing a virulence that lays claim to many a young Black man, our bodies perpetually washing up on corners, and in alleys, across America.

Cyrus McQueen @CyrusMMcQueen · Oct 23, 2018
This morning Megyn Kelly defended dressing up in blackface by saying, "When I was a kid, that was okay"... Yeah, smoking cigarettes when you were pregnant used to be okay too... Took us a while to learn that certain behaviors ultimately compromise our well being. #TuesdayThoughts

⟲ 976   ♡ 3942

Overpriced clothing, though, is among the least of our problems. When it was revealed that Ralph Northam, Virginia's Democratic governor, had dressed in blackface, even using the picture of this lunacy in his medical school yearbook, it signaled that stereotypes of Blackness are bipartisan. In fact, this inanity appeared to cut across ideological and socioeconomic lines, with poor whites and even rich, educated ones like Megyn Kelly, and now Northam, having feasted on this foolishness.

Next, after Northam's yearbook came to light, and amid calls for his resignation, Mark Herring, his attorney general and second in line to become governor, admitted that he, *too*, had worn blackface at a college party, an admission that ratcheted up the absurdity as a parade of prominent white people now sought to get ahead of their prejudiced pasts. But, aside from the fact that as college-aged students they should have known better—as well as Northam and Herring attempting to minimize their actions by painting them, no pun intended, as homages to Michael Jackson and Kurtis Blow—what strikes me most is witnessing the outrage of white pundits who called for the officials' resignations as if their summations spoke for us.

The operative, by leaking Northam's yearbook photo, had engaged in an act of expediency, turning the subsequent fallout into political theater. With white Democrats soon tripping over themselves to make examples of the offending governor and attorney general, it obscured the obvious: that this sort of ignorance had gestated in a *blue* bubble.

Democrats' "virtue signaling" masked an inability to address stereotypes comprehensively, or even to allow *our* voices to lend comprehension to the discussion. It robbed us from providing much needed clarity—a moment where it could be edified that this is not just a Southern or a conservative problem, but rather one that is ubiquitous, an *American* problem infecting both bourgeoise and basic minds from Madison Avenue to Pennsylvania Avenue. For African Americans, such signaling points yet again to our inability to break through certain echo chambers—ones that pretty much *all* privileged people are guilty of erecting to insulate themselves. When white people on television, irrespective of partisanship, are more vocally upset about blackface than are Black people, it reflects a significant problem: our voices have once again succumbed to their desire to hear themselves speak first. With our opinions sacrificed, a majority satisfied with swathing itself in interpretations of Blackness, even interpretations of Black indignation, ends up magnifying our hurt—only in this case, through the distorted lens of hubris.

Cyrus McQueen @CyrusMMcQueen · Feb 25, 2019
I been tryna explain to people why black folks are upset with the Best Picture winner. Basically, imagine all your home movies were filmed from next door by your neighbor. All those important moments that shaped you were captured from a distance. You're tiny and barely in focus.

⟲ 263   ♡ 1584

Media and politics aside, this sort of arrogating can be readily observed in Hollywood. Using quirky Caucasian calculus to estimate Black value is almost routine in Tinseltown. Yet by being used as props, interracial friendships here serving as a device to tell *one* kind of story, this itself becomes tantamount to taking Blackness out for a spin. Like blackface, it operates like a joy ride, reinforcing the idea that we are mere empty vessels to be occupied by a public uninterested in really seeing us for who we are.

Nowhere was this more apparent, or more distressing, than in *Green Book*, a movie derived from the actual *Negro Motorist Green Book*. The travel guide created by Victor Green, a Black postal worker from Harlem, New York, had provided a lifeline for Black Americans traversing the nation's byways and backroads in the pre-Civil Rights era. The guide, established in 1936, would ameliorate the intrinsic threats posed to Black motorists during the Jim Crow era—its pages eventually listing more than 9,500 Black-friendly businesses, from gas stations and drug stores to hotels and restaurants. Given its unique history it certainly deserved to be portrayed more accurately than through the perspective of some stilted white protagonist. The legacy of Sundown Towns—all-white counties where a bell rung at sundown signaled that Black domestics and laborers had to leave the area, or face violent retribution—illustrates the recurring dangers inherent not just in driving while Black but in *living* while Black. The perils of merely existing, back then as well as now in Trump's America, signifies Hollywood's desperate need for more thought provoking stories highlighting this glaring link between our past and our present, something films like *Blackkklansman* and *Get Out* captured superbly.

Ultimately, the automobiles at the center of these heartwarming yet hollow tales of reconciliation, whether it be *Green Book* or, three decades earlier, *Driving Miss Daisy*, signal a broken-down conveyance incapable of moving us all forward. When "white saviors" occupy the driver's seat, equality takes the backseat, no matter *who* is pictured driving. Therefore, blackface and the myth of the white hero are inextricably linked. This maelstrom of mendacity, this typhoon of tropes, of stereotype used to paint inaccurate pictures—projecting our inherent inferiority while upholding white America's implicit sense of superiority—culminates in an indisputable pattern of destruction. Perhaps the placement of cars at the center of these two Best Picture winners is actually fitting: both films take us for a ride, and the vehicles, like our very image, seem to exist solely to propel this distortion—or even to serve up cheap laughs, in one instance providing the setting for a distasteful lesson on how to eat fried chicken, as if we really are little more than a carnival-like attraction.

These sorts of invidious displays are, of course, as old as the movies, going back to the first talkies, bringing to mind Al Jolson's *Jazz Singer* and its images of a Black heaven replete with pork chops growing on trees. Yet Hollywood still gets mileage out of this bullshit, Blackness no different than bumper cars as the worlds of film and fashion simply, illogically, go in circles. Or maybe a demolition derby would be a more apt metaphor: these troublesome tales told on screen leave our true image bent, dented, and demolished. With our real identity unrecognizable after such seemingly inconsequential amusement, this entrenched pattern is perpetuated; this damage having been easily exacted under the *guise* of entertainment.

By inserting a white protagonist, a flawed yet infallible hero who tackles race from that perspective—bringing audiences along for the improbable journey—both the character and the watching crowds can continue ignoring the disastrous implications of this societal construct, all while *projecting* a semblance of personal growth. In these instances, Black folks marvel at white Americans' propensity to wallow in their own perspectives, opting for the shallow end as if they must ease into the deep pool of our collective history, conveying their profound aversion to immersing themselves *fully* in the unsparing waters of truth. Whiteness operates sort of like a wet suit, a protective barrier, an impenetrable layer that keeps many at a comfortable remove from us and our chilling reality—while undermining the almost superlative strength we must possess in order to endure. Deathly afraid of their role, of the bitter, biting agony presented by our shared past, they recast themselves, pussyfooting around history's edges, while remaining impervious—many prioritizing their own personal comfort over any authentic progress.

Here a funny yet fascinating thing occurs: many get so close to the issue that they actually appear to be addressing racism—a task so commendable they rack up accolades for the endeavor. From certain angles, these road trips and morality tales pull off the trick of making it seem as if white Americans are tackling this unwieldy problem and even embracing *us*. In actuality, though, they do neither. Being that communication is actually a two-way street, those individuals remain woefully removed from any verity whilst promoting the grandiose notion that they are purposefully connecting with Black Americans and our shared and trying history. Yet if you get close enough to inspect the product, you see we have in no way moved forward. You discover no definitive contact, no *real* embrace. That arm is not around us at all. They are just patting themselves on the back.

16

R-E-S-P-E-C-T

How can I endeavor to ponder a system of subjugation knowing that as I sit here writing this, a male in a world constructed and fortified on patriarchy, I unconsciously contribute to a dynamic that prioritizes me and my examinations at the expense of my sisters? How can I be so bold as to believe for one moment that my perspective, or any male perspective, is either warranted or wanted in the discussion of gender inequality? This imbalance goes back millennia and has shaped the world, and role, I inhabit. As such, I am inclined to listen if not stand aside rather than undertake this virtually impossible undertaking. But how could I elucidate on the egregious legacy of white Americans furthering a system that has imperiled my people without acknowledging those parallels and reflecting on a comparable underclass as it pertains to women?

As I highlight the shortcomings of a society that elects a fraudulent, foolish, facsimile of a man, I would be remiss if I did not mention that his ascension came at the expense of a brilliant, deserving, supremely qualified woman. That America had to endure an unprincipled investigation into Hillary Clinton while she was running for the presidency would be unfair enough without the added ingredient of the ignoramus she ran against compounding the deception by churlishly encouraging the spread of misinformation. Before becoming secretary of state, even before her 2000 Senate candidacy and 2008 run for the presidency, Hillary had endured concerted Republican assaults while serving as First Lady of Arkansas and First Lady of the United States. By the time Republicans tried to blame her for the deaths of a U.S.

ambassador and three other Americans perpetrated by coordinated Al-Qaeda attacks on U.S. facilities in Benghazi, Libya, their decades-long onslaught had already inflicted irreparable damage to her reputation.

With the subsequent GOP investigation into her use of a private email server, the pall followed her around—much like her rotund, profane opponent during their second presidential debate. Most anyone with eyes or any enduring sensibility observed with disgust the manner in which Trump's unseemly presence lingered just over Hillary's shoulder throughout their debate. Purely off-putting was how he encroached upon—stalked—the former secretary of state as her measured, thoughtful responses to a host of questions inspired his jowls to contract.

His adolescent upstaging movements would have been notable even under normal circumstances, but that they unfolded two days after *The Washington Post* released the Access Hollywood recording of his infamous admission that he would grab women "by the pussy," audio so audacious, so unnecessarily ribald, not to mention improper and ultimately illegal, it made his behavior that evening even more egregious. A crude man, an admitted misogynist, his physical presence telegraphed his contempt not just for his female opponent but for *all* females, his barely contained belly cutting off the distance between them, his pear shape and unnaturally long tie betraying a man desperately overcompensating for all his shortcomings. That he would go on to excuse the captured audio as "locker room" talk before launching into attacks on Hillary—once again retrieving that favorite Republican punching bag, former President Bill Clinton—he would attempt to deflect from his disrespect of women by, low and behold, *disrespecting* a woman. His stupefying decision to then roll out several of Bill Clinton's accusers at the very moment his own sordid past was catching up with him was tantamount to watching a dog eat its own shit in an attempt to get rid of the mess, completely oblivious that this very action cemented his status as a primitive beast.

The *Access Hollywood* tape created quite the ripple, the crude candor it captured threatening to strike a much-needed blow to this blowhard and a campaign that shocked sensible people the world over. But this was but one gross display in a lifetime of gross displays. It takes little imagination to ponder the dozens, if not hundreds, of women targeted by an arrogant, unfeeling, entitled, enabled, callous, and ultimately worthless individual who uses economic might to both facilitate *and* absolve his misdeeds. Over sixteen women would come forward before

Election Day to report untoward behavior toward them, from Jessica Leeds, who the future president touched inappropriately on an airplane in the late 1970s, to Bridget Sullivan a former Miss New Hampshire, who detailed how Trump would casually stroll through the dressing room during the Miss Universe Pageant to view the undressed women. All the overwhelming signs pointed to a vile, repugnant man who victimized women for sport. The *Access Hollywood* audio capturing his braggadocio threatened to dash his presidential ambitions, yet other audio, captured during an interview on *The Howard Stern Show*, was even more indicative of his pathology and overall unworthiness as a candidate and as a man.

Trump possesses little to no nuance. He projects, he assails, and he openly displays his disrespect toward minorities and, in this instance, women, with *incontinence*. He has no desire to veil his venom or appear in any way respectable—this a lack likely spirited by his wealth, his race, and a lifetime of zero accountability. In referencing the Teen Miss USA pageant, his admission to Stern that he was "allowed" to go backstage because "I'm the owner of the pageant and therefore I'm inspecting it" is the evidence that Trump is likely guilty of Sullivan's accusation, as well as a host of others that may never come to light. I conclude that Jill Harth, Rachel Crooks, Cathy Heller, Kristin Anderson, Jessica Drake, Jennifer Murphy, Mindy McGillivray, Temple McDowell, Tasha Dixon, Karena Virginia, Ninni Laaksonen, Natasha Stoynoff, Cassandra Searles, and Summer Zervos, in addition to the women already mentioned, all told the truth because Trump, the transparent loser, had effectively told it as well.

His subsequent admission to Stern—"I sort of get away with things like that" in addition to his declaring, "I'm the owner"—was the most revelatory and gave me the most pause. This psychology not only inspires his abusive behavior; it is also the same dangerous mindset, regarding women as possessions, that an unfathomable number of males, from investment bankers to incels, possess.

Guided by this same mental and moral deficiency, Trump forced himself on writer E. Jean Carroll in a Manhattan department store's lingerie section during the 1990s. In 2019, when she revealed in *New York Magazine* her fateful encounter with the boorish bastard, bringing the number of public accusers up to eighteen, she distilled his privilege and predatory motivations down to one plain and perfect moniker: "rich boy." Her painful recollection of their violent encounter—she describes how the future president "lunges at me, pushes me against the wall, hitting my head quite badly," before describing how he "thrusts his penis" inside—is disturbing enough on its own without further reading in painful detail about the "colossal struggle" that ensued before she knees him and flees the dressing room.

He remained nameless in that moment, but the "rich boy" we have all come to know during his years in the political arena has shown through his coarse behavior that he will similarly force his way onto us Americans and proceed to violate everything we *too* hold sacred. In many ways, Trump's whole presidency has felt like nothing more than one long, drawn out assault. And we presume that on that afternoon in Bergdorf's, the "rich boy" assumed he would "sort of get away with things like that" just as he had countless other times; just as he did in November of 2016.

That Trump got away with the assault on Carroll for 23 years is a testament to the insulating power of race and privilege. That he would keep skating justice, impervious to any repercussions from his slippery actions, means the prerogatives we afford status are more responsible for his enduring freedom than his professed innocence or even the slipshod defense he soon mounted by claiming that Carroll was "totally lying." Even more revealing than his rebuttal was his subsequent assertion, "She's not my type," words so utterly, so unnecessarily unkind. While distracting from the fact that sexual assault has little to do with appearance yet *everything* to do with power, Trump confirmed that he views women in a subservient and purely physical capacity. It telegraphs the heartless nature of this particular "rich boy," along with the society that enables him, and others like him, to ride roughshod over people and principles. Reducing women to a "type" would be problematic on its own without that underlying projection all but certifying his guilt on top of it—a denial that pretty much cemented it was, indeed Trump, who was "totally lying."

Cyrus McQueen @CyrusMMcQueen · Oct 16, 2018
Stormy Daniels is no different than the country... Trump's fucked us, denied it, and then gone on to insult us... #horseface

⟲ 438   ♡ 1515

As the world watches, many men of privilege within Trump's orbit now find themselves in handcuffs for a host of criminal activities. With the arrest of billionaire financier Jeffrey Epstein, it culminating the tireless work of *Miami Herald* reporter Julie Brown, who persistently shined a light on his egregious shenanigans, the public could connect the dots between sexual violence and those using their influence to facilitate it. When her work led federal prosecutors in the Southern District of New York to charge Epstein with both sex crimes and sex trafficking of underage girls, his power, privilege, and predation finally fell under a microscope. It suggested that his closeness with Trump extended beyond their moneyed Manhattan and Florida circles to, more aptly, a shared pathology, one exacerbated by caste. An Epstein accuser, allegedly recruited into his sex-trafficking ring when only 16 years old and working as a spa attendant at Mar-a-Lago, Trump's eponymous South Florida resort, is but one of the many connections between the commander in chief and the dead financier. But where Trump lived less than a mile from Epstein in Palm Beach and would profess his friendliness with the felon is not nearly as shocking as his babble in *New York* (the magazine in which Carroll ultimately detailed her assault) that Epstein is a "terrific guy" and "a lot of fun to be with. It is even said that he likes beautiful women as much as I do, and many of them are on the younger side. No doubt about it—Jeffrey enjoys his social life."

Trump's ability to plug his foot in his own mouth with regularity is well known, yet audio or some other form of evidence unearthed from his sordid past always seems to corroborate his worst impulses. His unctuousness only further confirms our worst impressions of him, it leaving a sentient public *repulsed*. Whether it is *Access Hollywood* or *The Stern Show*, Trump showed his own predilection for young models just as Epstein had, his tell of "type" as opposed to an outright denial of impropriety leading us to deduce his likely attack on *any* woman, regardless of "type" or even scenario. Besides, if a changing room in a public setting could not curb his impulses, why would a private beach, packed with vulnerable young women behind the gates of a multimillion-dollar estate? One with a host enabling his predation?

The answer, of course, is as definitive as the guilt of the defendant. Epstein's ability to secure a mind-boggling plea deal granting him federal immunity in 2008 is almost as disturbing as the realization that it was brokered by none other than Alexander Acosta who worked closely with Epstein's attorneys and, some ten years later, would serve as Trump's Secretary of Labor. The sheer fuckery is flabbergasting when you consider that after it was *confirmed* Epstein sexually abused over 30 girls, it only led to his serving 13 months in a county jail—a veritable slap on the wrist considering his abject heinousness. What it revealed about race, our broken criminal justice system, and the corrupt network of facilitators involved, left me *seething*. Given Epstein's certifiable guilt, his only serving a year can never jibe with the fact that his victims, like Trump's, will carry this trauma around for the remainder of theirs.

Thus, the bad behavior of "rich boys" brings me back to E. Jean Carroll and that afternoon in Bergdorf's. Upon reading Carroll's revelation, and digesting the despicable actions of the man-child at the center of it, I came to a painful realization: New York incarcerated Antron McCray, Yusef Salaam, Raymond Santana, Kevin Richardson, and Korey Wise—the Central Park Five—for an assault they did not commit, while their most vocal accuser was assaulting women in New York dressing room stalls. We cannot view Trump, Epstein, or the complex network of corrupt men and women who keep guilty men like these out of prison separately from the innocent Black boys whose guilt these very same corrupt men and women manufacture and ultimately certify. The tragic tale of the Central Park Five is uniquely American, and therefore impossible to isolate from the tragic history shaping our sociopolitical reality—one that all too often turns vulnerable young Black men and vulnerable young women *into* victims—prey for those entities intent on fucking them.

Because of the proprietary relationship that wealthy men exhibit in relation to women's lives, echoing a very specific pattern historically established with Black and Brown bodies, I conclude that just as Trump manipulated the many preexisting, unresolved problems pertaining to race to get elected, he exploits a similar dynamic when it comes to women and the longstanding gross imbalance between genders. Given the overwhelming overlaps of racial and gender inequality, this theme of ownership over another's physical being cannot be considered mutually exclusive. Each problem is perpetuated by those who are not wealthy or powerful in the traditional sense, yet who assume that mantle because of a designation placing them above all others—in one case, because they are white by birth and in the other because they are men by birth. Having consolidated power while sowing discord and perniciously claiming that women are inherently inferior, men lay claim to their lives, legacies, and reproductive choices; it becomes virtually impossible for many, despite incremental progress, to shake free of this nearly prehistoric stigma, to shatter the glass ceiling that, even a century removed from suffrage, remains unbroken and arbitrarily high above their heads.

Hillary herself, despite these overwhelming odds, amassed three million more votes than her opponent, yet failed to capture the presidency because of the Electoral College, that antiquated system implemented, ironically, to supplant the popular vote out of a fear of factions and corruption. America's past *is* what has compromised its future. James Madison, the "Father of the Constitution" and, like Thomas Jefferson, a hyperbolic, hypocritical slave-owning scoundrel, insisted on electors instead of the popular vote, pushing a proverbial boulder down the Hill that has steamrolled progress ever since. With Madison's formula for calculating the number of electors in each state, the crafty cretin has shaped every presidential election since—but not before he would go on to address the "Negro" population, which he also deemed to be of "a serious nature" as it pertained to population counts. As a landowning, slave-owning Virginian, he designed his plan to ensure that the more populous, and more progressive, white Northern states did not overshadow a Southern state like Virginia, where slaves comprised roughly half of its population. Thus, he embedded the three-fifths compromise—counting each slave as three-fifths of a person—into his proposal. Virginia, as a result of this quizzical Caucasian calculus, would garner a significant number of electoral votes, bolstering the influence of a backward South, eventually helping usher in the presidencies of not only Thomas Jefferson but Donald J. Trump as well. The past is, indeed, often prologue: racism and misogyny, the very hate that has long kept women and people of color from power, stifling change for over a century, reemerges in this new millennium. We have again witnessed this disastrous dynamic misshape the outcomes of our elections; not once but *twice* within a 16-year window.

Cyrus McQueen @CyrusMMcQueen · Jun 6, 2018
With Hillary's emails they made a mountain out of a molehill... With Trump's treason, they're trying to make a molehill out of a mountain...

⟲ 862   ♡ 3229

At the core of all this is the theme of ownership, which is what inextricably links Women's Rights and Civil Rights. This historic tradition—toxic white masculinity using and abusing bodies for personal pleasure and capital gain—has shaped America even more than its mighty coastlines. It is a paradigm that emboldens an evil, vile, and loveless man like Trump to continue his own pattern of abuse. Given his history of unchecked entitlement, his ascension in public life would now run concurrent with the primitive behavior he continued to display, and hide, in his private life. Yet the stunning *Access Hollywood* tape and the numerous women coming forward to relay their traumatic run-ins with the Republican frontrunner was unfortunately tabled by a media that simply clamored for the next scandal this clown would create. And here he would pull from his bottomless bag of tricks, and tweets, to simply roll the campaign circus from city to city, rally to rally.

The twenty-four-hour news cycle is now supplanted by an eight-hour one, with two or three Trump scandals dividing a single calendar day, the morning outrage made old by the advent of the midday horror. Notoriety, the once unfortunate reality of political life that destroyed candidacies, bafflingly feeds and grows his. Each day on the campaign trail found Hillary forced to field questions about her fuckin' computer, even as Trump was tweeting nonsense, infecting our politics with invective, callously dismissing not only his opponent but every woman who came into his orbit through bloody hyperbole. The gross double standard governing our society would ultimately affect who the nation chose to govern our society.

Yet a cloud of suspicion also began emerging out of his campaign and his subsequent election: likely evidence of unsavory behavior in a hotel room in Moscow, it a grim forecast of what was to come. Not long into his presidency, Trump's predilections for porn stars and paid sex became his worst kept secret. Here, many soon found themselves holding out hope that the storm created by his brief dalliance with a certain Miss Daniels *would* finally capsize his wayward ship.

A year after the scandal broke, Michael Cohen, Trump's longtime lawyer and fixer, testified before the House Oversight Committee and proffered receipts—reimbursement checks the just-elected president had made out to him in his indelibly imbecilic handwriting. It seems that Cohen and Allen Weisselberg, the Trump Organization's longtime CFO, had paid Daniels to remain silent, marking the first evidence of Trump's obfuscation in the matter. With $35,000 checks, Trump and his minions simply sought to silence the woman. The irony was not lost on me, nor on a nation of aggrieved women, as we drew the unmistakable parallels between this act and his election, both aimed at silencing women's vital voices.

The tawdry details of a bum engaging in an extramarital affair shortly after his wife gave birth to their son compounded his unrivaled brutishness—notwithstanding that the mushroom man viewed women as conquests, their bodies nothing more than buildings to occupy temporarily before figuratively slapping his name on them in a filthy, frivolous feast for his simple mind. But in contrast to the silence of Sarah Sanders, Kellyanne Conway, Kirstjen Nielsen, Betsy DeVos, or any of the tragic women in his employ now enriching themselves at the expense of women's progress, a rumble within the populace *would* soon be felt. Demonstrations arose across the country, a primal upheaval, a purging from the poison being forced on a proud, resilient country and its even prouder, more resilient women. Less than 24 hours after his sparsely attended inauguration, even before he set about diluting the Affordable Care Act and engaging in a host of other dastardly deeds, women around the world showed their solidarity with the Women's March on Washington. It was heartening to watch women like my wife and my mother—among countless coworkers, friends, and family members— taking to the streets, rebutting this boorish man, assuring that we would be wasting no time in remediating this historical blunder. Over 200,000 people filled the National Mall, with some five million more descending on Chicago, Los Angeles, and many other cities and towns. In my own NYC, the sea of pink hats dotting Fifth Avenue, not far from his eponymous building, resembled flowers in a vibrant garden, blooming once again after a particularly vicious winter had appeared to snuff out all discernible life. It was proof that America, whether we realized it or not, was already on the road to recovery.

Cyrus McQueen @CyrusMMcQueen · Jan 20, 2018
I ain't gonna lie, I forgot the #WomensMarch2018 was today... I'm tired, hungover... But when your wife bursts into the room and says 'Get your arse up!' You know what time it is... #WomansMarchNYC

⟲ 138   ♡ 1007

Of course Trump's treatment of women, his attempts to cover up his misdeeds during the nascency of his presidency, with his term in office not so much taking off as careening off the tarmac, was not the only sign that patriarchy was heading toward crashing and burning. It is almost inevitable that a coterie of repugnant Republican men—the misogynists who flocked to frolic with the big orange bird, their matching feathers ensuring their protection in the vast safety net that the nest of his Administration provided—*will* be undone by the very feminine forces they so violently try to repress.

When not one but two ex-wives accused Rob Porter, a political aide, lawyer, and Trump's then-staff secretary, of physical and emotional abuse, it shocked many Americans who were apoplectic that the White House not only employed a serial wife beater despite his well-known abusive background, but that the president had tried to incubate this most rotten of eggs. Jennie Willoughby, Porter's second wife, would go on to pen a *Washington Post* op-ed detailing the horrific abuse both she and Porter's first wife Colbie Holderness had suffered. Her efforts would resonate despite a callous attempt by Trump and then-Chief of Staff John Kelly to disregard these assertions—the very same ones she had *already* leveed during Porter's FBI background check.

With her legitimate claims summarily dismissed—even before Kelly went on to misrepresent them as only "emotional abuse," minimizing her trauma as well as Porter's culpability—Willoughby rightfully went ahead to describe in detail the very contours of abuse. She thus framed the dialogue the only way it should ever be presented: from the victim's perspective. "The constant and repeated insulting, degrading, ignoring and undermining of someone's intelligence, looks and choices is abuse," she wrote. "It is insidious, demoralizing, paralyzing. It is real." She was speaking not as a scorned woman, as Kelly mischaracterized her; she was speaking for women from all corners of the globe whose lives had been marred by the scourge of misogyny and maltreatment.

It is no mystery that Kelly, that crusty lobster-like crustacean out of the salty Boston waters, is an unrepentant racist; yet he, too, appeared to operate under the bullshit premise that femininity, like racial equality, is a threat. His desire to diminish Willoughby's declaration as "just the accusation of a messy divorce" echoed his epically awful reaction to Frederica Wilson, where he would denigrate the Congresswoman, labeling her an "empty barrel." Thus, when Willoughby wrote that abuse "represents an extreme and targeted form of bullying, one that damages the victim's sense of self-worth and creates a fear of retaliation for standing up for oneself," she could have been easily speaking of Porter, the president, or even Kelly *himself.*

That a hollow man like Kelly tried to minimize guilt and mischaracterize one woman's nightmare as a dream is proof that we must braid the struggles of women *and* people of color into a mighty rope to lasso beasts intent, even hell bent, on inhibiting our futures. Toxic white masculinity and abuses of power are an American hallmark, a menace imperiling the lives of women and all marginalized people since the Mayflower docked off of Plymouth, some four hundred years ago. So, in examining this history more closely— as well as Kelly *and* Porter's Bay State past—something in me would be awakened.

Given the DNA of the country and those aforementioned dogs, a reality predicated around the abuse and misuse of others, one sees it is not unique to Trump's administration. Yet that both men were brought up in the city of Boston *was* too conspicuous to disregard. For the most densely settled population of intellectuals to produce a perplexingly underdeveloped mind like Porter's, a sick puppy prone to cruel, violent, and basic behavior, would be disturbing enough without the added wrinkle that the White House, of all places, is where he would ultimately be allowed to flourish.

Trump's willful ignorance in this regard is what secured Porter's place on Pennsylvania Avenue, along with Kelly's—men rejuvenated and rewarded for their fealty—it having only helped expand a degenerate's fiefdom. But that Trump, like Kelly, heaped praise on Porter after he resigned, even entertaining the notion of bringing him back to the White House—"[he] says he's innocent, and I think you have to remember that"—is less notable than the fealty Porter and Kelly clearly forged with one another. Their shitty bro-mance was likely *informed* by those commonalities forged in the Commonwealth of Massachusetts.

I keep returning to the unmistakable parallels between these abusive men, in the process uncovering, as Willoughby so perfectly presented, the presence of a common "fear of retaliation for standing up for oneself." These words resonate with me on a cellular level because I and countless others, in Boston and elsewhere, have been forced to stomach the arbitrary, abusive whims of men emboldened by badges, titles, and power to control the bodies and destinies of the descendants of suffragettes *and* slaves. As a member of this historical underclass, I myself would need to possess a great deal of willful ignorance to not recognize that a campus cop who relentlessly shadowed my shadow was, basically, John Kelly, or that the garbage man on my childhood street, a man embodying the very filth he was tasked with collecting, *was*, in effect, Rob Porter.

This is why the maltreatment of women is something I have never been able to tolerate—even if I can only claim to understand a scintilla of their experience through my own at times fractured sense of self-worth. I recognize what it is like to be reduced by the actions of men, those who snatched right out of my throat the voice I have worked a lifetime to establish, back alleys and bathrooms in these instances almost synonymous, along with the symbiosis of the victimized, be they Black or female, our bodies made vulnerable by the combined threats of violence and devaluation.

When news of the college cheating scandal broke in March of 2019, Porter immediately came to my mind, not least because his own trajectory as progeny of two Harvard administrators had probably secured him a legacy acceptance. Regardless, the privilege that paved his path to success, like those celebrity children who benefitted from breaking all the rules, very likely stunted his maturation, impinging on any potential to grow into a person of integrity. In this regard, the Blue Bloods and blue-collar citizens of my birth city, despite differing economic realities, share a chromosome when it comes to abusing privilege, it almost uniting them in their dogged defiance of progress.

That Porter's father made his bones in the administration of George H.W. Bush, he of Willie Horton infamy, is also of note. Bush used the anomalous tale of Horton, who raped a Maryland woman while on a crime spree during a weekend furlough from prison, to undermine Michael Dukakis, his Democratic rival in the 1988 presidential race. As governor of Massachusetts, Dukakis had supported the furlough program, a fact that Bush used in a shock-and-awe attack to capsize his campaign and presidential aspirations. Porter, comparable in age to me, would have been growing up in Belmont, Massachusetts, during this time—the same period in which I was coming of age in Roxbury. Yet he would go on to witness his father profit personally and politically from this corrosive fearmongering, his family fortunes thus inextricably tied to the American mythos of Black male predation. That Porter himself would go on to work for a president who also glommed onto this perturbation, projecting his own unfounded fears to reinforce this heavily trafficked trope and create a specter of guilt around the innocent Central Park Five, cannot be disregarded. It is hard to overlook the hypocrisy—that two beneficiaries of privilege capitalized off stereotypes against us, as they themselves went on to engage in brutal behavior against women.

Cyrus McQueen @CyrusMMcQueen · Jun 18, 2019
Good God, did ya hear Trump's Central Park Five statement? The way he disregards DNA evidence, I'm amazed he ever claimed Tiffany and Eric...

⟲ 260   ♡ 1565

Where conservatives weaponized the tales of Willie Horton and the Central Park Five, it is Porter, the serial abuser, who evokes yet another tale of tragedy, this one also unfolding out of Massachusetts in 1989. That year was historic in myriad ways, from the massacre in Tiananmen Square to the collapse of the Berlin Wall. In a month that began with the Black Friday stock market crash, followed shortly thereafter by a major San Francisco earthquake, my American city would come to experience aftershocks of its own after a man-made disaster knocked everything else off the front page, its ghastly denouement felt to this day by those who lived through it.

When Charles Stuart, a yuppie Boston native who made a living as a furrier on Newbury Street, got in his car to bring his wife home from birthing classes, he unbridled an evil in a city still contending with its fraught and unfortunate past. Indeed that posh thoroughfare where Stuart worked was mere miles yet worlds away from where this story would unravel. In Boston, the chasm of race could be easily reflected in a very short distance, highlighting the immense disconnect that exists between the residents of a relatively small city. On the evening of October 23rd, Stuart would turn down a dark street in my Roxbury neighborhood with his pregnant wife Carol beside him, yet when they emerged a few miles away in Mission Hill, *each* had sustained life-threatening gunshot wounds. After police and ambulances arrived, Stuart would fatefully relay that a Black man had carjacked them and proceeded to steal all their valuables before shooting both.

Hell unleashed is an apt appraisal of what transpired in a town immediately unglued at the prospect of a Black man killing a pregnant white woman—its police force transforming into an occupying army overnight. With the city's long, horrible history with race now playing out in real time, it once again placed the city in the national spotlight for all the wrong reasons. Forced busing coming before my time, this crisis marked my introduction to an electricity in the city's streets, all powered by a profound, almost *shocking* animus. As a 10-year-old, I was now old enough to better process everything I was observing, even if the adults around me failed to fully articulate this sudden tension. I recall coming home after a marathon day of school and after-school programs to witness my mother and my uncle engaged in an excited conversation, the local news blaring in the background as they went back and forth, exchanging expletives while never taking their eyes off the screen.

I immediately knew the gravity of the situation because my churchgoing uncle never cursed, his language in this instance betraying that he was completely unnerved. I had been hearing the name Stuart a lot, but up to this point, it had been background noise to me, since it had nothing to do with Ninja Turtles or Transformers. Moreover, I had yet to connect his name to his effect on the city's Black citizens. I remember feeling compelled to call my uncle out for saying a bad word, but my childish motivations quickly dissolved when my mother turned to him, her furrowed brow telegraphing her concern, imploring him to please watch himself. "You gotta be careful out here, Glenn, these white folks don't play!" Her impassioned plea was triggered not only by her worry for her only brother, a recent transplant from the Midwest, but also because of what turned out to be an exhaustive search by police for the gunman.

My mother was well aware of the inherent dangers presented by a rabid Boston, having arrived in the city at the height of the busing crisis in the early 1970s. A woman well versed in the city's history, she once pointed out with pride the William Lloyd Garrison House, nestled a stone's throw from my childhood home on Highland Street in Roxbury. That Garrison, the tireless abolitionist and editor of *The Liberator*, was instrumental in the struggle to end slavery is notable. Just as important, his altruism and advocacy placed him in the crosshairs of a morally stunted Boston mob: several thousand dragged him through its cobblestone streets, he fortunately escaping the threat of tar and feathers and grave injury on Boston Common. Thus, a century and a half prior to Stuart, neither my mother, nor anyone with half a brain could ignore that racially motivated violence in this town was an old tune. That a leading 19th-century intellectual, a white man, could be on the receiving end of such malevolence suggested the high potential for incomprehensible calamity to ensue once the gloves really came off.

For a city that loved to celebrate its often-brutal past, learned, perceptive people like my mother knew, on a cellular level, that its unlearned, unfeeling citizens possessed the particular willfulness necessary to *repeat* that history. In no way would she prove more prescient than now as police would start pulling Black men out of cars and department stores, off of busses and out of buildings, shaking down entire swaths of the city, violating civil rights as they doggedly, determinedly chased the shadows. It did not matter if it was Roxbury or the whiter section of Dorchester where we now resided, a fact likely reinforcing our fears since blue-collar ignorance of a different sort had already made itself known on our block. All I know is that for several weeks, while Stuart convalesced, the streets sizzled like a fuckin' frying pan. White folks turned up the heat alright, and it felt like we would all burn before it was over.

Race having derailed Governor Dukakis's national ambitions, it was only a matter of time until Boston Mayor Ray Flynn would feel the tension. His own administration and thinly masked political aspirations would be affected by a failure to reconcile not only our city's issues regarding race but, in this specific instance, how seriously these issues had been compounded under his stewardship. As Jim Vrabel has highlighted in *A People's History of the New Boston*, Flynn had already alienated Roxbury residents when they discovered his "secret plan" to redevelop Dudley Square. But it was his laissez-faire attitude with respect to policing that sealed his reputation among Black residents and, ultimately, his political fate. "All the progress that had been made to heal the city's racial wounds was jeopardized in Flynn's second term," Vrabel writes. "First by the Boston Police Department's implementation of a 'stop and search' policy to try to combat the crack cocaine epidemic that was sweeping Boston and other American cities at the time, and then by the handling of the bizarre Stuart case."

This tragedy of Shakespearean proportions played out to a dramatic conclusion one cold, grey January day. Walking loudly and unaware into the kitchen, I was promptly told to shut up. This theme would play out again and again throughout my childhood, whenever I walked in while major events were on TV, the adults all glued to the screen. It happened when Magic Johnson abruptly retired from basketball and, shortly after, when the cops in the Rodney King case were acquitted. This one evening, as we watched a little black-and-white set on the kitchen counter, the ghastly image was of Charles Stuart's body being pulled from the Mystic River for the world to see. He had flung himself off the Tobin Bridge after his brother revealed that Charles was the one who had killed Carol, her unintended pregnancy and his fear of the financial strain motivating her murder. He had attempted to cover it up by reaching for race, knowing that his lie would spark the hallucinations necessary to obscure his crime. That day remains with me some thirty years later, the lie at the center of the television screen bigger than all the lives touched directly and indirectly by this tragedy. One man's objective evil had telegraphed a society's failings, reducing both grave sins to Black and white.

Women routinely suffer abuse at the hands of men like Rob Porter and Charles Stuart, men they *know*, despite any prevailing narrative to the contrary, the convenient foil of stereotype presenting public cover for any number of heinous private transgressions. But halfway through the year 2017, rumblings turned to a chorus and began to shake the lies, shattering the pristine images that far too many men had cultivated in service of perpetrating their misdeeds. A growing cacophony of women rose to a crescendo, drowning out those preposterous cries and forcing many men to experience karma in action.

When #MeToo became a hashtag, shaking the firmament on which the patriarchy had been constructed, the seismic shift may have appeared to come out of nowhere, but this upending actually arrived after building momentum over many years. In fact, civil rights activist Tarana Burke had coined the term "Me Too" over a decade earlier to raise awareness of the prevalence of sexual assault in our society.

Movie producer Harvey Weinstein became the first notable name attached to what eventually became a national reckoning. It would elicit a much-needed purging—a moment long overdue given the centuries-old abuses systematically leveled against women. Yet just a short time earlier, it would have been nearly impossible to imagine the cavalcade of women now coming forward and finding their voices, exposing the systemic predation carried out by legions of gutless males.

In many ways, it was the new virtual highway of communication that helped morph the moment into a full-fledged movement. The traditionally powerless now began tapping into a platform devoid of gatekeepers or diminishers, the almost unfettered power of social media indispensable to shaping our social discourse, to *amplifying* long-suppressed voices. It has proved a welcome assist in creating an expansive network for women to share their stories and concerns, while also building a community of support connected and strengthened through its awesome global reach.

On my own Twitter timeline, increasingly peppered with testimonials from my followers, one woman's tale of what she had endured throughout her working life would be corroborated by another commenting on that post with her own story of abuse, sometimes at the hands of a family member or close confidante who used his familiarity, proximity, and reputation to inflict abuse.

I could not help but recognize the glaring parallels that ran through so many of these stories. A boss or a mentor, a coach or a teacher, even a stepparent, had waited, often in plain sight, for the right moment to exploit a relationship, a woman's vulnerability, or simply abuse the very power he wielded for the purely pathetic purpose of his own sexual gratification. It was eye opening and soul stirring to read about the reprehensible, unconscionable behavior of men whose moments of selfishness rippled over a lifetime for these women.

One of the most heart-wrenching lessons revealed by the outpouring on Twitter and Facebook was how brief encounters could create unending damage, one man's boorish misbehavior an albatross that his victims were then forced to carry with them. The weight of these encounters would tether the victims to a profound trauma indefinitely, this continuing pain and its many manifestations resembling the contours of PTSD. With the women in my own life rounding out this chorus, many sharing their pain for the first time, this moment would expand even further. It was a release as much as a reckoning, this existential concern exculpating the victims instead of the men whose actions had long gone unexamined, and been deemed inconsequential.

As social media gave this redressing a forum, the moment provided me and many other men opportunities to listen fully, to be present in new ways, forced to recognize how our own unprocessed attitudes contribute to this pervasive problem as the roles we occupy and do not contest are often predicated on the persistent subjugation of women's worth. Similar to the many ways in which racism remains uncontested due to the unconscious contributions of many within the white community, who remain detrimentally unaware of their privilege, I had to begin owning up to my own shortcomings and acknowledge how I too benefit from a position that elevates my wants and viewpoint at the expense of women. It is a familiar feeling, yet a tough pill to swallow, to bear witness as the women of the world, represented through social media's seemingly boundless reach, illuminate my own inherent biases and educate me on the bases of freedoms I enjoy. Like those white folks whose privilege often comes in spite of Black pain, my life, too, is grounded in a problematic paradigm.

Here is the awesome potential of #MeToo and #TimesUp, not simply to give some their warranted comeuppance, but to force upon men their necessary accountability. Just as important is the dialogue, the deep, nuanced conversations these moments generate with your average male, those who might not be hurting women but still have to recognize that they are likely not doing enough to improve the matter or *alleviate* hurt. That many women share their trauma for the first time means that many men now must digest a similarly revealing notion, facing the fact that, for a lot of us, this is the first time we actually stop to consider everything they endure.

This long-gestating change is bringing our society's colossal failings into focus along with our own unconscious indifference. Witnessing women heal invariably highlights the very blinders and behaviors we have adopted as males; in a world designed around their detriment, the great lesson is that, through increased awareness, we men might finally eschew old patterns and habits. Catcalls and wolf whistles, these sad heirlooms, this sort of mindless, adopted deportment that many men have almost blindly inherited, are in desperate need of reappraisal. And here the beautiful unforeseen benefits of our cultural reckoning are further realized as that more sentient society it is producing *improves* us, with many now encouraged to *not* pass down the wrong lessons or the worst kind of patrimony.

While women seek and receive a semblance of justice and many men learn the myriad of ways we have consistently failed them, we begin to experience the society we always had the promise to become: one evolving toward tolerance and accountability, equitability and respect. In the same historical moment, though, that image of what we can become is consistently, sadly obscured as the president and a phalanx of toxic forces engage us in an epic tug of war. Here, as revanchist forces bear down, progressives our forced to dig in our heels, day after day, as we fight tirelessly for the soul of this country.

If Trump's election marked an almost primal cry by that gray and dying network, recoiling from signs of racial parity, we can view their feverish resistance to #MeToo as a direct response to the growing remediation of patriarchy. Hillary Clinton's sizable popular vote win had undoubtedly brought this matter to the fore, augmenting those very substantial fears. Of interesting note, #ImWithHer and #ImStillWithHer was *still* trending frequently on Twitter more than a year *after* the election, a fact that likely unnerved Trump despite his repeated insistence that his electoral win was legitimate.

But it's pretty clear that Republicans don't dwell in the same world as the rest of us. This much became certain in 2017 as they appeared to rebuke our reality by promoting a slimy, sinister, serial rapist. When Roy Moore emerged as the Republican candidate in the special election to fill Jeff Sessions' vacated Senate seat, his path to victory appeared almost guaranteed after having beaten Luther Strange in the Alabama primary. Not only was Moore running in a deeply red state, but Trump had immediately transferred his support to him after the primary. Never mind that "strange" was a more fitting name for Moore, his subsequent campaign against Democrat Doug Jones would serve as a test of not only his viability but, in many ways, Trump's *own* influence less than a year into his presidency.

By all signs, Trump's own questionable past with women had not curtailed his political aspirations so, it was predictable, as multiple women now accused the former judge of inappropriate relationships, that Trump would double down on his endorsement even as some Republicans began shifting their support. Here the hollow GOP battle cry of "Drain the Swamp" reached ironic levels, as Moore, clad in a leather vest that only added to his snakelike, swamp-like reputation began barreling ingloriously toward the bog the GOP was promising to drain.

The embattled Trump, who desperately needed the sort of insulation that only a Republican senate majority could provide, soon began downplaying the litany of credible claims against Moore. His callous dismissal—"He says it didn't happen. You have to listen to him also"—echoed a prevailing theme. This inclination to not believe women but, conversely, the *harshest* men imaginable had now become the strident president's signature.

When nine women came forward to reveal Moore's host of violations against them, ranging from sexual assault when they were underage to his relentless pursuit of inappropriate relationships with them as teenagers, his history came to resemble that of the very president supporting him. Trump's own troubling behavior of walking in on scantily clad beauty contestants seemed to mirror Moore's now heavily publicized past transgressions in which he was known to troll high schools and local malls in the '70s and '80s—with reports even emerging that one or more of these locales had actually *banned* him outright for his illicit behavior. But that one man's word could be given credence over the voices of several women was not only a page ripped right out of Trump's playbook, it turned out to be the glue binding all patriarchy.

Still, with the eyes of the country, and the world, trained on Alabama, the Republican machine worked overtime to stuff their ill-fitting candidate into an empty Senate seat. Here, the square peg of Moore's candidacy became juxtaposed against the image of his more dynamic and deserving Democratic rival. Doug Jones's history of implementing desegregation measures signaled that this election *could* represent a righteous remediation of the racist Sessions.

Jones's eventual and unexpected win—in spite of Trump's full throated support of Moore—in a state, it should be noted, Hillary Clinton had lost by 28 points, signaled a monumental victory for the soon-to-be senator *and* for progressives countrywide.

Significantly, when Jones became the first Democrat to represent Alabama in the Senate in twenty years, African American voters and, specifically, African American women, proved instrumental in dragging the state forward. They got the electorate out to vote, and Jones pulled off a narrow victory, winning by only *two* percentage points. African Americans comprised roughly 30 percent of the state electorate, but 96 percent of Black voters cast ballots for Jones (a two percent increase in turnout following the 2012 general election). His success is attributable to the grassroots canvassing carried out in areas like Birmingham, Montgomery, and Tuscaloosa, but more specifically, to the work of those aforementioned women. Notably, this block of the Democratic Party consistently shows up to the polls *and* encourages others to follow suit—possessing a fearlessness that underscores the often extreme measures taken to suppress black turnout.

Whether it was Barack Obama or Bill Clinton, Jimmy Carter or Lyndon Johnson, the success of the Democratic Party—in Alabama and throughout the nation—is tethered to this faction of female leadership, even if the same women have gone mostly unacknowledged or, at best, insufficiently appreciated for their impact in fortifying the base. Ida B. Wells and Fannie Lou Hamer, Claudette Colvin and Rosa Parks—American society is defined by the tireless political activism and civil rights work that women of color have selflessly engaged in, particularly in a subversive South. I would even argue that this collective of women consistently saves this nation *from* itself. Having had the privilege of traveling throughout the South to meet a number of activists who had played crucial roles in the Civil Rights Movement, many who remain active in politics, I can personally testify to the awesome force wielded by women of color who put boots on the ground in *every* election, whether for something as big as Congress or as small as comptroller. With ignorance blanketing much of the South like the kudzu along a Mississippi highway, this invasive species obscuring objective truth, it is active community participation—those staffing phone banks, knocking on doors, conducting voter education workshops, and getting folks to and from the polls—that is making the difference in the Democratic Party's ability to pull out victories, *despite* the odds.

Make no mistake: Black women are the oil that makes the Democratic machine run. Though often relegated to the backseat in more ways than one, they steer us *away* from calamity when it comes to unmitigated disasters like Roy Moore, leaving little question as to *who* is driving the country forward. But that Moore dominated in rural pockets of the state, especially among white voters and even college-educated white women, evinces our great cultural divide. Despite Jones' improbable victory—despite it being objectively clear *who* was the better candidate, as was the case with Clinton's campaign against Trump—that men who abuse women routinely run neck and neck with women and their advocates reveals a distressing dynamic about power and the continuing effects of toxic masculinity on our politics. That Clinton accumulated three million more votes than Trump yet lost in several states where white women carried the corrosive candidate over the finish line signals that it is time for Americans to engage in a more nuanced, more difficult national conversation about *why* exactly we are regressing as a society.

Cyrus McQueen @CyrusMMcQueen · Jul 14, 2018
I still can't get over Gohmert's pointed remarks at Peter Strzok... Thank God for Bonnie Watson Coleman. Where would this world be without Black women to cut through the bullshit and call it like it is... "Uh uh, you are outta line! You BEEN outta line! You take your medication?"

↻ 1282 ♡ 4867

Though no group is monolithic in its voting, the number of white women who vote against their own best interests is in many ways reflective of the overall success the GOP enjoys aligning economically depressed voters with their free-market platform. Though these sorts of electoral curiosities have long impinged progress, in the era of #MeToo, with the remediation of misogyny and patriarchy very much on the ballot, and a diverse, convincing cross-section of women emerging, many anticipated that unifying voice to rebut such inane trends. Yet 63 percent of white women cast ballots for the undeniably disgusting Moore, compared with the 98 percent of the state's Black female voters who went for Jones. This profound disconnect indicates just how and why the grip of toxic white men endures. The role of race in our politics, and in the history of wealth consolidation, cannot of course be minimized. In many ways, it is as responsible for shaping party affiliations as the groupthink that permeates pockets where economic power overshadows those entrenched patterns pertaining to gender roles—that which prevents women, even white women, from wielding unfettered sociopolitical power.

It is discomfiting to recognize that even among women in the era of #MeToo, there is such a discernible difference between women of color and white women in this respect. All too often, the contours of feminism take on a different depth depending on which dynamic voice captures that all-too-elusive megaphone. Although abuse is doled out nearly equally—no female escaping this societal scourge, no woman unaffected by those forces that prioritize boys in boardrooms, bedrooms, and classrooms—the reactions to those legitimate concerns are often, sadly, commensurate with the race of the victims. Often women of color suffer doubly because, beyond our fucked-up gender roles, their race and ethnicity compound their plight, rendering them invisible despite their noticeable suffering. Because they are Black or Latino, no one seems to *hear* them scream. The #MeToo movement Tarana Burke started in 2006 gained national attention only after the notoriety of so many men made these cases, and the cause, more newsworthy. And while discussions about the movement have grown to encompass a larger conversation surrounding how stardom and the corrupting, enabling forces of fame and wealth in many ways facilitates abuse, a necessary, more nuanced discussion needs to be had about *why* women of color, and their plaintive cries, remain unheard.

From inner cities to rural counties, domestics and undocumented women workers toiling away in low-wage jobs endure unconscionable abuse without resources in place to combat workplace harassment, their plight often exacerbated by a socioeconomic reality that keeps them ostensibly powerless. The historic horrors of bondage aside, where bay windows and fainting couches often provided a peek into our discomfort from a comfortable remove, white women in the Western world have invariably benefitted from a narrative that prioritizes their looks, lives, and voices, their perspectives and, yes, even their pain, over their more diverse counterparts whose race and femininity are fetishized if not ignored by an editorial and entertainment juggernaut that relegates them to the back pages and the background of the American consciousness. Whether it is sexual mistreatment or the slipshod manner with which the medical establishment has handled many women of color—as just one example, *ProPublica* reports that Black women are 49 percent more likely to deliver prematurely than white women—implicit and explicit biases affect every area and stage of these women's lives.

Historically, this chasm between white and Black progressive women's movements existed long before message boards and smart phones could telegraph the gulf, long before suffrage even, as the nascency of feminism in America, linked initially to temperance and religion, became increasingly tethered to race. The 19th Amendment was ratified upon the backdrop of a record number of lynchings, the murders of African Americans resulting from that combustible formula of white fear and the fallacy of Black male predation. Thus, white feminism would almost solely be defined by the adjective separating it from the sisterhood of all. With Separate but Equal thriving for nearly another half-century post-suffrage, African American women had to wait for women's rights to encompass them—the weeds of division inhibiting any widespread growth.

Cyrus McQueen @CyrusMMcQueen · Jul 14, 2018
Black domestics been taking care of white folks children for centuries... then those same children grow up and don't take care of black folks... 🙌

♻ 105   ♡ 581

In no way has this schism been more apparent than in the 2018 candidacy of Stacey Abrams. That year, the Georgia Democrat and former state representative ran an impressive, effective campaign for governor, embodying not only the tumultuous history of Black political activity in the South, but also the tenacity and will power required to combat the ever-evolving forces of voter suppression. The daughter of Civil Rights workers, Abrams knew all too well the pernicious attempts to disenfranchise Black Southerners through gerrymandering and a host of underhanded methods. Depressingly, her neck-and-neck race against a Republican—his own candidacy strengthened *by* said methods— would see sharp practice used to again neutralize a Black Democrat. These sorts of Southern shenanigans, this kinda modernized monkey-business, saw literacy tests now replaced with "exact match" policies. Where at one time, a grandfather clause could use your own grandfather's last name against you, in our new era, your ballot could be discarded based on the difference between, say, McQueen on one document and Mc Queen on another. Craven methods long utilized to hamstring progress—be it having to state the number of beans in a jar or the bubbles in a bar of soap—had been all but transformed, reemerging to again nullify a significant portion of the Black electorate.

Brian Kemp, Abrams' opponent, in his other role as Georgia Secretary of State, had the audacity to withhold 53,000 voter registrations, the vast majority of which belonged to African Americans. Thus, Blacks make up one-third of Georgia's electorate yet withstand *all* of the discrimination. Considering that only 54,723 votes separated Abrams and Kemp, it was unequivocal: the secretary of state used his office unfairly to gain a victory. Subsequently, a U.S. district court judge would declare that the Atlanta suburb of Gwinnett County had violated the Civil Rights Act of 1964, while another U.S. District Court Judge went on to declare that rejecting the absentee ballots *was* unconstitutional. Yet the myriad of methods employed to maintain white rule, including racist robocalls and disinformation campaigns, unfortunately did the trick. Abrams eventually, and reluctantly, conceded even though the Republicans' voter suppression efforts *would* go on to be verified.

That a brilliant Black woman succumbed to concerted attempts to minimize her unmistakable effectiveness is yet one more reminder of those debilitating racial dynamics at play in our politics. And it signifies the reforms necessary for clearing these almost insurmountable hurdles moving forward.

But malfeasance aside, with white women in Georgia voting for Kemp by a 3 to 1 margin, it clearly suggested that Abrams' race, *not* her gender, had galvanized them to cast ballots against their own best interests. By factoring in the large number of African American women who not only supported Abrams but Hillary in 2016, it telegraphs that Black women's support for white female candidates is not in question in American politics; the real question appears to be, when will white women bring themselves to fully support Black women? This gulf between Black and white, reflecting our centuries-long divide, goes a long way toward explaining what blocked both Abrams *and* Hillary from ultimately attaining power.

Like those African American conservatives who enjoy economic success, and who parrot the principles of the ruling class despite its deleterious impact on our community, those women who voted in large numbers for Trump, Moore, or Kemp suggest the need to identify and defeat comparable coopting forces in favor of one penetrative, truly unifying political voice. The Republican platform and the role of *Roe v. Wade* in shaping the politics of many women undoubtedly contributes to this chasm, especially in the South, but as long as this moralistic stance overshadows the greater issue which is men's control over women's reproductive destiny—we will see the power of all men continuing to come at a cost to women everywhere.

17

And Still I Rise

That a woman's right to choose now stands on precarious footing is attributable to the fluidity and interpretation of our laws, but mostly, it is a testament to the unrelenting desire of those in power to retain godlike supremacy despite their own fallibility. This conversation, despite the monumental 1973 *Roe v. Wade* ruling, has never been put to bed. Much like the Second Amendment still provides men with the power to destroy, this very decision disrupts their insatiable desire to control who gets to *live*. Again, this belief that women's bodies are inconsequential, even upon conception, their inherent power imperiled by the conception of men's absolute power, means that the dialogue long surrounding abortion, and its recurrence year after year after year, is less about women's rights and can be more accurately framed as men's irrepressible, incorrigible designs on that right.

White men in America have historically claimed the right to choose who procreates and who perishes, who is important and who is not, who matters and who does *not*. That Supreme Court ruling wrested a crucial power from the hands of these men. The resulting decades of discourse around this *settled* issue, with Georgia, Missouri, Louisiana, Alabama, and other states enacting restrictive, absolutely bonkers abortion bills, indicates how deeply that decision has unmoored these small-minded men. Many had gotten so drunk on that power that when a drunk teenager and future judge exercised this inferred control over a woman's body, it placed his destiny on a collision course with the future of women.

It is difficult to discuss Brett Kavanaugh and the seat he now fills on the U.S. Supreme Court without first mentioning Merrick Garland, whose nomination to that lofty position Mitch McConnell and a Republican-led Senate stonewalled, enabling Neil Gorsuch to become Trump's first conservative nominee to fill a vacancy on the High Court. The Republican plan to stack federal courts with right-wing judges had been playing out so successfully that by the time Kavanaugh, the binge-drinking, privileged poster boy of Chesapeake Bay, became Trump's second nominee to the bench, it was almost a foregone conclusion that the Senate would confirm him. But where few outside legal circles had questioned Gorsuch's merits for the High Court, the problematic predilections of Kavanaugh, his fellow Georgetown Prep alumni, made the question of overall *fitness* a topic of national debate.

It was no mystery that Kavanaugh's appointment would create a conservative majority on the court, this conspicuous outcome clearly influencing McConnell's decision to block Garland. Yet that Kavanaugh would hold the decisive vote potentially upending *Roe v. Wade* now further polarized an already *severely* polarized American populace. With a slight Republican majority in the Senate and considering what Kavanaugh represented in terms of conservatives' designs on upending precedent and reversing decades of progress, his confirmation hearing would rank among the most consequential and closely watched proceedings ever.

By now, Trump's support for the worst men had become both a pattern and of great concern. Kavanaugh's confirmation and, moreover, his belief in unfettered executive power, were portentous—a move likely to insulate Trump from being removed from office. The president's bureaucrats had come more to reflect our fractured times and the fractured man behind these questionable nominations than any discernible sense of virtue or civic duty. All this set the stage for a monumental showdown as these outstanding concerns would reveal an ineradicable divide; the court of public opinion now enlisted to help decide the judge's future. In a hyper-partisan congressional landscape, however, the decision over Kavanaugh's fate rested in the hands of one hundred senators, that lingering disquiet concerning not simply his worthiness but *what* he represented. Just days after it became known he would, in fact, be Trump's choice to replace Anthony Kennedy on the bench, an event from his buried past, and the pain that it had created in one woman's life, would be unearthed and telecast for the world to see.

Before Christine Blasey Ford relayed her story of being sexually assaulted by Brett Kavanaugh to Congresswoman Anna Eshoo—before it was then brought to the attention of Senator Dianne Feinstein—she had kept the torturous memory mostly secret for over thirty-five years. Her desire to retain her confidentiality was compromised only after media rumblings concerning new allegations against Kavanaugh led reporters to her door. She then made the painful decision to go public, telling her truth to *The Washington Post*.

Ford's bravery in relaying her story of the assault, at the home of a mutual friend when she was 15 years old, is undeniable. Her revelation—Kavanaugh had pinned her down, covered her mouth, and groped and violated her—was difficult enough to hear, yet she further disclosed an added fear: given his heavy inebriation, he could very well have suffocated her in the process. That his ne'er-do-well accomplice would relish in this assault, their laughter adding insult to grave injury, their boorish revelry a disdainful accoutrement to their criminal behavior, is what stood out most in Ford's testimony.

That Kavanaugh had been spoiled rotten by circumstance—his privileged life attending private schools where overindulgence and unaccountability stunted maturation and contributed to his self-centeredness *and* self-destructiveness—made Ford's revelations not only believable but, given what soon emerged about his time at Yale, indicative of the kind of conduct that appears to be the norm in those elite circles. When Ford could not escape the microscope of a Senate Judiciary Committee hearing, her truth, and its meaning for women everywhere, would expose our nation's outstanding issues with sexual violence.

Most of us first saw the Stanford psychology professor at her swearing in for the Senate hearing. The proceedings, presenting the only hurdle on Kavanaugh's fast track toward the Supreme Court, meant her own life would yet again be impacted by his privileged trajectory. The stakes could not have been higher as Ford shouldered an almost impossible burden. Her veracity was no match for the machinery in place to undermine her testimony, including Trump's heartless tweet that, were the allegations true, she would have reported them at the time. Chumming the waters, Trump almost ensured that not only would conservatives toe the line, but also that a feeding frenzy would deny her any semblance of justice in the heavily partisan proceedings. That the FBI did not conduct the thorough investigation she requested prior to her appearance meant that politics would taint this moment and her truthful admission, her legacy defined less by what she revealed and more by what her testimony would reveal about our nation and our politics.

Left to our own eyes and minds to judge, Ford's immediate impression and subsequent testimony cannot be mistaken. She was believable. As Ford relayed the events in that bedroom, she transported me—and every sentient observer—back to that summer afternoon in Bethesda, Maryland in 1982. Her honesty would only be underscored by Kavanaugh's grandstanding hours later, the boozehounds babble helping only to buttress her sobering testimony. The past bringing them together for this moment of reckoning made her truth that much more pronounced, especially when those watching from home juxtaposed it with his juvenile posturing.

This brilliant academic and mother, navigating a torturous past in real time before a Republican-led Senate likely to disregard her honesty, made my heart ache. In that moment, she was my mother and sister, my wife and friend; she was every woman made to suffer in silence—a woman who, by exposing her truth knew it only exposed her again to those very men that our patriarchal system enables and protects.

Ford's testimony, her heart-wrenching yet clinical description of her violation at Kavanaugh's hands, answering in excruciating detail questions about not just the nature of the assault but also how she processed it, how it *seared* into her memory, would not be easily forgotten. Her probity was that palpable, her story *that* resonant. Yet Republicans would waste little time turning the momentous proceedings into political theatre. By casting Rachel Mitchell, a career prosecutor, to cross examine Ford, Senate Majority Leader Mitch McConnell assigned the political hack the task of not simply questioning the professor but, of ostensibly, *upstaging* her. Though both were women, only Ford was working on behalf of women that day. This awful theme, which had played out in the general election and in state politics, in the news media and on morning television, stood front and center once more as conservative females would again play a crucial role in thwarting advancement. But where Trump's success would be tied to Kavanaugh's, their troubling pasts and power grabs uniting them, women like Mitchell played a pivotal part in ultimately diminishing the danger these men pose. Under the fire of these hired female guns, we would again see women's progress succumbing to self-inflicted wounds.

Arizona Senator Jeff Flake temporarily ran interference for Ford, promising to hold out his vote in favor of an FBI investigation into her claims. Yet it was a promise as hollow as his ill-fated walk across the aisle to temporarily halt the Kavanaugh vote. Flake merely turned the moment into a matter of self-aggrandizement *instead* of a thorough appraisal of the ill-suited judge. Thus, it was only after he stated his intention to vote "Yes" on Kavanaugh that Ana Maria Archila and Maria Gallagher, two fearless and undeterred activists, acted, confronting the spineless senator in an elevator. Adding yet another indelible moment to the already memorable proceedings, Archila pleaded with the senator that she "recognized in Dr. Ford's story that she is telling the truth." She continued: "What you are doing is allowing someone who actually violated a woman to sit on the Supreme Court. This is not tolerable. You have children in your family. Think about them."

This incredible scene, it capturing the gravity of what Kavanaugh represented and what this moment meant to the lives of all women, even those in Flake's life, would leave the namby-pamby senator exposed. His inability to even look Archila in the eye magnified the egregiousness of the GOP effort. It would betray his utter flaccidness as a man and as an elected voice, his inability to live up to his awesome responsibility corroborated days later when, living up to his *name*, he flaked—changing his "conditional vote" into a "Yes."

Flake aside, Senator Lisa Murkowski, a Republican from Alaska, went on to issue an expedient yet principled "No" vote on Kavanaugh. However, all hope was quickly crushed when Maine Senator Susan Collins would make a similarly expedient yet unprincipled vote to place the beer-loving bastard on the bench. The Collins vote pointed to yet another uncomfortable truth in an episode marred by uncomfortable truths. Those men opposed to female autonomy could sadly, maddeningly, continue along their ignoble path because a handful of conservative women, empowered to cripple that cause, aided them. The lasting image of the proceedings would be Collins leaving the country hanging on every muffled word in her long, prattling way to a " Yes." Much like Governor Kay Ivey would later do when signing a bill making

253

it a felony to perform an abortion in Alabama even in cases of rape or incest, the nation would have to sit back and watch as a powerful woman proved instrumental in undermining the power of *all* women.

Cyrus McQueen @CyrusMMcQueen · Oct 5, 2018
I don't know what's shakier, Susan Collins voice or her morals... #FridayFeeling

♻ 439   ♡ 1756

As the world witnesses renewed attacks on women in legislature after legislature, the decisions of those like Collins and Ivey are proving impactful. With the spate of TRAP laws—Targeted Regulation of Abortion Providers—states have begun methodically chipping away at women's reproductive rights throughout the country. As Republicans do all they can to suppress the Black and Brown population through sentencing laws, deportations, and family separation, it stands to reason that the very people they seek to chasten when it comes to abortions are those white females also critical to that sustained majority. In other words, white control, this centuries-old campaign, is realized only *by* controlling the bodies of women and people of color. It is a paradigm I cannot help but re-highlight considering the clamor to pack courts with judges that will uphold this tacit objective. For conservatives, the tomb and the womb represent viable avenues for limiting diverse life on the one hand, and growing white life on the other. One can easily argue *this* has been the driving force behind our laws and our politics for the past fifty years. But whether patriarchy sustains prejudice or prejudice ultimately sustains patriarchy, the end result is the same: All women lose.

Central to this issue are attacks on Planned Parenthood, which provides a multitude of invaluable health services to our nation's women. From cancer screenings and infertility services, to STD testing and treatment options, its clinics are integral to ensuring that American women receive great general care and health education. Planned Parenthood's critics have long obscured the overwhelming necessity of the organization's services to all women. And if Republicans have their way, forcing many more women to have babies they cannot care for, it introduces a consequential subtext to this discussion. Because pursuing an education and a career track places women in direct competition with men, it is easy to discern *whose* primary interests are served by keeping them as second-class citizens—or in this instance, pregnant and resultantly, *out* of the workforce. Anything that takes the onus off men, while simultaneously making it harder for women to advance economically, is too conspicuous to dismiss.

Thus, the decision concerning a woman's choice—and therefore who sits on the Supreme Court—extends beyond misleading language surrounding embryos and when life forms, and everything else it has been reduced to. It is a decision concerning the future of the country, with ramifications not simply for women but for the nation's wealth inequities, a chasm that only promises to worsen. It is no mystery that Republicans are loath to fund Head Start, support paid family leave, or endorse commonsense welfare initiatives in conjunction with all these babies being born. Quite the contrary, if left to their own devices, they would force women at or below the poverty line into an even more precarious financial predicament, the ability to climb out of said trouble, or even survive, implausible.

"Pro-life" has proven a far more persuasive moniker than pro-exploitation, though the latter seems to better describe their aims. Fettering social mobility, securing an underclass, ensures that a baby born into a world without many options will be left to the mercies of those who have set themselves up to capitalize on those vulnerabilities. It has become painfully apparent that their plan to use you later can only be accomplished by using your mother now.

Cyrus McQueen @CyrusMMcQueen · Oct 6, 2018
Daylight Savings came early this year... We basically turned the clocks back five decades... #KavanaughConfirmed ⌐ https://t.co/fBlazOgdod ⌐

⇄ 330   ♡ 894

If the 2016 election set the stage for Republicans to stifle progress, the 2018 midterms presented an occasion for our country to begin purging itself of the poison slowly eating away at our identity. Though tales of a Blue Wave had been hyped, even sensationalized, pre-election, the outcome of the midterms, marked a country that was on the road to recovery. In spite of that debilitating loss two years prior, we were finding, rather fittingly, that this fight for the future of our nation was indeed being led by a diverse, dynamic, and determined cadre of women.

Though Trump's rise seemed to telegraph a trend where conservative causes and candidates were becoming viable the world over, the shock of his far-right brand of nationalism soon *invigorated* a new generation of progressive leadership. As I watched the election returns from my living room, that most scintillating quote from Maya Angelou came roaring to mind: "You may write me down in history with your bitter, twisted lines. You may trod me in the very dirt, but still, like dust, I'll rise." Great purpose had been enkindled in our nation. Like a veritable phoenix emerging from the burning embers Trump's fiery tenure had caused, Democrats went on to capture 41 seats on this night, transforming not only the House of Representatives but several state legislatures in the process.

This historic election was even more remarkable considering that many historic firsts were ushered in with this new Congress. On the night of November 6, we witnessed the election of the first openly bisexual U.S. Senator, Kyrsten Sinema of Arizona, and the first openly gay U.S. governor, Jared Polis of Colorado. A GOP whose anti-LGBTQ+ stance defines its pitiful platform lost seats of power to the very people who, through fear mongering, it so fervently oppresses. Sinema's presence even suggested at first a loosening of Mitch McConnell's death grip on the Senate, although the GOP actually gained seats with the defeats of North Dakota's Heidi Heitkamp and Missouri's Claire McCaskill, among others. Still, even these losses were tempered by the incredible gains transforming the House of Representatives, turning the election into a referendum on not only Trump but also the patrimony of white males on our electoral politics.

It is important to reiterate that the results of the 2018 midterms can never be viewed outside the context of the 2016 election and its unfortunate outcome. Nevertheless, that the GOP's attempts to stifle change and silence Hillary's voice led women across the country to find theirs, many seizing office for the first time, means that those concerted efforts to end one woman's promise created a glorious kerfuffle. Hence, we can reframe the story of the election: it was the historical occasion when, because one woman had been held back, many more moved forward.

Indeed, we had searched for solace in the first twenty-four months after Trump rose and the rest of us fell, as GOP control of both houses of Congress—in addition to the judicial branch—left the Left with very little wiggle room. We watched the tempestuous man-baby shit all over our Constitution and use its pages to wipe himself, his petulance that much more untenable with Mitch McConnell and House Majority Leader Paul Ryan, heads of a coequal branch of government, abdicating their responsibilities. By empowering this bum-ass president, their coddling yielded tax breaks for the wealthy and a dramatic conservative intrusion into our federal courts.

Yet the reality of having a fractious president with unchecked power, *is* what engendered the huge midterm turnout. The results in New York, Massachusetts, Michigan, and Minnesota immediately telegraphed the seismic shift occurring in the House of Representatives. Upon realizing we would now have congresswomen named Alexandria, Ayanna, Rashida, and Ilhan, my heart nearly leapt out my damn chest! Dude, I fuckin *danced* into the kitchen to refill my wine.

It is difficult to overstate my joy in seeing this new congressional landscape. After we had traveled through the deepest of tunnels, these women, with their pride and their inimitable incandescence, promised to lead us all out of the darkness. That the nation elected its first Muslim congresswomen in Rashida Tlaib and Ilhan Omar, its youngest ever congresswoman in Alexandria Ocasio-Cortez, and its first African American congresswoman from Massachusetts in Ayanna Pressley—the undeniable progress that these women represented felt that much more profound given the regression it summarily signaled for Republicans. That the aforementioned freshmen, along with Jahana Hayes, the first Black congresswoman from Connecticut, Illinois Representative Lauren Underwood, the youngest Black woman to serve in Congress, in addition to Kansas Representative Sharice Davids and New Mexico Representative Deb Haaland, the nation's first Native American congresswomen, respectively, had *all* seized power, their victories felt even sweeter upon news that the number of Republican women in the House fell by ten. Seeing congresswomen who looked like you committed to fighting *for* you was awe inspiring—especially in contrast to those jaw dropping photos they would often release of GOP Congresspeople. Those snapshots of homogenous House members engulfed by their equally homogenous staffs always felt like staring into a glacier—this feeling confirmed by the chills these pictures would usually send down your spine.

Representation truly matters! It is impossible not to feel a kinship with these freshwoman representatives, given their brilliance, boldness, and the undeniable fact that they succeeded in an electoral system that often excludes candidates like them almost exclusively because of race and gender.

I feel a particular fondness for Ms. Pressley, the new congresswoman out of Massachusetts, not just because she represents my hometown but because she unseated Mike Capuano, a 20-year

Democratic incumbent, in a race hardly anyone thought she should run yet alone could win. But earlier she had created an opening by consolidating a base in Roxbury, Dorchester, and Mattapan, forging an impressive grassroots ground game in that oft-overlooked section of inner-city Boston to become the first Black woman elected to the Boston City Council. I am awestruck by Pressley and those in her congressional class mostly because, in cities like Boston, with their deeply entrenched political patterns and dynasties, such "audacity of hope"—to borrow the title of Barack Obama's book—made the difference in their forging long-gestating change.

When the traditionally powerless become powerful, as had played out on a national level with Obama's election, the traditionally powerful struggle to reconcile how a person like that could skirt every booby trap and succeed. That is when the privileged call into question notions of hard work, merit, and aptitude, and, in the case of Obama, something even as irrefutable as a birth certificate. Yet here we have Congresswoman Pressley, who dropped out of Boston University to work at a hotel to support her mother, and Congresswoman Ocasio-Cortez, who graduated from BU and then worked in the service industry to support herself and her family, completely undermining the paradigm of privilege whilst, conversely, establishing themselves as true paragons of virtue. Both women have subverted the traditional road to power and prosperity in America.

Comparable to how diversification—whether in education, entertainment, politics, or, for that matter, any field—often inspires the privileged to cry foul, that women of color succeeded inspired childish, churlish attempts to besmirch them. In an era of gerrymandering and redistricting, measures that ensure progress ebbs rather than flows, it did not take long for these triumphant women to become embattled. Soon, those at war with progress seized on their newest target: Alexandria Ocasio-Cortez.

Cyrus McQueen @CyrusMMcQueen · Jul 1, 2019
I don't wannna hear shit about AOC, a young Latina who overachieved in America where she never had the benefit of the wind being at her sails, while we celebrate Ivanka Trump who's importance has been inflated and who's lack of savoir faire has proven an international disgrace...

⟲ 2156　　♡ 9613

It is difficult to discuss the vitriol directed at a firebrand like AOC without first considering the qualities that so inflame the GOP's fearful attacks. Not only do her age and ethnicity place her at odds with a mostly homogenous and ancient collective of men, but just as noteworthy is her marrying this polarizing otherness with a fearless radicalism. That she was elected at the age of 29 certainly rankles that patronizing element within the patriarchy: they do not consider *any* woman as intellectually equal, let alone a woman of her age and background. Nor would they overlook that AOC, like Pressley, pulled off an incredible grassroots campaign in an oft-overlooked, diverse section of the inner city. And that she too unseated a ten-time incumbent many thought she had no business taking on to become the first of her generation to make it to Congress—and all before the age of thirty—augments their ire. It is this boldness—to not only seek power but to dare unseat a white male career politician, obliterating patterns of obsequiousness often associated with women and people of color mindlessly demurring to those who long occupied these roles—that *really* makes Ocasio-Cortez scary. When considering how unspoken rules control us all, that she came roaring out of the gates proudly declaring herself a democratic socialist, while proving herself a tireless advocate of the working class and the working poor—unapologetically, unabashedly, maintaining her belief in Medicare for all, abolishing ICE, and advocating for the Green New Deal—is why she became an enemy overnight to those dinosaurs diametrically opposed to her from across the aisle.

Imbalance is maintained through obedience: when this proud woman of color flipped the script, inspiring those born outside the predetermined parameters of privilege, she shocked not only New York but conservatives the world over. Echoing the catchphrase uttered decades earlier by Shirley Chisholm, the first Black woman elected to Congress, Ocasio-Cortez is too "unbought and unbossed." I felt heartened that AOC's meteoric rise in no way suggested the Bronx native would rest on her laurels, as she participated in a climate change protest outside Nancy Pelosi's chambers on her first day in Congress—this before going on to address the government shutdown in her very first speech on the House floor. I sat raptly as C-Span aired her memorable remarks: "The truth of this shutdown is that it's actually not about a wall, it is not about the border, and it's most certainly not about the well-being of everyday Americans. The truth is, this shutdown is about the erosion of American Democracy. And the subversion of our most basic governmental norms." *Chills.* Here she was highlighting the president's shortcomings in the face of these so-called men, those in his

Republican coterie who had done nothing but appease him, pointing out the irrefutable fact that *they* were sabotaging our democracy.

The GOP recognized that she was likely to erode the very foundation that had been fashioned at our expense. Consequently, their bleached-blonde propagandists and those in their bully pulpit began to paint the young congresswoman as a saboteur—this their unabashed attempt to hijack the narrative. It is truly ironic, if not hilarious, that overachieving politicians like Ocasio-Cortez, much like Obama, whose brilliance cannot be belittled, routinely, if not instinctually, are held in contempt by some of the most contemptuous, worthless individuals imaginable. And as occurred with the former president, the vengeful men and women within the GOP soon turned petulant. Like their comments on Obama's choice of hamburger garnish, we again saw them use the superficial to tarnish a superlative individual. Thus, Ocasio-Cortez's suit, like Obama's tan suit and his use of Dijon mustard, caused quite a commotion among conservatives who rushed to sully a spotless Democrat. AOC is the latest politician to prove that being meaningful is to be made to endure a myriad of meaningless attacks. But that her outfit would be deemed too expensive for the working-class hero only highlights the hollowness of her detractors. Pulling a page out of a prehistoric playbook, they tried to reduce her using some simple, sexist, and elitist criteria based solely on appearance. Here, I would be remiss in not repeating how greatly she overachieves in an America that chronically undervalues women of color like herself—a nation that has also shown a predilection for criminalizing and encaging Hispanic people. When their external appearance, cultural identity, and class affiliations do not otherwise find them incarcerated in the prison of stereotype, those like AOC upend these skewed narratives, thus forcing white conservatives to recalibrate.

We also cannot overlook the glaring reason the congresswoman distances herself from her haters. Having amassed an incredible following on social media, expertly tweeting truth to power, she could compound that appeal having *gained* traditional power—all this giving her an advantage over those critics whose lack of authentic engagement on these platforms leaves them vulnerable. With her clapbacks against the journalist who tried to create controversy around, of all things, her coat and jacket and, later, against those who tried to use an endearing video of her dancing while in college to weaponize the insignificant, the millennial congresswoman routinely *takes* power right back. When she eventually posted video of herself dancing right into her congressional office, Ocasio-Cortez undermined the insipid while her over four million Twitter followers enjoyed a laugh at their expense.

Cyrus McQueen @CyrusMMcQueen · Jan 4, 2019
Funny how they're tryna shame Alexandria Ocasio-Cortez for a video from when she was 18... if you wanted to view a video of Melania Trump when she was 18... well, you'd have to be over the age of 18... #FridayFeeling

♻ 3296   ♡ 9320

It is the clear threat these women pose—challenging white conservatives while also encouraging an as-yet-to-be quantified (but obviously significant) number of young women and men of color to follow in their footsteps—that led Louisiana's Republican Senator John Kennedy to label them the "Four Horsewomen of the Apocalypse." Even if Rep. Tlaib had not provided a riveting assessment of Trump, righteously intimating her desire and that of the Democratic camp to "impeach the motherfucker," her objectives would have likely ranked second to the fact that Muslim American women like herself and Rep. Omar won office in a country intolerant of that outcome. It is why a specific level of vitriol has been directed toward both congresswomen. Though ethnicity links all four freshwomen, the Muslim faith of Tlaib and Omar provides an undoubted accelerant in conservative circles. Conflating their religion and terrorism, the GOP seeks to continue exploiting the American deaths suffered on 9/11—their malignant politicking resulting in death threats to these women.

Yet amid ballyhoo chants of "send her back" among Trump's irascible rally goers, the congresswomen did not back down and, given their party's majority in the House, they subsequently gained leadership positions. Delightfully, AOC, Pressley, and Tlaib were soon serving on the Oversight Committee where, to the consternation of conservatives, Tlaib could now buttress her profane promise and actually *begin* investigating "the motherfucker."

Still, Tlaib's language and Ocasio-Cortez's dance moves proved far less material after Michael Cohen's congressional testimony revealed the true existential danger these House members posed for Trump. First, Cohen gave a quivering admission in response to AOC's pointed question about Trump's inflating the value of his assets in an attempt to defraud insurance companies. Then, his answer to her follow-up query, asking "who else" among Trump's staff knew about these manipulations, implicated Trump Organization executives Allen Weisselberg, Ron Lieberman, and Matthew Calamari. As a result, the president was less likely consumed by the race and religion of these women and more by the likelihood that, much like that nest atop his head whenever he embarked on Marine One, they were churning a mighty wind that threatened to lay bare his gross coverups.

In the face of his unyielding criminality, his administration would always look to distract through discrimination. His turning up the heat on the most vulnerable—the men, women, and children escaping penury to find themselves in a purgatory of his making along the Mexican border—would impel the new congresswomen to begin *defending* the defenseless. Trump making fodder of the innocent in an incessant attempt to feed his base, meant they had little time to waste when it came to addressing these human rights abuses.

Yet in the weeks following the Fantastic Four's visit to the southern border—where Rep. Pressley announced unflinchingly that the detainees "are welcome here! And that we love you! And that we will never stop fighting for your dignity, for your humanity, and for the preservation of your families"—Trump utilized all 280 characters at his disposal to tweet that the representatives should "go back and help fix the totally broken and crime infested places from which they came." The notion that he would declare that Tlaib, Pressley, and Ocasio-Cortez "originally came from countries whose governments are a complete and total catastrophe," given that these women hail from Detroit, Chicago, and New York, suggests that just as he had promulgated the lie linking an American-born Black president to Kenya and the Muslim Brotherhood, he was going to egregiously conflate these American-born elected officials with the very subjects he was seeking to delegitimize along the border.

These sorts of sweeping generalizations, this "one size fits all" racism is not uncommon from a president ignorant of facts and, more specifically here, *actual* geography. Given the starved minds within his constituency, Trump knew it necessary to simply feed their emotions—especially since they were never going to concern themselves with stubborn things like facts. Yet this sort of truculence is indeed telling. Where Trump delights in slamming two Muslim Americans, an African American, and a Latina, he was less inspired to roll up his sleeves and swing in quite the same way at the Jerry Nadlers, Adam Schiffs, and even the Nancy Pelosis in the House. Though equally critical of him, because they were *not* women of color, each represented a less desirable punching bag for the torpid Trump.

Unsurprisingly, AOC, Pressley, Omar, and Tlaib did not take these attacks lying down. No, they hit *back*. When the worldwide rebuke his racist tweets engendered led "the Squad," as they had affectionately been dubbed, to hold a press conference to address his hate, Rep. Pressley, cutting through Trump's bullshit like a hot knife through butter, implored us, the progressive community, to keep our guard up. "This is a distraction, this is a disruption on our leading and governing," she remarked, her well-timed counterpunch providing much-needed clarity and reminding us not to abandon all technique in an all-out brawl— especially when the bellicose president enjoyed hitting below the belt.

Cyrus McQueen @CyrusMMcQueen · Feb 27, 2019
In case you're missing it AOC, Ayanna Pressley, and Rashida Tlaib just got a buncha tighty whiteys tighty whiteys in a bunch... Rep Meadows tried to argue it was reverse racism to call out racism and Cummings had to bang the gavel and restore order... #DoMyLadiesRunThisMothafucka

⇅ 245   ♡ 1214

Although we can now deduce that Trump was alluding to Rep. Ilhan Omar when he mounted his hackneyed "go back to where you come from" offensive, the Somali-born congresswoman and, specifically, her Muslim faith was exactly the chum he needed to entice his followers. This is why he, again, reserves a special level of vitriol for the Minnesotan. Yet for a president and a political party aligned with men and women chanting "Jews will not replace us" to change bait in an effort to lure the base with this notion that Omar is anti-Semitic (and thereby anti-American), this tangle of lies, though apparently contradictory and thus invalid, *still* finds the fish jumping right into their boat. This Republican ploy to paint Omar as the enemy, given that those on the extreme right had already proven equal opportunists, shooting up both synagogues and mosques the world over, is not nearly as jaw-dropping as the corrosive idea that a woman of color, who had long ago emigrated to America, did not belong. Thus her religion and birthplace, though appearing to underlie this strain of Nationalism, is ultimately tertiary in my opinion. Given the godless bottom dwellers in the GOP's waters, and the unmissable African-American phenom in their midst, I believe their castigation is engendered mostly by gender and skin color.

This coarsening of political discourse is all the more curious when we consider how Trump's current wife Melania, herself an immigrant, helps promote this flawed, fucked-up double standard that suggests those like her somehow *do* belong. Considering the virulent xenophobia defining his administration, for Trump to pose that chain-migration is acceptable, at least as it pertains to those hailing from Eastern Europe, is downright infuriating. By positing that this Eurocentric fulcrum leaves those like Melania Trump beyond reproach—all while denying the same to accomplished women like Omar—leaves those like me bristling at a glaringly racist appraisal that once again applies a *lesser* value to darker Americans. The emaciated minds of his base assign more value to a nude model from Slovenia, no Einstein by any stretch, than to an astute African American woman elected by the voters of Minnesota's fifth congressional district. The GOP uses Omar's head scarf and Somali heritage to distract from her message and platform to eliminate student loan debt, provide a living wage, and make housing more affordable for all Americans—efforts that *should* ingratiate her with those drowning throughout middle America, the very men and women flooding Trump's rallies who have been left shipwrecked by the GOP's policies.

Comparable to Colin Kaepernick, whose crime is that he is not a criminal, Omar's transgression is that she is not a terrorist. America simply appears to have no room for a conscientious Black man or an impressive Muslim American woman who dares challenge conservative America's corrosive hypocrisy. They can only exist as the enemy and, as such, a woman who had picked up neither a bomb nor a machine gun has her words weaponized by the very man who, ironically, inspires his followers to pick up bombs and machine guns. It is all too easy to portray a U.S. congresswoman as anti-American because America cannot *see* her as anything else, despite her serving the United States in the House of Representatives. Just as the Trumpers usurped and used the flag against Kaepernick, almost overnight they declared the congresswoman to be an enemy of the people. Those very same folks on the far right—those who declare that "Jews will not replace us"—now play both sides of this incurable bifurcation within the American electorate. Through their shrewd duplicitousness, it continues to be "Us versus Them."

The Fantastic Four found themselves outsiders on Capitol Hill, however these congressional "firsts" differ little from others who have shattered societal barriers. That several members of the freshman class had the compounded burden of gender and ethnicity certainly undermined their arrival: thus, the argument was soon mounted that the women were somehow out of their element. This would even lead to articles in *Politico* in which one anonymous House Democrat was quoted, remarking of AOC, "She needs to decide: Does she want to be an effective legislator or just continue being a Twitter star?" Though haters are inherent to the topic of change, these sorts of comments, this kind of detractor, can be placed within a larger historical context. Whether it is Jackie Robinson integrating Major League Baseball, or even Barack Obama rising to the presidency, exemplary people of color are made to endure all kinds of carping. Thus, the emergence of true game changers sees every cudgel imaginable employed to dull their impact. As evinced by the anonymous House Democrat above, trailblazers will even see members of their own team try to cry foul—as did many of Robinson's fellow Dodgers early on. Though society invariably benefits from such growth, we should never underestimate how unsettling it is for some to witness that new ground being broken.

Yet, where women like Pressley and AOC bring to mind certain heroines, for me, their tenacity and reputations as fearless firsts evoke yet another indomitable woman who triumphed in a world that she was born to disrupt: my very own grandmother.

Cyrus McQueen @CyrusMMcQueen · May 10, 2020
Just got off the family Mother's Day Zoom call... My grandmother's the best... She had her dress on, makeup... and before we log off she goes, "Y'all be safe and if ya go out make sure you gotcha mask and stay away from folks... Don't listen to the government, listen to grandma!"

⟲ 1999   ♡ 15903

Born in St. Louis, Missouri, in the year 1934, my darling Norma Jean would enter the world while our country was in the throes of the Great Depression. Because she was Black and, more important, because it had been established that whatever misfortune befalls white America is exacerbated and exponentially worse within our ranks, she was thrust into a predicament that skewed close to penury. St. Louis in the 1930s was a city defined almost exclusively by a flawed theory of racial separation. Here, seventy-seven years after the landmark Dred Scott Supreme Court decision established that people of African ancestry had no legal claim to either U.S citizenship or freedom, strictures to manifest this idea resulted in a social order that shaped the country she would come to know. That Scott had tasted freedom in neighboring Illinois yet would suffer his devastating loss in both Missouri and federal courts—

that decision setting the stage for both Civil War and its Separate but Equal aftermath—is of grave importance. That historical through line, establishing that African Americans had no rights, served as the official blueprint for a codified system of disenfranchisement that would stretch for over a century. It ensured that any Black person born in the middle of this continuum would, like Scott, be unfree despite the 13th, 14th, and 15th amendments to the Constitution.

Where World War II found America mobilizing against forces attempting to use race and eugenics to facilitate genocide—my grandmother was forced to contend with these glaring hypocrisies as she navigated the confounding labyrinth of a segregated U.S. city. As a little Black girl coming of age in wartime America, she would end up experiencing this epic contradiction first hand. Sitting on her sofa one bright afternoon last summer, I observed a woman on what was the eve of her 85th birthday, as she revisited this grueling epoch.

One of the first things you notice about my grandmother is her striking, objective beauty. Eight decades have in no way diminished her glaring appeal. Time, if anything, has merely underscored it. She radiates. Her aura palpable; her presence *commanding*. As the coffee percolated and the pound cake was plated, something instinctual told me to go grab my iPhone. Just as modern technology has proven an auxiliary in capturing raced based crimes of the present, I imagined it could, in this very instance, assist in documenting those of the past. As my Uncle Glenn began slicing into the Schnucks lemon pound cake, I pressed record and sat back as my grandmother proceeded to slice into the ironies of history. "We couldn't go to the Fox, or any of the white theaters, but the German prisoners could," she now relayed from her living room, mere miles yet a lifetime removed from the epicenter of downtown St. Louis. "And that used to boggle my mind! They wouldn't go with the general public, but they had a special time for 'em and sometimes you'd see them being marched up the street on Grand, and they could go in there."

Her revelation rocked the house. As I attempted to process it, I observed how the weight of this disclosure, even some seventy-five years later, was still so heavy, so burdensome, that it knocked her back in her recliner. As an octogenarian, sharing her story some three-fourths of a century after the fact, wiping the dust from that awful memory laid bare its tragic implications. It exposed her pain, those particles of time having bestrewed a picture in her mind that remained crystal clear, still shocking and sorrowful. "And I said, I'll be daggone! There's a prisoner of war can go in here and I can't?!" The inherent irrationality prompted the slightest of chuckles from her as she relived this uncomfortable memory for our edification.

For the formidable and stoic woman seated before me, sifting through this dirt like an archaeologist excavating America's brutal, buried past, the ridiculousness she unearthed needed no further commentary, not in this moment, so she let this colossal absurdity linger in the air. Her momentary silence spoke volumes, her slumped posture corroborating that the unwieldy load of this lifelong albatross still weighed her down. Several more disquieting seconds passed before she finally, decisively, cauterized the wound. "But that's, that's the way it was."

When discussing history, we often portray the past using sepia tones. Like certain photographs, this rose-colored hue can distort, glossing over those more problematic and unsparing aspects, reducing a bygone era to a one-dimensional, self-serving appraisal in an effort to sell an inauthentic, yet more palatable, picture. That our historical gray areas, thus tinted, can produce an inaccurate tally means that my grandmother's words, and those of others who lived in that fold, close to the margins, and who kept receipts like bookmarks in this collective past, are integral to us students of history and our endless quest to find an ever more accurate estimate of America and its unresolved past. For a nation that readily sacrifices its own in order to secure the rights of others, the irony that a segregated army, fighting for a segregated country, bestowed upon its foreign adversaries a level of respect that remained foreign to those like my grandmother belied the discomfiting fact that, postwar, it took another twenty years, and a crucible at home, until we finally acquired civil and voting rights.

The notion of human rights kept returning to me as I listened to her, her furrowed brow telegraphing that, all these years later, after a lifetime of struggle and survival, and even eventual triumph, she was still wrestling with it all, still searching for a way to articulate for me, and even perhaps for that little girl with the golden eyes somewhere deep down in her, the singular sensation that only such colossal contradictions could elicit. "I'll have to think of a word. The feeling— Not depressed. Not despondent. *Disturbed.* I was disturbed spiritually," she finally uttered. "Because here I am a citizen, a good citizen. Never done anything wrong and here is your enemy that has tried to destroy you, that you're treating better than a person who loves you."

Her heavy assessment caused me too to sit back as I attempted, rather naively, to help her shoulder this enormous burden in the moment, to relieve her by providing my unnecessary and inferior insight. But when I went to speak, alas, nothing came out. My loss for words was apropos, for I would only have derailed her momentum in this moment. My sole purpose, revealed through the sacred space she had created in this unassuming suburban home, was simply to bear witness, to provide stillness and silence so as not to obstruct this porthole into the past.

I sat with the rapt attention of a med student as my grandmother, this oracle, masterfully and methodically deconstructed this matrix with surgical precision. "But to think about the mind, that's what always bothered me, how is the mind like that? How's your *mind* like that?" As she commenced dissecting the cadaver of race, the pressure from that load soon giving way to her precise examination, her albatross was alleviated, however briefly. As she carved up the diseased mass for study I watched as, now invigorated, she suddenly sat up in her chair while continuing her elucidation. "How's your mind that you can trust me with your most precious possession, your child, okay? You can give your child to me to care for, right? You can trust me to prepare your meals that you're going to eat. But you can't trust me, or care for me enough that I can sit next to you? Something's wrong with that picture. Something's wrong with that *thinking!*"

Her lesson complete, this rhetorical query provided its own, if discomfiting, answer. And for this neuroscientist and her prized pupil, diagnosing the problem became an end in itself. The conclusion, though dissatisfying, though disheartening, evinced that, over a lifetime that stretched 85 years, from segregation to Trump's inauguration, despite the host of doctors and treatments our country had thrown at this particular cancer, she had never witnessed its complete remission, only its reconfiguration. The absence of a cure belied the fact that she, like her mother before her, and like my own mother after her, had expended a great amount of energy learning to somehow cope with the disease.

This very realization had now thickened the air between us. As the light leaked through the living room blinds, in this moment, I saw plain as day, that the crux of the Black experience can be boiled down to spiritual work. Who can say it is not the work in which we have been actively engaged *since* West Africa—this inner endeavor to preserve that bit of ourselves that is not directly exposed to calamity; this force that we can guard and protect despite privation; this energy that belies our brutalization and the very bodies perpetually sustaining blows. My grandmother, through her generous, nourishing reminiscence, identified what the work really is and always has been. Whether we are slaves or sharecroppers, domestics or day laborers, our true work is a *spiritual* work. To be Black in America is to be bestowed with an eternal flame. And as a people, as she so brilliantly illuminated, our duty, as was hers, is to not allow that light to *dim*. Watching with bemusement as insult was tethered to our injury, the irony of self-professed god-fearing people unleashing unfairness upon us, our loved ones, and our communities, both methodically and mercilessly, there is no doubt you could become disturbed; your spirit could even flicker from the gusts created by this disgustingness. But ours is ultimately a fire that is inextinguishable, though it may appear indistinguishable from the hellish inferno that challenges, and at times engulfs, that very progress.

I now see that a conclusion I had long ago drawn, about the inevitability of our figurative demise, needs reconsidering. Her shining example makes me realize that, however intense, hate can never rival the intensity of *our* burn, especially given the accelerant our ancestors provide us and the fuel unwittingly supplied by centuries of segregation, suppression, and even this simple-ass president. So when it comes to matters of *inevitability*, I would argue, our defeat is not nearly as assured as our survival and eventual *triumph*.

Nowhere did this prove truer than when history called upon my grandmother. Even in a country that has often resisted treatment, the times periodically produce a groundswell when progress chips away at the arbitrary distance between two worlds. In 1949, Cardinal Joseph Ritter mandated that the Archdiocese of St. Louis desegregate its Catholic High Schools, his proclamation coming a full five years before *Brown v Board of Education*, the landmark Supreme Court decision that, subsequent to Dred Scott and *Plessy v Ferguson*, sought to remove the dark pall those improbable decisions had cast over the country. My grandmother became one of a handful of outstanding Black students to transfer from her all-Black high school in Kinloch to the all-white Rosati-Kain Catholic High School downtown. Here, her status as one of the first Black students to integrate, and eventually graduate from, a previously all-white school would bear lessons far greater than any that could be gleaned in any of its classrooms.

Familiar themes of isolation and, more accurately, invisibility, resurfaced as my grandmother relayed to us the unspoken work she had to engage in, corroborating my own tale of transparency some fifty years after hers, this unfortunateness having doubled our workload as the white peers we learned alongside had a reprieve from the supplemental education we were forced to undertake. It was chilling to discover how closely my own trajectory paralleled my grandmother's, that cold indifference of our peers, those unmovable barriers, betraying only a modicum of change despite the half century separating us.

Given she was serving up incredible food for thought, I had completely neglected my cake and ice cream. I looked down and saw a small puddle was now threatening to breach the lip of my saucer. I quickly disposed of the melted remnants and, seeing the pot was now full, poured herself and I two cups of joe. 'How you wan't your coffee Darling?' "Give it to me black baby!" she shouted back. With a smile and two mugs of fuel, I dashed back to the living room to continue the class. "Mmmm." Taking a long sip, she placed the cup down on the table beside her, and promptly picked up the lesson.

Here she began to reveal how her sense of creativity had in many ways saved her, it helping buoy her during this rocky period. I soon learned how she too had channeled her frustrations into art—this leading to yet another stunning admission after an afternoon full of stunning admissions. Having just integrated her new high school she disclosed that, upon submitting a poster for a school-wide art competition, she got her first taste of subterfuge. "I did my poster, turned it in, and just so happened to be walking by the art room, and there was *my* poster laying on the desk. And the nun told me, 'Oh, I'm so sorry, I forgot about it.' Can you believe that bull?" Now, most stories would likely end with this bothersome outcome. But if I have come to expect anything from my grandmother, it is that that magical woman never ceases to amaze. What she divulged next, peppered by chuckles and a still palpable defiance—which she thoroughly relished in—caused me, too, to titter. "So I submitted it myself… and guess what? I won!" That she absorbed the nun's disrespect yet possessed the presence of mind to, in the same moment, grab her poster and submit it herself, a mighty alchemist who transformed prejudice into first prize, showcased her adroitness at taking the indignities she was handed, of which there were many, and spinning them into *gold*.

To not allow disrespect to damage you to the point of dejection is indicative of the fire needed to withstand the awful pettiness of an obdurate public. As I have learned through my own battles with gatekeepers, those in these positions often possess stupefying levels of disingenuousness, many having come to confuse their mediocrity for magnificence. As a Black American it is not a matter of if but *when* we will cross paths with these sorts of charmed yet indolent individuals—those who, again, do not actually *count* our buckets to begin with. As my grandmother showed, being the best among those whose own sense of preeminence is secured through prejudice and separation requires in us a level of resourcefulness and even ingenuity to secure that which we deserve, especially given the manner in which our merits are almost reflexively undermined. My grandma discovered the only recourse is *not* taking any shit; not bending; not making jetsam of our virtues, especially when doing so would compromise the integrity of our vessel, sacrificing the very ballast one *needs* to move forward.

Such was the case when she refused to sit in the back of the school bus on a field trip to Jefferson City. I said, "Uh uh, this ain't right... Glenn?!" My uncle promptly popped his head around the corner. 'Yes mama?' "Here, heat this up for me, son." Though it was still daylight, well over an hour had passed. In the time she had weaved in and out of these anecdotes, her coffee had gone cold. She handed my uncle her mug and, in that split second, I recall being briefly concerned that she was going to get sidetracked again. You must remember that, with a Black family, any large family really, these sorts of intergenerational gatherings get *raucous*. It is a cacophony of conversations and asides, laughing and hollering, squawking and singing. And as the matriarch, there was so much activity constantly buzzing around her—aunts and cousins coming and going, everyone gravitating to her light, wanting a piece of Norma Jean. I mean, I could not blame them. Hell, I wanted her all to myself too. But I *needed* to hear what happened. Almost instantly I noticed my cousin Christina approaching her with a photo album and, quickly grabbed it from her. "Wait, grandma, finish telling me about what happened in Jefferson City?!"

Back on track, she would now share how, after boldly sitting up front she found, upon arrival, that the handful of outstanding Black students chosen to visit the State Capitol could not attend the reception with the others and had to eat in the basement. "I said, 'I'm not eating in a basement! I'm above that! And if I'm qualified to be outstanding like the others here, then I should be equal with them. This is not equal!'" By this point, the racket around us had thankfully died down. As my uncle returned with her chalice the Queen, soon reenergized, would share how she brusquely, nobly, walked straight out of the State House, grabbing her fellow Black classmate. "I said, 'C'mon, we're leaving!'" The words which followed would help paint a poignant picture, it a tribute to her mettle, one which easily brought to mind the poem *Invictus*. With her evocative words, the majestic woman before me detailed how her and her friend decided to go ahead and hold their *own* celebration— to recognize "each other"—just the two of them, two brilliant black girls bloodied, but unbowed, sharing a Coca-Cola on the Capitol steps.

Having rattled off the abasement she had to bear, both those booby traps she had to sidestep in public and the hijacks those pirates dressed as clergy mounted on her in private, I began to marvel more and more at the superhero in my midst. I also began connecting her unwillingness to compromise, which underpinned this power, with ultimately giving her the ability *to* fly. Here, she brought up her participation in Glee Club, the one extracurricular activity she *was* granted permission to participate in, revealing that a nun warned her not to be "too conspicuous" before one performance. "'Don't turn your head and move too much, because you're so noticed,'" she recalled the nun saying. "Isn't that something? In other words, I was going to stand out too much. I may not have been the only Black girl at the school, but it was definitely because, you see, I was the most defiant!"

In the denouement to these, her tales of disregard and disrespect, she topped them all with one final, fitting accoutrement, a cherry as deliciously defiant as the woman herself, it a testament to her most valiant journey: "And do you think I listened?!"

A strong Black woman, a matriarch, a grandmother is an absolute treasure. There is no better word to describe a figure who fully epitomizes such wisdom, strength, benevolence, and elegance. You can point to your own existence as a reflection of the bright, shining example they set, a lustrous paragon who has guided your own improbable journey, a flawless gem who leaves you no resort but to remark on your unmistakable good fortune. For having been blessed with not simply a maternal figure but a juggernaut, a woman who has gallantly, selflessly, incontrovertibly held it the fuck down, who possesses oracle-like powers, raising a family of future college graduates while she herself went back to school to become one is not something to understate. Put simply, older, beneficent, magnificent Black women possess the uncanny ability to leave us feeling better, knowing better and, ostensibly, *being* better.

It was distressing to not only hear firsthand about the unfairness to which she had been subjected, but to also come to the blistering realization that, above all, this scourge had metastasized. Her plight to be seen, like mine, like all others dropped into a cauldron of homogeneity, had merely evolved from having your art submission sat on to having your writing submission disregarded. That her tales of a time long past left me momentarily dispirited was due in no small part to the sadness of her admission but also to the even sadder realization that things had not sufficiently changed in seventy fuckin' years. Most writers, performers, and artists of color still can point to their own examples of the Glee Club, where being unapologetically Black, too culturally obtrusive, is a threat that can cost you. Consider what unfolded with the actress Gabrielle Union, summarily dismissed from her position as a panel judge on *America's Got Talent* because her rotating hairstyles were deemed "too distracting." It suggests that our struggle is, in many ways, a sad heirloom, this unfortunateness *inherited*. And because this problematic dynamic is still very much in play: we watch as those who choose to not be "too conspicuous" are often rewarded for their obsequiousness. This willingness to reflect back to privileged persons an innocuous image, one more closely resembling their own likeness, sees some tamping down their flame, consciously providing softer lighting simply so these dull contemporaries can look better.

Witnessing how many of us, across all industries, often suppress our power in deference to power, I draw the unmistakable connection between my grandmother, on the eve of her 85th birthday, and those dynamic women of color in Congress on this, the eve of the 2020 election. Considering the fire many firsts must maintain, especially operating under the long pall of race, it suggests that dwindling yourself in any way to make your impact palatable is to compromise not only your potential but that greater promise you represent.

For those righteous women of color, whose improbable rise is invariably rocked by turbulence, their steadfastness in the face of offense is essential—especially given the ease with which real change can be scuttled, sent straight to "the basement," if you do *not* remain vigilant.

18

This Shit Won't Go Down

Cyrus McQueen @CyrusMMcQueen · Sep 16, 2019
Trump's tweeting about "Obama Netflix" cause he knows ain't nobody tryna pay to watch anymore of his whack ass reality show... Unless Fox News gets into streaming... then what we talkin bout? Orange is the New Crack? Things Are Stranger? Russian Gall? Making a Hamberder?

343 2080

The ramifications of the 2016 election, our legitimate fears, were all but certified as by 2018 it became undeniable: something was desperately wrong with Trump. Ever the more mercurial, he fired off hundreds as opposed to dozens of tweets, his weekend flurries, his churlish calling cards, now evincing increasingly erratic behavior. These gross displays sent the signal that, despite his usual deportment, his conduct was indicative of a nadir: we were likely witnessing the unraveling of an American president.

We entered a world where axiomatic truth could be axed, logic summarily discarded when it was incongruent with a president's chicanery, and all of us raised to tell the difference between fact and fiction watched as an unstable man bent the world to fit his reality. In the weeks following his idiotic idea of purchasing Greenland, he stubbornly ignored geography, weather patterns, and the scientifically based predictions of the National Weather Service to service his falsification that Hurricane Dorian would hit the state of Alabama.

The childish flourish of #Sharpiegate, seemingly otiose at first glance, takes on added meaning when you recognize that Alabama *is* Trump country. Yet that the state is vital to his success is not as notable as the fact that his electoral success there *derives* from fear. His hold over his statewide supporters has been like that of an abusive husband—making them afraid to leave him, creating an atmosphere that their lives will be worse without him, forging the false impression that the world is really what is scary and dangerous, *not* the toxic environment he has fashioned. Trump's control over those within its citizenry rests on his ability to convince them that what is harmful is harmless and vice versa. As evidenced by his endorsement of Roy Moore, he will always sacrifice the best interests of those within the state before lessening any of his momentum.

Yet the storm rages on. The mounting list of sophomoric displays suggests only one logical conclusion about Trump, about this entire era: we have *all* been held hostage by a fuckin' fool for the past four years.

Donald Trump is an embarrassment. I have expended every appropriate adjective I can think of to describe this unrepentant jackass, leaving me with the most fitting, most encapsulating, most precise summation of his stumbling, bumbling walk across the world stage: he is an embarrassment. But as the world watches a discombobulated fool alter weather maps, using a black marker to justify his lie, like a child who tries to cover up a mess by making a bigger one, the fear he seeks to instill in that irascible portion of the electorate is no match for the even greater fear that each and every aggrieved American feels upon digesting the discomfiting truth: we have an unremitting disaster sitting in the Oval Office.

Nearly four years into his term, Trump has thoroughly eroded any sense of normalcy. Be it his common outbursts or the outrage it engenders, the sophomoric way he insults those he deems beneath him, punching down as a petulant rich kid is want to do, the result is impossible to deny: his presidency is an insult to our greater intelligence. That the abnormal has become normalized, I cannot help but agree with the great Joy Reid, the indefatigable journalist who perfectly encapsulated this greater danger, remarking of this era, "One of the things it has done to me is, it's kinda robbed me of astonishment."

In fact, Trump has carved out a whole new sliver of journalism, creating an entirely new category of coverage: Petty News. By all estimations, he is Pettydent of the United States. And, as the real estate mogul's fractious output consumes the Fourth Estate, the tedium he generates registers on the faces of just about every talking head. Those working within the medium are forced to focus intensely on the crimes behind the lies, the misdeeds behind the misinformation, the disaster behind the distraction, so as not to be sidetracked by every shiny object he tosses out.

In a nation inundated with shenanigans, I have recognized a far more unsettling fact: when you pause to think about it, we have actually forgotten *more* of Trump's misbehavior than we can collectively bring ourselves to admit. In crafting an obloquy of his obnoxiousness, I have had to resign myself to the fact that we have descended so far down the rabbit hole that his scandals have a shorter shelf life than the milk in a NYC bodega. Given his overwhelming intolerance, the sheer volume of shit he produces, I, and most people, completely forget about far too much.

Because Trump is such a fucked up, irredeemable man, he has reduced the Oval Office to a bully's pulpit, a pitiful reflection of what it was even when the similarly dimwitted W was its occupant. Yet what is even sadder is that we are all, as Joy Reid alluded, becoming *dulled* to a dullard's behavior. His scandals now bleed together. A knot of nonsense and unbecoming behavior, a gross, unsightly entanglement of pitiful and dishonest displays. Day in and day out. Week in and week out. (Gasp) Year in and year out.

As I plumbed the depths of my social media output ranging from that period when this shadow was first cast in mid-2015 to the present day, I have discovered that the consistent theme, the rusty needle that his needless, juvenile behavior can always thread, is that he, time and again, displays zero compunction when it comes to doing wrong. Thus, the only dependable aspect of this era, the only thing you can actually set your clock to, is that you can count on Trump to *not* do the right thing. If there is any definitive take on this president, it is that when it comes to right and wrong, the man arguably does not know the difference. His penchant for creating collateral damage when he tries to cover for his crimes has since become a hallmark of his presidency—his chronic missteps always engendering a witless, fruitless attempt to redirect attention *away* from his glaring indecency.

Yet it is his deft ability at not only burying his initial crimes but deluging the public record with additional ones that suggests we are unlikely to ever get to the bottom of his epic criminality. Given a preponderance of scandals, by the end of every news cycle many Americans can make neither heads nor tales of them. And whether it is Gorsuch and Kavanaugh on the Supreme Court, Mnuchin in the Treasury, Barr in the Justice Department, or Pompeo in the State Department, it is clear that, even if Trump *were* to be taken to task, virtually every layer of government now insulates him from any comeuppance. And even if little of his blatant, in-your-face corruption is methodically thought out or executed, we are talking about flagrant violations of the Emoluments Clause—whether it is Mike Pence staying at Trump International Golf Club in Doonbeg, Ireland, while on government business or, in another instance, more than fifty military servicemen staying overnight at his Turnberry, Scotland, resort during a refueling stop. Sickeningly, a U.S. president turning his tenure into a cash register before our eyes, signals that we as journalists and writers—and even those members of the greater public who daily take to social media to object publicly to his objectionable behavior—perhaps all of us criminally bury the lede. Perhaps this nightmarish chapter in American history begins, and will end, with the obvious: Donald Trump desires, above all else, to profit from the presidency.

Though he criminalizes Black and Brown people, even Black and Brown children, he essentially does so as a diversion, distracting attention from his, and his children's, *rampant* criminality. Ironically, by his emphasizing us, indulging the verisimilitude of our villainy, be blinds his supporters to the real criminals. Whether it is his daughter immediately, and magically, securing Chinese patents, including 16 new trademarks, to facilitate her own business and eponymous brand; his installation of his high pitched son-in-law in the West Wing, security clearances be damned, in order to secure Saudi and Qatari funding for any number of his moribund properties or wishful projects; or even his sons Tweedle-dee and Tweedle-dumber who ostensibly run his corporation in his stead yet are likely shills who, when not engaging in high crimes and misdemeanors with Russian assets, drove his so-called charitable foundation into the ground with avarice and mismanagement—it is now unequivocal: the First Family is a crime family using the WH to trade the Trump name for access. Here, a comparison to the Corleones is apt, except even the vicious, fictitious mobsters in Mario Puzo's *magnum opus* operated with a code of ethics; these grifters, invariably and noticeably, do not.

Cyrus McQueen @CyrusMMcQueen · Aug 24, 2020
Have ya seen the lineup for the #RNC ⧉?? It's just Don Jr, Eric, Tiffany and Ivanka... ooh and I almost forgot, Melania... It's just a sad ass testament to nepotism and mediocrity... it's like they're stumbling into the final season of their reality show and facing cancellation...

⟲ 356   ♡ 1754

As we follow the money, Trump's tangible financial troubles help explain why he found himself in a hotel room in Moscow back in 2013—and why he ultimately got in bed *with* the Russians. Much has been made of his dalliance with the Russian president and those oligarchs who greased the well-manicured, moisturized palms of Paul Manafort to facilitate his election, but in the years we have been dealing with this boil on America's ass, his coverups and coconspirators have so consistently sidetracked us that we tend to overlook the catalyst of this cataclysmic series of events that tests our democracy.

Trump, the shiftless tabloid-star-turned-politician, needed not only race to get elected, but he also desperately needed Russia's help. To understand how a reality show has-been has become our reality, we have to recognize that it was only through a foreign adversary—and his lifelong adversaries here at home—that he could piece together this winning formula. Where African Americans and Russians both represent traditional threats to white conservative America, part of Trump's genius was recognizing that white conservatives *would* ultimately be willing to reignite the Cold War with us. Right-wing populism would provide him with an aperture. A New York hustler, he knew a sucker when he saw one: a disaffected middle America *made* the perfect mark. Where his pathology may have prevented him from using people of color outright to achieve his sinister desires, he knew instinctually, given both his past and America's own problematic history, that he could use us in yet another way to achieve his end. Thus, he set about disrupting the electorate through scaremongering. Taking the focus off one common enemy, he then placed it all on the *other:* by exaggerating the threat we pose, he diminished the true existential danger of the Kremlin.

Seeking the help of a hostile foreign power is not a foreign concept to a career criminal, especially one for whom cutting corners and sharp practices are second nature. Getting into bed with the Russians in 2016 was a no brainer given that he had been in bed with them since the 1980s. Where his U.S. buildings may have been bereft of Black and Brown people, his antipathy to things foreign to his white world certainly was *not* the case when it came to Russians. His much-mentioned, well-concealed taxes, his decades of manipulations, his operating the Trump Organization in many ways as a front for Russian criminals—who themselves used his property to launder their own ill-gotten gains—presaged his behavior in politics and later as chief executive. Given the nebulousness surrounding his taxable earnings, the years of concerted dishonesty when he was already robbing the government in a private capacity, it makes all the sense in the world that he has continued this treachery since becoming head of government. Whether Trump exploits certain Russian entities or those entities exploit him, whether it is his own hubris or Putin's that has led to this outcome, it is undeniable that each enjoys this profitable partnership. This racket had played out for decades, yet it now yields more lucre—that greater plundering facilitated because both men can exploit a clamorous white America.

Though many, including myself, attempt to artfully convey how our history was hijacked in the last presidential election, our future rewritten like the plot of a Robert Zemeckis movie, we can boil down those unfortunate events, which have all but returned our nation to the 1950s, to one simple fact: Russia needed the United States to remove the crippling economic sanctions we and other nations had imposed after its 2014 invasion of Ukraine. Even before that, the Magnitsky Act in 2012—named for Sergei Magnitsky the Russian tax advisor whose anticorruption efforts led to his murder by Russian officials—had *banned* Russian human rights abusers from traveling to this country. When Obama signed that act into law, it gave Trump and Putin a common enemy and, thus, a common *problem* to overcome. We cannot minimize the existential implications of either country's predicament in this regard, nor the dire steps each would engage in to ameliorate their untenable positions. Though we can rightfully frame 2016 as America's rebuttal to Obama and racial progress, we also must bifurcate this historical outcome to include the incontrovertible objectives of the Russian Federation to erase his indelible impact.

Russia desperately needed Western deep-drilling technology to procure natural resources and help them fortify their outdated industrial model—as well as Putin's iniquitous plans. The Kremlin discovered the shortest route to this outcome would be *through* the pockets of America's conservatives. By enriching Republicans like Senate Majority Leader Mitch McConnell—who, through an intermediary, secured $200 million from a Russian aluminum producer to fund an aluminum plant in his home state of Kentucky—Russia incentivized him to block a bipartisan effort in the Senate to maintain the penalties. With McConnell freeing Trump to then lift sanctions, Kremlin-linked businessmen soon revealed that the party of family values possesses no values at all—at least none that will not sink to the bottom of the Black Sea if you load them down with enough bags of cash.

Things became funky the moment Republicans realized they could achieve their ends by bringing in a critical third party: their embittered white constituency. Crucial to this game plan is the continued fealty of those within their states and districts who, post-inauguration and married to the Trump brand and agenda, make known, in no uncertain terms, their unequivocal, unwavering support for his moribund presidency, despite the mounting evidence that what is advantageous for the Kremlin is certainly adverse for the United States.

The relaxing of sanctions, this unquestionable victory, was predicated on the movement of cash, a savvy investment of, say, $200 million up front reaping potentially astronomical profits for Russian industry leaders and unscrupulous Republican politicians down the road. What has played out in Washington is tantamount to a three-team deal, similar to what is routine in the National Basketball Association: multiple players and multiple moving parts, in many instances cash and future considerations, are exchanged, often changing the entire culture and face of a franchise in the process.

Though Trump and Republican leaders struck a Faustian bargain with the Russians, the deal appears mutually beneficial on the surface. Their white constituents, convinced the country has been restored, ignore the gross implications of this dalliance. Their revanchist impulse so blinding, it obscures the very fact that our democracy has been compromised—this version of America, at best, ersatz, our own brand *devalued*.

Connecting these dots reveals a rudimentary yet compelling picture: Russia was instrumental in restoring the wealth of an American real estate tycoon who had been $4 billion in debt in 2002. That tycoon-turned-reality-star-turned-candidate would, in turn, take on the task of restoring the whiteness of those who supported his presidential run, thus restoring their *sense* of wealth in the face of America's rapidly changing cultural landscape. Yet it was mother Russia who was poised to be the big winner, their unfettered interference in our elections notwithstanding.

In many ways, our new world resembles a Russian doll. If you could crack open the globe, you would find Putin nesting just beneath the surface. Investigate a little and you see Putin's power fortified by Trump's. Look into Trumpty Dumpty's shell, cracking it open, and you discover his own perfidious power predicated on the continued proliferation of white power. Yet if you put this puzzle back together, you find the Russian president undoubtedly, invariably, pervading every layer. Russia's presence in the Balkans, parts of Africa, and the Middle East—and in Ukraine—reveal his Machiavellian, mad desire to control this very globe—and the unmistakable fact that *he* now affects nearly every part of it.

Cyrus McQueen @CyrusMMcQueen · Jul 13, 2018
Mueller just indicted 12 Russian Military Officers for the DNC Hacking... Which does not bode well for Trump's performance review with Putin next week...

⟲ 257   ♡ 903

Many Americans reached a tacit understanding of all this after Robert Mueller's appointment in May 2017 as special counsel, our entering into an unspecified covenant with the enigmatic investigator. Though it was impossible to litigate the intangible sociopolitical implications behind Trump's White House run, anyone with half a brain knew that financial improprieties likely linked to election improprieties. Given the oft-employed yet accurate directive to "follow the money," one could plausibly get to the bottom of any criminal enterprise, be it in the executive branch or outside. But the long gestation of Mueller's investigation belied the anticlimactic drop of his *Report on the Investigation into Russian Interference* in March 2019—as it was immediately followed by Trump's crooked and corpulent attorney general, William Barr, redacting the fuck out of it before declaring that it magically exonerated the president. The wrecking ball we had all expected to destroy Trump's house of cards turned out to completely, and maddeningly, miss the huge mark. The collective public *gasped*.

I must disclose my own disappointment with this unforeseen outcome. Like the rest of the country, I had built up my expectations, waiting anxiously for the other shoe to drop. Mueller and Trump were, at this point, so associated with one another, the images of both so dominating the headlines, that these 70-something men had become inextricably linked like adversarial bookends. With normalcy shelved, our Constitution and laws became sandwiched between them. We saw principle tilt, as party affiliations determined which man, which dichotomous side, our members of Congress would ultimately align with.

The stoic, silent Mueller, career public servant and ex-Marine, appears, on paper and off, to be the opposite of the privileged, undisciplined Trump, a man who, military deferments notwithstanding, is a deft take on Kurtz, Joseph Conrad's literary villain and the evil inspiration behind the colonel in Francis Ford Coppola's *Apocalypse Now*. Though Trump fancies himself a Godfather, be it how he speaks or how he carries himself, he unmistakably skews closer to the Brando interpretation of Kurtz. Be it his gait, his lunacy, or the way he seems stranded on an island unto himself, surrounded by sycophants and mercenaries, it is clear he, like Kurtz, has secured a level of deference due to his mercurial displays. Yet despite the noticeable fear Trump's frequent outbursts engendered, his hold was in no way absolute, and he indeed appeared poised for a great fall. We waited for Mueller, a man right out of central casting, his military career and war experience expertly suiting him for this lead role. With the firing of FBI Director James Comey and Deputy Director Andrew McCabe, and with a Justice Department turned on its head with the appointment of William Barr, Mueller traveled up river, in relentless pursuit of a manic, unmoored slug.

Given the great contrast between the two men, Mueller's worth appeared appreciable, especially upon it being established that he was dealing with a president who was, in many ways, evil incarnate—a man who belligerently compromised norms, sinisterly violated the office, and mercilessly attacked our vulnerabilities. However, despite a report that was damning (despite what Barr claimed) and the subsequent news that its eponymous author would appear before two congressional committees, facing bipartisan firing squads, Mueller's mythology left us underwhelmed, if not completely let down, by the time the smoke cleared. This amalgam of Lincoln and Superman, this mighty hero who had appeared indefatigable in our collective vision and our collective wishes, who we had no doubt would save America in the nick of time, was obliterated by reality as we watched the 74-year-old man meander through a marathon day of questioning. Even if his work would ultimately speak louder and better than he could, as I watched his appearance on the Hill unfold, I could not help but feel that even Mueller himself had anticipated this unfavorable outcome.

Watching Mueller felt much like watching a vestige of America's past. A man unbothered by the vicissitudes affecting our sociopolitical landscape, imbued by notions of truth and integrity, his virtues spoke volumes even when his physical voice could not. That laudable idea of "country first"—one that, in all honesty, has struggled to resonate in post-1960s America, a nation polarized and preoccupied with placing the individual over the collective, profits over principle—was seemingly unearthed alongside the gaunt, gray-haired public servant that day on

Capitol Hill. But unfortunately for Mueller, that uniquely American archetype and those special qualities on full display, exhibited under the bright bulbs like some precious antiquity, now appeared noticeably dated under the unforgiving media glare.

This was proven by the presumption underlying his entire investigation, the principle upon which he predicated his conclusion: the belief that a sitting U.S. president cannot be indicted. Though he was unquestionably working from precedent, this inscrutable inference of Mueller's dismayed us, especially after Charlottesville, the Southern border, and sharpies. Here was a president who courted and conducted disaster as if he were some malevolent maestro, a crook who had made it *abundantly* clear we were now in unprecedented times. Though much would be made of Mueller's 400+ pages of deep dive into the compromising of the 2016 election, devoting the second half almost entirely to Trump's clumsy attempts to circumvent the investigation at multiple intervals—be it firing the FBI director or the ham-handed, even hilarious, way he attempted to deputize his dickish underling Corey Lewandowski, ordering him to fire Jeff Sessions—it was the first half that chilled us the most in its painstaking documentation of Russia's concerted attempts to undermine the wishes of the U.S. electorate. Indeed, for the specific purposes of my own pursuit of truth, neither the bog our swamp rat of a president resided in, nor his repeated attempts at chewing off his own foot to escape the trap he found himself in, proved as important as those cracks his election had exposed. It would be those gaping holes that desperately needed filling to prevent this rodent, or future ones, from infesting the White House ever again.

When I finally got my hands on the special counsel's work, I was stunned not simply by the myriad ways in which the ratty Trump had attempted to rip, claw, and extract himself from the coiled spring that pinned him down, but also by his ability to further ensnare himself, and others, in traps that had not even been set. Whether it was those attempts to fire his way out of the mess after his well-documented meltdown and maneuverings subsequent to Sessions' recusal, or even his blatant admission to NBC's Lester Holt that he had indeed fired James Comey specifically because of the whole "Russia thing," Mueller's findings corroborated that Trump was basically daring someone, *anyone*, to stop him.

Yet I ended up tabling my frustrations as it pertained to the bold cover up, all so I could focus, in earnest, on the nightmare chronicled comprehensively in the first half of Mueller's dense report. I have to search for a word—bemused immediately comes to mind though dejected is probably better—to describe the feeling that washed over me upon reading that by the end of the 2016 election, nefarious Russian actors had deliberately targeted and likely affected *millions* of Americans. Mueller revealed that Russian interference had actually begun back in 2014 with the creation of the Internet Research Agency (IRA), its sole purpose *to* sow political discord. That the company ran numerous fraudulent accounts on Facebook and Instagram, accumulating hundreds of thousands of followers, reaching up to an estimated 126 million people, was only slightly more distressing than discovering that its Twitter presence was responsible for engaging roughly 677,000 individuals with their duplicitous output. When Twitter later linked nearly four thousand accounts to the IRA, accounts that posted damaging memes and misinformation about Hillary Clinton, with tens of thousands retweeting this misleading content, it was coupled with the revelation that some of these shady characters had gone on to undermine #BlackLivesMatter and other legitimate causes. In many instances, they identified themselves as grassroots activists; in others, they posed as progressive people of color for the purpose of turning rallies in various cities into furtive opportunities to exploit racial tensions.

Cyrus McQueen @CyrusMMcQueen · Apr 18, 2019
I'll tell ya this much, all these fuckin redactions are the first time we're seeing anything black in this Administration... #MuellerReport

↻ 972   ♡ 4970

By now it is irrefutable: the Trump nightmare links inextricably to the Obama dream. But be it Trump's championing of Birtherism, or his rapacious efforts to undo Obama's policies, successes, and impressive legacy, many remain unaware that where Obama taught us an edifying lesson on the virtues of harmony, reconciliation, and change, his revolutionary ascension also provided his enemies with a lesson on how to *win*. His formula, a multimedia approach as dynamic at the time as his message of Hope, proved effective. It was his widely disseminated and motivating slogans, indeed the indelible digital imprint of this majestic leader—not merely transforming our sociopolitical landscape but social media *itself*—that furnished future political campaigns with an invaluable tutorial. It is safe to reiterate: there would be no President Trump if not for President Obama. Yet this succession, due in large part to race, also links to the very blueprint Obama had created—one that an ignominious Trump campaign purloined, enabling a caustic candidate, and a corrosive conservative message, to succeed.

In this context, I cannot overstate the impact of Cambridge Analytica or its crucial role in harvesting data for mad men like Trump and his advisor Steve Bannon, men who weaponized information for the specific purpose of turning platforms like Facebook into a cultural battlefield in the lead up to the 2016 election. The political consulting firm based out of Great Britain, specializing in data and digital communications, had proven its mettle with work the company's CEO Alexander Nix had done to promote the "Leave EU" movement. That very disaster proved to be a dress rehearsal for the American shitshow that followed shortly thereafter. With the success of the conservative digital strategy, Brexit foreshadowed Election 2016. Once these men figured out how to win, how to usurp protocols and play people in this unregulated landscape, it was only a matter of time until the world would reflect those visions playing out in their diabolical minds.

Sadly, much of the public has yet to recognize the links between the British firm and monsters like Steve Bannon, who, as a former vice president of Cambridge Analytica, fulfilled his wish to wage a culture war once he got his meaty claws on the type of data that could reshape both sides of the Atlantic. Even if Mueller felt he could not conclude that the Russians used Trump polling data to meddle in the 2016 campaign, it is clear that then-campaign manager Paul Manafort, operating as an intermediary, handed over specific data related to battleground states like Pennsylvania to known Putin associates. It does not take much to conclude that where there is smoke, there is likely fire—an indicator here that life can be stranger than fiction. Trump, Manafort, and Bannon could have come right out of a Tom Clancy novel. They were the bad guys in a Bond film. Hell, Bannon, the blotchy, corpulent misanthrope, full of delectable idiosyncrasies like sporting two dress shirts at a time, while affecting the posture of an invidious global mastermind, even *resembled* one. This walking contradiction, this self-professed genius who was pedestrian enough to buy into pseudoscience and eugenics, is an anti-globalist who paradoxically wants to rule the globe.

Bannon's behind-the-scenes work, muddying the waters, reducing Clinton's worth, and enhancing the truculent Trump's estimation and viability, confounded me and most progressives. At the time, I could not imagine how this self-destructive, mercurial candidate could get elected.

Yet in hindsight, it appears that everything went according to script. They utilized Obama's social media approach, misappropriating what happened organically in 2008, and then weaponized the new information they gathered—before gaining the help of the Russian Federation to buttress these objectives and wreak all-out havoc.

Cambridge Analytica had even courted a member of Obama's very own team to impart her knowledge for their knavish purposes. The young woman who had played a crucial role in his 2008 campaign and in refining his social media imprint now helped the firm identify "persuadables": those independents who could be groomed via targeted messaging and thus corralled into the conservative camp. This sort of psychological warfare was especially effective when utilizing data that platforms like Facebook had harvested through personality quizzes and the like. Cambridge Analytica rounded out the psychological profiles of these potential swing voters, distilling information down to the states and districts where it mattered the most. This enabled Trump's camp to fill in a picture that crystallized as they painted these voters into a corner, turning blue states red and securing the 270 votes needed to win in the Electoral College.

As the sheer magnitude of the disinformation campaign to elect Trump came into ever clearer focus, my own memories of random memes of Hillary behind bars and of Mexican gang members, images that had flooded the Internet and even found their way into my notifications in response to some of my anti-Trump tweets in the buildup to 2016, now flooded back to me. I processed how and why we had arrived at this point. Silly imagery that I had naively considered innocuous, that I had dismissed given its glaring distortions and obvious embellishments, turned out to be a hell of a lot more consequential, given that it crossed not just discerning eyes but was landing before many who were easily manipulated. The autopsy of 2016 was ghastly: this company had identified those who were on the fence, especially in places like Wisconsin, Michigan, and Pennsylvania, and inundated them with negative ads. It set up emotional dominoes that it could then knock down one after the other. By convincing enough voters that they had come to their opinions organically, they were, in turn, *impelled* to spread this nonsense.

The great conundrum—the Obama voter becoming a Trump voter—is less implausible when we consider the massive efforts to control what these voters saw and, more importantly, *thought*. Stealing an election is easier after you steal minds. Between British datamining and

Russian subterfuge, the lasting lesson I take from these efforts to turn the world upside down is that we must never underestimate the element of fear. Our nation went from change to mange, from tremendous to horrendous, because fear is one hell of a motivator—even more than hope in some cases. Though hate is inorganic, fear *is* organic. It is instinctual, often illogical, and given the candidate whose personal life it shaped, given the way it manifested in his political life, I can now see more clearly how those who had embraced hope and the magnanimous man who proffered it could trade it all for an ignominious man who had nothing better to sell *than* fear—a man who would go on to rule by it because *it* ruled him.

Though I identified how we got to this point, I was unsettled, struggling to reconcile myself with our new normal. Along with virtually anyone who lived through 2016 and still struggles to live through this period now, I often find myself out of breath, the pressures of enduring this tenure drowning me in a tempest of emotions. Considering how Trump rides the wave, having surfed it all the way to D.C., I become unwell at the far more difficult to digest notion that we have been played. That recurring theme, too, reveals itself in Mueller's report, which now reads like the death certificate of a terminal country. It is abundantly clear that the forces evincing our inexorable decline confirm my assertions that Black progress—virtually all progress—is tumbling helplessly downward in America's rip current, while wealthy white Americans, they the sole beneficiaries of inequality, inaction, and indifference, continue to frolic just above this frothy torrent.

Cyrus McQueen @CyrusMMcQueen · Apr 18, 2019
Umm, if they can consistently prosecute countless black men for 'Intent to Distribute' I think we should be able to prosecute one President for 'Intent to Obstruct'... #MuellerReport ⊐ #TrumpColluded ⊐ #BarrCoverUp ⊐

⟲ 1170   ♡ 3926

A multitude of factors helped Trump fortify his echo chamber, including clones busy propagating his message, but a large and determined camp of us discovered our very own megaphone through social media. And it is here where I would scream to all corners around the globe. The rank and file of the Resistance usually echoed back my anguish in those brief moments when Trump's backward cadre were not disseminating their own disgust, attaching his hyperbole to our summations in a feverish attempt to bog down any thought-provoking threads with invective. Given the now-constant flood in this new era, it made for a situation where, oftentimes, we would not see the forest for the trees, this quandary compounded by an inability to determine whether this rotten output derived from a diseased shrub or simply a fake one. With Russian bots ever-present, their network of branches far reaching, I admit to getting lost in a jungle of fake accounts from time to time, my vitriolic rebuttals landing before a thicket of both real and fake eyes.

Mueller himself highlighted in shocking detail this new reality, since borne out in our new world and this new cultural landscape. Upon digesting the fruit of his labors, those of us who had often gotten lost in this labyrinth resigned ourselves to the sad fact that, more often than we might want to admit, we likely had been embroiled in fights with some unnamed foreign adversary posing as a punk-ass American.

Flashbacks from this murky battlefield revisit me. Memories arise of my screaming into my keypad, hands trembling as some Carolinian—or Comrade—opened fire, their letters like bullets culminating in a mighty barrage, a vicious salvo, N-words and F-words turning our phones and followers into readied battalions. At times, I would lament the precious time squandered on one troll or several, Twitter never failing to supply ample reinforcements as these antagonists, hiding behind hatred and empty avatars and bunkered down in their mothers' basements, fired off one missive after another. Whether their attacks were personal or political, these snipers prided themselves on the kill shot—be it your race, your career, or the notion "you're not even funny" or should just "move to another country." They would never fail to draw first blood or withdraw first, their intrinsic cowardice prompting their retreat from any subsequent engagement—but not before lobbing that four-letter grenade into your replies: #MAGA. Furious, you took chase, on the hunt, firing indiscriminately at any who dared embed themselves in this heated exchange, your response readied like a bayonet and sharpened to a deadly point for both efficiency and maximum effect. Yet after zeroing in on their tunnel, after stooping to an embarrassing low, after darkness eclipsed you, after twisting yourself into a pretzel to taste revenge, then and only then would you rip through the dog tags and hashtags to discover that the person cowering at your fingertips had 2 Followers.

The battle lines drawn, mounting evidence suggested that Resisters were persistently, perpetually, under attack from all sides, this rampant confusion at times producing entire Twitter threads where progressives wound up eating their own. Thinking back to 2016, I recall how a slight difference of opinion dredged up by one awful event could culminate in vicious hand-to-hand combat between allies. Whether it was the DNC email hacks or the fallout when the FBI relaunched the Clinton probe, these moments always inspired calls for defection. In some instances, for example, someone would foolishly try to corral troops into Jill Stein's ragtag outfit; others would use that very moment to reveal they still took orders from Bernie, despite his losing the nomination and no longer leading this army. #NeverTrump and its converse #NeverHillary would then trend almost immediately, these neutralizing forces underscoring this polarizing intensity and contributing to the likelihood that fuckery was afoot.

A couple years later, I still found myself facing down Democratic mutinies, those very Sanders supporters—high on absolutism and the unassailable belief that his leadership and vision were beyond reproach—unwilling to sidestep those very same booby traps that had so decimated our numbers in 2016. Even some two years removed, the news of the Obamas' purchase of a Martha's Vineyard mansion was inspiring vociferous objections among certain progressives, some charging that our president and his wife had turned their backs on working people to join the 1 percent. Yet, I must admit, I was left with the sneaking suspicion that *this* prolonged division may be more the result of deliberate calculus instead of random coincidence. With white progressives *and* conservatives on social media weaponizing Black wealth, it an underhanded exercise that only reinforced a white status quo, given the confusion these grievances created—and considering the undeniable presence of bots—I could not help but wonder whether *some* of the combatants were simply waving false flags.

Whether that was the case or not, what *is* undeniable is that, as a Black progressive in this day and age, you can often find yourself fired upon by both Trump *and* Sanders armadas. Given our pugnacious politics, you can easily become besieged by these broadsides. Left shell-shocked, the resultant bewilderment, that feeling of profound disconnect, betrays the fact that we have once again been set adrift. Subsequent calls for unity amid this firefight can even prompt an ambush, your timeline riddled with self-righteous shrapnel, the flurry of ensuing blocks further evidence of friendly fire as allies and adversaries alike fall victim to the moment—thus confirming the often-nebulous dynamics of our social media crusade. It evinces not merely the inestimable toll of embroilment but a more disorienting fact: it is practically *impossible* to see clearly in the fog of war.

On this veritable battlefield, virtue signaling and "what about-ism" usually cancel each other out, as those lined up opposite or even next to one another in a landscape littered with landmines blow themselves to pieces. Neither camp cedes, or effectively gains ground, forcing you to conclude that any so-called victory in this virtual conflict, any argument or dialectic proven, is more inconsequential than critical, more *pyrrhic* than productive.

This sort of combativeness is now *de rigueur* online. Though the speed with which perpetual strife can be instigated and sustained on social media has emboldened such embitterment, a multitude of longstanding factors contributes to the divisiveness. Critical is that the furious and disaffected have long found the structure they so secretly crave through an unwavering commitment to dogma. Left and right sort of dissolve in a shared sense of imprimatur that prevents passionate, often younger, folks entrenched in ideology from recognizing that not only do they clutter the poles but also that, as a consequence, they leave tremendous ground between themselves and the lane the majority will travel. This passion, this power of conviction, is wonderful—and painfully familiar. However, it breeds a propensity for degeneration, disintegration through perpetual disagreement, a defensiveness that easily graduates to *offensive* deportment.

Unwavering conviction can easily become a set of handcuffs, fettering the freedom that can only be established through cultivating fellowship and acceptance. I long ago learned that waging a social media battle is an exercise in futility if not coupled with a semblance of electoral consensus, the tide of war remaining unchanged, that fleeting sense of self-satisfaction tantamount to splashing around in an ocean to no great effect.

Cyrus McQueen @CyrusMMcQueen · Oct 30, 2019
Right wingers are tryna fault the Obama's for buyin a house on Martha's Vineyard? Given all the black families who own homes there what's the problem? I mean do they consider black home ownership elitist? What, you supposed to be 'keepin your head above water' on the South Side?

⟲ 380   ♡ 2189

After primaries end and debates are held, our presidential elections reveal their true intention: establishing which faction of the electorate will further patriarchy for another four years. To not highlight this disheartening and ironic outcome would be derelict. Here the metric of white college-educated males versus white non-college-educated males, the polling data clumsily rolled out in an attempt to determine which partisan winds will carry us forward, obscures the more obvious takeaway for those within my encampment: our impact is being undermined once more by the calloused sourcing of such sour criteria. Race, yet again, proves crucial in establishing the *perceived* importance of particular voices.

However, with regard to leadership, the vision that seeks a diverse backing, this sort of myopia is inherently problematic. The almost flippant belief that one does not need to speak specifically to the problems of Black America, or embrace that fastidious element of the base, reeks of the off-putting privilege that, despite enticing rhetoric, reflects the enduring problems of patriarchy and race. Given the corporeal consequences of these elections, with Black and female autonomy ostensibly on the ballot, liberal entities that pit their ideals against our very bodies do little more than elect to undergird white privilege—this outcome fulfilled through the inanity of third party votes and protest votes for candidates *out* of the running.

Again, one can speak neither passionately nor persuasively about that broader human struggle without speaking to *our* struggle, or the sin which has metastasized in this country over several centuries. For a people whose impact has long been reduced, who long to have their race and individuality graded using a proper loupe, white candidates who overlook those qualities—either consciously or unconsciously—are anathema to a community that finds no comfort in the peripheral gaze. "What have you done for me lately" is more than a catchy tune whenever those seeking control fail this all-too-important test when it comes to acknowledging and showing compassion for the Black Democratic base.

Still, having witnessed the knife cut both ways—be it progressive infighting or Russians posing as both liberals and conservatives, running interference and stoking tensions, while creating incredible discomposure—it is *here* that the true importance of Mueller's document is most evident. Not in the report's ability to sink a presidency, as we had perhaps convinced ourselves it would, but for educating us on how a facsimile of reality could easily enter into our history books. Mueller corroborated that we were all, undeniably, pawns in a systematic disinformation campaign orchestrated at the highest levels to reward a villain and amplify his vitriolic message, while thousands of unnamed bots provided a flank to his gross maneuvers. Never did I feel we were fighting a losing battle with fear more than after I perused Mueller's masterwork, discovering the sheer magnitude of the Russian campaign to hack not only servers and social media but also the very minds of the most impressionable within our stratified society—those men and women dwelling just beyond the demarcation point in our inveterate divide.

Two decades ago, Malcolm Gladwell touched on these very themes in *The Tipping Point*. Though the award-winning writer produced this bestseller long before we would witness a conspiracy play out in our computers and on our phones, well before smartphones, he presciently observed that the Internet and email offered a level of immunity given the sheer volume of information and people constantly vying for our attention. In many ways, he pointed toward the very problem that would manifest from these new modes of communication. Citing psychological findings that "groups who communicate electronically deal with dissenting opinions very differently than groups who meet face to face," Gladwell highlighted how people "holding dissenting opinions expressed their arguments most 'frequently and persistently' when they communicated online." Where it was once difficult to attract the attention of any one individual given the expansiveness of our personal networks, the advent and proliferation of social media make it far easier for people to sequester themselves in vast bubbles of group think— faxes and email giving way to more personalized and curated networks of friends and likeminded individuals.

This unintended consequence of social media exposes Americans to manipulation. A generation prior, telemarketers sold us products over the phone, but in our new reality their equivalents sell us ideas and opinions. Further, since virtually all of us have lived online for the better part of a decade, telegraphing our tastes, our wants, and our likes, often in service of Likes, it was simply a matter of time until our immunity was compromised. This has exposed us deeply to bots and trolls, the new telemarketers, who know exactly who we are, what we want, and, more important, what we want to *hear*, thus rendering many of us utterly defenseless. Here, depending on one's objectives, be the agenda negative or positive, pushing a person's buttons is as easy as pushing a few buttons.

What unfolded in 2016 in many ways reflected what Gladwell further spoke about: "Epidemics create networks as well: a virus moves from one person to another, spreading through a community, and the more people a virus infects, the more 'powerful' the epidemic is." Given this astute assessment, what is "Make America Great Again" (or QAnon and Pizzagate for that matter) other than evidence of a great epidemic, like the Great Influenza a century prior, the virus that claimed over 50 million victims and touched every segment of society? The sad implication, however, is that Trump's network did not spread its disease hand to hand; MAGA does not infect the body's cells; rather, the sickness has been proliferated via the cellphones we *hold* in our hands.

The parallels are undeniable, as I discovered during my own volatile, often vicious, back and forth's with Twitter bigots—a development that is playing out to ironic levels during the coronavirus outbreak. As folks "frequently and persistently," in Gladwell's words, express opinions online they would not state in person—opinions that even go against their own best interests—it becomes clearer how those pummeled with far-right, or even far-*left*, propaganda, having this information fortified in hermetically sealed social networks, go on to spread the disease to the larger community. Thus is created an even bigger bubble, the newly brainwashed infecting those around them, because they are wholly convinced that nothing is wrong with them.

19

Funny Business

Cyrus McQueen @CyrusMMcQueen · May 29, 2018
Good for ABC! As a comedian there is a profound difference between punching
up, and punching down... Some people kick the marginalized. I choose to kick
the margins in the hopes of expanding the perimeters which for far too long have
kept black folks on the outside looking in...

⟲ 169   ♡ 910

With warring entities encamped on virtually every available platform transforming social media, our greater discourse soon permeated the comedy landscape as well. Trump's presence had so inspired vociferous objections to progress and parity across the board that, men operating within the microcosm of that particular community now appeared determined to reflect back this unruly development—championing their right to be as wrong and ill-informed as the man spouting doggerel from the highest office in the land.

Though this element of comedy has long been viable, the nation got a taste of the problematic dynamic when *Saturday Night Live* hired, and subsequently fired, a conservative comedian: his history of distasteful embellishments of minorities not going down well with folks craving healthier fare three years into the Trump presidency. Almost as soon as it was announced that the comic in question would not join the cast after all, the fallout was swift and severe. Suddenly, maladjusted men began to cry foul, the feverish objections on Twitter almost resembling a Tea Party-like groundswell. The noticeable change evinced by #BlackLivesMatter, and #MeToo had triggered something primal in conservatives, those existing both inside and beyond this performing microcosm.

Yet the conservative railing against "Cancel Culture" typifies a shared grievance not unlike the lamentation Trump himself expresses when conducting his orchestra of invective. It reflects a person who secures their sense of self through superciliousness. For a white male comic who already has a platform, it makes a certain sense to augment this perspective. Their peremptory nature allows them to look down on whole groups of people whilst literally looking down on an audience full of people. Thriving in this exalted space is the closest many of these comic men can get to omnipotence in a post-modern, post-Civil Rights America. It is their way of, like their fathers and grandfathers before them, achieving an elusive, outdated version of the American Dream, their way of experiencing, if only in ten- or fifteen-minute increments, what it is like to have no competition in the workplace.

To me, the image of the white picket fence is apropos in this greater context: it symbolizes not simply white flight but the hallmark of homogeneity, fittingly representing entrenched societal barriers that have come crashing down. For these individuals, a desire to reclaim a once-heralded position informs their need to resurrect the very same dynamics that *secured* that position. It suggests that whenever dominion and privilege are protected by keeping equality and accountability at bay, any sign of parity or responsibility will be viewed as lamentable and, in this regard, laughable.

Taking into consideration that the vast majority of Black folks are doing better than our parents and grandparents, at least concerning education and the corresponding opportunities this breeds for upward mobility, the opposite is bearing out for many white men. Where women's rights and civil rights have irrevocably transformed the American workforce, many of these men rue those advancements, overlooking how their own stagnation results not from racial or gender equality but from greater wealth inequality, a situation compounded by factors like outsourcing and automation. The American middle class, that postwar 20th century phenomenon, has never been more threatened than it is now: that suburban middle ground, which many comfortably inhabited, is imperiled, economic precarity undermining the American dream. In my estimation, it is this development, highlighted in a National Bureau of Economic Research study, *The Fading American Dream: Trends in Absolute Income Mobility Since 1940,* that fuels much of the animus. The findings, that children born in 1940 had a 90 percent chance of earning more than their parents, while the odds were half that for children born in 1984, help us understand the erosion of America's middle class and the racial dynamics that this erosion exacerbates.

Therefore, it is not only puzzling but paradoxical that Trump should be the self-proclaimed champion of the working class when he and his children reflect the converse. The family exemplifies the auspicious tendency for the well-heeled to hoard wealth, both he and his father displaying a propensity for promoting ne'er-do-well progeny to positions of importance despite a lack of true merit. Like many throughout middle America, those aggrieved comedians, by disparaging diversity, overlook that none of *us*, irrespective of race, are billionaires impervious to the vicissitudes of capitalism. And, being stuck on the same economic rung, we will likely all continue to remain here until we look up rather than over.

For many individuals positioned atop a pecking order, that stereotypes continue to inform insipid takes on those beneath them in our socioeconomic hierarchy is symptomatic of that larger issue pertaining to an inability to cope with newly realized intergenerational deficits. Yet it is *this* downward mobility, the whirlwind created because these men cannot claim to be doing better than their forefathers, that causes the clamor, this desire to reach for disdainful ethnic embellishments of the past. It is their way of knocking their competition down a peg. Such caustic humor serves as a security blanket, simultaneously providing comfort and honoring a long-lost history, it comparable to the behavior of generations of Southerners who, no matter how distasteful their regional legacy, refuse to let a bygone era vanish.

Whether these humorists rail against #MeToo, "Cancel Culture," or the whole notion of political correctness, it is but a vexation prompted by their having lost their fathers' prerogative to flaunt and fortify unfettered power. The pernicious perpetuation of stereotype is their feverish, albeit futile, attempt at resuscitating that force. However, while both arrogance *and* ignorance influence such sardonic humor, this well-honed riposte is informed *not* by their knowing no better but mainly by the fact that they have not *done* better. By holding on to hateful distortions in the name of comedy, they convince audiences, and even themselves, that their preeminence is in no way imperiled. But it is because diversity now whittles away their sway that this form of jejune jocularity remains, one of the last chips to fall. Like Al Jolson's jazz singer clinging to blackface to satiate benighted crowds, these humorists are unwilling to let the shit go, instead clinging dubiously to disdainful ethnic embellishments despite our changing times. Even though they can no longer legitimately look down on women or Asians or African Americans, they defiantly insist on doing so anyway, their indignation amounting to a form of protest. It is insolence inspired by their own obsolescence. But given that it took centuries of protests for marginalized persons, the butts of their jokes, to combat and correct unfair treatment in the first place, these infantile displays are ironic. Umbrage is the only way for these parties *to* justify ignorance and conveniently ignore objective truth. And like the 45th president, many will fashion an alternative, subjective reality, a facsimile of an imagined 1950s landscape where they can simply erect picket fences, or premises, rather than allow change to seep in.

In examining men like this, we see further proof of a ploy that has become essential in the post-modern era, all roads leading back to the very crucible that produced the Civil Rights Act of 1964. There were once-tangible legal barriers and pernicious intangibles that buttressed our perverse social construct. Judges and juries made it easy to espouse corresponding falsehoods, the law almost corroborating their veracity. But post-Civil Rights and the establishment of true voting rights—a situation that declared us ostensibly equal—ghostly ideas and horrific clichés have to do *all* the heavy lifting. In theatrical defiance of our discernible progress, comics and common men now work as one to shore up their conviction that we are *not* equal citizens, that we "should go back where we came from"—essentially re-litigating legal decisions from bars and stages, much as the president does from the White House. Here, sophomoric jokes restrain advancement through ribaldry, many appearing determined to pull women back also, their right to control their own bodies not nearly as strong as the hold these men wish to maintain—the objective being to secure a manner of obedience; thus they assert illusory control through half-baked, highly prurient comedic bits.

It is truly odd that, after contravening newly established rights and standards, many of these "funny" men present themselves as the injured party. But whether on social media or the performance stage, this predisposition to harangue, to air hollow grievances, betrays how much easier it is to play the victim than it is to *be* the victim. Again, the overwhelming signs suggest that these toxic males want a redressing of race and gender entitlements simply because they are left in a world without the advantage. As with Trump, they weirdly perceive that lack as tantamount to victimization. These malcontents' denigrations of gender and color confer on their comedy some intrinsic power to victimize, regardless of economic reality. Losing that authority thus makes them victims. They misconstrue and mistake losing the power to control others for being powerless and controlled. Yet perhaps most surprising, these childish protestations leave in place a harsh fact: when you have never been truly invisible or voiceless, it is easy to assume you were meant to be seen and heard. But far too many of these "bros" have never faced the discomfiting fact that maybe, just maybe, they have nothing *useful* to say. When people who predicate their value on some inorganic societal mutation that prioritizes one perspective almost exclusively and at the expense of anyone who does *not* share that distorted measure, it can spark anger, resentment, and an all-out tantrum from those who cannot grow the fuck up when forced to take off those training wheels and find equilibrium on an even track.

Cyrus McQueen @CyrusMMcQueen · Jan 18, 2020
This Meghan and Harry news is powerful... You got white folks in America who cling to race because it provides a sense of primacy... This dude is willing to give up ACTUAL primacy... the castles and servants and regalia... and all because he loves a black woman... it's exemplary.

⟲ 2515   ♡ 14732

The nihilism and disillusionment produced by such regression permeates popular culture to the point that, perhaps every ten years or so, we find ourselves inundated with a new batch of movies or projects that speak specifically to this societal canker: these conveyances open a porthole into the psyche of the increasingly unmoored white American male adrift in an immutable sea of progress. From *Taxi Driver* to *Falling Down*, *Fight Club* to *Joker*, despite the makeup or Mohawks sported by the protagonists, these tales capture the zeitgeist mainly in addressing this thinly veiled grudge. However, their probing of discontentment often reveals such content to be duplicitous. This tired rumination on the tortured white male, the cliché these creators prod the public into embracing—this unspoken idea that these men deserve more from a society that turns its back on them—is, in and of itself, intellectually dishonest. It is histrionics by those who wish to eschew our very history, reinforcing the battle cry, the primal scream, of those seemingly relegated to the periphery, exploring a rage that belies centuries of racial and sexual dominance.

Yet where that constant produces chilling real-life examples of misfits and malcontents exacting violence in every pocket of the country, the cinematic tales are anemic in contrast, nothing more than fallacy forgoing a deep dive into the entire notion of gender and racial supremacy. By cleverly marketing these vehicles as revenge fantasy, exploring the raw emotions of these effete characters—instead of the inconvenient politics underlying their perturbations—this one-dimensional fare merely nibbles at a symptom of a grave illness, one that portends the worst for a society prone to providing wrong solutions rather than addressing their true problem. As a result, these character studies do not so much draw you into fictitious struggles as much as they present compelling, even if unintended, pictures of our fractious country—a country whose character *can* legitimately be called into question. For what would these leading characters settle on, after all of the calisthenics and the physical transformation? After the haircut and after losing the girl? When they are done peacocking and talking to themselves? The auteurs behind these tales paint their protagonists into a corner: anarchy and mayhem appear to be the only escape, the only tangible resolution, violent destruction the best way forward for the backward thinker.

For these comics and other artful exceptions, their compelling tales of outcasts and misanthropes ignore a glaring fact: whether it is Madison Avenue or middle America, movie houses or magazine stands, the ballad of the white American male, that roaring saga, has continued on its distinct and undeviating course at least since 1776. Despite much ballyhoo, despite a cultural reckoning and trends pointing to the contrary, that beat goes on. This hegemony has never been under any real discernible threat. Not in my lifetime. Not when African Americans represent one-seventh of the U.S. population yet more than one-third of its prison population—and not when preeminent institutions like Harvard enroll more legacy students than Black and Brown ones. Even when navigating the extremes, the effects of color *still* compound even the most disparate of predicaments.

We merely need to look back one hundred years: read *The Souls of Black Folk,* the seminal work of Harvard graduate W.E.B. DuBois, and you will discover that the damaging impact of discrimination is perpetual, the dilemma of white supremacy persisting for centuries. A person of color negotiating our bifurcated reality, both then and now, cannot do so "without being cursed and spit upon by his fellows, without having the doors of opportunity closed roughly in his face."

Though class concerns in America are also outstanding, the racial reality suggests that where census tracking might convince our white counterparts that they are losing, those who are divorced from opportunity, and in many instances, from freedom itself, see a constant reinforcement that they are likely *to* lose. As with Trump, this pother may result from the obsession over the exceptional among us, with many lifting their noses at the flavorful change the Obamas of the world embody. However, these fractured men overlook that it is precisely their otherworldliness that secures such dispensation; the Obamas are exceptions rather than the rule. When it comes to brilliant Black men and women, their detractors see *only* the Black, not the brilliance. Additionally, those like Trump who delight in singling out those like his predecessor—even openly questioning his Harvard placement—never admit that while those outstanding men and women like Barack and his wife Michelle follow all the rules, mediocre men like themselves break them. And therein lies the lie, the very falsehood that neither a foul-mouthed Trump nor his toffee-nosed nationalists own up to. Though legal segregation ended over fifty years ago, the side doors and backdoors are *still* labeled "whites only."

In a haunting incantation from *Hamilton,* the words of the great Lin Manuel Miranda resonate, forcing us to consider who has never been barred from "the room where it happens, the room where it happens, the room where it happens, the room where it happens." If we take an incisive look behind the scenes, we can spot a pattern at work in those entrenched attitudes that keep people of color just beyond the threshold while *literally* opening said doors for white folks. Furthermore, whether it is a film crew or those areas of upper management in an investment firm, those settings *clinically* bereft of diversity, it is easy to see who is *not* represented, who is invariably left behind. Whether it is politics or popular culture, the misleading impression that men who can find their reflection, in abundance, in board rooms and writers rooms, from *Fortune* 500 companies to Internet startups, on Wall Street and Capitol Hill—that they are somehow fighting uphill battles is a counter-narrative that brings idolaters to propagate spurious propaganda, with fiction strangely regarded as fact. But that plight, however solipsistic, however skewed, still appears to be most important, that pain still registered, that voice overpowering the chorus of people of color, women, and members of the LGBTQ+ community ululating from the void of America's background.

The reality of white male dominance thus proves unyielding but layered, inhabiting the face of both the status quo and the underdog. With the conventional feeding on itself, those whose race, gender, and sexual preferences imprison them along the fringes eat scraps, barely satiated on crumbs of hope and a brighter future.

TWEETING TRUTH TO POWER

At some point in my personal recent history, I remembered that I am a standup comedian. This realization could not have come at a better time, the world under Trump having become so unbelievably serious. Though I continued to humor in a 280-character comedy club, my thirst for a live audience, for the visceral, palpable exchanges that are endemic to the performance stage, had gone unquenched for too long. Yet in preparing to jump back on stage, I recognized that the world had changed. Had the rules of stand-up comedy also changed? Did a particular strain of piousness now run through the greater culture in natural response to the Trump presidency?

Still, I was not too concerned, given that the new mood mostly stifles those men who, as I pointed out, mock the marginalized and delight in punching down. Coming from a rich Black comedic tradition—and after a minstrel era in which our forced deportment belied our palpable frustrations—I operate in a more salubrious climate, one that affords me as performer the opportunity to defiantly punch *up*. So I kind of welcomed this period and the world's increased appetite for the "pull no punches" kind of comedic truth those who inspire my work have expertly served up for several decades.

The fact is, a humorist is part sociologist, part philosopher, part cultural anthropologist. Pillorying this particular president embodies, in part, that rich legacy. Being a Black comedian is a most dynamic reflection of being a Black American, and because we are on and forced to operate from the socioeconomic bottom, strictures that long inspired our resistance and tempered our resolve help to inform *this* unique period. That singular reality infuses this most redolent of art forms.

Our special license to examine the human condition courageously, communicating the findings in our distinctive, evocative cadence, sets comedians apart from other artists. Life is not always black and white: it can be both probable and improbable, clear-cut yet messy, and very often those murkier aspects of our existence, our conflicting and confounding gray areas, inspire the kind of art that grips audiences. We comedians can engender a primal reaction in real time because those keen observations and distillations, the ironic delicacies feeding our craft—those inconvenient truths reflected in our personal experiences and those of the collective—provide the basis for forging a strong bond with said audience. It is *this* connection that enables us to go on a most gratifying and illuminating journey together.

Being that comedy is inherently political as well as deeply personal, it is often through a comics' personal failings that audiences come to recognize their own, self-examination augmenting their willingness to identify and explore those even *greater* failings. Our ability to hold the mirror up to ourselves enables us to then turn it around on them and the society we live in. That said, a room full of strangers typically grants us this tacit consent *solely* if we are willing to say not just what they want to hear but, rather, what they *did not* know they want to hear, this series of surprises earning us the permission to probe deeper. Established commonalities having created a pool, we can go far beyond surface and superficiality.

During this deeper shared journey, our having identified ironies large and small, and having established trust, a comic can wade into the biggest laughs—as long as we, of course, relentlessly deal in the currency of honesty. Again, we invariably earn and can thus afford these concessions only when we first present unvarnished truth. Though there is plenty of shallow humor, and shallow humorists who happily splash around in superficial waters, it is those who are not chary of plumbing the depths of verity, that more daunting immersion, who generate the *greater* response; that greater reward is their compensation *for* their courageous endeavor.

From Moms Mabley and Redd Foxx, the continuum stretches to truth tellers like Richard Pryor and Dick Gregory (and is incarnated in the present era in deliciously defiant warriors like Dave Chappelle and Chris Rock). I am well aware of this legacy of African American humor and humorists who have found levity in even the darkest, most depressing reality, under the most poignant of circumstances. Therefore, the lyricism through which I often lambaste a mushroom-dicked mothafucka like the president, this fuckin copper Caligula, is my *channeling* those predecessors, my way of honoring our past by inviting them to speak through me during this, our problematic present.

Among all these distinguished predecessors, I would be remiss to not underscore my unparalleled love and unbridled fascination with one Richard Franklin Lennox Thomas Pryor, that singular voice who harnessed so acutely the Black storytelling tradition. This unique form of testifying—something paramount in the Black experience, extending from tribal traditions to the diaspora, a spirited engagement that often takes the form of holding court yet can easily transmute into elaborate send-ups about family, community, and existence—unfurled almost magically in this majestic and wiry champion. That he could wield lightning, shocking the callous and sentient alike with his electrifying honesty—bearing witness as he pulled back the curtain on Black America to entertain with a charged, albeit delicate and nuanced, look into the often-discordant layers of race—was part of his sublime mastery. But that within those layers was embedded an obloquy, a matter of factness, his palpable defiance lending a sociopolitical crease to his art, rendering it crisp and resplendent, is what really made him an idol to me and so many others.

Witnessing Pryor juggling these elements could be jaw dropping. In one of his most candid recordings, the album titled *Is It Something I Said*, he launches into a bit that is eerily ironic, almost speaking to our present and what we face with the 45th president. He begins with a riff on Richard Nixon being received in jail: "What's happening, Tricky Dick" then segues into a staggered dissemination of the distinctive dilemma we face as African Americans. Pryor, reflecting the awesome potential for Black comedy to both entertain and enlighten, hilariously discloses his own struggle, yet he shrewdly connects it to the greater struggle of other Black men—here assembled in one specific courtroom. He posits, "You go down there lookin for Justice, that's just what you find: *Just* Us." He dissects the politics of privilege, in this case a crooked president skirting justice, while sending up how that justice would play out, before sharing his own deeply personal rumination—this culminating in a sobering indictment of both the criminal justice system *and* race itself—and all within one minute! It is a testament to his sheer, unrivaled brilliance. Scott Saul, author of *Becoming Richard Pryor* speaks specifically to this singular talent when he writes of Pryor that: "Onstage he is mesmerizing. You feel, in the audience, that you're plugged into the socket of life— that you're seeing not a single man onstage but rather an entire world in roiling motion, animated through a taut experiment in creative chaos and artistic control."

Pryor's acuity was forged by the inelastic reality of Black poverty and prejudice, this giving birth to those salient and singular takes on it. When considering how we have taken a step back as a society, his redolent output is more relevant than ever. Given the reality of Black life and racial strife, these factors unchanging, Pryor's impact, his *importance*, has only appreciated. For those of us who continue to deconstruct the matrix of supremacy methodically, laugh by laugh, I vow to never let go of those sonorous voices in my ear. Those like Pryor—and like my own late father, a product of Black urban life in a pre-Civil Rights America, who also reflected its post-'60s excesses, his resonant, well-curated comedic voice honed in the back alleys and gambling rooms of Roxbury—continue to resonate with me on stage; he is part of a group that anchors my performance from the celestial wings.

Though I am disinclined to be ribald per se, I am prone to punctuating my act with the right amount of profanity. My adroitness with all the words showcases my concomitant education in both the suburbs and the inner city, my sets reflecting DuBois's dissertation on double consciousness. Those conflicting forces, which form our comprehensive Black reality, influence this quest to present our most authentic selves to audiences. Here, the Black comedic perspective reflects that deep desire to neither sublimate our "older selves" to satisfy Eurocentric tastes nor eschew our Western influences and thus inaccurately render Black life. By sharing dispatches from our encampment, communiques that the white world is not usually privy to, I and others recognize an added benefit: a chance for audiences to see the world more accurately through our eyes instead of through their own distorted gaze. Because impressions of Blackness have long been one-sided, by proffering a unique profile, almost curating these notable contours, Black artists can guide outsiders around our cultural totems, aspects that the gatekeepers of mainstream culture often misconstrue and misrepresent. Be it poverty or privation, deprivation or even destitution, our unsparing look into the shadows of American life—along with the oppression from which it is cast—transforms this herculean endeavor, and those whose talents I revere for taking up this task, into a testament to bravery. Those who boldly explore the dark thereby expose America's deception by shining *their* light on it.

Plato would be proud of Pryor and that faction of Black philosophers who grabbed microphones to deliver their elegies. Because they were unafraid to go further and, moreover, because their mirth was, in effect, informed by the filth littering America's fucked up, forgotten fringes—a perimeter that both primes and amplifies our screams—I take it as my mothafuckin' duty to honor this prospecting tradition. Having benefitted from their groundwork, and because the forces augmenting the reality of Black life have not fundamentally changed, I, in a word, *vow* to not be politically correct. Besides, what is my roasting of the boorish swine at 1600 Pennsylvania Avenue other than my thumbing my broad nose at political correctness?

Cyrus McQueen @CyrusMMcQueen · Mar 24, 2019
The way most Americans are feeling right now in light of the #MuellerReport
and Barr's findings is the way most people of color have perpetually felt
throughout the history of this country... This is a familiar feeling... As Richard
Pryor said, "There is no Justice... Just Us"...

⟲ 618   ♡ 2171

The opportunity to once again take the temperature of the country soon presented itself. For me, a living breathing patient in the form of a large live audience is always preferable to digital correspondence. I relish the chance to study in real time how humor affects the human body, to observe the blood rushing to their faces, the lines forming from their cheeks to their chins, their mouths agape as they are fed one line after another. There is nothing better than beholding a satiated crowd, stuffed and fully satisfied from the comedic fodder being served up.

These delicious visions nourished me all the way down the shore, my hunger to jump back on stage about to be rewarded with a feast in a familiar location. Yes, I was returning to South Jersey, the scene of the crime, the same venue where, a year earlier, I had reenacted the Boston Massacre for a middle-aged, mostly older audience, the guffawing geriatrics unprepared for the physical demands I placed on them. Yet as I counted down the exits on the turnpike, nervousness set in. Would it be the same? Would this crowd prove as welcoming as the last? After yet another year of the Trump presidency, would my observations remain salient and satisfying to an older audience? I had pieced together several new jokes, repurposed from my Twitter set, embellished and fleshed out for maximum effectiveness on stage. Yet though they had succeeded online—likes and retweets corroborating their viability—disseminating it all in real time was not unlike walking a tightrope. Every step had to be well timed and perfect, or I would face a ghastly demise. No comedian enjoys dying on stage and, despite the science and repetition we apply to it, it remains an art form and thus unpredictable, kill or be killed the binary option.

I furtively retraced my steps, arriving to another sold-out house, retirees sipping rosé, the men clad in a rich palette of turquoise and peach button-downs. As I paced the hallway behind the back tables, sensations from the year before returned to me. The audience began emanating approval to the emcee in the form of raucous cheering and whistles. As he lay groundwork, I recalibrated and shifted things around. The feature act went on, presenting gems not too dissimilar to ones embedded in my leather-bound notebook. I held mine up to his in the moment, comparing and contrasting, before determining that my precious stones bore enough of a resemblance that the patrons would likely buy mine, too. That would be my way in now. General jokes about the weather, not unlike those about sports, would, I hoped, provide my perfect springboard into another warm reception.

The knot in my throat threatened to constrict my breathing as the host announced me, but the muscle memory of vaulting onstage soon took over. My body began moving without my consent. The previous comic having addressed the inclement weather gave me an anchor for my opening joke—a yarn about white weathermen vilifying black ice while never mentioning the destruction caused by regular ice. Almost immediately I heard the boom: that all-too-familiar, oh-so-welcome sound after your words detonate an explosion of rolling laughter. I was back! Opening on race, with my comedic examination of societal contradictions eliciting that big of a reaction, it reduced any lingering fear that was keeping me from being fully present. I proceeded with the pyrotechnics, transitioning seamlessly into growing up Black, being Black in an interracial marriage, even the silly way racism propagates through such technological advancements as autocorrect. Every punchline popped, the clapping hands convincing me that not only did my truth go off, but that it was *landing*, the distant rumble reflecting the slight delay as my gospel rippled throughout the venue.

The sweat began to trickle down my forehead, a drop landing on the screen of my phone when I checked to see how far I had ventured into my set. Already at the 42-minute mark, and despite the discharge, I had yet to launch into any Trump material. With less than twenty minutes to bring this flight in for a landing, I addressed the orange elephant in the room. "So, I gotta ask, how do we feel about Trump?" The response was nearly unanimous. Boos began to emanate from the bombed-out crowd, this corroboration all I needed to begin lighting the fuse for the finale. "Can ya believe Trump says he isn't racist? Says he's the least racist person you'll ever meet?" The disdain slowly began cresting, the hisses preceding the very sound that would immediately follow ignition. "I dunno. If it looks like a duck, and it walks like a duck. . ." I then paused for pacing and to provide just the right amount of distance from the setup. I could feel the anticipation mounting as they waited for me to deliver the punch. "And it's named *Donald!*" BOOM! The cracking of thunder reverberated throughout the crowd of flushed faces. I remember the heads of those around the stage darting from side to side as each person found comfort and confirmation in the laughter of the person beside them, this stunning visual adding a compelling layer, rolling laughter from the crowd leading to this rewarding display, the sea of happy faces resembling rollicking waves.

I did not hear the different kind of boos at first. The ones comedians dread. You would have been hard-pressed to hear any signs of disapproval in that extravaganza, but perhaps my inner ear was attuned to, even anticipating, such a response. That all-too-real possibility that had preceded my journey and lingered just over my shoulder throughout the evening, was indeed transpiring. My fears would be confirmed when the applause died down just enough for me to make out a faint "fuck you!" from near the back. Almost immediately, the sea parted and I could make out shadows of figures rising, sounds of commotion supplanting the more favorable noises that had been drowning it out. I observed those looks of satisfaction suddenly morph into looks of concern as every head was soon rubbernecking toward the back of the room. I had already begun my next joke and, so as not to telegraph my own disconcertment, pushed on through. To my consternation, the joke failed to land. My mind immediately began racing as I feverishly sought a way out of this turbulence. I started thinking of retorts, loading the chamber with a few deadly comebacks, just in case I had to start firing back. But alas, no one was paying attention to me; all eyes were now trained on this table of six disgruntled Trump Supporters from Cape May. As they continued their hijack, I could now definitively make out the "fuck you's." The manager began to hustle them from the venue, but under the burning stage lights, what was likely a matter of seconds felt to me like an eternity.

But before I could recover, let alone retaliate, magic occurred. The audience, my charges, stood up to protect *me*. They heckled my hecklers, steadily at first, then in a precipitous downpour drowning out the disruption. Folks on either side of the stage rose to their feet, their own booing raining down on those being ejected. A table at two o'clock, followed by a table at nine o'clock, rose, the octogenarian occupants creating an omnidirectional phalanx. The fervor by which they slowly but surely rose to the challenge moved me to my core. I was rendered speechless. I remember once reading about a school of dolphins that had encircled a swimmer to protect them from an approaching great white shark. This felt like that. Before long, every table was shielding me from the attack, these older men and women a rampart of reassurance, absorbing this vituperation. To my eternal surprise, nearly everyone around me began clapping, encouraging me to "keep goin!" The disdain redirected at the saboteurs, the ringing endorsement directed toward me, heightened the dissonance in this surreal scene. The group of six finally exited, and I will never forget the exclamation point that one woman provided as she pointed toward their empty table and yelled, "They couldn't handle the truth!" And then, as if she could not warm my jaded heart any more, this vivacious woman with the animal-print blouse implored me, "Keep goin hon!"

Having taken to stages both minuscule and massive, from bar basements to a Hollywood soundstage, from shows with over one thousand people to those with only *one*, this stands as my most rewarding stand-up experience ever.

However, I cannot help but note what this heartwarming display suggested about our greater discourse three years into a presidency that had coarsened dialogue—polarizing our society and those living in it. It proved to me that surprises *can* come when I least expect them and from those I least expect to provide this sort of corroboration—the kind that forces you to recalibrate your perspective. With another general election on the horizon, this discovery warmed me on my wintry commute back to the Big Apple. If a young Black man and a room full of older white Americans can reach a dynamic consensus amidst those pockets of divisiveness, then not only does it forecast something favorable but it also suggests actual hope for our American dialectic. If that very showroom, operating as a microcosm, reflects dynamics progressing throughout the American macrocosm, then the unimpeachable truth, born out of the unyielding, inflexible laws of comedy, and through this very act itself, almost ensures that this country is gonna be alright. It is a potent reminder that there is but *one* truth and it is ultimately impervious to misinterpretation.

"Fake News" may be Trump's churlish, often successful attempt at muddying the waters, but when it comes to verity, that ingredient indispensable to our art form, there is little room for confusion when presented with such palpable concord—when the lowly estimation of him *has* been verified by most. He may get away with "Fake News," but no comedian gets away with fake laughter, especially when you have a live, liquored-up crowd. And, yes, a repudiation of him and his influence can indeed spread throughout a large group.

20

Call In The Plumbers

Throughout my time writing and tweeting, Donald Trump has lied and aggrandized, augmented his brand at the expense of U.S. taxpayers, abused the very power he was vested with, and eroded any sense of decorum, decency, or normalcy. In the process, he has also become the third U.S. president to be impeached by Congress. Yet that he had coasted through 73 years with zero accountability, his wealth earning him dispensation to erode the solvency of others while his wealth grew, suggested a pattern unlikely to change when he transitioned, at least nominally, from business to politics. Indeed, we soon learned that the president leans on leaders of countries with the same temerity with which he has bullied the vendors for his casinos and other properties. Where the business world's lack of oversight enabled his hurricane to gather momentum, checks and balances, that mighty monitor of our own system of government, would provide us the only readily available measure to impede this out-of-control man from prompting further calamity.

If you were a betting person, or simply as prescient as House Speaker Nancy Pelosi, who intimated the man would be "self-impeachable," you would place a hefty wager on Trump's eventual self-immolation. But if you pay close attention to the motif the odious builder routinely etches—a pattern of skullduggery ensuring that he always meets his material and mercurial wants—you will also recognize how he often relies on the law or, more specifically, an unscrupulous gaggle of high-priced lawyers, to facilitate his desired end.

Considering that the casino builder lacks tact, that he always runs roughshod over people, we knew we could count on him to replicate this invidious behavior in the White House. His indecency and indelicateness suggested that it was only a matter of time before he reduced the role of president to one of mere self-remuneration. That he has devalued *another* valuable East Coast property in the process can be chalked up to a long-established pattern of brazenness. Thus, his plan to improve his reelection chances—and concomitantly cover up crimes that got him elected—would see him dispatch another weaselly attorney, this time to oversee yet *another* situation in which he had fucked someone. But his diabolical plan, to have Ukraine's newly elected president Volodymyr Zelensky investigate his likely Democratic rival Joseph Biden, surprised me more than I thought possible; his treachery entangling individuals at *multiple* levels of our government.

The incriminating evidence soon poured in, making it clear that Trump believed he could pressure Zelensky to impugn Biden—the biggest obstacle standing between him and four more years in the White House. To facilitate this, Trump would create a specter of criminality around the work Joe's son Hunter did for Burisma Holdings, a Ukrainian gas company. Trump's actions here speak to the behavior of a person too weak, too ineffective to win an endurance race that places inordinate demands on any candidate's inherent gifts. Operating from a fundamental deficit when it comes to the intangibles that we observe in so many other presidents—qualities like inspiration, sophistication, and legitimacy—Trump had no resort *but* to cheat. Here he would simply replicate the formula he has applied his entire life: prevarication, distraction, and, when all else fails, *disruption*. For the mercurial real estate mogul-turned-politician, disaster *is* the go-to model, his most effective blueprint for success. It is the very template from which the plan to withhold military aid to Ukraine would hatch.

After Robert Mueller's testimony on Capitol Hill, the denouement to his investigation and the release of his eponymous report—a report that, it must be reiterated, had not exonerated Trump; it simply failed to indict him—the expedient presumption among Washington Republicans was that their most crooked champion had dodged a bullet. Upon the end of that day's hearings, every conservative pundit on television was puffing their chest. It was almost certain that, as we watched the special prosecutor walk off into that majestic D.C. sunset, Trump too felt more invincible than ever. It is now clear our outlaw president felt emboldened enough to carry out his criminal act in regard to Ukraine once it became clear Congress would *not* be bringing him to justice after all. Hell, I would argue that it was precisely because he had not been charged for his election improprieties that he felt free to then *pin* those improprieties on Ukraine.

Yet what was truly maddening, and what left Resisters collectively scratching our heads, was how Trump pressed on in spite of his legal tumult, proving adroit at replenishing his well of criminal coconspirators. Exit Rick Gates, Roger Stone, Paul Manafort, and Michael Cohen; enter Mike Pompeo, William Barr, Mick Mulvaney, and yes, the bootless, toothless, former NYC Mayor Rudy Giuliani. The new but questionably improved rogue's gallery of henchmen rotated in to do their crime boss's bidding, this time with many of them bearing official government titles and operating comfortably from the confines of the Justice and State departments.

Given Trump's rotten objectives, and considering that his infamous phone call to Zelensky came less than 24 hours after Mueller's testimony, the rather unambiguous backdrop was filled in even before a whistleblower complaint painted the damning picture. Yet in this phone conversation, where Trump plainly asks Zelensky for help with "the Biden thing"—before volunteering the services of the imbecilic Giuliani to help find the trail of crumbs the gang had scattered between the former vice president and his son Hunter—it is evident he had already begun spinning a self-entangling web. His criminality is so robust, so layered and involuted, that his crimes, like his lies, buttress one another.

That he undoubtedly enlisted his own staff to alter scheduling and handle evidence related to Ukraine—this for the specific purpose of promulgating rumors that would improve his reelection bid—meant he had likely impelled White House employees to violate the Hatch Act *before* he even got around to this tangled business of withholding military aid. As we now know, the groundwork for the solicitous call, and the crimes therein, was in place well prior to Zelensky's swearing in: Trump's chief of staff Mick Mulvaney later admitted his own involvement, disclosing that Trump had mentioned to him the "corruption" narrative pertaining to the DNC hacks before confirming to reporters, "That's why we held up the money."

Quizzically, Mulvaney attempted to brashly explain away their brash criminality, positing, "We do that all the time," a statement as illuminating as his subsequent announcement that the White House planned to hold the next G7 Summit at Trump's Doral Country Club. I mean, the fuckery was flabbergasting. Trump's temerity cut those of us who thought we had grown calloused to his chronic wrongdoing. In one short press conference, Mulvaney betrayed how the Emoluments Clause *and* the Hatch Act were mere afterthoughts to an administration determined to carry out ever greater acts of criminality. However, it was this sort of brazenness that would in many ways inspire what did happen next: The House Judiciary Committee taking the momentous and necessary step of drafting articles of impeachment. It was as if Mulvaney's truculent words, "Get over it" primed the historic, righteous response that followed this ignoble foot-swallowing—despite his futile attempt at extracting his leather oxford from his mouth to try to walk it all back.

Trump's egregious actions, the crux of what led to the impeachment inquiry and subsequent vote, were solely—it bears repeating—the actions of a profoundly worthless man seeking to insure himself from an almost preordained failure. Freezing roughly four hundred million dollars in aid—incidentally, right in line with the roughly four hundred million dollars in aid his father had provided him over a lifetime—reflected the ebb and flow of funds it took to provide the incapable Trump with a desperately needed advantage.

Cyrus McQueen @CyrusMMcQueen · Sep 27, 2019
What're the odds that a political party, which launched multiple investigations into Clinton's secret server, would find themselves defending a 'Crooked' President who, lo and behold, hid the transcripts of his Ukraine call on *drumroll please* A SECRET SERVER? 😬 #CrookedDonald ⌨

⟲ 1251   ♡ 4049

It would soon be proven: Trump deliberately delayed $391 million worth of aid to Ukraine, both medical funds and military equipment, including rocket-propelled grenades and sniper rifles—items instrumental to the country's ongoing fight against Russian separatists. That he used the prerogatives of the presidency to shore up his own hopelessness is what resonated with me most in the moments after it became clear that impeachment hearings would take place. As our government ground to a halt, forced to unearth this chain of events, a clear-cut picture emerged: one day after closing the chapter on foreign interference in the 2016 election, Trump picked up the phone and opened the chapter on foreign interference in the 2020 election.

Again, an incriminating timeline of events—events that, try as he might, he could never explain away as happenstance—cemented the case against Donald J. Trump. The facts would never exculpate him, as they established quite definitively the converse: a mere 90 minutes after the Zelensky call, the doofus did indeed delay that aforementioned aid. Thus, he set in motion events that would ensnarl the Pentagon, State Department, and, upon the brave act of a whistleblower, the U.S. Congress.

Considering Russia's annexation of Crimea, its borders repeatedly violated by hostile Russian actors, the irony was inescapable: a president who caused such a pother over border safety in the southern United States, who expressed such a fixation over "invasion," now purposely disregarded not only a legitimate threat to Ukraine but also the subsequent steps our Congress took to ameliorate that threat. Putin had compromised not only Crimea's government but *ours*.

These new developments would only bolster the assessments that Vice President Biden aired back in 2015: "Russia continues to send its thugs, its troops, its mercenaries across the border, Russian tanks and missiles still fill the Donbas." With everything that has since transpired, it was *this* very appraisal, followed by Biden's full throated assurance, that has proven to be most consequential: "The United States will continue to stand with Ukraine against Russian aggression. We're providing support to help and train and assist your security forces, and we've relied on and rallied the rest of the world to Ukraine's cause."

Regarding a country like Ukraine—whose purported "corruption," it must be reiterated, the corrupt current U.S. president could not give two fucks about—it is undeniable that our chief executive's decisions catered exclusively to undoing the work of the Obama/Biden administration. Yet the shocking nub of it all, of grave importance to our own country, is that Trump's desire to improve his own political future ran parallel with, and was now indistinguishable from, Russia's political concerns and future. We must also consider the countless individuals within the GOP who, ignoring this peril, adopted Trump's chicanery and further enabled his treachery, seeking to fortify their own power by placating him. But the epic criminality of it all—Trump having not only colluded with Russia to compromise 2016 but then *using* those ill-gotten gains, his very presidency, to bribe a country into investigating Biden—is almost dizzying. His further attempts to pin blame for 2016 on Ukraine would find him colluding in order to cover *up* that initial collusion, all as he took steps to try to compromise 2020.

It still unnerves me: if one scrupulous public servant had *not* come forward with an official whistleblower complaint—throwing up a roadblock to prevent a careening, out-of-control president from dragging America further down the road to unmitigated disaster—Trump would have barreled forward on his inexplicably dangerous path until he left the rule of law, American autonomy, everything that distinguishes us as a democracy, unrecognizable and pulverized in his wake. The whistleblower complaint is unequivocal: "In the course of my official duties, I have received information from multiple U.S. Government officials that the President of the United States is using the power of his office to solicit interference from a foreign country in the 2020 U.S. election." The complaint lays bare, rather succinctly, the precursor to the inquiry that produced that most historical of congressional rebukes, the momentous occasion in which a decisive impeachment vote questioned the integrity of the U.S. president.

Cyrus McQueen @CyrusMMcQueen · Oct 10, 2019
BREAKING NEWS: Two Associates of Rudy Giuliani were just arrested for campaign finance violations related to Ukraine and seeking dirt on Biden... I'm not saying it's the beginning of the end but, if this was a Scorcese movie, you'd be hearing The Rolling Stones right about now...

⟲ 729   ♡ 3555

Paramount to the eventual case was the role of toothless Rudy, Giuliani's name appearing three sentences into the whistleblower complaint. Concerning said solicitation for interference, and the call to investigate one of the president's main domestic political rivals, it states: "The President's personal lawyer, Mr. Rudolph Giuliani, is a central figure in this effort." Giuliani had already traded-in his caché as "America's mayor," squandering currency he had accumulated post-9/11, to be a full-time Muppet on Fox News. When not spouting doggerel on those airwaves, he was the busy hired gun for a coterie of international criminals—engaging in backchannel deals to oust Venezuelan President Nicolas Maduro in one instance; using his relationship with Trump to force then-Secretary of State Rex Tillerson to intervene in the prosecution of a gold-trading Iranian-Turkish client in another. Clearly, he was in no way chary when it came to spreading conspiracies for a little lucre. That those instances were precursors to the brash maneuvers to undermine Ukraine's leader, and later ensure that a State Department under Mike Pompeo would do his illegal bidding—it reveals that Trump was not the only one operating from a diabolical template.

That the vampiric former NYC mayor would be a central figure in Trump's impeachment is unsurprising. Giuliani is himself a hubristic and amoral man with a huge head and little principle, a man who has, inarguably, built a career on the undue suffering of others. Given the generation of Black men lacerated by the shards of his "broken windows" policy of policing, who had their freedom summarily squeezed between the rock of stop-and-frisk and the hard place of those corresponding Rockefeller sentencing laws, watching him amass *more* casualties to service his own illegality and questionable endgame, felt somewhat predictable.

Given all that unfurled after the now infamous July 25, 2019, call between Trump and Zelensky, the illuminating three words of their conversation, "talk to Rudy," represent the most consequential dot connecting every subsequent detail of this criminal conspiracy, the whistleblower complaint, and a picture that had begun to crystallize long before Trump even picked up the phone. Alongside those furtive efforts to incriminate Burisma Holdings, it is now known that Giuliani's other objective was to tout the ongoing conspiracy theory citing Ukraine's involvement in hacking the Democratic National Committee. Critical to these ignoble efforts was Giuliani's quest to incriminate CrowdStrike, the cybersecurity firm that did work for the DNC and, more important, discovered that it was Russia, not Ukraine, behind the 2016 security breach. Operating as an unfettered outside channel, an intermediary able to work with surrogates inside the Trump administration, Giuliani could *will* that particular conspiratorial falsehood into existence, even if the intelligence community and Mueller had already corroborated CrowdStrike's findings: Russia was solely responsible for the DNC hack that precipitated the release of 20,000 internal Democratic emails prior to the 2016 presidential election.

Zelensky never stood a chance: Trump was hellbent on historical revisionism, on minimizing Mueller's findings and Russia's pertinence to his own presidency. As leader of a much-maligned Ukraine—given the force wielded by his hostile neighbor and the ignominious U.S. president working on its behalf—Zelensky was already between a rock and a hard place on May 20, 2019, the day he officially took office. A *Washington Post* report from October of that year corroborates this, detailing Trump's plans to pressure Zelensky from the moment he assumed his duties: "Trump instructed Pence not to attend the inauguration . . . an event White House officials had pushed to put on the vice president's calendar—when Ukraine's new leader was seeking recognition and support from Washington."

Although Vice President Pence later denied being aware of any attempt to dig up dirt on the Bidens, plausible deniability flew out the window the minute Energy Secretary Rick Perry supplanted him to observe Zelensky's swearing in. Trump was playing hard to get, withholding both U.S. aid *and* recognition, even refusing to host the newly minted leader until Zelensky made it clear he would do something, *anything*, to improve the boorish U.S. president's reelection bid. Those outside and inside channels, be it Giuliani or Pence, were instrumental in priming Zelensky for the moment Trump would take him to task— the moment he would be charged with changing objective truth to service their craven objectives.

The simultaneous attacks on Burisma Holdings and CrowdStrike soon reached a farcical level, exhausting even the steadfast, a malaise setting in despite earnest attempts at keeping up with all the disorienting chicanery. With the Fox News 24-hour propaganda machine in full swing—eschewing logic to twist heads around the uneven stories routinely offered up by this imbalanced president—the GOP got out in front of the upcoming hearings by painting Biden as the guilty party.

The president's team soon launched another bizarre narrative: that Ukraine was hiding *additional* information pertaining to Burisma Holdings. Given that Hunter Biden had once served on the gas company's board, it was almost predictable the inert president would target the son of his prime political challenger. We do not need to watch nature documentaries or hear the euphonious voice of David Attenborough to know that calves in the wild are typically the most vulnerable, especially for predators ill equipped or, in Trump's case, *incapable* of taking on bigger prey. Trump, Giuliani, and his pack of hyenas knew that an ambush on Biden's son ultimately hurt Joe.

Biden's own historic address to the Ukrainian Rada in December of 2015—when he cited the Orange Revolution and the country's historic refusal "to back down in the face of rigged elections"—would be augmented by what has since become a most consequential rebuke to Trump and company. After drawing parallels between the United States and Ukraine, and our shared "battle for our independence," he went on to state, "It's not enough to set up a new anti-corruption bureau and establish a special prosecutor fighting corruption. The Office of the General Prosecutor desperately needs reform." The vice president, having contextualized the overwhelming crises facing both our countries, herein identified the very grievance that would graduate to full-fledged sabotage four years later. Indeed, Biden's impassioned speech highlights that there was but *one* common enemy. This would fillip both the forecast *and* challenge he issued: "America and Europe now stand together united in our commitment to impose tough economic sanctions on Russia," Biden stated. "The false propaganda that the Kremlin is disseminating in an attempt to undermine Ukraine and fracture Europe's resolve will not work."

It is laughable that a conservative base mischaracterized these very public efforts, and Biden's unassailable prognostication, all while eschewing the incriminating context of Trump's own motives. Biden's predictions have basically crystalized, as Russia and its proxies have created an inauspicious future for both Ukraine *and* the United States.

Yet it was awfully easy to get lost in the labyrinth of conspiracy, the veritable forest of dumbfuckery made all the more confusing by the growing number of shady characters whose heavy involvement in this case, and prevention from testifying, encumbered House leaders from shining a light on Trump's transgressions. However, anyone needing help finding their bearings could always expect a likely assist from the indolent Trump and those sinful motives that remained noticeable despite the brush. Guided by Democratic leadership in the House, Rep. Adam Schiff, star of the impeachment inquiry, methodically gathered the breadcrumbs, presenting them to the public once hearings were underway. The congressman's oracle-like carriage and political savvy were indispensable, his guidance instrumental, in keeping his colleagues *and* the public out of the weeds.

Cyrus McQueen @CyrusMMcQueen · Jan 24, 2020
I tell ya, three days into this trial, the most memorable aspect has been the undeniable gravitas of one Adam Schiff... Nothing against Jimmy Stewart but, fuck it #MrSchiffGoesToWashington ⸣

⟲ 471   ♡ 2465

Again, the whole reason Trump dragged us down this dirt road is indisputable. As the whistleblower complaint substantiates, our sloth-like president saw an opportunity to kill two birds with one stone: perhaps one phone call would cover up misconduct past *and* present. His "perfect call," this improvised device, the discussion that threatened to blow up his presidency, echoed his Sharpie stunt. Once again, he drew all over the map, only this time scribbling arrows pointing to Ukraine.

Trump's grift, his hustle, his all-too-consequential game of Three-card Monte, depended on stacking the cards—which is precisely why Burisma became the newest, biggest, baseless distraction since Benghazi. It was the commotion Trump needed once he identified his mark. Getting folks to turn on Biden meant they would fail to notice his criminal efforts and it would give him time to further manipulate the 2020 outcome.

But let's circle forward here for a moment. Much as Trump was too weak to take on Obama in the 2012 general election, he also was too ineffectual to take on Obama's VP come 2020, particularly in states like Pennsylvania that he narrowly won in 2016. Thus, a man incapable of meeting the challenge alone summoned help from his little friends, those dildos like Giuliani who jump at any opportunity to fuck someone. Trump's efforts, it bears noting, seemed also to be compelled by the fact that people genuinely *liked* the avuncular Biden. Much like the bottom feeder had used Birtherism to attack the beloved Obama, he sought something, *anything*, to lessen the distance between himself and the former vice president.

In fact, there is an unspoken but otherwise inarguable subtext between Trump and Biden: Obama was critical to the ascension of both, his own historic rise stimulating both Trump and Biden's eventual bids. But where Trump could not stomach being upstaged by his predecessor, Biden dutifully *chose* to play second in command to our magnetic, transcendent Black president. That a white male from Trump's generation had not only suppressed his ego but buttressed his younger Black counterpart speaks to an unimpeachable character—a counterbalance to Trump's bigotry. Though this under-appreciated act earned Biden great currency with our community, long overlooked is how rare indeed it is to see such subordination from a white politician of a particular age, regardless of party affiliation—especially considering how easy it is for racial identity *to* undermine ideology, with parity routinely sacrificed to the precepts of a white power structure. But with the Black vote indispensable to Biden's primary success in 2020, and Trump's white, non-college-educated vote in clear jeopardy, Biden became particularly vexatious *because* of this fact. By merely appealing to *one* demographic, by failing to grow his base, Trump was now clearly in trouble.

Having never cultivated even a modicum of strength, Trump was chary to call on his own will. Never in his life, from birth all the way up to Birtherism, had the wealthy toddler *truly* been tested. This did not bode well for a flaccid incumbent heading into a general election, the sort of contest that would place inordinate demands on any candidate, their strengths and weaknesses inevitably laid bare through the rigors and microscope of the campaign. Remember, it takes a truculent Trump a considerable amount of effort just to *appear* normal, and even then, his uninspired attempts at connecting come across as mawkish. Whether he attempts to display sincerity or orchestrate genuine interactions, his long meander across the world stage has only reinforced our knowledge that the man has not a redeemable bone in his fuckin' body. His efforts to combat these shortcomings through subterfuge establish incontrovertibly that not only do debilitating fear and self-doubt rule Trump, but, as mounting impeachment evidence suggested, he *knew* he was incapable of winning on his own.

By the time December of 2019 rolled around and public testimonies began, it was abundantly clear that women, and in particular, those scrupulous public servants driven by a sense of moral and civic duty, would do their damnedest to ensure that the prurient politician did not skirt justice. Yet such bravery ran contrary to what we witnessed from congressional Republicans, that body of emasculated men across the aisle who, though serving in a coequal branch of government, had been penetrated by this president. Thus, another unforeseen outcome of the hearings was the manner in which these women shattered gender associations: where the GOP's men discernibly feared Trump, Nancy Pelosi repeatedly and at times *literally* stood up to him. But given the bulwark that these beta males represented, be it Rep. Devin Nunes running interference on the House Intelligence Committee or Mitch McConnell scuttling witness testimony come the Senate trial, I could not overlook her steadfast resolve. "His wrongdoing strikes at the very heart of our Constitution," Pelosi emphatically stated. "Our democracy is what is at stake."

When Speaker Pelosi authorized the House Judiciary Committee to draft articles of impeachment, it highlighted not just her own integrity but also that of former Ambassador to Ukraine Marie Yovanovitch, whose probity was crucial to this very outcome. Soon, the impact of both women would appreciate in this same crucible. With Capitol Hill deluged with dynamic women like the former ambassador, this unique moment in our nation's history was not lost on those of us observing the proceedings. Nor was the fact that problems for the poised career diplomat all began the day Trump identified *her* as standing between him and what he wanted.

Yovanovitch's pointed, concise, believable testimony brings to mind another momentous appearance on Capitol Hill, one also disastrous for Trump. Three years earlier, in a weighty backdrop to the impeachment proceedings, Sally Yates, as acting attorney general, had pried back the curtain to expose Russian trespasses—and had likewise found herself relieved of her duties. Her unceremonious removal likely provided the Trump White House with the very template they later utilized to eliminate Yovanovitch's similar threat. Given that the GOP had rebuffed Yates as "an Obama person," her very testimony and those partisan attacks on her previewed what unfolded with the former Ukraine Ambassador.

In reviewing those earlier events concerning Yates, a stubborn timeline supplies the context for establishing Trump's ulterior motives. After alerting the White House of National Security Advisor Michael Flynn's susceptibility to blackmail—his having engaged in nebulous paid work in both Turkey and Russia, even attending Russian galas conspicuously seated next to the Russian president—Yates found herself on the chopping block a full two weeks *before* Flynn did, despite his deliberate lack of transparency and subsequent guilty plea. Given what has occurred with Ukraine, we can now view Sally Yates as a sibyl. Her chilling words—"You don't want your national security adviser compromised with the Russians"—are nothing short of prophetic considering that the Kremlin *would* go on to usurp both Ukraine and the United States, Eastern Europe in many ways serving as a dry run for their growing and aggressive presence in the North Atlantic and elsewhere. And considering that the National Security Council also factored heavily in the impeachment hearings—with the revelation of National Security Advisor John Bolton's unwillingness to play ball with Trump and Giuliani, his own forced resignation appearing preordained—it tangentially related to the circumstances leading to Flynn's earlier departure. This greater framework inextricably linked Yates and Yovanovitch—as did Trump's past and present efforts to ensure himself an auspicious future.

When Yovanovitch found herself under that same partisan scope as had Yates, facing character assassination for being truthful, she would nevertheless convince the country of her veracity. Her undeniable grace shone through the smoke in the Capitol, her stately bearing speaking volumes in between her measured answers. The damning testimony—revealing Giuliani's efforts to conduct a "smear campaign" that undermined U.S. interests and assisted a host of questionable characters—painted a damaging picture, it eventually supported by the dribs and drabs of additional evidence that leaked out.

The world would soon learn that Giuliani had outsourced his conspiracy grift to his own set of underlings, tasking two Russian-born businessmen, Lev Parnas and Igor Fruman, with trailing Ambassador Yovanovitch. But Parnas had left an incriminating trail across Europe, on hotel stationery no less—their furtive activities betraying a rather glaring motive, one at the very nub of the entire Ukraine scandal: "Get Zalensky to announce that the Biden case will be investigated."

Though the brazen intent of these men was clear, Trump used the occasion of Yovanovitch's public testimony to fire off a flurry of brazenly intimidating tweets, further inculpating himself. And when not sullying his official role as head of government with Twitter twaddle, he was deploying stooges like Ohio Rep. Jim Jordan to obscure his objectives. The world watched with disgust as the disheveled Jordan, buoyed by his boss's tweets, badgered the truth-teller with a meandering, meaningless diatribe, insisting that the career diplomat was *herself* part of a coterie of anti-Trump officials. But Yovanovitch, wielding truth like a machete, cut surgically, effortlessly, through Jordan's bullshit, capping his folly by simply positing, "I'm sorry, was there a question there?"

Jordan's petulant attempts at derailing her testimony did little to obscure the real reason they targeted Yovanovitch: her anti-corruption efforts. In truth, as ambassador, she had strongly supported measures to curb Ukrainian malfeasance—in particular, she had supported the work of the National Anti-corruption Bureau of Ukraine and its surveillance of then-Ukrainian Prosecutor General Yuriy Lutsenko—making that much clearer the reasons behind her ousting and, more important, the entities who stood to benefit most from it. Lutsenko had failed to arrest Konstantin Kilimnik, a Russian operative who had worked closely with Paul Manafort—and whose pivotal role in compromising the 2016 election Robert Mueller had himself identified.

With Lutsenko, the crooked prosecutor general, and Giuliani, the crooked former federal prosecutor, enjoying a mutually beneficial arrangement, they created a morass that would float D.C.'s swamp rats in conspiratorial bullshit. Of course, this all ran counter to Biden's own words, which in many ways previewed these subversive attempts to sabotage his presidential bid. Having drawn attention to "both the unrelenting aggression of the Kremlin and the cancer of corruption," we would now watch, rather ironically, as that "cancer of corruption," that very same "aggression," spread to the U.S. Congress—the manufactured mud the GOP gathered, used to try to now taint Biden.

Ambassador Yovanovitch pointed to this during her own testimony. She corroborated that a similar "alternative narrative" had been utilized to sully her in service of a singular purpose: to throw everyone *off* Russia's scent. Given that all roads undoubtedly led back to the Kremlin, it became obvious to those of us keeping score that Biden and Yovanovitch were targets because of one axiomatic commonality: both had upset pro-Russian forces in Ukraine and the United States.

Quizzically, the president attacked those Americans nobly engaged in fighting Russian corruption and manipulation, all before labeling them as corrupt themselves. We were now thoroughly ensconced in a post-truth era, where a political scandal could be orchestrated *without* any actual improprieties. Tasking immoral and amoral attorneys and politicians with creating new facts, often on the fly, was now par for the course on Capitol Hill—a development that we would see play out to a disheartening denouement in Trump's Senate trial.

Yet Lutsenko's role in trying to sabotage Mueller, and later Yovanovitch, would reveal something compelling about this entire controversy. Where honorable, dutiful public servants, like Yovanovitch or Biden, use their positions to serve the public interest, there are diametrically opposed bookends, like Lutsenko and Giuliani or even Flynn and Barr, who have no scruples when it comes to polluting our politics—who elect to *use* their powers to support private interests. When wealthy and notorious individuals align with a wealthy and notorious president, those whose sense of duty is far less vital than the axes they have to grind, we see plenty of men line up, eager to chop down a great democracy for a little bit of paper currency.

Yet what would soon prove satisfying is that, amid the unforgiving glow of impeachment, the gaggle of cocky individuals Trump had sent to Eastern Europe came home to roost one by one, these stool pigeons cooing and cawing while cooped up in the Capitol for the hearings that would decide his fate. And although the usual suspects had their moments under the media glare, those individuals who had *not* acquiesced to Trump helped turn this moment into something more noteworthy: an opportunity for Americans to observe, with their own eyes, what *true* patriotism looks like.

When Lt. Col. Alexander Vindman testified before the House Intelligence Committee about the Zelensky scandal, he followed nobly

CALL IN THE PLUMBERS

in the footsteps of Yovanovitch, calling down upon himself the very same gauntlet the career public servant had herself withstood. Watching the decorated Army officer and top Ukraine expert, his gravity bowled me over. Vindman's stately carriage, deportment, and even his opening words set an immediate tone for his testimony: "I have dedicated my entire professional life to the United States of America."

When the compelling 43-year-old read a prepared statement, addressing his own father's momentous decision to flee Ukraine, with him and his twin brother in tow when they were merely three years of age, he reminded us of what America represented at its best. As he spoke of his father's bravery (inadvertently highlighting his own), his words resonated: "Dad, my sitting here today, in the U.S. Capitol talking to our elected officials is proof that you made the right decision forty years ago to leave the Soviet Union and come here to United States of America in search of a better life for our family." In that instant, Vindman not only provided insight into his own motives but also drew attention to those outstanding dynamics that had influenced both his past and this present moment. The Purple Heart recipient capped this emotional aperture, assuaging his father's concerns along with our own: "Do not worry, I will be fine for telling the truth."

Vindman's almost palpable virtue would have come across even had he not been resplendently clad in his dress uniform, adorned with a plethora of medals and ribbons highlighting his rank and career of service. However, it was the testimony that followed that would *really* speak to his gravitas—while highlighting the dichotomy between the distinguished officer and his Republican inquisitors. When Devin Nunes, the ignoble California congressman, addressed him as Mr. Vindman, the combat veteran quickly retorted, "Ranking member, it's Lieutenant Colonel Vindman," an admonishment so perfectly executed, it prompted a standing ovation from me in my living room.

Vindman soon disclosed that, upon hearing of Trump's desire to smear Biden, he had reported it twice to his superiors, going on to state that he found Trump's behavior "highly unusual" and the phone call itself "improper." Vindman's follow up, that he had reported Trump "out of a sense of duty," was particularly telling as the converse was now playing out before our very eyes. Nunes, the unruly ranking committee member, was here now abdicating his own duty in favor of partisan parlor tricks, his cowardice contrasting starkly with Vindman's inviolability in this moment.

Cyrus McQueen @CyrusMMcQueen · Nov 19, 2019
What's truly incredible is, when you really think about it, Vindman was born in the former Soviet Union and decided to work on behalf of the United States... Donald Trump was born in the United States and decided to work on behalf of the former Soviet Union... #ImpeachmentHearing 🔗

⟲ 3367   ♡ 9182

With such profound unseemliness exposed to the world, I could not help but consider these congressional hearings profiles in courage as, one by one, patriots at every level of government, every layer Trump had sought to infect with sycophantic, corruptible intermediaries, were proven to have *resisted* his subversive efforts.

When Fiona Hill, a former senior director on the National Security Council, was deposed and then testified publicly before the Intelligence Committee about developments pertaining to the Ukraine scandal, her regal manner and potent acuity also evoked impressions of Sally Yates. And that the Russia expert had, like Yates, served in both Democratic and Republican administrations spoke directly to *her* unassailability: her reputation as an intelligence analyst under Bush and Obama preceded her. Considering her impeccable record, that Hill found herself the target of threats in the lead-up to her testimony sadly paralleled what Yovanovitch had experienced only a few days earlier. A discomfiting fact was becoming a broken record: Russia and a compromised GOP appeared to be the sole beneficiaries of silencing these women. Hill herself addressed this during her testimony, remarking with sobering impact, "We can't let this stand. . . . And I don't think anyone here thinks we can let this stand."

Hill was as well versed in the tactics of Vladimir Putin as practically anyone in our national security apparatus, suggesting that the Kremlin expert's resignation from the NSC a week shy of Trump's shakedown of Zelensky may have facilitated that inglorious outcome. That her departure coincided with Trump's incriminating phone call helps corroborate that stubborn timeline of events, Trump's plausible motives and the curious circumstances surrounding her decision to leave apparent despite the conspiratorial thicket the GOP tried to then create. Hill spoke to this muddling, addressing her inquisitors directly: "Some of you on this committee appear to believe that Russia and its security services did not conduct a campaign against our country—and that perhaps, somehow, for some reason, Ukraine did."

Hill followed this unsparing redressing with a superb distillation that clarified the Kremlin's motives and, in the next breath, demystified those of House Republicans: "This is a fictional narrative that has been perpetrated and propagated by the Russian security services themselves," Hill said. "The unfortunate truth is that Russia was the foreign power that systematically attacked our democratic institutions in 2016."

The firing of Yovanovitch, a bona fide expert on Ukraine, followed within two months by the resignation of Hill, the foremost expert on Russia, proved those efforts to drive out patriots and nonpartisans had worked. Those who stood to mitigate Putin's destabilizing effect on American foreign policy had been neutralized. Thus, Hill used her time under oath prudently, *reiterating* the objectives of Russia's security services: "They deploy millions of dollars to weaponize our own political opposition research and false narratives. When we are consumed by partisan rancor, we cannot combat these external forces as they seek to divide us against each other, degrade our institutions, and destroy the faith of the American people in our democracy."

With Hill's words essentially reading like the autopsy report of our demise, the outcome of Russia's outside attacks could never be viewed separately from that self inflicted damage, the devastating blow republican brass would ultimately cause, and carry out from inside, their very own country.

Perhaps most incriminating, most immutable, and most unmissable in the entire Ukraine scandal and the subsequent impeachment is that none of these developments occurred until *after* it became clear that a Biden run would be disastrous for Donald Trump. Given everything that has unfolded, we can pinpoint the genesis of the Ukraine plot to that short period in the late summer of 2018 when a *Politico* poll gave Biden a seven-point lead among potential voters. Shortly thereafter, Giuliani officially began his "consulting" work with Parnas. Giuliani's own meetings with Lutsenko and his coordinated strategy sessions with Parnas at the Trump International Hotel in D.C. appeared to represent an insurance policy in the event of a Biden candidacy. Thus, in March of 2019, when the former VP revealed, albeit inadvertently, his intention to run, it was rather conspicuous that Lutsenko then opened those spurious investigations into Burisma and the 2016 election. That Yovanovitch was informed that Trump had "lost confidence" in her mere hours before Biden's formal announcement is itself too curious to dismiss, especially as this was precisely when their subterfuge began to snowball.

The fact remains: those "attempts" to root out corruption in Ukraine had not crystallized at any point during the preceding two years when Biden was a retired politician living out his golden years in Wilmington, and Trump, with the power of the State Department and the Pentagon at his disposal, easily could have addressed this so-called corruption diplomatically or through other legitimate channels. With Ukraine's borders fodder for Russia's rapacious movements, our own illegitimate president's objectives, running concurrent with Russia's, would run *counter* to those of Ukraine's reconstituted government.

Cyrus McQueen @CyrusMMcQueen · May 22, 2020
At this point you gonna have to come up with a lot more for me to not vote for Biden... you better come up with a buncha bodies in his basement or some shit... and even then I might be like, 'Well, what did they do?'

⭢ 1427   ♡ 7159

That anticlimactic, maddening developments in the Senate would supplant the apparent denouement to the Trump presidency can never erase the fact that on December 18, 2019, nearly three years into our nightmare, the alarm had been sounded. Because of the stated abuses, the House of Representatives formally impeached Donald J. Trump by a vote of 229 to 198. The preamble to this historic rebuke, codified by the resonant and impassioned words of Georgia Congressman John Lewis, spoken a half year before his death, lent a powerful counterweight to Trump's later acquittal. Anchored by a palpable gravitas, Lewis's blistering elucidation gave goosebumps to all who bore witness. The Civil Rights icon, who had faced down bigotry and corruption over a storied career, reminded his fellow members of their unequivocal charge: "Our nation is founded on the principle that we do not have kings. We have presidents. And the Constitution is our compass," Lewis preached. "When you see something that is not right, not just, not fair, you have a moral obligation to say something. To do something."

The 79-year-old leader, whose life embodied this coda, lent a sage-like element to these final proceedings, filliping the momentous House vote with a sobering reminder *of* that greater imperative. This edification would prove particularly relevant when the GOP, inebriated off equivocation, blatantly abdicated this very responsibility during Trump's Senate trial.

Still, perhaps no individual was better suited to issue forth this chilling sentiment than Lewis himself, given his familiarity with sacrifice and the almost superlative bravery that had led him *to* this very place. Life rarely demands from anyone what it did from John Lewis, repeatedly, almost greedily; over 80 years, his better angels perpetually battled with America's worst. Indeed, the life arc of a child born to sharecroppers in segregated Alabama, an icon long before he became a congressman, mirrored the curve in the very overpass that provided the setting for his greatest sacrifice. It is nearly impossible *to* articulate the contours of that calamitous traverse on that brutal Sunday in 1965 when Lewis and 600 other marchers pushed forward on the Edmund Pettis Bridge.

I have been privileged to visit this historic site, along with the nearby Voting Rights Museum, on numerous occasions. To call it hallowed ground would be most appropriate. Though I have always traveled there during the month of July, when the humid Alabama air hangs like a blanket, the thickened atmosphere surrounding this crossover derives from the spiritual density *in* the very air of Selma. Being there is to be tickled by history's touch. The past is superimposed over the present, that sleepy town waking up as you find yourself bound by the gravity of the day in question. Its history quickly comes alive if you are quiet enough *and* willing enough to pay close attention. The bumps that pop up along your forearms, the tingle in your neck—they are all a palpable indication that you have embarked on a psychic journey, it a successful trip when you realize you have been delivered to the other side.

Having recreated the march with several groups of students, I have found that one of the first things you perceive as you step onto the Edmund Pettis Bridge is its noticeable arch. Though the bridge itself is short, the bow of the oxidized overpass briefly obscures what lies directly ahead. Not until you near its very apex does a view of the other side appear. Here, you find yourself solemnly stepping with the marchers, reverentially placing yourself in their shoes, if just for this brief exercise. And though the terror itself *is* conjured, try as you might, it is virtually impossible to imagine what greeted Lewis and others as they approached the halfway point and the Alabama State troopers came into focus. The sight of that intimidating phalanx, smacking billy clubs into their hands—Lewis being smacked *with* that terrifying image before continuing on for a few frightening minutes—is almost indescribable. To be all of 25 years old, to have your heart in your throat, to know you are about to *feel* the very fire ahead, yet you *keep* going one bold step at a time—it is *unfathomable*. Because he and others walked bravely into that waiting inferno, where the flames of animus and the teargas embellishing this hellish portrait soon enveloped them—this incendiary passage incentivizing the passage of the Voting Rights Act—suggested that he would not be afraid to meet *this* historical moment head on either.

Back in the Capitol, more than fifty years removed, Lewis continued to move forward. "Today, this day, we didn't ask for this. This is a sad day. This is not a day of joy," he sermonized before building to a powerful peroration: "Our children and their children will ask us: 'What did you do? What did you say?'" This man whose life work was carved out of this moral obligation—whose contention with the devaluation of flesh would find his separated from his body due to the instruments of those vicious troops, it creating a river of blood and a most chilling parallel to the Alabama River below—understood better than any in that congressional body that red states had earned their crimson distinction *through* bloodletting. Though representatives from those muddled districts were defying justice once more, Lewis knew the path toward a more salubrious future went *through* them, it only able to be realized by marching boldly ahead *despite* them. He knew that the road though uncomfortable, though frightening, could not be bypassed or even bifurcated; there was but *one* way forward for him and his colleagues. "For some, this vote may be hard," he concluded. "But we have a mission and a mandate to be on the right side of history."

Despite the moral high road that Lewis and his fellow Democrats would travel, despite the impeachment vote and the evidentiary proof of Trump's abuse and obstruction, it was abundantly clear from the start that Senate Republicans would facilitate a miscarriage of justice. That the GOP overrode any form of consensus, even in procedural matters, represented for *us* their diabolical plans to fast-track a Trump acquittal. Much like the man on trial, these brazen men, in this greater moment, evinced a staggering paucity of integrity.

Cyrus McQueen @CyrusMMcQueen · Jan 14, 2017
#DonaldTrump says #JohnLewis is "all talk, no action"... There's a difference between bleeding for the country and bleeding the country dry.

t⁊ 1108   ♡ 2003

It is almost impossible to put into words what followed, despite the inevitable conclusion. Now on the other side of that affront, immersed in the miasma of the imprudent outcome, to say that I and most Americans were disheartened does not do justice to our feelings. Words can never encapsulate the hollowness that accompanies, and is unique to, having to stomach such overt injustice.

In this questionable tribunal, with Chief Justice John Roberts presiding over an otherwise momentous disgrace, the virtue of the select group of House leaders anointed to combat the GOP's dark defenses conveyed the epic undercurrent to this epoch-making showdown of good versus evil. The House managers waging this battle felt like the congressional incarnate of the Justice League, while those Republican forces they were up against seemed almost fictitious in their fitting, fully embodied nefariousness. Yet nothing could change the unfortunate fact that the Senate trial of Donald J. Trump, given his almost forgone acquittal, was a sham, stuffed in a farce, wrapped in some straight up bullshit. It was a multifarious embarrassment, a turducken of blithe and blatant fuckery.

Having exhausted any reserves I have left to articulate this partisan-fueled disappointment, I am resigned to simply highlighting the great words and works of those like Schiff, his dutiful presence operating in many ways like our nation's moral compass. The efforts of him and the Democratic leadership, though battling the mighty current of a coopted GOP, became a beacon in this rocky moment in our nation's history. Their actions serve as an edifying chart, providing for future generations an archive of the dynamic attempts taken *to* lead this country out of the rapids and away from the precipitous fall promised by such irresponsible stewardship.

In contrast to a president whose tenuous relationship with verity generated incredible mileage out of specious terminology like "Fake News," Schiff invoked the greater importance of the work in which we were embroiled. In his closing argument, he reminded all who were bearing witness *of* that greater charge, saying pointedly, "If the truth doesn't matter, we're lost."

Yet the immoral moves of both Trump and McConnell nullified the moral efforts of House managers and Senate Democrats, their obfuscation blocking both Mick Mulvaney and Mike Pompeo from testifying. The fix in, it forced us to digest this injustice as well as the undeniable fact that those germane to the crime—like the president himself—were guilty as sin.

As the proceedings devolved toward their predictable, disheartening denouement, the House managers reminded the American people of the inconvenient reason that had brought the nation to this moment, the oft-obscured yet axiomatic crux to Trump's rise and fall. "The Russians are at it as we speak," Schiff admonished from the Senate floor, reminding all who had lost sight of this president's destructive trajectory and those entities most responsible for igniting it. His rhetorical flourish made obvious the clear and present danger facing our country, as well as the brutal evidence of not only Trump's hypocrisy but also our own should we allow such callous wrongdoing to continue. "President Donald Trump gave his word he would drain the swamp. And what have we seen?" Schiff mesmerically posed. "His personal lawyer go to jail. His campaign manager go to jail. . . . I guess that's how you drain the swamp."

Yet the world now braced itself for the coming undoing, the Abuse of Power and Obstruction of Congress Articles ultimately failing to garner the two-thirds majority needed to depose Trump. But that vote, indeed the coverup to come, can never obscure the luminous eloquence of those like Schiff, and the other House managers, their moves indelible in the wake of Senate Republicans' nadir and their earnest attempts to redefine this outcome.

Though the collective impact of those House managers resonates, the inspired words of Brooklyn's own Hakeem Jeffries have left the most lasting impression with me. The passionate, precise dissection of the president's defense by the person representing New York's 8th Congressional District perfectly frame this moment for all of perpetuity. The insipid query of Jay Sekulow, lead outside counsel for Trump's impeachment—"Why are we here?"—instigated the jaw dropping action that followed. Indeed it was the attorney's temerity, his flippancy, which would give rise to Jeffries' thunderous jam: "We are here, sir, because President Donald Trump elevated his personal political interests and subordinated the national security interests of the United States of America. We are here, sir, because President Trump corruptly abused his power and then he tried to cover it up."

Future generations will certainly ask where we were when Rep. Jeffries punctured the bloviate Trump defense lawyer, rattling the scales of justice in the process, as he hammered home, for those eyes bearing witness and those that had yet to open, both the importance of this moment and the crossroads our government and nation had reached.

Jeffries' words were searing, his colossal undressing building to a climax: "And we are here sir, to follow the facts, apply the law, be guided by the constitution, and present the truth to the American people. That is why we're here, Mr. Sekulow."

This invigorating opprobrium having reached a righteous crescendo, the congressman garnished it with a profound peroration, this selected cherry supplied by yet another native son of the borough: The Notorious B.I.G. The fierce finality to his reprimand would herein ripple across the country: "And if you don't know, now you know."

21

The Joke's On Us

It takes me awhile to locate my hair clippers today, shaving being rather redundant given my career and place of residence. The bag containing my home barber kit is buried beneath the sort of jetsam closets generate: clothes, old clothes, books, random beanies, a scarf with tag still attached to it, Christmas gifts long ago dismissed. Beards are somewhat ubiquitous in my beloved borough, the accoutrement of choice for men dwelling in this urban oasis, a signature of both hipsters and blipsters, a sign not just of virility but that we likely reside in this modern Bohemia, that we belong. Having adhered to this unwritten rule, my own whiskers possess a certain coveted Brooklyn imprimatur, mine a mane typically ascribed to pirate captains, impressive for its volume and somewhat severe angles. A now-distinct part of my identity, it has even achieved an imperial quality, my chin follicles flowing to a mighty jut, its dagger-like point deliberately lifted from my majestic idols like Malcolm and Bill Russell.

"There they are!" Finding my buried treasure, I proceed to the paper-towel-lined bathroom sink, rubbing alcohol at the ready. I extract my tool, uncoil its thick black cord, tap into the juice, and hear that long-lost hum. After a few minutes of mowing, a familiar face greets me, one I had not laid eyes on in nearly five years. The Samson-like remnants now filling the sink, I take in my shorn mug and am immediately reminded how small my chin is. Suddenly, I am 18 again. Baby-faced. I hate it. Weakened, my eyes struggle to adjust to my unearthed jawline. I am soon locked in my own gaze, the mirror magnetized; I can barely turn away from this familiar stranger. It evokes a feeling similar to when you return home after a long trip, that odd sensation that everything is the same yet briefly rendered new again. But here's the thing: I had no desire to go on this journey, to meet my clean-cut twin, but extenuating circumstances, matters more pressing than my own vanity, had prompted this momentous shearing.

As of this writing, and this dreadful face time, the world has turned completely upside down. We are embarked on a very strange trip indeed. Any previous lamentation of the Trump era, regardless of how warranted, certainly did not take into account how much farther down the rabbit hole we would all descend, and oh how much worse it would indeed all get. As I stand beneath the dim bathroom light, getting reacquainted with my reflection, I know this new face will face the grim, twisted new reality we suddenly find ourselves in.

The spread of the novel coronavirus has upended the world. Murmurs out of Wuhan, China, quickly graduated to a full-fledged global pandemic, leaving no pocket of the East, or the West, North, or South, untouched by a calamity unleashed like a biblical plague to punish us for all our perceived sins, of which there are far too many to count. The death tolls doubled, then tripled, and now tick up relentlessly. Global GDP's plunge while the inhabitants of our marble in space shelter indoors, away from one another. With every patch of our terrestrial plane impacted, we watch helplessly as the virtual world fulfills its promise to supplant the real one; what was once optional is now in many ways our *only* option as sites like Twitter and Zoom become viable lifelines to an uninhabitable outside world.

But you cannot spell pandemic without panic and, I am fuckin' scared. Like *really* scared, for the first time in my life. Of the unseen. Of the unknown. Of the fact that I cannot run to the store or breeze past a stranger without putting my life on the line. Those effortless vestiges of normality that I now know to be beautiful, that I appreciate in ways I never did previously, have been rendered lucid by a crisis that has created percipient distance between the before and after, the then and now, the relatively untroubled way we once were and the unmissable, embattled way we now are.

It is only through hindsight, thrust into an unmitigated hell, that we recognize how halcyon those pre-pandemic days really were. This reappraisal, of course, runs concurrent with our resultant and frightening remolding, facilitated by an epoch pivotal in each of our lives. This multigenerational menace, which promises to redefine us, will bisect the historical record as well, its arrival distinguishing with stark clarity how incontrovertibly and comprehensively our world has altered. Our life and times will be herein reclassified by the Biblical scourge that has rent it: *before* COVID-19 and after.

To undergo a metamorphosis of this scale usually requires time, yet the trial that promises to fundamentally transform our society unfolded seemingly overnight. Coronavirus advanced like a rebel army, its abrupt charge overwhelming a jejune, unsuspecting populace, this unforeseen development leading me to romanticize that sudden loss of the precious mundanity that only peacetime provides. Ours is a condition that perhaps only those who have been beset by war fully understand: with safety no longer guaranteed, the will to survive is the prime dictate. Dispatches from the frontlines corroborate this unfortunate comparison, as the casualties, a phenomenon long associated with war, become an all-too-real byproduct of this upheaval, the courage we long associated with soldiers now displayed by a new incarnation of war hero. We watch those medical personnel answer the call to duty, placing their lives on the line, willingly enduring combat, braving those invisible bullets threatening to penetrate their PPE, all in a selfless attempt to mitigate the almost inevitable tragedy. Here, the poignant, somber opening sequence to M*A*S*H seems appropriate to our own burgeoning pathos. The association proves more than apposite as field hospitals, endemic to the battlefield, pop up in places like Central Park, with medical students fast-tracked and retired personnel reenlisting to see us through this crisis, or at least till we can firmly establish the enemy's retreat.

In a post-9/11 world, this equal opportunity killer vaults over every notion we engender about terrorists or enemies. A novel virus the likes of which we had never seen before has breached our trenchant silos, nihilistic in that it is ruled by neither religiosity nor ethos. It penetrates every line of national and cultural demarcation, an enemy that neither recognizes nor respects walls, borders, and any arbitrary claims of dispensation. All of mankind finds itself drafted into this conflict, a people long divorced by phenotype forced to align due to overriding, unbreakable bonds of genotype.

Our shared biology illuminates that prescient, declarative line indispensable to our very own inception. "All men are created equal" takes on added pertinence as we are all rendered potential fodder for this ravenous contagion. The idea of deadly droplets dancing in the air, waiting to turn your lungs into a mosh pit, invading and eventually conquering your breathing apparatus, has grown increasingly apparent, this overpowering prospect more than enough to entrap you in breathless apprehension.

Though I am fortunately free from infection, the thought of plague plagues me without relent and, by all accounts, I am starting to lose it. Already prone to melancholy, that the world now reflects my murk in earnest thrusts me into overcompensation, seeking and even manufacturing any light I can, knowing I cannot afford to go dark at a time like this. But those palliative efforts are no match for a degenerative climate that threatens to extinguish an already precarious flame, this situation, our isolation, almost promising to create an inevitable gust.

Yet this is a time when being pragmatic, regimented, helps me contend with the otherwise untenable. I eagerly focus on those factors I can still control: the home takes on the feel of a barracks, disinfectant stations and piles of supplies proffering everything needed to survive this interminable conflict. Still, bottles of hand sanitizer placed strategically by the door, the sofa, and the bed do not slow my heartbeat when thoughts that the contagion has crept in, that I have missed a spot, ensure that a cold bead of sweat drips down my neck, sending a chill up my spine. Which brings me back to the mirror and the youngish-looking man pulling an N-95 mask over his face.

My wonderful wife Leanne, the mighty preparer, took the whispers out of Wuhan as a presage and procured several of these masks the moment she was convinced it was not "a hoax" or would just "miraculously go away," as our imbecilic president blithely volunteered. In her forward thinking, she secured a box on back order, a prudent move as we would eventually divvy up the contents among those more vulnerable members of our outfit—her folks and my folks, a friend who was asthmatic, another who was pregnant. Her prescience was a lifesaver, our parachute on a flight that was goin' down, and by early spring surgical masks would arguably be more precious than Fabergé eggs. Yet, alas, the elusive, highly coveted treasure of the N-95 does *not* provide complete coverage—and protection—if you have a beard.

An unwillingness to roll the dice and risk my life put manscaping most definitely in the cards. So I shaved that shit without hesitation, brothers and sisters, and positioned one of those indispensable N-95s over my fresh face. But though it fits snugly to my jaw, as I pull it on my mind briefly wanders to the unwelcome prospect that, as a Black man wearing a mask, I am about to venture into an unpredictable world in which hoodies fillip illogical reactions. Always aware of those hallucinations based on race, I must consider whether even a public health measure can diffuse that hard wiring, those explosive fears that might profile me in the worst way, and at the worst time possible. Regardless, I stretch the elastic over my head and affix the mask to my mug. Fittingly, I realize that it is actually constricting. The damn thing is "bloody aggravating," my wife corroborates in her Scottish brogue. My breathing labors and my glasses immediately fog, prompting me to muffle "Fuck this!" into the mirror. Opening the medicine cabinet, I come upon the solution, press two pieces of plastic to my pupils, and we are off!

We head into the hallway after ten days of zero human contact aside from the two of us in an extended Netflix marathon of it doesn't even matter. Placed in dual confinement, enduring the harsh sentence in a one-bedroom apartment, the hours had scarily blended together into a miasma. This beast had soon consumed entire 24-hour increments of time greedily, almost effortlessly. The paucity of daily purpose altered time as we knew it, and multiple days blended into an endless one that neither of us could make heads or tails of. Whatever was gnawing away at the clock gnawed away at us. Somewhere along the way, during this endless day, we ceased to be individuals defined by habit and reason, so, resisting unsustainable torpor, we devised a plan to bust out. Our depleted rations also dictated that we must brave this brave new world sooner or later. Whether it was boredom or merely Ben & Jerry's calling our names is immaterial. We readjusted each other's masks, put the building door behind us with a generous dollop of Purell, and, with her sanitized hand in mine, swiftly marched to the tunnel.

Immediately amplifying the intensity of the moment was our inability to shake the feeling of isolation reinforced over several weeks, it greeting us the very second we exit the building. Turns out the sorrow had decided to linger, like a party guest who could not take the fuckin' hint. Having already consumed so much, it now accompanied us the rest of the way, that unpleasantness standing in where a kaleidoscope of captivating and energetic New Yorkers used to be.

This feeling is further reinforced when we soon realize that, in a city of eight million souls, ours are the only two floating down our street. We barely make it a block before the impression we are starring in our own post-apocalyptic science fiction film becomes all too real. We are the last two people on Earth, our need to forage an action that will not only save ourselves but all civilization—or at least, that is how I entertain myself to short circuit the steadily encroaching anxiety—it and that singular feeling of forlornness stalking us both as we bravely make our way.

Thus, a quiet block compounds our disquietude. You would think that, being free from prying eyes, these emotions might offset each other, but, my mask soon pumping like a party favor, the likelihood they are actually conspiring to make me hyperventilate becomes more real as each breath is eerily audible amid the acoustics of the pleated fabric. It is almost as if I am plagiarizing myself, my movements in this moment dictated more by memory than by any honest or authentic intention. And considering how I had also just become my own doppelgänger, each step I take weirdly feels as unfamiliar as it does routine. That we are also less than a mile from a macabre locale where bodies had been unceremoniously piled up in U-Haul trucks skews us closer to those hellish allusions; evidence of overwhelmed morgues and funeral homes suggests that this disconsolate news and our own proximity make this a passage akin to Dante's travels in hell. We check in with each other halfway, our eyes conveying melded reassurance and uncertainty, betraying this busy inner conflict. But we manage to pass through that awful intersection and, facing the nebulous future head on, put past discomfiture behind us by boldly turning the corner.

The stunning images captured on celluloid in movies like *I Am Legend* and *12 Monkeys* are no match for the reality which greets us. We have to contend with the actuality of shuttered businesses we had only recently frequented. A block that used to buzz, especially at this time of morning, barely mumbles. We bypass one after the other: our local pizza joint, the indelible smell that once greeted our nostrils, gone given the mask covering our faces and the store's closed and freshly graffitied grate. This perpetual shutterdom showcases a bunch of budding artists as almost overnight would-be Basquiats and Banksys have commandeered every inch of these steel canvases. The scene replays itself at the Jewish delicatessen, its chocolate croissants and bagels long gone, that wonderful scent buried in the graveyard of memory, entombed beyond a mask and yet another shuttered grate, this with a note taped to it, CLOSED the only word I can make out in big bold marker. The city that never sleeps has been administered a powerful sedative; the few people who do materialize move with caution. The mellow journey we have made countless times takes on the pulsating tenor of a suicide mission, the short subway ride to the supermarket, two stops, enough to strike fear in both our hearts.

Where the mandates of employment typically throw men and women together, the hoards of New Yorkers performing the morning pilgrimage to midtown, that deluge of diverse bodies, is reduced to a conspicuous trickle. A nearly empty can of trepidation has replaced a 4 Train; usually sardined, the steely resolve of commuters has been supplanted by the visage of uncertainty covering the faces of the few unmasked passengers aboard. I feel like a tourist visiting an unfamiliar city. All the anxiety associated with navigating New York, especially for first-time visitors—those irrational fears that often register on the faces of Midwesterners desperately trying to follow the subway maps clenched in their trembling hands—suddenly feels familiar as I nervously register every movement being made. We are robbed of any local confidence we once wielded as we inch along this muggy underbelly with an intense wariness. My wife Leanne now nestled safely next to me on the inside seat, I clock everyone who subsequently enters and exits the silver snake, doing my desperate best to be aware of where the venom might come from. Suddenly the door rattles and a homeless man passing between cars raises my pulse. He clears his throat and the few fish scatter faster than when you tap against the tank; he might as well have taken a pin out of a grenade for our own mortality flashes before our eyes due to this basic, involuntary act. His innocuous gesture proves incontrovertibly that the fear always spreads faster than the contagion (and you could rightfully lament that that itself is the real detriment). I massage my wife's knee, desperately trying to assuage her palpable fear, and we somehow, with bated breath, survive the hourlong five-minute ride.

We emerge from our hole and survey a scene no different than before. Once busy streets produce only a handful of pedestrians. The threat still omnipresent despite the evaporation, I grab her hand to navigate the perilous maze to Key Foods, almost militaristic in both my sense of duty and the commands I find myself barking out. "Stay behind me!" "Follow me!" I feel my top lip begin to puddle from the condensation under the mask, my nerves compounding the percolation. My head is on a swivel as well, as I frantically process every degree of the concrete panorama unspooling before us. The brick trees feel almost like a canopy framing my tunnel vision. An old white woman approaches from eleven o'clock, prompting us to quickly cross the street. My steering my wife away from clear and present danger feels tantamount to tiptoeing around land mines in Laos—both of us are doing our damnedest to evade a vicious jungle ambush.

It dawns on me that I had likely elicited the same gutless reaction from countless white folks throughout my life, back when we sported figurative masks to navigate through hostile terrain, that contagion called race something we had also learned to operate around. I allow myself to recognize the delicious irony, and even promise to laugh about it . . . later. And though it will provide a reprieve, however brief, in that thickened moment, my senses both dulled and heightened, I cannot help but note that fear is, again, a very, very real thing, be it ultimately illogical or not.

The moment we breach the mechanical doors, bedlam greets us. It is instantly evident why the streets are so empty: everyone is in here! The omnipresent surgical masks now obscure the kind, familiar faces we were used to observing—people watching, that most entertaining of Brooklyn pastimes, has swiftly become a relic of the past, like the dodo and dead languages or, as the world soon laments, handshakes and hugs. It reinforces one of the first lessons I gleaned from this cataclysm: our vanity is the first to be scuttled. Given that we would jettison the joys of human touch, the stress of survival renders the material immaterial, cuteness in such a climate utterly superfluous and therefore expendable. Aisles that once operated as de facto runways are gutted. Society's collapse has precipitated a morass, promoting the grocery into an epicenter of sheer frenzy. Shopping carts are parked in perpetual gridlock, the human traffic that accompanies each nearly circles the store, producing a rage endemic to the BQE at five o'clock. The normal rhythms of my vibrant, blended community have been drowned out by an inimitable staccato of confused chatter, it discordant with the steady, sonorous beat we all usually followed. Upon discovering there are no more eggs, West Indians, Jews, and Latinos all exclaim disappointment in their respective patois, creating a cacophony of confusion and contempt. "Mira" and "Oy" and "Raasclatt" are repeated in the pasta aisle as well, its ransacked shelves reminiscent of the old tv show "Supermarket Sweep," several feet of options reduced to two boxes of lasagna noodles and one creased and punctured offering of large shells, it appearing to have been kicked up and down this pitch at least a few times. I overhear the same Rasta, upon spying this paucity of pasta and rice offerings, unload a barrage of righteous shrapnel, "Babylon" the one word I can discern from this patter of indignation, soon followed by a clear and chilling admonishment: "Amerriccaaah will NEVVAH be de same!"

THE JOKE'S ON US

The sage-like premonition barked from beneath his crown of locks sticks with me as the tilt of his overfilled cap disappears around the corner. Although many of the items on our list go unchecked, we replenish most of our rations in a haze and get the fuck outta there.

Coronavirus has become the *magnum opus* of a fetid administration—the noxious swan song of a plebeian president and his miasmic MAGA movement. Yet in a moment where Trump had already left us malnourished for normalcy, how ill-fated that a global pandemic would unfold to exacerbate it all. The losses we had already suffered almost primed us for this insufferable period when pandemonium has become routine, yet no one could anticipate an already erratic period devolving even *further*—and in such seismic fashion. But could anyone have scribed a more apt end? A more fitting conclusion to a spectacular devolution? Not to oversimplify things, but the pathos this ordeal has engendered merely augmented an already sad, sad time when balance and reason were brutally far away.

But it is unbelievable how the once unimaginable, fodder for far-fetched Hollywood output like *Outbreak* and *Contagion*, has overnight *become* our narrative. The theme I have visited often in this book—racism and the rise of Trump resembling a disease befalling the West—has materialized into a *literal* pandemic, interrupting the stories of our lives. An *actual* plague undoes a man who has plagued the conscience of progressives with his unabashed rapaciousness and overall unpreparedness. We who are living through this gray new reality use fitting descriptors, words like dystopia and apocalyptic; however, it is almost impossible to describe this calamity, one that is, ironically, *ineffable* more than anything.

I go back to the morning after Election Day 2016 when a pall descended, Trump's arrival presaging the withering world we contend with today. Now traversing anemic streets, observing storefronts and restaurants empty of customers, once-vibrant thoroughfares from Bedford Avenue to Flatbush depressing facsimiles of what they once were, I can declare that Brooklyn, my beloved city, is very much on life support. Fear registers on the faces of passersby; a requisite distance is kept by all. A reluctant grin here and there belies that folks barely make eye contact as if a glance could be contagious. An era forged on irrational fears has graduated to one defined by, and replete with, rational, *incessant* fear. Early news of the death tolls in Italy, nearly 400 in one day, is soon supplanted by the death tolls in New York City, nearly 800 in one day. Dispatches from overwhelmed hospitals the world over paint a grim picture: hospital workers reduced to tears; quarantined Italians communicating through song, their fellowship operating at a remove, as folks huddle equidistant on iron balconies.

Yet that very scene provides a wondrous converse, supplying the first of what become countless outpourings, this euphonious offering giving us a surprising peek into the resilience and incandescence of the human spirit. Though immersed in pain, drowning in sorrow, we ameliorate our condition through unplanned camaraderie, uncovered in our courtyards, communities, and, as we increasingly discover, our computers. A fettered global community moves forward, however incrementally, finding a tangible way to warm one another, utilizing our undying flame, a most underestimated asset that is nonetheless a permanent fixture and boon to the human continuum. We see these unforeseen moments repeated in different cities and in different languages, from balconies in Barcelona to brownstones in Brooklyn, and they are all compelling evidence of our intrinsic, unbreakable bonds. We observe the need, the primal, powerful need of all living things to persevere. Something as simple as harmonizing with your neighbors during a discordant time, the communal ointment applied to sooth our deep wounds, *is* inarguable proof: life *always* finds a way, beauty inveterately seeps in *despite* the ugly. Given how COVID-19 further cripples those more vulnerable members of our society, we watch as those long deemed expendable quite ironically prove themselves indispensable, this crisis conveying the essential, undebatable value they have *always* brought to the table.

Nevertheless, the sky has fallen; this feeling is unshakable. Dissatisfaction with Trump and the way things had been going, however warranted, seems almost trite in comparison to the crippling of entire cities and countries. Indisputably, *all* humanity is now hobbled. This shared reality, seemingly unfurled from the mind of Phillip K. Dick or Rod Serling, confirms our connectivity in a future so bleak that even when we had previously sacrificed so much, we had never even *imagined* surrendering human-to-human contact and companionship. We were already meandering through a technological age that left us parched, thirsting for the authentic, irreplaceable satisfaction of personal interactions. Ours is a time when self-checkout and self-checkin have eroded those personal exchanges generations had taken for granted, those dependable stitches in our social tapestry conducive to warmth and a tangible sense of community. When economic mandates changed bottom lines, our collective fabric became threadbare, precipitating a plunge into insolvency for those low-tier workers hovering perilously close to the bottom. Jobs that had provided a decent living evaporated, while the inevitable deluge of debt rotted a working class that could not escape its unceasing torrent. Yet we now suffer the divorce of that human family, after having already gone through a lengthy separation.

Paradoxically, iniquitous decisions at the top have helped fashion a new normal, one in which our technological addictions disconnect us more and more, our reliance on gadgets instead of one another compounding this inexorable spiritual regress. As technology finds ways to satiate our wants, it simultaneously reinforces our desire for more, and the chasm that only *it* can fill steadily grows. Our new identity—as consumers first—estranges us from our time and, before long, from ourselves. The dopamine rush when a package arrives or our phone lights up addicts us, our now living in the moment *between* notifications, real life reduced to this ever-dwindling time.

However, as we suffer the strict penalty of social distancing, we soon realize how inferior all that artificiality is. Swiping right or launching into colloquy in our virtual villages of followers feels wholly unfortunate given that family and fellowship, as well as that age-old replacement found in our local bars, restaurants, and the homes of dear friends, are things of the past. Where a bottle of wine and solving the world's problems used to be on the menu, we acclimate to a real world corked for the foreseeable future. Our forced solitude generates an intense forlornness, especially because Facebook and Zoom have this funny way of reinforcing isolation—our loneliness curiously magnified even when we ostensibly *have* the world in our pocket. Though I remain a prolific tweeter, it is hard to deny that these shortcomings are evident, especially as the real world, the big beautiful world that, though frustrating, though challenging, though often disappointing and distressing, never once ceased to be meaningful, magnificent, and, most of all, *viable*.

Despite the wonders of the Internet, our intense depression has been triggered *because* our wonderful world is now off limits. And as our ordeal pushes up screen time for children and adults alike, I must consider whether this problematic factor of 21st century life will only grow disastrously worse if the loss of personal contact is an enduring consequence, one signaling increasing digital dependency. And we also need to consider the ugly concomitant development, the unforeseen consequences this will have on Black America: the probing question of *who* has access to high-speed Internet is ever more pertinent. When learning and working from home become standard, it aggravates longstanding inequities; a community thrust deeper into disarray is unlikely to adapt quickly to this new world order.

Cyrus McQueen @CyrusMMcQueen · May 15, 2020
Kayleigh McEnany says Obama's pandemic plan 'was insufficient' which is why it was 'superseded by a President Trump-style pandemic preparedness response plan'... Really? And how's that workin out? Seems he'd rather let 85,000 people die than listen to a black man. #TrumpHasNoPlan

⟲ 3980　　♡ 12429

We have reached a point in the pandemic where I must confess that the thesis to this book feels somewhat unimportant. However, the correlative relationship between infection and inequality, and those overlapping casualties to come, make these arguments quite apposite. As this work has come to fruition, a didactic on our great imbalance, one predicated on disruption disguised as order: an unforeseen disaster pushes us to the precipice of collapse. Our economic preoccupation and social inaction, having long allowed our maladies to manifest, now brings our situation to critical mass. With our ongoing tumult hinting at a reckoning, those outstanding debts are perhaps no longer being excused. Our arrogating has engendered a righteous remediation; our forced humility a sign the universe will no longer put *up* with our bullshit. Our socioeconomic iniquities and ecological inaction have produced nothing but a warming planet and a cooling among a polarized populace. It indeed feels as if our own bad behavior has sent us to our rooms, where a much-needed timeout might provoke a heartfelt penance—or at least enough reflection that we figure out whether we *are* willing to grow—if we really are determined to coexist more equitably and respectfully moving ahead.

If the path to recovery is forged in that instant when all is lost, then, with death descending on every pocket of our republic, with human totals giving a running account of this forced awakening, our eyes opened by this alarming moment, will we now, I wonder, *truly* transcend? With greater society taking a step back, this pandemic is an unmissable opportunity for us to take a giant leap forward. Nothing so highlights that we were on a road to nowhere than this barrier that has forced us all off the road. Though I have likened it to hell, for the vast majority of us this trial actually skews closer to purgatory. And as we look deeper during this pause, as we spy on that world just beyond us, it now at a hearty remove, I ponder whether our new transparency will soon enable us to behold it all with greater clarity—at least sufficient enough that upon our remolding, our eventual reunion finds us constructing new levels of respect and appreciation.

I have extrapolated on our social ills like racism and sexism, yet I also must highlight how this moment reveals the malignancy of our narcissism. Those pointless aspects of our lives, those mindless routines that consume so much of our energy, are rendered rightfully irrelevant. The time we devote to our hair or makeup, fashion and the charitable gaze of strangers, the fleeting and empty approval of others, is suddenly moot as the reality of this pandemic estranges us from one another. The meaningless mask we have cultivated for society has been literally replaced as so much of society has thoroughly broken down. With so many throughout the world thoroughly reappraising what is of true value, a most scintillating quote from Benjamin Franklin takes on added relevance: "The eyes of other people are the eyes that ruin us." Given our dull new normal, the words of the 18th century statesman pierce, especially his honest conclusion: "If all but myself were blind, I should want neither fine clothes, fine houses, nor fine furniture."

Indeed, "back to basics" rings ever truer upon the reshuffling of our priorities. We are impelled to redefine rather starkly the essential and the nonessential. With the vital ingredients to our well-being whittled down to food and shelter, to our very own health and that most indispensable blessing we call *love*, we discover that not only have these wholesome contents appreciated, but they were all we ever really *did* have.

The empowering legacy of the humanitarian and ecologist Henry David Thoreau comes to mind. Thoreau, who deliberately employed a method of social distancing as he deliberated on the human condition and society's ills, knowing isolation could service enlightenment, wrote: "Most of the luxuries, and many of the so called comforts, of life are not only not indispensable, but positive hinderances to the elevation of mankind. With respect to luxuries and comforts, the wisest have ever lived a more simple and meagre life than the poor. The ancient philosophers, Chinese, Hindoo, Persian, and Greek, were a class than which none has been poorer in outward riches, none so rich in inward."

As we find ourselves in either mandatory lockdown or self-quarantine, Thoreau's quest for self-improvement offers a perfect tutorial for a stir-crazy citizenry who, reflecting the fast pace and demands of our hectic modern world, have so chronically avoided themselves.

Now, envision the fervor with which the ecologist would take up the issue of global warming. And how he would rail against this age of smart phones and computer technology. Might we regard as prescient his awareness of the dangers the then-bourgeoning industrial model posed, with its resultant markets increasing our socioeconomic divide? Have we not now witnessed their subsequent collapse, the intrinsic fallibility of these inconstant metrics, betrayed by an act of nature? Thoreau knew that the verisimilitude of invincibility afforded to wealth and status are not impervious to those immutable laws rendering *all* living things vulnerable, our existential commonality signifying that those grips on levers of power are precarious, conditional, and, therefore, *inauthentic*.

Though I can only imagine Thoreau's righteous indignation at our self-absorbed digital age, with an era of selfies supplanting the sort of self-actualization he championed, he still leads me to ponder whether more than a century and a half after his death, as we all shelter in place at a remove from our neighbors, if we might draw the same righteous conclusions. Though we are far removed from the world that gave birth to *Walden*—or *Civil Disobedience*, with its piercing didactic on the virtues of environmental responsibility and transcendentalism—perhaps his teachings are more relevant than ever, especially as our derelict president, his ineffectiveness opening the floodgates, highlights both the necessity of self-reliance and our responsibility to chisel at these monoliths. To ensure that progress *can* continue despite our government's shortcomings—and because we are left *to* fend for ourselves in so many ways—maybe we can all recognize, as Thoreau stated, that we as a people represent the "independent power, from which all its power and authority are derived."

THE JOKE'S ON US

Perhaps the selfishness that drove our vote in 2016, the criteria we foolishly applied and naively considered paramount, that which revealed the oft-inherited ways we had chosen to behold our fellow men and women, will wither as well, its imprecision herein registered as we are painfully, indefinitely, separated *from* them. In this crystalized moment, the aforementioned resplendence of the human family has never appeared more objective or enticing than now, when our scope has shrunk to *us*. And although resilience gets us through the day, it *is* that collective hardiness, the harnessed strength of the human family, reflected through both our forced innovation *and* sacrifice, that will ultimately power us past this setback. Looking out for our own materialistic and flawed self-interests is rightfully rendered as an ignorant and inferior motivation, especially as that greater interest, that of our peerless survival, is rendered paramount.

Those larger lessons are unmissable, considering that folks who did not line up to vote now line up at Costco, desperately overcompensating amid the fallout of COVID, our civic action, or *inaction*, having left us all defenseless. This regrettable clamor, an indirect result of our own infectious complacency, evokes an even more poignant lesson: we really are all in this together. This calamity exposes our lack of selflessness *and* awareness as supermarkets become epicenters for showcasing these unyielding sins, society's chronic ills adding up as we again check out. Here, our predisposition to hoard instead of help forces the needy to again go without, as a handful of us stockpile toilet paper and hand sanitizer at the disastrous cost it exacts on the many.

At this moment, when the world is indoors, I am also reminded that actual walls have roughly replaced those invisible ones, long standing between us, arbitrary social distancing penalized with a nominal yet comparable mandate. At a time when children are detained and encaged along the nation's southern border, that we are locked in our homes, prevented from leaving, separated from our own families, is itself an irony too delicious to eschew. The great threat the virus poses to America's prisons notwithstanding, given the number of people locked up unnecessarily in our country, decades of cries for reform landing on deaf ears, the average American now feels what it is like to be unfairly removed from society: we can indeed glean profound lessons from all of this. Yet even the greater implications of a warning to shelter in place become otiose when you consider that far too many still live without the luxury *of* a place—and with a real estate catastrophe looming and millions unemployed, the prospect of millions of evictions remains a chilling potentiality.

COVID-19 ensures that the constrictions our social constructs have long exacted on the marginalized now afflict all. That feeling of being trapped and hopeless, vulnerable and scared, forges a frightening new day for a segment of society slowly learning that its caste is impermanent. Moreover, these fissures in our greater mold suggest that privilege itself will suffer a rude awakening. Conversely, for those of us long pathologized, forcibly segregated from higher socioeconomic rungs, we do not need any forced sequestration to betray these arbitrary absurdities. Despite our fevered climbing, we remain painfully aware that self-segregation is superfluous, that those peremptory attitudes we had long deferred to are utterly trivial.

As all across our strata endure a prolonged, unwanted separation, the words of Dr. King, a person quoted throughout this text, again come to the fore. I can think of no admonition either more prescient or more perfect than this: "We must live together as brothers or perish together as fools." Whites who would not commiserate with Blacks now find they cannot commiserate with whites either. Those problematic, infected bubbles they had manufactured are replaced by a different kind, quarantine betraying the insignificance of the former *because* of the stringent reality of the latter. When one is forced to self-isolate, when one's race, gender, and dispensation disappear, their sway, their so-called influence, manufactured roles, and titles evaporating, when a nebulous generational scourge and an even *more* unclear future nullify all leverage, when folks are left with *themselves*, the absence of the *other* finally determines if they ever had any actual presence.

This is why we see the clamor to reopen early, red state governors echoing this pitiful sentiment. Coronavirus came along, a mighty equalizer momentarily leveling rich and poor, conceptually at the very least. With profiting placed on pause, the rich find *this* more frightening than the encroaching virus. Yet I venture to suggest that this ululation to end lockdown boils down to a basic fact: they cannot stand themselves. Afraid of that greater discovery, business leaders and basic minds alike echo White House calls for reopening. Many share the president's spiritual bankruptcy and, finding themselves at the end of their ropes, are unable and unwilling to scale that mountain within. Like Trump, they want to return to business as usual because they cannot stand to *not* be ahead. Many need the economy to reopen because they would rather risk it all than suffer any form of collective reduction. Equality in death is preferable to any semblance of equality in life, this skew fueling their deleterious attempts to place financial losses on par with those inconceivable, and incomparable, human losses.

Though the White House understates the human tally, *that* immediate impact, the growing casualties of COVID, creep ever closer, ensuring that none of us are unaffected. Be it your best friend's grandmother; your wife's cousin's daughter; your friend's friend's brother and his wife; your mother's former coworker; your wife's good friend and her husband; a fellow comedian; the bishop who officiated your wedding; the bouncer and the bartender at the bar you frequented—the latter, a beautiful man brutally young, felled by this monster at age 35—the deaths hit closer and closer to home. I observe Facebook and other virtual vigils graduate into virtual memorials, everyone gathering to pin prayers or remembrances, a deft chronicle of an unfolding crisis in unparalleled times.

It is inescapable, the tragedy of COVID touching everyone, it forming a concentric circle of casualties and rocking *everybody's* world. Death is, as always, the nonnegotiable price of living. Yet witnessing suffering, and in many cases, people facing the unnerving prospect of dying alone, levies a most exorbitant cost on all of humanity at once. We are now all forced to contend conceptually, and quite literally, with the cruel stakes of both a brutal contagion and our own heightened susceptibility.

22

"IT IS WHAT IT IS"

As a nation poses the question "How did we get here?" the genesis of our latest calamity, much like those preceding it, betrays a president's culpability—his excuses engulfed by a flood of irrepressible facts. At a March 13th press conference, when questioned about the lack of widespread COVID testing—a query highlighting his glaring mishandling of the catastrophe—Trump blithely responded, "I don't take responsibility at all." His ineffectual statement was jarring but all too predictable. For a man who never takes onus despite taking an oath of office, his pitiful admission, his usual lame palliating, is squarely on brand. In all honestly, had he owned up to a mistake, it would have been *more* of a sign that the world is coming to an end.

This is all the more maddening when we note that our white nationalist president gutted the national infrastructure for combatting and containing the proliferation of infectious diseases. Early in his rule, Trump unceremoniously scrapped the global health security team that President Obama had initiated upon the emergence of Ebola and other epidemiological crises. It is all rather quizzical that Trump fired the NSC's pandemic response team, yet had *zero* problem using the agency to go after Ukraine. A real threat crept up on America while our president was nefariously concocting one to damage Joe Biden. This and shades of Ukraine echo in his subsequent decision to defund the World Health Organization. That he had left our country vulnerable pre-pandemic, and set out to cripple the WHO in the middle of this crisis, speaks to his hellion-like proclivity for slinging unnecessary mud in an effort to make himself appear clean. Because the WHO, like Ukraine, had not done its best to make him look good, Trump held up funds—compounding the corporeal toll and all because he placed his political future over the future of the people.

In the midst of this full-scale disaster, Trump, predictably, has reached for the shield of Obama. Yet his attempts to pull the former president down neglect the very fact that the Birther is on his own. His desperate attempts to resurrect the previous administration's handling of H1N1 are spirited by the futile belief that Obama detractions can dwarf the disaster unfolding in real time. The lack of testing, a problem his moribund coronavirus response team does not address, is apropos: in this moment when Trump's presidency and leadership *are* tested, he fails miserably. Our doughy president has failed to rise in a heated moment—a test from which no president is exempt; passing it is crucial to history's grade. In dismantling the White House pandemic office, in his effort to undo everything Obama, Trump created his *own* undoing.

But by now, we all know the damage he can leave in his wake. Consider, for example, his indecorous impact on Atlantic City. It is rather unsurprising that the man who did not want to pay his casino vendors does not want to pay for ventilators either. Trump resembles—in that case, as in presiding over a pandemic-stricken America—the smug converse of King Midas, his deleterious imprint ruining everything he touches. Because mistakes and missteps are so woven into the very fabric of his life, they form a lattice that leaves his failures indistinguishable from the image of success he presents. This, of course, results in the confusion that cushions his inevitable fall from the public's good graces when his scandals metastasize. This survival tactic, critical to his comfort, has fueled those subsequent efforts to protect his self-image. This ability to habitually lie to himself, resulting in his inability to discern *or* accept the difference between right and wrong, means he has zero compunction when it comes to then lying to the American people. It broadcasts the eventual, incessant spread of misinformation during a critical time when his words are of far greater consequence than in his casino days.

Yet his half-baked attempts at self-preservation—like his ploy to minimize COVID's epidemiological wallop—were nullified on April 4, when a damning *Washington Post* report established that, beyond a shadow of a doubt, Trump was *very* much to blame for the ballooning crisis: "The U.S. was beset by denial and dysfunction as the coronavirus raged," reads the headline. The article goes on to state: "The Trump administration received its first formal notification of the outbreak of the coronavirus in China on Jan. 3 . . . [yet] it took 70 days from that initial notification for Trump to treat the coronavirus not as a distant threat or harmless flu strain…"

That Trump fumbled the COVID-19 response for at least a full two months was made clear by Secretary of Health and Human Services Alex Azar. Having briefed the president about the growing threat on January 18th, Azar found his efforts torpedoed as the overgrown toddler launched into a tantrum about immaterial matters. Impervious to the critical moment, and nestled in the Petri dish that was Mar-a-Lago, Trump berated the HHS secretary over a completely *unrelated* issue. This, coupled with news that a late January memo from Trade Advisor Peter Navarro also warned Trump that the virus could graduate to a pandemic—a revelation precipitating the formulation of the White House's otiose task force—disclosed a president full of shit when he later posited coronavirus is "something that just surprised the whole world."

On the heels of Navarro's memo, the National Security Council had *also* warned of a "cataclysmic" event brewing in China. Trump's much ballyhooed travel ban, put in place in March, pushes that imperishable timeline back even *further* as we learn these warnings dated back to November: Trump actually knew of COVID-19 in *2019*. Given our immersion in congressional hearings at the time, with the news that NSC members were undermined for not using their resources to further his Ukraine ruse, we can certainly formulate a supplemental hypothesis: Trump's mishandling of the COVID crisis can be attributed directly to his craven misuse of the agency. With further reports corroborating that U.S. intel warned Trump about the virus threat more than a dozen times during the months of January and February, his subsequent decisions are clearly nothing but duplicitous. His reaction to all this information was to *misinform*, to dismiss it publicly as a "Democratic hoax," proving his mendaciousness beyond a shadow of a doubt. Squandering *multiple* opportunities to protect the American people, he demonstrated his disinterest in living up to either his oath *or* his intrinsic duty despite his repeated yarn suggesting he acted in a timely manner.

On April 11th, *The New York Times* further detailed Trump's glaring dereliction, running its report under the unambiguous headline: "He Could Have Seen What Was Coming: Behind Trump's Failure on the Virus." According to the article, the administration's public health experts recommended that Trump warn the American people and urge steps like social distancing. "But the White House focused instead on messaging and crucial additional weeks went by before their views were reluctantly accepted by the president—time when the virus spread largely unimpeded."

Cyrus McQueen @CyrusMMcQueen · Mar 24, 2020
This dumb fuck just said, this outbreak shows you "how important borders are"... Umm no, quite the opposite you bombastic simpleton... it shows that borders are ostensibly bullshit because as JFK so eloquently posited: "We all breathe the same air"... fuckin idiot #PressBriefing

⟲ 475   ♡ 2033

Perhaps the only benefit of Trump's ignominy is that it introduced us to Dr. Anthony S. Fauci, director of the National Institute of Allergy and Infectious Diseases, who joined Azar in the White House's new interagency task force. An expert in epidemiology, his four decades of experience have been indispensable in this precarious moment. No doubt, the sagacity of Dr. Fauci has helped offset an erratic White House. Amid the president's persistent mishandling of the crisis, the tireless doctor has put out fires almost as quickly as Trump can set them—these bonfires in the White House briefing room a direct consequence of the president's attempts to gaslight the American public through an unseemly recurrence: his period of daily Coronavirus Task Force briefings.

For weeks on end, Trump resembled a hostage taker, forcing a quarantined public to suffer foolishness and desperate propaganda displays. His 6 o'clock briefings provided all the reassurance of seeing a septic tank overflow—such events made even more alarming and off-putting when we watched this crap leak into the Rose Garden, Trump bandying about bullshit almost effortlessly, his only discernible motives seeming to be how much *worse* he could make matters. Experts like Dr. Fauci found their salient voices enveloped in the president's equivocating, their honesty and impartiality overshadowed by Trump's insipid sound bites. Recall, Dr. Fauci had already addressed the House Oversight Committee, positing rather unambiguously that "the system is not really geared to what we need right now." The doctor used that moment to speak to the failure of our government to get ahead of the testing dilemma—an issue that still plagues the administration even as countries like Germany and Korea have surmounted this hurdle—yet Trump simply used *these* occasions to lie his ass off, repeatedly blathering that the United States has "tested more than every country combined."

Our moribund reality began to feel more and more like Groundhog Day every time Trump emerged for his daily prevarication. We would watch, for the better part of the hour, as he repeated what "a tremendous job we're doing" before the assembled sycophants dishonorably echoed him, to our collective dismay. Observing Trump go through the motions, sleepwalking through his duties, day after day, was its own form of insanity. But watching experts and officials pander during a pandemic is what really heightened my ire, it no longer reserved solely for the tangerine tyrant taking up space on the screen. I soon trained my visceral and warranted contempt on those grown men and women who simply elected to *heighten* the farce, those mouthpieces insulting our collective intelligence as they callously misrepresented his.

To say that Trump was all over the place during the briefings would be an understatement. His inability to stay on topic was indicative of a man well aware that his political survival now depended on changing the subject, the Three-card Monte analogy still applicable; distraction crucial to the New York hustler's survival. But it was almost painful to watch him whenever Dr. Fauci took to the podium, his posturing unpalatable when the adults were speaking. Given Trump prioritized expediency, while Fauci was focused on the existential threat, you could almost see the wheels turning in his addled mind in these moments. Here he would stand to the side of the lectern swaying like a five-year-old forced into a brief timeout—his deportment that of a hard-headed child who had been reprimanded, his undeveloped brain working overtime to figure out how to still secure his indelicate wants.

This was, of course, the crude impetus behind the plea offered up, the hollow excuse Trump soon repeated *ad nauseam*, that 2.2 million Americans could have died if it were *not* for him. His positioning himself as hero betrayed the utter villainy at hand: these deaths were not nearly as important to him as *outlasting* the political disaster.

However, even if we are to share his dubious optimism—that millions more would have perished if not for him—this is a president parsimonious when it comes to empathy. His repeated failures to acknowledge the human toll suffered on both sides of the ventilator suggest he would take a casual approach to *any* number of casualties amassed. This textbook tactic of proven abusers, bragging about the positives of a negative situation, minimizing pain through the portent of more, has imprisoned many a defenseless American. Yet given the choice between rhetoric and reacting, he stubbornly yammers on. The unimpeachable recommendations of scientists have no appeal for an impeached president consumed with distancing himself from the unceasing deluge; so he elects to neither mitigate this downpour nor defer to those experts in the field of infectious diseases who *can*.

Because the moment is too big for Trump, he rises to it the only way he knows how: through chaos. Tearing down everyone around him, offering up one explosive falsehood and contradiction after another, his improvised device relegates the experts to his shadow. Thus, he boldly recasts himself in their role—despite his pig-ignorant suggestions constantly blowing up in his face. Placed on the same platform as brilliant scientists, he confuses his vacuousness for value, even if he is undeniably, almost cartoonishly, out of his element. In these moments we feel like we are watching Frankenstein's monster pretending to be the doctor instead of the stumbling murderous blockhead we all know him to be.

With Trump, self-aggrandizing is always part and parcel of the game of distraction. However, with hundreds of thousands dead, distracting others appears to go hand in hand with his equally pressing need to distract *himself*. His fragility is so glaringly profound that he roundly disregards the reality of life and death to service his fractious reality show. Yet his focus on his own reflection in the water, with Americans flailing all around him, betrays a president himself floundering, rendering transparent these attempts to keep scrutiny at bay by drowning himself in praise.

Whenever an intrepid reporter dares break the spell he has cast over his "yes" men and women, pressing the president over his failure to take the crisis seriously or get tests out, we can count on his usual riposte: it is either a "nasty question" or the press is not fair to him. This curated behavior betrays his temperamental inner child, evidence that the 45th President cannot keep it together even for 45 minutes. His petulance amid this pestilence worsens whenever it is a reporter of color who dares read him receipts or, in a few cases, read his very own words back to him. Thus, PBS's Yamiche Alcindor and CBS's Weijia Jiang find themselves locked in his crosshairs, their race and gender ensuring that he will, almost reflexively, undermine either reporter. Following this off-putting practice, Trump usually commences with interrogating *them*, betraying his umbrage at exposure. His bigoted attacks are him bridling because these women of color are not only noticeably better at their jobs than he is at his, but because they challenge *his* juvenility. His innate inferiority undoubtedly fueling the unmasked contempt, he quickly peppers them with questions like "Who do you work for?" before appending run-of-the-mill insults about their career trajectory.

Sometimes the president allows the reporter to finish asking about his attempts to undercut governors or turn COVID testing into a competition between countries. Yet here, in his primal need to "unhurt" himself, he hits back with bromides: "You people" or "Ask China." Babbling his unabashed prejudice, he promptly dismisses the reporter before prattling on, the diatribe that follows, his verbal incontinence, an unsightly scene in which he expounds on his disgust. Because the media and minorities are the crux of his perceived mistreatment, this predictable pattern plays out to its own illogical conclusion—and our collective disdain.

With an African American or Asian American reporter inspiring his most churlish retorts, it evinces a president not only unraveling before our very eyes but one who has concluded that his best defense is to *be* offensive. Amid an uncontrolled crisis, he just plays the hits, farting his way through these performances. As MSNBC reporter John Heilemann has described him, rather aptly, Trump is "like a political fat Elvis," content with doing "a lot of schtick." As the sagging politician tosses out barbs like paper towels, matters devolve, the press pool's clamorous objections leading to another part of the almost routine absurdity: Trump proceeds to disrespect the rest of them with a flourish, before defiantly, fractiously, walking out.

However, with Trump, the truth always rests just beneath the surface, in danger of breaching that well-maintained artifice—those like Yamiche and Weijia always threatening to offer up those honest reflections of him. It makes the lesser queries posed by other media members *that* much more infuriating. Afterward, as they toss it back to their colleagues in the studio many here attempt to parse Trump's words, trying to extract meaning from a meaningless harangue. I am forever amazed at their propensity to fail us all with fulsome pother in these moments. Their unabashed attempts at extrapolating on farce, dissecting his disrespect—while remarking favorably whenever he manages *to* impart a serious tone, be it ever so briefly—leaves me agitated. Otiose posits—"What do you think the president meant?" or "What do you think the president can do?" or "If you were the president, how would *you* try to appeal to those undecided voters?"—stunningly, superfluously, waste air time and energy. By posing such redundant questions time and time again—this collective rumination and undue fixation belying the damaging rhetoric and demagoguery at hand—they *choose* to augment the disaster.

After too many years of this obtuseness, of the media's many attempts to rationalize Trump's chronic irrationality, of many affecting a tone suggesting that what we see can possibly be interpreted differently, I cannot help but ask: *why* are they content with consistently burying the lede? It is inarguable: the man is worthless, hopeless, and completely *irredeemable*. With 200,000 deaths recorded by the end of September, that some so-called journalists continue treating him with kid gloves, or giving him the benefit of the doubt, when Trump himself flagrantly doubts scientists and statistics—and anyone who does not corroborate the lies in his mind—indicates that they are almost as derelict in their stewardship as he is. Objectivity flies out the window when you have a president who is *this* objectively dangerous. It is almost *too* easy to call him out on his hyperbolic distractions and consequential inaction, *especially* when makeshift morgues have become routine and his lack of leadership promises this could be our continuing reality.

I found myself tuning to these briefings to view his disgrace on full display, picking apart his heinousness rather effortlessly. As I dissected his bullshit from the comfort of my living room, relishing in schadenfreude and hate-watching every fuckin' second of it, I even literally guffawed—especially when he would posit something inane like, why don't we just "sanitize" the N95 masks because "we have very good liquids." I honestly remember thinking, "What's next; this motherfucker gonna tell people to just douse them in bleach and ammonia, then put them on and *breathe* in deeply?" That I, in many ways, telegraphed his staggering foolishness, and the dangerous suggestion to come—when he actually *proposed* injecting bleach to kill the virus—was both jaw-dropping and disturbing. To our collective bemusement, Trump soon forced science to compete with pseudoscience in a finite space and critical time when the superfluousness of the latter often subdued the importance of the former. These remarkable developments suggested that neither I nor anyone else should underestimate his bottom. With Trump, it *always* gets much worse.

Trump is a most tragic figure. Gallingly oblivious to his dreadful stewardship, he demands praise *after* hitting the iceberg. In a theater of ubiquitous death, his repeated insistence that others are at fault, despite the warning signs, despite squandering every opportunity to steer us clear of catastrophe, is not lost on most—especially when, after impact, the motherfucker *still* refuses to sound the alarm. The MAGA movement now akin to the Hindenburg, Trump, indistinguishable from the Captain of the Titanic, our country indubitably totaled, the objective disaster of his tenure has been realized.

As he predictably delves into his bag of tricks—pushing magic pills and potions, waving his arms as if casting a spell to hypnotize the benighted— we see him once again reach for his spotless predecessor to cover his blemish. After his having scrapped Obama's pandemic response team became widely publicized, and derided, that he *still* goes back to that well, is baffling. Yet, here he would offer up #Obamagate, half-baked postulates of conspiracy, undercooked in the heat of the moment. Only to his chagrin, *no one* bit. Whipped up in a pinch to please his base, he was proffering bullshit during a period when Americans are flocking to food banks. But, watching a president clearly starved for excuses, these most rotten displays give me much food for thought. Chewing on this, I derive delicious satisfaction from, and grow increasingly satiated by, the realization that 2016 had given him exactly what he wanted. Trump, so disgustingly jealous of a Black man, so obviously envious, campaigned to take his prize. And lo and behold, they had *given* it to him. And here he has it, the presidency—did not really want it, to be honest, but just *had* to have it. And he has now taken that prize and *completely* broken it.

It is absurd that it has gotten to this, that we have been reduced to *this*. Because 2016 placed the bloated ignoramus on par with his brilliant predecessor, the only way Trump could work a job he was wholly unqualified for was to besmirch the job *that* predecessor had done. But by lying that "the cupboards were bare" or that he had "inherited a disaster," he would attempt to distance himself from the unrelenting disaster *he* was responsible for. By degrading both Obama and the experts, objectively smart people, in his childlike mind, it therefore meant *he* did not have to compete with them.

Cyrus McQueen @CyrusMMcQueen · May 9, 2020
Trump's full of shit... says Obama left the cupboards bare... Please, Obama left that shit looking like the pantries you be seein on that fuckin extreme couponing show... Trump basically scrapped all of it... didn't even attend briefings on emergency response during transition...

↺ 454   ♡ 1894

Despite reaching for Obama; even though he was tossing out quick fixes and medicinal quackery, the greater problem—the lack of comprehensive testing and a cure—remained high on most Americans minds. In a *New York Times* Opinion piece, Laurie Garrett, a Pulitzer-Prize-winning journalist and best-selling author of *The Coming Plague*, wrote specifically about the lack of decisive measures being taken to combat the crisis. Garrett's no-nonsense assessment—"We need either a cure or a vaccine" in order to get a handle on the pandemic—augments her similarly spot-on take of Trump's mishandling of it. Her admonishment that he is "the most incompetent, foolhardy buffoon imaginable" encapsulates a president who leaves much to be desired under normal circumstances, never mind when he leaves us with a vacuum when Americans most need leadership.

Among Trump's myriad of monumental missteps, perhaps none is worse than his decision to ship 18 tons of personal protective equipment to China during the infancy of the pandemic. His diminishing our national stockpile during that initial, critical 70-day period increased the undue burden he ended up heaping on America's governors. That he would, ironically, scold them throughout, leaving them to procure ventilators and respirators themselves—after months of ignoring these shortages and preventing our meeting the ordeal head on—positioned the United States to play a desperate game of catchup with a crisis that was soon lapping the globe. His further flippant assertion that he is "not a shipping clerk"—before callously labeling state officials who took him to task over the lack of federal assistance as "complainers"—left many state leaders in the untenable position of having to fend for themselves.

Because Trump turned acquiring PPE into a popularity contest, he thrust blue state governors into a veritable quagmire. Andrew Cuomo soon described to a rapt audience how his own efforts to secure masks were doomed by the very dynamics that erupted the moment Trump chose *not* to seize the supply chain. Cuomo, in daily briefings actually worth watching, disclosed that the price of the masks had jumped from 85 cents to seven dollars as New York contended with both a global shortage and the federal government's inimitable delay in filliping mass production of these items.

The stunning lack of any coordinated White House effort to shore up these concerns left states to cannibalize one another, forced to bid against each other, and even FEMA itself in some cases, for PPE as if this were a fucked-up, depraved challenge on *The Apprentice*. In other words, the White House's imprudent decision, enabling private enterprise to undercut overriding national needs, exacerbated the public health crisis.

History will show that our casualties mounted in this unfortunate epoch because Trump played favorites—rewarding flatterers like Florida Gov. Ron DeSantis, who dragged his heels on flattening the curve in order to puff up the president. And with those very red state governors, be it in Florida or Texas, underpinning Trump, teasing that they are relaxing social distancing measures out of a desire to open up the economy—we can now juxtapose their indelicateness to the actions of their more sentient counterparts in New York and Michigan, those like Gov. Cuomo and Gov. Whitmer, who inevitably mitigated the spread, given that each was consumed more by the "human cost" and its inherent precedence.

But because Trump is buoyed by enablers, he is able to then pass his days coming up with whichever adversary can best distract from his almost Herculean ignorance. As one-fifth of America is now out of work, and many of the rest work from home, we watch from our living rooms as he posits that the problem is Gov. Cuomo, or the news media, or China, or Obama, or whomever else swirls around his addled mind— at least until that particular press conference, tweet storm, or campaign rally passes and he begins the indecorous cycle all over again, spinning the same revolving door of excuses and scapegoats. Shades of Ukraine even reappear: Trump advised Vice President Pence *not* to call Michigan Governor Gretchen Whitmer, amid the crisis, because he felt she did not "appreciate him." His misogyny and menace, pitiable before parking lots and convention centers became triage units, sees that incontinent need to hurt women now incurring an even *greater* consequence—his disrespect impairing the lives of *all* Michiganders.

Yet after anointing himself a "wartime president" and COVID the "invisible enemy," it was clear that he could not contend with a virus that was impervious to his connivance. His delusions of grandeur, ever the more pitiful in these moments, are not simply bad given the disruption coronavirus has brought to the average person, but because first responders and medical personnel, sacrificing without tests, many reduced to reusing masks over and over, are being dispatched to the frontlines to fight this "war" *without* the proper weapons. Considering that lives attach to each discourtesy, each one an individual who might have been spared, the sobering impact of this pandemic, and his immaturity, will be unforgettable.

On a day when NYC experienced 799 deaths in a 24-hour period, one of them was my best friend's father-in-law, who lost his battle with COVID-19 in the very Queens hospital Trump had only briefly acknowledged between baseless assertions that America's PPE shortage might be due to hospital workers' stealing masks. The very moment I received the text announcing that Mr. Calvo's life had been cut short, the doting family man yet another loss in a growing list of unfathomable losses, that saddening news was quickly followed by news of Trump's latest indecency. The indescribable tragedy of a loving grandfather forced to spend his final moments alone, intubated and without his loving family at his side, while the president touted that the ratings for his latest press briefing were "through the roof," aggravated my already raw emotions. I stared blankly at my phone. Before that family could even begin to absorb their titular loss, their lack of closure would be enmeshed with his lack of decorum. These problematic notifications blended together on my screen as the record of a single sad day, a reflection of this unbearable moment in time, the greater absence of a soul now latticed with the president's lack of sobriety. Trump's indelicateness incongruent with the ineffable toll of these outcomes, his actions on the front and now the back end produced nothing but a glut of unspeakable anguish.

Cyrus McQueen @CyrusMMcQueen · Apr 9, 2020
My best friends father-in-law died last night from this fuckin virus and the President of the United States is on television bragging about his fuckin ratings! I hate him with every fiber of my motherfucking being!! 💀

⟳ 2261   ♡ 14420

The president relegated COVID-19 to his back burner, as even those tangible losses could not break his preoccupation with a likely loss in November. Considering how fallacies about Mexicans and Muslims had powered his improbable rise, it was almost predictable that a hateful tenor would soundtrack another White House run. It is why mere months after effusively praising Chinese leaders for their response to the crisis, Trump began pinning blame *solely* on them. With the pandemic and his reelection running concurrent, he needed to distract from a tanking economy, pitiful poll numbers, and Joe Biden's looming larger and larger before him.

Considering how coronavirus began as a "Democratic hoax," it was only a matter of time until he promoted it to a "Chinese Virus." With Trump's racism so all-consuming, it was almost inevitable he would couple an invidious component to an already virulent contagion. Their viciousness now runs parallel, xenophobia adding a superfluous strain of social stigma to a ubiquitous health crisis. He has brazenly replaced an enemy that cannot be seen with one that *can*. An intrepid photographer soon captured an image of a Trump speech with the word "corona" crossed out, and the word "CHINESE" boldly written over it, confirming this doctoring. This axiomatic tactic to misinform, a Sharpie reincarnation, reveals that he will indulge in the most basic behavior, and stoop to any low, to remain simpatico with his base.

Woodrow Wilson failed to acknowledge the Great Influenza that gripped the nation a century prior, giving this new presidential abdication an eerily familiar feel. Where Wilson feared the flu would take focus off the Great War, Trump takes steps to ensure that nothing distracts from the culture war he conducts. Seeking to bury his monumental mistakes in the process, our "wartime" president follows right in Wilson's tracks, wielding nationalism as a cudgel. Flat caps have been replaced by MAGA hats. And just as Wilson inspired thugs to corral draft dodgers and terrorize those considered leftists, the raucous protests occurring at this president's urging, suggests how much our history is actually a broken record.

With Asian Americans experiencing a drastic uptick in hate crimes, accosted and spat upon because our broken president feeds a collective paranoia, scapegoating draws attention *away* from him and the bourgeoning catastrophe. Because hate courses through his veins, he reframes the "war" by tapping a palpable fright, validating the often-violent recoil of his peanut gallery. Employing sophistry to combat actual occurrences, a man unwilling to handle reality endeavors to craft an alternative one—one he continues to prioritize, even amidst a generational scourge, out of its benefits to *him*. Though very much weakened, a Republican bulwark somewhat insulates him from both the facts *and* his own accountability, permitting him to mount these sorts of doleful attacks.

The sort of divisiveness that is crucial to the Trump brand contributes to the nation's literal and analogous losses. At a moment when our commonality has never been more apparent, his concerted effort to separate people essentially ignores and aggravates the act of nature that almost forces our coagulation. He, thriving on disorder, disregards every logical step a normal chief executive would take. Instead of conciliating, the pig wallows in his own filth, augmenting the disrepute.

Other ne'er-do-well presidents have withered during crises. Reagan immediately comes to mind, with his flat-out refusal to address the AIDS pandemic during the 1980s. Trump somewhat rekindles the stigma that eventually attached to AIDS, misnamed "gay cancer," in his hellacious insistence on referring to COVID-19 almost exclusively as the "Chinese virus." And as before, the egregious actions of a sociopath, a purely political animal, deliberately aggravating underlying sociopolitical factors, ensures that the problem will only get much worse.

Cyrus McQueen @CyrusMMcQueen · Jul 31, 2019
Seriously, FUCK Ronald Reagan! We went from an actor President to a reality show President with the Jed and Jethro war machine sandwiched in between. 16 yrs of prosperity with Clinton/Obama but everyone acts like the 80's were great. Shit, I recall folks doin better in the 90's!!

⟲ 523   ♡ 2911

For an incorrigible sliver of our populace, facts still instill more fear than the virus itself. We watch as the legitimate terror of contamination, and scientific projections of a second spike in infections, breeds vociferous opposition. With this slow-moving disaster enveloping the country, Trump upstages the virus at almost every turn, tainting untouched pockets by roundly downplaying its veracity, exposing more Americans to his fiction than to the disease itself. Having violated his sworn oath, this ongoing perjury usurps health protocols, his now infecting an even larger number of Americans through his Twitter twaddle and his desperate campaign stops.

Scientists caution against relaxing social distancing too soon, but their projections of "needless suffering and death" fail to register with those who succumb to Trump. That his is a base that banks on the undue suffering of others—and long attributes their own insolvency to ethnic instead of economic factors—is precisely why his threatening invective drowns out the threat of silent infection. We watch helplessly as a merciless pathogen continues along its bipartisan war path, swamping Texas and Florida with an inevitable uptick in infections. Yet Gov. Abbott and Gov. DeSantis, Trump's veritable toadies, follow his disastrous example instead of actually *leading*, each focusing on businesses instead of taking care of business. Given COVID's cruel stakes, the clamor to reopen creates a morass for Republicans, mortality a direct consequence of the party's chronic immorality.

A *Washington Post* report details this maddening trajectory, observing that older Americans are concerned about coronavirus—unless they happen to be Republican. This speaks to a perturbing notion that our politics are now so polarized, so entrenched in partisan salvos, that there is nothing pugnacious outlets like Fox News will *not* fire on. Their eschewing scientific evidence is a corollary to their subverting truth itself, sacrificing it to buttress their binary platform, *us* versus them. Chronic contrarianism has eroded their audience's immunity, diminishing any ability to discern right from wrong—even in moments like this, when social distancing is in *everyone's* best interest—and when their clown prince is full of shit.

Yet in our 24-hour news cycle, many roundly accept the lies of a man and a party in the face of facts—the very standard that should govern all life. This is *maddening*. It is why I have *no* love for conservative leaders: they know the difference between truth and lies. If their spouse lies to them or one of their children, whether about something either big or small, they probably notice. They *address* it. When someone lies to you, either they want to protect you or they do not *respect* you. Could it be that Fox protects those billionaires whose iniquitous global interests are thus served by protecting the Republican base from the truth, from the reality of a multicultural world that is heating up and a wealth chasm that is growing? I conclude that those very entities lying to them—who get them repeating lines like "Lock Her Up" and "No Collusion" and "Chinese Virus"—ultimately do not respect the men and women within this base. And *that* is what is truly pathetic about the world, or the facsimile of one, of Fox and its mouthpieces. They simply do not *respect* their viewers.

For Republican politicians, the matter of flattening the epidemiological curve, our immediate and existential concern, fails to supersede the more pressing matter of their own political survival. Impelled to cosign the president's fable, to go down with the lie, keeping up certain appearances takes on ever greater importance. It is why they question and eventually jettison mask-wearing—so *Trump* can save face. As the *New York Times* has highlighted about Trump's disturbing contribution to a growing trend, "He is not alone among Republican officials in eschewing masks or downplaying their benefits, behavior that political scientists believe has encouraged a partisan split in who wears masks."

Since conservatives need to obscure this monumental calamity unfolding with shocking force before our very own eyes, they simply rely on what has worked before. So, despite life and death, the cruel stakes of COVID, they devolve the pandemic into hyper-partisanship: eschewing social distancing measures the newest way to "own the libs." Whether triggered by anti-science diatribes and demonization or the threat of gender and racial parity, with coronavirus leaving many helpless and hopping mad, they direct their pent-up animus toward one or all of these traditional targets. Yet when stay-at-home measures meets with such *inspired* belligerence, it suggests that notions of freedom are actually a red herring and there are likely darker issues afoot.

Despite the death totals in Detroit, where the coronavirus eviscerates the Black community in particular, disgruntled white men, their armed militias clad in rebel flags, descend on the Michigan State House, an occurrence both shockingly incongruous, yet, at the very same time, felicitous given America's repetitious history. It brings to mind events that unfolded in 1943, when race riots in the same city ignited when recently migrated African Americans filled newly available defense jobs. Our actions to help that war effort presaged this current unrest: upon decades and decades of stratification, today's white mobs bridle at the efforts to win this latest war. Given the parallels, the developments in the Michigan Capitol bring to mind Eleanor Roosevelt, who, during the aforementioned turmoil, memorably posited: "I suppose when one is forced to realize that an unwelcome change is coming, one must blame it on someone or something."

But we can juxtapose those frontline workers—the ethnic minorities comprising most of Detroit's bus drivers and delivery people, nurses and plant employees, who have to keep working—with the amplified petulance of Trump's feral followers and their desire to open the floodgates of infection by reopening early. It is a stunning reminder that in America, you have Nationalists, those seemingly living to die, while the marginalized, bereft of economic power and options, must contend once again with the invidious prospect of dying just so we can *live*.

But being that the state of Michigan, which Trump won in 2016, is essential to his reelection, coronavirus and calls to reopen provide him with a wedge, enabling his base attempts to force resentment politics onto the state ballot. Gov. Gretchen Whitmer is thus one more Democratic female he seeks to undermine to fan the embers of his culture war, (an occurrence which has had dangerous ramifications as 13 domestic terrorists would later be arrested and charged in a conspiracy to kidnap and kill the governor).

Yet here again, we see Trump reach for social media as an accelerant, his caustic dissemination promising to ignite America's racial powder keg. Firing up his volatile base, he foments infernos with tweets like "LIBERATE MINNESOTA!" "LIBERATE MICHIGAN!" "LIBERATE VIRGINIA!" States whose Democratic governors opt to align *with* science rather than with him see his umbrage surge, his base abetting this shabby offense. His having already impugned these leaders' response to COVID, these swing states forecast the battle to come in November. With the president hedging, consumed not with coronavirus but with his own personal crisis, he tries to transform his chagrin into an electoral advantage. But by conflating COVID-related protocols with violations of freedom and liberty, these flimsy ideals manage to override his failure—as the pandemic, and the humiliating way he has handled it, succumbs to tribal politics.

It is in no way coincidental that pleas to reopen the economy come when staggering data corroborate the havoc COVID-19 is wreaking on Black America. In cities with large African American populations—Philadelphia, D.C., Detroit, New Orleans, New York, and more—fatalities climb at an alarming rate. It leads me to surmise that the clamor to return to business as usual has everything to do with *who* is dying. The arbitrary decisions doctors are tasked with, over whose life to save, begin to plague my conscience, considering that our bodies may not fit into those existential boxes, our value again incommensurate with those who have traditionally appreciated. And considering the significant number of African Americans on the frontlines, the nurses and orderlies in these overwhelmed, undermanned hospitals—America's dearth of PPE exacerbating their exposure—it almost ensures that we are absorbing more of the impact.

By the month of April, disturbing numbers corroborated both COVID-19's ominous trajectory and its imminent threat to Black America. In the state of Michigan, where African Americans comprise 14 percent of the population, they accounted for 40 percent of COVID-19 deaths. In the city of Chicago, though African Americans comprise only 30 percent of the state population, they accounted for 70 percent of COVID-related deaths. With death rates consistently higher for African Americans, it suggests that a community already vulnerable due to a myriad of underlying factors—be it hypertension, higher incidents of multigenerational housing, or denser living conditions overall—had been primed for an epidemiological catastrophe. Considering we do not receive the best care during the best of times, an oft-maligned community finds itself short of defenses. Far too often, circumstances give us neither the option of staying home from work nor the luxury of going to the doctor upon becoming ill. By the time we seek treatment, it is already too late for many of us.

The immediate reality as infection rates soar is that the outbreak reinforces America's longstanding inequalities, the contours of COVID indicating that indelible color line. While no race is exempt from infection, the disproportionate concentration along the margins sees those victims of relegation contracting and succumbing to the contagion at alarming levels. Though many preexisting factors, again, contribute to this imbalance, the morbid outcome remains the same: the disease is annihilating Black and Brown Americans at a staggering rate. The Brookings Institution confirms this: "Death rates among Black people between 55-64 years are higher than for White people aged 65-74."

Here, COVID conjures up unwelcome recollections of Hurricane Katrina, those memories *still* raw. I lament that yet another son of privilege has been elected against the will of the people, Trump's ineptitude, like George W. Bush's, contributing mightily to the human losses sustained. In 2005, Black bodies were macabre buoys done in by the rising tide of disregard; in 2020, we sadly witness another act of God, these two almost Biblical tragedies defined, and compounded, by a Republican president's disgrace. Penury had primed our community, in many ways a tinderbox, to explode when the matches of fate were lit. Pestilence turned out to be that spark, as New Orleans would see a flood of unnecessary deaths again unleashed upon its low-lying shores.

As I repeatedly state, the devaluation of Black bodies carries over to essentially any crisis. It is why the cries surrounding today's decimation of the Black population, even when issued at alarming decibels, fail to arouse greater sympathy. But those Black losses aside, it is the greater indifference to death that is *most* responsible for our nation's roundly tolerating COVID-19 and the causalities it amasses. Predictably, a novel virus is no match for the outstanding illness of idiocy. Here, the sentient and the senseless within our populace again face off, the tolerant forced to contend with intolerable, feeble ideations of "freedom" maddeningly overpowering that greater imperative: the preservation of *all* American life.

Yet I keep coming back to that ostentatious scene at the Michigan State House, those disturbing images and deeper connotations almost failing to compute. It is no great mystery why the epicenters for rejecting masks and social distancing are the very same ones in which we see a rejection of commonsense gun control measures. Again, African Americans, the disproportionate victims of both gun violence *and* coronavirus, must contend with the dissonance of a benighted, bellicose citizenry mobilizing to facilitate a morose outcome. It truly feels like the demons descended on the Capitol to ensure that COVID, in this case, could *finish* what it started. Which is part and parcel of why they now pit the virus against the Confederate flag and freedom: this conflict is actually *in* our American algorithm.

White men carrying nooses and trying to force Blacks back to work remains America's answer; this proffered solution remains the *real* problem. It indeed brings forth eerie evocations from preceding centuries. Parallels to the Civil War are innumerable; COVID summons a time when we were both expendable and indispensable to the U.S. economy—our free labor irresistible to an irascible populace who would rather *die* than relinquish it. Our current developments resurrect America's age-old quandary, that unresolved conflict of morality versus money. Only here, those working for *next* to nothing and those who stand for nothing, these dichotomous forces, rekindle age-old contradictions amid a ballooning crisis. It again speaks to the notion that COVID-19 is but a manifestation of that greater malady. And as we contend with a racist president and those governors undergirding his madness—this too will likely produce historical echoes too sonorous to dismiss.

Yet those greater implications of COVID-19, and those whose money secures their dispensation from this latest war—the ruling class staying home as the underclasses fight it out—make it almost inevitable that poor, gun-toting whites *will* bring the battle once more. But when vulnerability, belies volatility, it eventually renders even the barbarous powerless—placing all in the untenable position of facing a virus that cannot be intimidated.

Cyrus McQueen @CyrusMMcQueen · May 2, 2020
It's ironic how much conservatives love the military... I mean, you had Michigan protesters clad in camouflage fatigues... they're carrying combat grade weapons... Yet none of em could bring themselves to follow orders... 🌚

⟲ 525   ♡ 2303

The shared outcome of a divergent hypothesis, prejudice versus pestilence, given their corrosive overlaps and the overall collective detriment, suggests that conditions created by the former facilitate the devastation caused by the latter. But whichever one considers more ruinous, their symbiosis is undeniable, both bringing great disruption to Black America, eroding our numbers at a staggered tempo.

That our list of casualties promised to be greater was critical to the forecast I had made upon Trump's win: I posited we had *everything* to lose. Though I, and most in my outfit, swallowed that tough little pill, it is a gradual poison like the hydroxychloroquine Trump carelessly pushed, digesting this reality has too proven detrimental to our hearts. Having barely endured his tenure, the inevitability of contamination now engenders an even greater discomfort. We have been set up to die and, left tenuous by this president and with many more casualties to come, that brutal undercurrent to these United States is unavoidable: racial inequality always has, and always will have, corporeal ramifications. We see this reflected in the inflamed public health crisis and in the arduous road to economic recovery, as both continue to boil down to *whose* body is worth *less*.

23

Black Lives Matter

Where Trump's election brought to bear the inveterate recurrence of America's racial discord, COVID-19 lays bare our deep and correlated economic divide. Those on the frontlines, despite having gone too long without a living wage, are proving unequivocally that they are the *essential* bedrock of our society. It is the sacrifices of those overlooked, undervalued men and women, the very fingers of the working poor, that keep the proverbial dyke *from* cracking.

Yet our crisis is compounded because monetary value is wrongly attached *to* human life—reducing us by inauthentic metrics like purchasing power or consumer value, our portfolios, paychecks, or 401k's. Thus, the divorce of people from both their time and their money, the primary objective of commerce, has been dealt a brutal blow by COVID. Ironically, consumer confidence, which long sustained Western economies, has pretty much been shattered, especially as we realize how precious and fleeting our time here is. This is why pleas to reopen businesses are so quizzical. The sky may be falling, but, because profits are as well, business leaders expect us to focus on that incommensurate loss. Yet those who allow the economic imperative to supplant the epidemiological one appear oblivious to the fact that life as we know it will never be the same *until* public health is everyone's priority.

In this moment, I cannot help but remember that slavery was a business: being Black affording me that much needed perspective. The most heinous, hellish rationales were used to defend what is intrinsically indefensible. With the calls to reopen businesses, and the president's command to reopen schools, even as infections climb throughout America, the iniquitous again proffer up innocent bodies for sacrifice. Even as the heavens demand their pound of flesh, those capitalists who try to demand theirs have yet to awaken to the profundity of this multigenerational reckoning, one which finally places our focus on what is of *true* value.

It is easy to argue that we have long endured a bastardized normal, one that haunts our entire waking life, the incorporeal plaguing us with ghostly measures. An unquantifiable human existence has been inexplicably diminished to numbers preceding a decimal point. For far too long, we have deified wealth, glorifying the takers over the givers; for far too long, we got away with it. But now we see how our monomaniacal focus on the individual comes at a deleterious expense to the collective. At its core, ours is a selfish society, our debilitating sense of entitlement both engrossing and defining us, evidenced by the reluctance of many an American to amend behavior so as to flatten the epidemiological curve and ameliorate this protracted crisis. Yet that a president's ineptitude has precipitated the collapse of markets, it brings to mind those who flippantly, flagrantly, dismiss his racist disposition, his pathologizing and negative impact, all *because* of its positive impact on those 401k's.

Though *schadenfreude* is inapplicable in this rumination—we have all lost in one way or another, any economic gain made during Trump's tenure disappearing overnight—one cannot help but conclude that those Americans betting on the long shot saddled themselves to a jackass, their wins nullified as they could barely enjoy all this "winning" before he bucked them all off. The gate had been left open, and their gift horse had galloped away, dragging away their gains, while it also allowed danger to seep in. Despite all the talk of walls and travel bans, a global economic crisis precipitated by a global health crisis has arisen precisely *because* political nearsightedness has left us all unsafe. A country committed to capital gain and rugged individualism always promised to be undone by an epidemiological disaster—this presenting the very challenge we observe when it is time for protocols and coordination with the private sector *for* the public good.

Americans who abandon their conscience when it comes to electing bankrupt candidates are *exactly* why a cabal of conservative pirates can maraud our vital infrastructures. But when we witness such axiomatic dereliction of duty—ignoring the early warning signs, electing a caustic candidate not ready for prime time—it makes those members of both the underclass and the ruling class who blatantly ignored his fomentations wholly complicit in this intolerable outcome. They have been indispensable *to* their very own destruction. When they empowered Trump to fire our nation's pandemic response team, they handed an assault weapon to a president with the comportment of a kindergartener. They toyed with fate, and he did what he was wired to do: destroy any and everything in his path.

To expound on this description, and their unwary choice, we can say that these individuals traded their votes and power for a few magic beans. Now, they cannot buy a brain when they most need it. Lest we ever forget, Trump is empowered to make bad decisions because his backers made a bad decision *first*. Allowed to get up onto a podium, he gaslights them with impunity *because* of the unholy covenant they have entered into. The president is incapable of absorbing the gravity of life and death situations, yet those voters, by electing him, by following his fiendish lead, showed they *too* are incapable of processing a critical, life-altering decision. They squandered their consequential vote, electing to indulge wickedness, pumping his malformed brain with the sort of hot air that only fueled his bloviation. They allowed *him* to skirt all rationality because they *themselves* long ago abandoned it. Being guided by resentment instead of reason, profits instead of principle, they are now unable to restrain an impeached president. When it is time to listen to numbers and experts and unimpeachable science, his ego has grown too gigantic, he has proven *too* incorrigible to be held accountable. They can now only get carried away together, despite the perilous fall to come.

Too many Americans sold out for a few fleeting years of feeling good, a "good" that is as questionable as the man who promises it. This good is indeed predicated on bad, as "fake" as the very descriptor Trump applies to the truth. That high had to come down sooner or later, yet his base refuses to accept that they are not superheroes, that they are not superior despite what the drug has convinced them: they are merely one of us, one of many now picking up the pieces and starting over.

A major component to Trump's success is that a wealthy white candidate embraces and espouses the racial tribal politics of poorer whites. It is part of his appeal. Part of his *magic!* They vote for him because they believe they are akin. He cast his spell and, four years in, his hold is unbroken, many operating as though they too are now rich— as if by casting their ballot, they had played the lottery, Trump's win construed as *their* windfall. Although they share none of his planes or properties, hotels or country clubs, they share his race, his *hate*. Yet that commonality flies in the face of truth: they essentially have nothing, and thus *are* nothing in Trump's eyes.

Conservatism is especially pernicious because it convinces its followers that less is more, its sheep to volunteer to be fleeced, willingly sacrificing their own growth in service of their oppressor's warmth. Conservatives prosper by championing, and eventually convincing individuals, that social identity is *binary*. However, this sort of stringent outlook goes against our very nature; we can readily observe the undeniable benefits of cross-pollination, immutable, inarguable natural processes resulting in vibrant, diverse ecosystems, something in which diverse species ultimately thrive.

Given that all living things are interconnected, any expectation that the human race is an exception, an advanced species defying this didactic, is unnatural and, beyond that, morally reckless. Such an inorganic, invidious ideology, by weaponizing our dichotomy, produces only perpetual disharmony. Ironically, so-called leaders get their flocks upset about the notion of subtraction when that is just what they sell: the idea that multiculturalism takes away from your own. By teaching that you will lose instead of the converse—that one stands to gain from such exposure and influence—they allow the fruits of progress to rot before them, willingly starving themselves, keeping better education, medicine, and even culture at a remove, many embracing philistinism as if they can extract virtue from intractability.

Ultimately, conservative leaders want to keep these individuals weak, to be satisfied with less, so that they do not notice that the powerful forces under this umbrella take more and more from them. Iniquitous developments like outsourcing and automation slowly evaporate jobs and resources, all while the focus remains on some imperious "other" rather than those disappearing opportunities. It creates frightening levels of confusion, blame landing squarely on Black and Brown people for both the loss of livelihoods and, curiously, the inability of this deprived monoculture to flourish. The illogical fear that identity will dissipate in diverse waters overpowers all evidence to the contrary. The beauty of a blended America, the inherent positives of hybridization, succumb to disastrous rationales, amalgamation sacrificed in service of sour, regressive homogenization.

Dissonance having created artificial distance between us, the pandemic reveals not only the absurdity of the chasm but also those additional and unnatural rifts created by great socioeconomic inequality.

As the upwardly mobile enter into limbo, unable to increase coffers, the downward trajectory for the rest of us clarifies the utter insignificance of their improper approach to life. Again, the irony is too powerful not to repeat. At a moment when everyone practices social distancing, the fact is, a different sort of social distancing had precipitated it all: the calcified divisions that allowed a whack-ass reality star to come in and fill that space left no middle ground, the fractures he exacerbates enabling those gaps to grow.

Because this virus is indiscriminate, slicing through our population like a scythe, it renders all the more nonsensical the thought of giving priority to tax cuts for billionaires over strengthening our medical infrastructure, even when so many individuals across our vast socioeconomic strata lie intubated, an invaluable breath from death. Yet Senate Republicans who have plied the one percent with money, do nothing but delay when it comes to subsequent coronavirus relief bills. As they drag their heels on helping average Americans when they need it most, such untimely intransigence constitutes an act of moral turpitude. Because they posit Medicare for All as a scary proposition, that long-con decades in the making, the weaponizing of health care sees medical costs rise even as earnings stagnate. And with 30 million Americans receiving jobless benefits and nearly 27 million set to lose their health insurance, the crisis again exposes and exacerbates our outstanding variances. That we still tether something as sacrosanct as health care to the fickle, capricious whims of employers makes the collateral damage of COVID a case of America's chickens coming home to roost, and at the worst time imaginable. Cooped up and out of work, we see this untenable imbalance, these psychic faults, reconciled by a physical expiation, this existential crunch indicating we *all* must pay the price of this public health crisis.

This upheaval is an undeniable inflection point, the great crucible of our lifetime. This trial of the human spirit mandates us to either continue down the perilous road of iniquity, which has left us all truly vulnerable, *or* take this pause to begin carving out a wider path, one that does not squeeze all into a single file, marching lockstep toward a plummet. Since none of us can advance or sidestep the pitfalls of a gig economy, this coming election, and those to follow, consequently provide opportunities to begin getting it right. I long ago learned the antidote to society's ills are found *through* interdependence. If I have grown more certain of anything in this time of great uncertainty, it is that we are more endangered, and at the same time more interconnected, than we ever realized.

I propose that notions of true interdependence—in both theory *and* practice, and not in some exploitative sense but rather as a higher socioeconomic consideration—*should* override those racial hallucinations and nationalistic malformations that have long lulled so many into a false and disastrous sense of normalcy. Lest we forget, the status quo only became a monolith because we allowed profits to supplant principle at every turn, creating structures that are unsustainable. As my brilliant mother Candelaria long ago posited, any semblance of peace *will* inevitably shatter whenever there is a chronic absence of justice. Conditional power has only been confused for absolute power because *we* have gone with the program. And as this cataclysm brings everyone's mortality to the fore, the idea that we would waste another fleeting minute, underpinning such profound imbalance, given our finite time here, highlights the *immediacy* of this necessary change.

Control over our globe and its harnessed energy has contracted to a handful of individuals, but we have an opportunity to subvert this standard—all while gaining a greater appreciation for the world that was never theirs to purloin in the first place. That we have often bartered those simple freedoms for a complex network of e-commerce and capital alchemy, social mobility and manufactured wants, proves that immediate gratification has helped cultivate an insular, utterly inferior world. As we are more aware than ever before, that insular world is inimitably eclipsed by the beautiful world just outside our doors—a world taken from us because we did not truly appreciate it.

Cyrus McQueen @CyrusMMcQueen · Aug 5, 2020
If Trump doesn't care about the people of America, why does he want to be President of the United States of America?

⟲ 1155   ♡ 6562

Though I had achieved a balance between information and entertainment in my life, the act of dispensing laughs during this time highlights how so much humor, or *certain* humor, does not really fuckin' matter. It is probably alarming for a comedian to utter such words, but this moment, this relentlessly serious, consequential moment, teaches me that a lotta shit just is *not* funny. And though the elixir of levity *is* definitely needed, perhaps now even more than before, the thought of grabbing a communal microphone and standing before a roomful of people certainly is not viable. I do not know when the pyrotechnics of a live show will be an option, or where the explosive laughter and flushed faces that anchor our light show will proceed, unmuzzled by masks and bandanas. And though it is missed, I would be remiss if I also did not share how the politics of the comedy business have become more unappetizing than ever, especially when the politics of justice are a far heartier pursuit, a more worthy toil than waiting on gatekeepers, those whose importance is inflated only because we convince ourselves they can validate our mother and father's inimitable creation. Besides, given our heightened mortality, we can best utilize this uncertain time by *kicking* those gates down. This is where our ability to communicate on digital platforms becomes increasingly vital, this an opportune time *to* be a creator—as Twitter and other vehicles are particularly viable given the brutal constraints of the contagion, and in that they constitute a driving force we can actually control with *our* hands.

As we slowly envision the world we want to come out of this, even as people lie dying, whatever reforms and greater perspective will arise, like a phoenix emerging from these embers, that greater evolution will hopefully mark a dying off of the sort of disposition and deportment it was time to lose. Like a forest fire that eliminates dangerous brush, thereby promoting new growth, maybe this moment will be crucial to self-correcting those combustible aspects endangering our socioeconomic landscape. Hell, perhaps this fire will even spark a true renaissance; the *soaring* Twenty-Twenties. Shit, a boy can dream.

Ours is a time when everyone takes selfies but far too few take time to really look at themselves. This is an era of conflict in television and music, when art succumbs to unhealthy competition, to those false idols we have chosen to embrace without audit. Much of this mind-numbing nonsense has been tendered by those who do not take the oath of artist seriously enough—who do not fulfill their charge as provocateurs, that necessary filter for the public consciousness, questioning power while imparting life-affirming, *positive* output, not just the fast food we cram into our minds and bodies, the shit that does not stand up to the brutal sieve of time.

As the casualties of COVID hit closer and closer to home, we recognize, more than ever, that tomorrow is a *gift*. Like a war from a half-century prior, the virus pulls the draft number of your neighbor or friend or the local bartender; in this poignant period, overwhelmed hospitals replace rice paddies as the epicenters of untimely, unnecessary death.

This begs the question: can we go back to the way things were? At some point, after we escape our dwellings, we will once again exercise the privilege of dwelling on the mundane, the meaningless, and the jejune, but *should* we pick up where we left off? Perhaps it was our lack of seriousness that got us here, where the maestro of that sort of mind-numbing output disguised as reality, that which facilitated and celebrated unhealthy conflict, turned viewers into voters. It was indeed problematic forms of escapism that sequestered us from our best selves, ensuring our wakeup call *would* be severe. In that regard, our current reckoning is very much like rehab, forcing us to face ourselves and the aggregate of our chronic neglect.

It is now useful to admit these mistakes and take ownership of our lives, especially as we reverse engineer our disaster to figure out where, exactly, we went wrong. It is also necessary, more than ever, to embrace the honest truth: because we no longer stood for righteousness or personal growth, we were poised for a great fall. This greater virus infecting our televisions and phones and, inevitably, our *minds,* severely restricted how much good we were actually taking in before we all began to deteriorate, spiritually, collectively, *and* quite rapidly.

Cyrus McQueen @CyrusMMcQueen · Aug 1, 2020
What're the little things you miss most? I miss sitting at a bar, getting a big juicy hand sculpted burger with some thick ass steak fries and tapping that stubborn ketchup bottle till it goes 'splunk'...

⟲ 122   ♡ 1909

The lingering question produced by this lockdown is whether this pause *will* trigger a reset and lead us to that necessary rebirth. This crucible *could* sublimate our society into something irrepressibly better, forced improvement a byproduct of being forced *to* go inside. I ponder, will this gestation give birth to a better citizenry? Will we realize we cannot keep going on the way we were? Whether it is those greater issues of inequality or our predilections to grant them a pass when we are pacified on piffle, inundated with inanity, perhaps, at the very least, we will no longer lose sight of the true beauty around us, because we are too busy seeking the perfect light for that selfie.

I find myself coming back to this hope: that this crisis will be a chrysalis, it resulting in more of us *flying*. The nub will be whether, as a result of all this dying, our differences and inequalities become further entrenched or we begin lessening the distance between all living people. Previous plagues led to a dramatic restructuring of entire socioeconomic frameworks: the Black Death broke the grip of serfdom throughout 14th century Europe, eroding feudalism throughout the continent. Though the human cost tallied to afford this comprehensive change was in the tens of millions, the unforeseen calamity gave birth to greater innovation and equality—art, science, and all of society resultantly advanced by leaps and bounds.

Centuries later, though, pestilence was indiscriminate, but the human family decimated by the Great Influenza of 1918 roundly disregarded this edifying lesson, reacting with man-made chaos instead. If the past really is prologue, that one-hundred-year rewind reveals that pandemics do not always rehabilitate society but can, conversely, increase our divisions. I lament the moment when the flu and world war served as invidious backdrops to widespread race riots. In Washington, D.C., and many other cities, returning white soldiers, hearing rumors of miscegenation, spewed whatever anger and fight was left in their tank on Blacks, this moral decay redrawing old battle lines. Later deployed to places like Phillips County, Arkansas, and yet another interminable outbreak, hundreds of those white troops assisted white mobs in murdering hundreds of Black citizens, among them returning Black GIs. Many were like Leroy Johnston, heroes of the Western front who, an ocean removed, found the war had not ended—them *forced* to reenlist and fight through an unmitigated hell here at home.

The 1918 flu pandemic was a dispiriting precursor to the Red Summer of 1919, the race riots that erupted throughout America producing yet *another* kind of Black Death. Many who had survived the war abroad succumbed to the one back on our shores—all because a racist president and a terminally racist America did not fully shake that sickness. Southern trees produced an abundance of strange fruit, culminating in a macabre harvest, Black bodies satisfying white America's bloodlust for a roaring decade. Who can fathom what it is like to be a member of our maligned outfit—then as well as now—when we must contend with *two* pandemics concurrently, the lines blurred between them, the deadly outcome of each therein similar? Black folks were inured to the worst and inclined to expect even *worse* when disaster upstaged Trump and his like. And when we see federal agents deployed to communities like Portland, Oregon, it is clear that he, otherwise starved of attention, needs to sink his teeth into *something*.

That so many Americans get sick while a sick man sits at the helm is almost too much irony to pack into one sentence. His cognitive, emotional, and spiritual deficits have placed us all in a deep hole. Those analogous themes highlighted throughout this text—about the cancer of racism, the pathogen-like aspects of our political factions, the disinformation infecting small groups and proliferating to larger and larger pools of people—all rise to new and ironic heights with the spread of this new contagion. As we contend with coronavirus, a nominal illness that mirrors the untreated sickness long plaguing America, our past, as always, is but an ominous prologue.

The city of Minneapolis, Minnesota, is one of several settings in history's latest repetition. Recalling the 1921 Tulsa Massacre's eruption in a post-pandemic America, and countless eruptions since, we can see that "Black Death" has recurred with greater frequency over the past century than any other, the absence of a vaccine likely due to the *color* of who suffers. But George Floyd's final moments, documented and disseminated to the world, even as an invisible contagion brings needless death, enkindled, I believe, a more sentient globe, one averse to any more superfluous loss.

These agonizing moments, this disease captured on video, recorded in a stark, unforgiving glow, this malignancy magnified and rendered with utter clarity for a public to behold—represents an auspice for change. It is as if empirical evidence finally verifies the pleas of Black America, our having long warned about the monster under our bed. Racism is indeed *our* nightmare, but our screams now rouse white Americans from *their* dream. Our struggles and strife, our lives and consequently our deaths had gone chronically undetected, but in an hour of hypersensitivity, Floyd's timeless ululation finally impresses that *this* is white America's problem to solve. Though he had called for his mother, they *appear* to hear him. It is as if the pressure applied to one Black man's neck has begun to loosen the grip of white supremacy.

Because our work is a spiritual one, we dedicate ourselves mostly to enduring, to staying afloat, treading in America's riptide, the current of inequality too strong for many to experience tangible progress. The supplemental work, the work of many like myself, therein becomes survival without internalizing this disregard, without playing proxy to white supremacy as we drift aimlessly, praying for a wave. And yes, we are exhausted.

When my sister Amber shared the link to the George Floyd video, I knew I did not need to see it. Amber is the one who usually breaks this sort of unfortunate news, sharing these headline-grabbing moments when police dispatch Black men. She had broken the news of Alton Sterling and Walter Scott, among countless others, so I knew what to expect when I saw a link followed by her text: "CAN YOU BELIEVE THIS FUCKIN BULLSHIT?!?!"

I refer to these as Amber Alerts, and no matter how you slice it, they are *never* good. Besides, why watch a movie I had seen before? *Especially* a bad one? A movie where I *knew* the tragic ending? Be it Eric, Philando, Freddy, or Tamir, Black murder is the worst kind of porn, briefly exciting the public's bloodlust but always resulting in an inauspicious outcome. I knew the immediacy these moments engender, the promise of change eventually dissipated right after the crowds as we could only brace ourselves for the disappointment of America returning, after weeks of televised unrest, to their regularly scheduled program.

An admittedly jaded man, I knew this story, its climax, its conclusion. I did not want to train my jaundiced eyes on this murder. To masturbate again to Black pain. To fuck myself emotionally in *that* way. So, it sat there. Unwatched. Until major news outlets ran the stunning video and a familiar face greeted me. George Floyd's murderer, no need to say his name, the killer who knelt on his neck for 8 minutes and 46 seconds: I *knew* him. Of course, I am *not* referring to the officer himself; no, I have never crossed paths with the pig. But I have certainly encountered his cloven brethren and, dammit, I *knew* that fuckin' look. That unfeeling, unnerving gaze he shot the camera. It gave me goosebumps because my sense memory blasted me right back to Boston. Suddenly, I was no longer in my living room, or in Brooklyn for that matter; I was rocketing *back* to college—to a dramatic reunion I in no way looked forward to, racism again a definite, most terrible time machine.

The murderer's head initially obscured by a car bumper, the video soon panned to reveal a raised eyebrow, its arch launching the dead cold expression he then shot the camera. I clocked the casual way the cop went about completing his task, the stunning efficiency, the both clinical and cavalier manner in which he hijacked a man's future. We all watched in horror as he turned over the hourglass and Floyd's life quickly seeped out of him in just under nine minutes, the murderer's mercilessness betrayed as he blithely rested a hand in his pocket, affording himself a modicum of relief during the routine dispatching. He was teaching the other officers to hunt. As he knelt into his dying buck, he even imparted a mischievous grin.

It was this unsettling image that left the lasting impression, as we observed prejudice trophied—comparable to the image we would get weeks later when an Atlanta police officer shot Rayshard Brooks in the back, then stood on his corpse after remarking, "I got him!" Just as they usually kick us when we are down, America's victors and its true victims—much like our resultant wounds—are usually delineated in black and blue. And where Floyd muffled a primal scream, an ultimately futile plea, for reprieve, for his mother, for God's Grace, and it could not break the barbarian's grip—it absolutely floored me. The haunting soundtrack to this American horror story left me breathless. Having barely come up for air upon learning of the murders of Breonna Taylor and Ahmaud Arbery, the nation again tumbled downward, "Black Death" again proving static, this unrelenting news suggesting it was merely the *manner* in which our murders are documented that actually changes.

Far too many harbor the invalid impression that all racists wear white sheets, never considering racism's chameleonic adaptability, it having gone *mainstream* after undergoing a deliberate and necessary ombré from white to blue. And though nooses are now outlawed, choke holds, administered ironically in this instance by those upholding the law, produce the same results, the *same* macabre outcome, thus marking a seamless transition. Black murder has entered a new millennium, where the arbitrarily skewed interpretation of our laws often precipitates the full weight of that law then crashing down on our necks.

This reminds me of a far less severe, yet telling moment years earlier during the U.S. Open. After penalizing Serena Williams to the point it cost her the championship, the chair umpire blithely remarked, "I was just doing my job." Now this loaded refrain, so often lobbed at us, *cost* George Floyd his life, this glib excuse used to justify taking a person's very last breath. Yes, I am fully aware there are levels to this shit. However, I am also aware that "I was just doing my job" is routinely proffered as some sort of panacea, it tendered to justify the most *overblown* reactions toward us. People of color are not long out the womb before we learn that the rules apply differently. African Americans and our white counterparts consistently experience different interpretations of justice: often we witness the very same rules used to excoriate us summarily applied to exonerate them. You would have a hard time arguing that rule enforcement, in practice, is *not* an effort to corral Black expression and constrain Black existence. Hell, we have all observed temperamental, petulant white males from Queens routinely indulged— their behavior disregarded—while we are almost mandated to be error free. Though the rules are malleable, with us, these arbiters usually resort to flexing, those same rules suddenly proving *inflexible*.

Yet in a moment when sports are on hold, I find myself noting the irony, as we watch the sport of hunting Black Americans *televised* to a sequestered audience. Surprisingly, this American pastime has lost much of its following, our vulnerability resonating, reframing the vile practice of profiling and predation. In an ABC News/Ipsos poll, 74 percent of Americans said they viewed George Floyd's death as a sign of a broader problem. It is beginning to feel like law enforcement and this zero-sum game *has* been exposed for all of its viciousness. During a time of coronavirus, Americans see that no amount of precaution or PPE can protect Black citizens from a pestilence primarily targeting us—a pestilence to which, they now realize, their race and privilege makes them mostly invulnerable.

Where a knee was the instrument of death in this instance, the violent force with which it pressed into organic matter is juxtaposed in my mind with the peaceful protest that led to Colin Kaepernick's career dissipation. The 49ers quarterback had knelt in silence, nothing but the organic earth beneath him, yet his gesture met with outrage because he had ostensibly crushed white verisimilitude; the NFL, Trump, and America only saw us occupying one position, and it was withering under their knee. Ours *was* the great American tragedy. Thus, the rules of this great drama dictated we must remain bit players and at the mercy of these murderous impulses. Predisposed to victimization, we would never take on the lead role, at least not for long. Fickle audiences simply would not go for it.

That raises an obvious question: what is it about *this* moment in Minneapolis that has sparked change? I could not have telegraphed these headwinds. No person of color could have. The murder of Black Americans had been captured before, with police brutality broadcast over at least four decades. At this point, being Black was like the worst fuckin' horror franchise of all time! Each sequel, more ghastly and preposterous. And, given how we often succumbed quickly, violently, while otherwise engaged in the mundane, this horrific output always remained true to form. Be it Rodney King's beating, or Eric Garner's final moments, these videos struck a similarly eerie chord—I can't breathe, the grisly, catchy audio; we now all knew it by heart.

Again, I, like many, wondered aloud, what is it about Floyd that has breached white America's defensive wall? Social engineering having long cemented our foundational disconnect, why does this snuff film leave a mark? What about this televised execution differs from those previously cited? How do *his* pleas penetrate the conscience of an otherwise *conditioned* public?

Going back to Kaepernick, I have long maintained that he was ostracized mainly because he forced white folks to look at themselves. Well, what the video of George Floyd accomplishes is, *it,* too, forces white folks to look at themselves. They have to accept what the mirror offers up; forced to hold that officer's long, uncomfortable gaze. This honest reflection suddenly obliterated what many had convinced themselves of over a lifetime, in denial of this greater ugliness: what they now witness is *unmistakable.* The shade raised, the light pouring in, those lids slowly part, their eyes opening wider as they struggle to adjust to this greater transparency. It soon envelops them; this video opens a window into their very own soul, the truth of their intransigence and indifference staring directly back at them conveyed, to chilling effect, through that officer's gurn.

A further significant reason this killing has traction is because we are staggering through a time when white Americans themselves are vulnerable. Pestilence has *awoken* sentience. As epidemiological and economic crises unfold simultaneously, a sociopolitical issue touches those who can normally avoid it. Perhaps business as usual has been finally interrupted *because* business as usual has finally been interrupted. The opium of sports and Black entertainment having long taken many eyes off the ball, in its absence the exceptional no longer deflect attention from the rules by which society mostly subsists on the unhealthy diet of our detriment.

Justice suddenly has nothing to compete with, our world of distraction ebbs; under the glare of the national focus, tears can now flow for a man and for a people unjustly sentenced to the prison of America's periphery. In lockdown, we get the nation's attention, making it a question of what exactly is the true threshold of this fandom? What is the level of dedication when it comes to *all* Black people?

Due to the darkness of COVID, and because we all ostensibly have been sent to our rooms, perhaps Americans can tackle this long-procrastinated assignment. This collective epiphany cannot help but evoke that adage long passed down by spiritual Black folk: the darkest moments come right before the dawn. With Floyd's murder coming on the heels of the brutal murders of Ahmaud Arbery and Breonna Taylor, both of which garnered national attention, we may have reached a tipping point. Yet this still does not fully explain why *this* captured killing captures the zeitgeist, it now promising to inspire a legitimate moratorium on racism.

No matter what, it has been quite the arc for a quarantined public to go from voicing concerns about not being able to get haircuts to taking to the streets to voice concerns about racial injustice. Though this evolution had been hinted at for ages, Floyd's murder, I believe, differs because white America has locked eyes with *pure* evil. Because we associate an officer with ideas of virtue given the oath to protect and serve, this archetypal American ideal breeding the longest standing and most positive of public narratives, from movies to television, the incongruity of witnessing one audaciously opting *not* to preserve life, but rather to take it insouciantly, intensifies the public recoil. In literature and even film, the villains who resonate most are those whose evil follows none of the clichéd contours, who neither scream nor project their malevolence, but rather communicate it through a whisper or an unnerving grin. We remember those evildoers who convey mercilessness through at times mordant humor, it cushioning their sociopathic tendencies—producing, paradoxically, an even *greater* discomfort in the viewer. Hannibal Lecter and Iago in *Othello* come to mind. Only *this* is a real-life Shakespearean tragedy, one where we too observed a contemptible figure set out to methodically destroy a sizable Black character.

Yet I am *still* surprised that this event shocks so many so deeply. I would be remiss in not disclosing my additional surprise upon receiving a plethora of messages from white friends and former coworkers, some of whom I had not heard from in years, their heartfelt confessionals not only establishing their repulsion to the murder but also contrition because they had not done enough to understand this pervasive problem. This very chorus, soon augmented by similar outpourings on Twitter, indicates how and why this moment promises to actually ramp up progress.

Cyrus McQueen @CyrusMMcQueen · May 27, 2020
There's a virus goin around disproportionately killin black people... it constricts your airways and leads to asphyxiation... it uses a billy club but often a knee or forearm... and masks can't prevent its spread... seems the lives of its victims have never mattered. #GeorgeFloyd

⟲ 748   ♡ 2233

This moment is different, I finally determine, because ours is a social media generation that has shrunk our world to the point that our Twitter and Instagram followings, our network of progressive voices, have become not only equipped to easily share these horrors, but, consequently, this has readied and primed those on these platforms to then take that tandem step toward action. I had actually seen this depression, this coming storm, forecast *through* social media. Those tea leaves, the analogous discontent reflected in the virtual world having served as an auxiliary, now help ignite social change in the real world. Young progressives can take that literal leap because a virtual world provides a viable template for the Resistance to organize *across* the world, wielding an invaluable tool to unite, communicate, and create an even broader coalition than was possible in 1968 or even 1992.

It is also important to note that, at this point, we are deep into the hyperbolic Trump era. The evidence of his hatred, the exhaustion of living day to day in a neofascist's reality show, makes us all more cognizant of this kind of wrong—and, consequently, much less tolerant of its promulgation. George Floyd's cries are indeed the plaintive scream the world finally heard, but his are ultimately tangential to others—those who know they might easily draw their final breath beneath a cop's knee, as well as those who may not yet are dying spiritually and just cannot *live* like this anymore.

The justice system having long had its foot on our throat, when George Floyd could not breathe, it was symptomatic of a lingering problem. Be it administered with a forearm or a knee, a chokehold itself is but a physical manifestation of an overwhelming psychic constriction. Ours is an already suffocating existence where, as I can attest, one routinely experiences some shortage of breath during their Western traverse. Our collective exhaustion now produces convulsions; our fevered, almost involuntary gasping, our unheard, unanswered pleas, find us thrashing about the country, because our cries, our deaths, keep falling on deaf ears.

Yet, as always, we further observe the images of uprising, of cities turned into cauldrons, used as flint to ignite the fears of a general public. Our visceral ire, programmed to inspire the ire of fickle television viewers, creates an emotional and moral detachment, enabling them to watch from an imperious remove. It is tragic the way property and meaningless wares are used to generate public contempt, utilized to negate both the cause and the very fact these outpourings are a legitimate recoil of those long deemed meaningless. And there is, of course, another distressing correlation: a people long relegated to the ideation of property now watch as politicians express consternation over the destruction *of* property. The sheer fucking ignorance, the colossal disconnect, of fixating on property damage when *people* are damaged—that they take lives while all we take *is* property—is maddening.

It is all rather ironic that this purging results directly from our consecrated destruction, systemic racism resulting in an almost routine demolition of Black life from LA to Minneapolis, Louisville to Atlanta. Yet that some take umbrage at appliances being absconded is fuckin' cheap, these misjudgments missing the true value of these outstanding moments. It is incredible how many fail to register that none of the items carried out of a Target or a fuckin' Foot Locker will endure 40 years from now—yet over that very same span, and absent a knee in his neck, George Floyd *could have*. This deficit of rationale from far too many Americans, this misplaced umbrage, suggests that when it comes to *certain* Americans, we are unlikely to bridge our increased chasm anytime soon.

The pathos these moments engender are intensified by the realization that, through insufferable coverage, we see flames of distortion forge our identities. The organic distress of the dispossessed, the endemic rage of Black Americans made fodder by the teeth of a ravenous criminal justice system, often proves *less* compelling than the need to feed certain narratives. Here, the melding of protest and riot leaves an inauthentic impression on many in the public, their ascribing color and contempt to what are mostly *diverse* and peaceful outpourings. In spite of opportunists and vandals of every race and denomination contributing to the surge, this counter-narrative of incursion is *more* expedient in this contaminated moment as Black protesters again incur *all* the negative scrutiny.

Particularly disheartening is that interlopers across the ideological spectrum exploit the groundswell, those with disparate agendas contributing mightily to both the chaos and the ensuing community destruction. The very fact that white nationals and even unidentified officers had been in the streets of Minneapolis, these nebulous entities running interference for one another, only adds to the discomfiture. Similar to the disparate voices I had observed going at it in my Twitter threads, the maelstrom in Minnesota saw progressive forces hamstrung by regressive ones. Sadly, for many in middle America, the lasting image of Brown looters would again obscure the Brown victims of a thoroughly broken system.

It is maddening to know that, once the smoke clears, our victimization continues, the larger issues of criminal justice reform and police accountability remaining unaddressed. Be it the incestuous relationship between police and prosecutors, or those dubious judges and grand juries who fortify this imbalance, it is clear that racist practices, policies, and procedures *are* likely to persist. When we digest the disproportionate funding for police departments, "public safety" coming at the expense of social services and education, the absurdities in no way sit well. They contribute mightily to the almost reflexive purging we witness, it incentivizing those growing calls *to* defund the police. It is as if Americans are just now regurgitating bullshit that has been shoved down our throats for decades. Add in the armored vehicles and grenade launchers, this thorough militarization, and juxtapose that with all the children operating without iPads or even Internet access— it is clear that our nation's great upheaval is *long* overdue.

A consistent investment in the problem instead of the solution wrought this public reckoning, it realized through decades of aggressive policing, racial profiling, and coordinated, well-funded efforts to fill America's prisons with people of color *instead* of our filling its colleges and universities. Given that a city's budget directly affects that city's future—and the future of *all* its people—we see how inflating the importance of the police is to the detriment of what is of equal or even *greater* importance. It is as if city hall were a womb and budget negotiations tantamount to vanishing twin syndrome. So many lives never even get off the ground because education succumbs to that bloated, inflated lobby gobbling up these vital resources year after year after year.

In America, crooked cops are as strong as the robust institutions protecting and validating them. That police unions are wholly complicit, *devoted* to propagating this very kind of injustice, guarantees the problem will go uncorrected. It is precisely why sadists and sociopaths continue to encamp comfortably behind the shield, safely ensconced in a culture that rewards the bigoted and bellicose. That these organizations are bereft of *any* accountability frees officers across America to continue the fully subsidized business of killing us with impunity.

Therefore, the complaint of Minnesota Governor Tim Walz, arguing the protests are "no longer about George Floyd, it's become about attacking civil society, and instilling fear," rang hollow. Considering the role of a militarized, unaccountable police force *is* to instill fear, the inherent irony of his words was augmented by the sight of National Guardsmen firing teargas and advancing on news reporters. Besides, none of his blether touches on the inarguable fact that the offending officer in George Floyd's death would have kept his badge and never incurred any charges had this horror *not* been captured. Because the blue wall remains unbroken, it takes people taking to the streets, an unmissable upsurge, to get results. In this country, protest and sociopolitical change have a causal relationship. America, by resolving to live with the canker of racial violence, would likely have let this flareup go too had not many determined that, stop, something is *disgustingly* wrong here.

Cyrus McQueen @CyrusMMcQueen · May 29, 2020
Trump said, "When the looting starts the shooting starts"? Twitter tagged it and Trump moves it to the official White House Twitter account... mind you we're in the middle of a motherfucking pandemic... We've now officially entered the Dark Knight phase of this presidency... https://t.co/tApV6dEWJ4

⟲ 1311   ♡ 4572

As a racist toddler pretends to be president, it is a foregone conclusion he will use our distress to again toy with progress. Trump, never failing to disappoint, soon threatened to sick "vicious dogs" on protesters. Here, impressions of the 1960s are unmissable, this tenuous time now echoing a historical rhyme.

But Trump has been showin' his ass now for the better part of five years. He has hit so many new lows, the only conclusion anyone can draw at this point is: he is bottomless, his ignominy inexhaustible, the real estate magnate *certifiably* low rent. As some in the media continue their futile daily practice of shoehorning an oblong president into a flattering silhouette, trying to normalize his every errant movement, these rhetorical queries seem finally to be exhausted with widespread protests. "What should we *expect* from the president?"—these attempts to telegraph a moment that will never come, building expectations he will never even *try* to fulfill, are finally, indecorously, replaced by reality.

Then comes the image of a petulant president scampering to St. John's Church like a glorified baby, flanked by his sitters and his coddlers, for an imprudent photo op—where he spins and flips around a Bible like a goddamn toddler attempting to hold up the yellow pages— this *truly* unbecoming visual *unforgettable*. Here is a president who draws all over maps with Sharpies, pushes aside world leaders so he can puff his chest, and even autographs Bibles. Though he has long seemed to shockingly metabolize scandal and our recurrent disdain, *this* current spectacle, this latest sacrilegious moment, is uniquely unseemly.

Yet it is nothing *but* the culmination of what has been promised since the day he descended that Trump Tower escalator in 2015. Charlottesville, his immoral equivocations, Birtherism—it all presaged this moment when he briefly barricaded himself in the White House, behind yet another unnecessary fence, holed up gutlessly in a bunker, inflaming the race war he had up to now been kindling.

Though he has locked children in cages, the image of a young white girl having her face doused with water outside Lafayette Square has roused residual contempt for a president who, moments before, had National Guard storm protesters to clear the way for his invidious photo op. In the lead up to this walk of shame, that he had gassed a peaceful gathering, forcing a diverse assembly out of the area before mounted police stormed in to finish the job, was haunting. Yet the lasting image in my eyes is this young woman having teargas rinsed from her eyes, a direct consequence of Trump's own contemptible decision, cementing both this moment and his superlative evil. Though it remains to be seen what if any legislation this primordial stimulus will effect—or if this set of protests will spark lasting change—we already see how far certain imagery goes toward captivating an obdurate public. Where the optics of dogs and firehoses trained on Black children disgusted a desultory public from their living rooms sixty years prior, the image of young white kids having teargas rinsed from their eyes—all as a president threatens to sick dogs on them, his heartlessness betrayed by his bullish desire to be *that* guy, evoking *those* historical sensations—promises that this, too, is a moment of special significance. Comprehensive change, an expanding consciousness, may be gestating right before our very eyes.

Are we finally witnessing the buzz saw of hubris dull, the chronic predictable recoil of "I'm not racist" losing its punch? Many young white Americans are exposing the fraudulence of that narrative as they stand shoulder to shoulder with Black folks, exposing themselves to rubber bullets and virulence in cities and towns across the country. Though the greater question of their sustained commitment is yet to be answered, in this moment they expose the moral bankruptcy of indifference, its coffers exhausted as those with no skin in the game redefine what it means to be allies, *anti-racism* the active, optimal, and, in many ways, *only* tangible way forward.

As George Floyd cried for his mother, it was no longer sufficient to simply not be racist; his pleas were too sonorous for tone deafness. It has become shockingly plain that, while that self-righteous shroud had provided a sense of refuge, insulating generations, it has left true progress out in the cold. Furthermore, the inherent anemia to "I'm not racist" no longer squares with the fact that police departments are breeding grounds for those who *are,* their unfettered power to brutalize and besiege a people secured under many an upturned nose.

This event leaves a conspicuous lesson sitting out in the open, as the children and grandchildren of freedom riders echo the movements of those who preceded them over a half century earlier. Their actions resurrect this greater importance of seeing progress through—of not disappearing into the monochromaticity of an upper-middle-class reality in which progress becomes a relic of the past, stashed away in the attic of a suburban home. We have all seen how worthless ideals become when they are out of mind. Despite periodically dusting off these recollections, a significant number of our predecessors are now disconnected from the promise they once embodied, change succumbing to conformity as they sit at a comfortable remove, languidly observing the uniformity they elected to supplant it.

America is in trouble now *because* Trump conflates diversity with adversity. This tactic proving wildly successful, he continues to undermine the aggregate *through* divisiveness. That souring American monoculture and his impending expiration date increase this desperation. His political future and the future of white conservatives blending into one, his existential concerns and their own are now inseparable. With troops in our streets, citizens in our streets, and a president pitting one against the other for his political survival, it feels as if we are leaning *into* autocracy.

The tent poles of our democracy, the rule of law itself, already have been undermined in our Congress and by Trump's very own Justice Department. Of the myriad consequences of his impeachment acquittal, perhaps most problematic is that it signals he is, for all intents and purposes, *above* the law. Putin and Trump are having the last laugh now that he is *completely* untethered to consequence. Because too few had stood up to him, he is emboldened to train America's soldiers on a new enemy: the American people. Thus, Trump places us all on a perilous road, not too dissimilar from the very ones that lead to Russia, the chilling irony being that our people are under attack by *both* presidents. There is certainly no middle ground, the way forward having been bifurcated. Our options here are simple. Egalitarianism or authoritarianism. Black Lives or Black Death. America or *Trump*.

The historical implications only increase the horror. Past presidents had deployed National Guardsmen to undergird Civil Rights, but we must swallow the historic inverse, observing protests torpedoed by a president who puts boots on the ground to *defang* progress. With federal agents swarming cities in unmarked vehicles, all to undermine advancement, it is a chilling auxiliary to developments within American policing, where the tenor of war has long been adopted. With men and women of color, young progressives, and even suburban moms creating a multicultural phalanx, a brittle president weaponizes the DOJ to try to break an organic consensus.

As COVID cases surge in red states, we again witness a president minimizing his own shame, downplaying his cratering disgrace, by overrunning Democratic-led cities with federal agents. Like his Fourth of July flyover, he needs the optics to mold the malleable, to minimize his terminal weakness by projecting the image of strength. The hellion parades his little army men through traditionally progressive places, these maneuvers likely a dry run, a brutal forecast of a chilling fall to come.

Perhaps my childhood in Boston, my proximity to history, attunes my ear to its echoes. With Trump using troops to extinguish dissent, and as we again and again witness the murder of Black men, the gross abuse of power and authority evokes certain timeless sensations. Contextually, I see a tangible, 250-year connection between the cities of Minneapolis and Boston—the death of George Floyd bearing a striking similarity to that of Crispus Attucks. Two sons of America, two forty-something Black men cut down in their prime, arouse profound feelings regarding not simply the use of excessive force but American probity *itself*. As the first person killed in the American Revolution, the death of Attucks, like that of Floyd, raised a vital question: who are we as a people? Will the quarter of a millennia separating these two inflections, March of 1770 and May of 2020, now bear an axiomatic consequence, with the revolutionary chain reactions each engendered permanently improving our society henceforth?

I must disclose, my skepticism was *still* unbroken after two weeks of protest: I disallowed any notion this centuries-long problem could be on a course toward correction. It was damn near impossible to resurrect my faith. One thing I had taken to be the gospel in my life, undeviating and unchanging, was that the propagation of privilege is *so* powerful, the derogation of Black lives and livelihoods *equally* as strong, I just could not envision America doing the required work. I also recognized something many whites were frugal about owning up to: disabusing oneself of a lifetime of supremacy is difficult, to say the least. Every aspect of white existence only reinforces this fallacy: where you live, where you learn, where you work, everywhere you *look*, everyone you look *at*, the *same*. When social engineering fuels an entire run, from sunrise to sunset, *not* acquiescing to those built-in benefits seems antithetical, to put it mildly. When every factor of one's life is handled with assiduous care, it considered, cultivated, and buttressed by a culture that promulgates the imprimatur that what *you* are is normal, you inadvertently *become* the fulcrum by which all subsequent considerations deviate. It precipitates a rejection of the *other*—nullifying their humanity, their opportunities. Consolidated power eventually creates a sort of herd immunity, where inequality and injustice beyond these confines likely no longer really affects you.

White privilege has been putting on weight for four hundred fuckin' years. It constitutes an American monolith, multifarious and omnidirectional, coming at Black folks in education, real estate, banking, and health care, facilitating our absence in much of the private sector, the lack of parity in fashion and entertainment signifying this invisibility, with the police and the courts fulfilling their end by *literally* removing us from the American scene. As I often maintain, to be Black is to vacillate between figurative and literal absence. Thus, racism is in many ways an octagon. Ideations of our inferiority built into the undercard ensure that between admissions scandals and a prison-industrial complex, no competition exists between us and members of the majority. Nah, we are trapped, left to fight it out with one another in those battle royals—be it for their entertainment or because we are simply programmed to take one another out, Vichy-like in our fealty to that strange, debilitating concept of supremacy.

Racial violence and racial indifference are equally important turnbuckles, mutually responsible for reinforcing a space of iniquity. But where many may escape catching a knee or a chokehold—though that danger is omnipresent—virtually *every* Black American experiences the torturing repetition of banging our heads against a wall, the insanity of going up against unmoving apathy again and again and expecting a better outcome. Where covert and overt hate both deliver the screw, because those subtler forms deliver the repeated, dulling blows of disregard, the toll it takes is not always visible to the naked eye. But because our American canvas is ultimately held together *by* this tension, it becomes a matter of *which* part of you—be it your mind, body, or soul—is going to feel it first.

Cyrus McQueen @CyrusMMcQueen · Jun 9, 2020
Stephen Miller is writing Trump's speech on race relations? Lemme guess... "It puts the cocoa butter on its skin, or else it gets the hose again"? 😐

⟲ 228   ♡ 1526

Though Black Lives Matter is splattered across my television screen, and I spy it on baseball fields and basketball courts—it is even emblazoned across the very street I cross every day—my mind vaults forward from the current day, entertaining whether this heightened moment will sustain its momentum. Will equality merely be a fad that slowly fades, with many uncommitted to its difficult execution?

Brooklyn is slowly reopening, and I cannot miss the banners unfurled from balconies, "Black Lives Matter" scribbled colorfully on sidewalks and in front of brownstones, these pastel chalks indicating that all ages seem to be enlisted in this cause. And as I traverse heterogeneous neighborhoods, they interlocked within a borough again blossoming under the July sun, this searing message, conveyed boldly, repetitively, in storefronts and bars, cafes and car windows, suggests the seed indeed has been planted in fertile soil.

Yet underlying these righteous displays is that pressing question: *who* will tend this garden? Who will rise with that sun, and get their hands dirty, when many have yet to awaken? As I am very much aware, our upcoming election burns brighter and brighter on the horizon; I remind myself that Brooklyn cannot be confused for areas in Ohio, Oklahoma, and Texas that are less liberal with their chalk—those pockets that contain less hospitable terrain.

My walk mirrors this greater journey, with those larger questions pondered during my stroll determining we have *much* further to go. As I reach the bottom of Brooklyn Avenue and step off the curb onto Fulton Street, I speculate whether white America will take that tandem step toward actual parity. And it may be that the economic imperative, this centuries-long problem, it predicating and preceding *all* matters of race, will determine if folks will really put their money where their mouth is. My great fear is that many will treat their tacit support as a panacea. Recognizing this futility, I ask myself, what good is a Black Lives Matter banner on your brownstone if you head back to an all-white office? Although it is reassuring to watch children writing Black Lives Matter on the sidewalk, if they go back to schools with no or only a handful of Black students—this commitment to the modicum thus reinforced—I wonder *which* lesson will stick. By the time they reach adulthood, this norm now ingrained, should we expect them *not* to replicate this in every aspect of their lives? The neighborhoods they choose to live in, the schools they choose to send *their* children to—can we honestly expect their surroundings to deviate from this embedded standard? Or should we brace ourselves for the dizzying inevitability, the disorienting aftermath of a cycle continuing, this repetition playing out four decades hence, our having gone around in circles simply because no one puts their foot down.

Although staggering numbers now take to the streets, it being necessary, and considerably cathartic, this reckoning inspires an equally pertinent query: *who* can we count on to be woke where they work? Taking part in a march or proudly rocking a bandana or button can trick one into feeling progressive, but what about their actions will engender *real* progress? It is one thing to dress the part, but something else entirely to be committed to the role. I worry that many are married to the *moment* where only the future will determine if they are married to doing more than the minimum when it comes to Black folks. With this surge soon to wane, with many thoroughly convinced they are part of the solution despite workplaces and even weddings reflecting a culture bereft of tangible change, I am concerned that many whites will settle on what is palliative instead of what is permanent.

As the murder and maiming of unarmed Black men continues with a sinister consistency, the bodies of those Black men devalued and feared stand in contrast to the notable exceptions: those Black athletes whose valued bodies are pivotal to the accrual of great wealth. When a Kenosha, Wisconsin, police officer shot Jacob Blake seven times, leaving him paralyzed, the recently renewed NBA season abruptly halted. These African American men, the roster of the Milwaukee Bucks, elected to sit out a playoff game, causing a ripple, the remaining matches on this late August evening similarly cancelled. It came to symbolize a resilient community and, in this particular instance, a microcosm of sentient, determined athletes taking back ownership of their Black bodies *from* NBA ownership. Because the majority Black league and these players are a direct extension of a beleaguered community, they force a league that touts Black Lives Matter on its courts to fully examine the veracity of their profession.

It introduced an exciting wrinkle to the evolving dialogue surrounding police brutality and Black equality, this an almost historical through line. Given the Black body has long been American detritus, it purposely, perpetually relegated, Black athletes, perhaps the only Black Americans *with* ostensible leverage, self-emancipated those bodies, threatening to dry up billions in revenue—in the process raising new concerns for white ownership. With WNBA, NFL, MLS, and MLB players postponing games and practices and picking up the baton, it hints that they are laying the groundwork for a new, albeit, proven paradigm. The Montgomery Bus Boycott that ignited the modern Civil Rights Movement was an economic boycott—its success tied to the financial blow it delivered to the city—so perhaps we are glimpsing what a bit of "good trouble" can lead to. Maybe the Bucks and the Lakers, the Trail Blazers and others putting sports on hold will *hold* white America's attention this time, encouraging white owners to exert pressure on city leaders and lawmakers—it finally loosening the Faustian grip of police unions and helping to end the American sport of hunting Black men.

These developments come back to a simple question: What's in it for *us?* While it warms my heart to witness the NBA bubble incubate leadership, those like LeBron James, fist raised, exemplifying the fruitful marriage of sports and activism, where a mostly Black labor force can spearhead necessary change, I ponder what lies ahead for those workforces bereft of such leverage? Those places where progress is truly outnumbered. Where discussions pertaining to parity remain awkward, marooning many on islands unto themselves.

Will we, I wonder, ever see the day Black lives *and* livelihoods both command the national focus? Because we can never achieve parity with quick fixes, highly touted yet ultimately hollow diversity initiatives can offer the illusion of inclusion without *ever* addressing the fundamental rot underlying most hiring practices. When it comes to white hires never really contending with the fires of deformation, will the unfolding dialogue therefore persist? Will folks continue to fixate on how many deserving white applicants lose out to "diversity hires" instead of the pernicious, prevalent consolidation of munificence? Will any ask how many qualified people of color have been passed over or, in all likelihood, *never* considered because opportunity continues to be a game of keep-away played among privileged people?

Because money equals power, and because America has depressed its darker brother religiously, assiduously, the economic blows our ranks have suffered telegraph who maintains the upper hand and *retains* power. If America *is* interested in cleaning its house, are companies willing to look at their recruiting and retention practices? How many are committed to honestly determining why the revolving door traps people of color at the entry level, blocked from the escalators and elevators that carry others to their corner offices of success? Perhaps we remain on a road to nowhere because fair competition is never the objective. Wherever one falls on the ideological spectrum, America's grossest national product has always been patriarchy and supremacy. That it persists for centuries is attributable to the fact that no one really wants to face this reality or, most of all, *themselves*.

Considering how during the pandemic Black unemployment has gone up even as the national rate began going down, I ponder so many questions: Where do we begin when the protests end? When school resumes and offices reopen? Will we simply return to normal, our variance passing for normal? Will progress pause between the hashtags? Will the paucity of diversity in boardrooms and classrooms resonate with immediacy? Will those subtle and insidious instances of our profound imbalance trigger the impulse for rectification? Or will comprehensive advancement be again defanged, those pressing calls for fair hiring practices muzzled, as the prospect of white Americans bartering less privilege for the sake of more Brown faces around the classroom and the conference room remains tantamount to a hostile takeover, and for certain entities, given their dogged indignation, *highly* improbable? Will our community remain bereft of opportunity because equal rights in education and employment fails to be the sexy crusade?

Is it simply our deaths that create traction, not our repeated, often futile, attempts to *live?* The fact remains that cameras very rarely capture our chronic strides and resultant rejection; when we are turned down for loans, jobs, and, yes, improv teams; when we observe that coterie of well-intentioned liberal entities routinely undercut altruism with their own entitlement. Because Blackness has been done in by the frugal gaze, the key to upward mobility resting in arthritic hands, dubious benevolence continues to mar our advancement. To certain progressives, Black opportunity *will* continue to represent a deficit instead of a surplus, their spiritual parsimony ensuring a marriage to the minimum, exceeding a quota *never* possible because it would then jeopardize their roles and overall opinion of our worth.

My whole existence I have witnessed the stunning efficiency with which gatekeepers can take your breath away with a "No" instead of a knee. Having now died a thousand deaths, how does one even resuscitate a life when your future, your hope for that invigorating breath of American prosperity, continues to be predicated on some desultory form of white goodwill? Or mercy? On a system dedicated to destroying Black life not enriching it? Will that most predictable ebb of opportunity, these avenues bottlenecked with Black dreams, these reserves as empty as those proffered gestures, result in yet again only a *dollop* of progress?

As many of us know all too well, only a handful of tokens can even start the game. So, no matter how promising the news copy, we elect to read *between* the headlines. The panting anticipation that accompanies our actuality does not promise to change overnight, so it is probably best practice to reserve judgement on this moratorium, to not allow the lullaby of promise to distract from the alarming reality. Despite this apparent sea change, we are still a public enemy, faced with the inscrutable prospect of continued toil outside the main arena, our lives reduced to expending all of our mental and spiritual reserves in an exhaustive race *with* race.

Thus, we opt to *not* believe the hype. Not just yet. When we have never managed to get out front, to edge that most formidable competitor, my 40th year on this planet coinciding with the 400th year of Black struggle on this continent, it predicts we will remain gripped in an inauspicious reality. We know we can set our clock to the cycle of racial injustice going around with an almost sweeping consistency—absent, of course, a *revolution*.

And so, we get angry.

It is undeniable: we *are* living in a unique era—not simply for our country but in the history of the world. And though this president, and his imprint on this indelible moment, will eventually become fodder for generations of future historians, if the reader gains anything from these hundreds of pages of traffic, it is that our past, America's torturing past is jam-packed with malefactors and motherfuckers. Moreover, much of this nation's output can be deemed cyclical. Though historians can whittle down the past to examinations of power and those who vie for it, successfully and unsuccessfully, certain patterns are unmissable. For instance: the inept are rewarded. With their stations oft inherited and secured, race and patrimony tend to operate very much like a wrecking ball, clearing an inglorious path for those otherwise bereft of bravery, skill, or spirit. Given that many also attain power dubiously, illegitimately, history is chockablock with tales of the wretched conniving their way to influence and notability. Indeed, our national annals teem with *these* sorts of men—men who were abject in their day and, depending on who regales us now, either have that infamy rightly inflated or dangerously reduced.

Cyrus McQueen @CyrusMMcQueen · Jan 23, 2019
Here's something I don't understand... Why does a Confederate sympathizer wanna give a State of the Union address anyway? 😒 #SOTU

t⟩ 476   ♡ 2422

Some of history's derelicts *were* truly Machiavellian in their political maneuverings. Many were even masterful enough, persuasive enough, that they captivated friend *and* foe alike—whereas others, well, I guess we are currently experiencing that converse: a leader who is irredeemable, indelicate, who otherwise *lacks* tact: a boorish man has bulldozed his way through our era. Our history books will eventually quote someone whose remembrances of Trump are as unflattering as he himself is of others.

Those books may even contain recollections like: he was "amiable and possessed of some acuteness, but the only person I have ever known who was wholly indifferent in the choice between truth and falsehood, honesty and dishonesty." Hell, I can even see that future history adding that he was "ever as ready to attain an end by the one as the other, and habitually boastful of acts of cleverness at the total sacrifice of moral character."

We can *easily* envision Donald Trump described in this manner. However, those musings are not a summation of the 45th president of the United States. In fact, the writer and the sorry subject he pillories are separated from us by nearly two centuries.

Those are, in fact, the words of Major General Winfield Scott from his 1864 autobiography, *Memoirs of Lieut.-General Scott.* The retired commander, one of America's greatest generals, having fought with distinction in the War of 1812, the Mexican-American War, and the American Civil War, was speaking of his one-time nemesis and fellow general in the Mexican-American War, Major General Gideon Johnson Pillow. Held in low esteem by most of his contemporaries, Pillow pursued an inglorious career in and outside the military—bankruptcies, treachery, blatant and scurrilous acts of defamation, scandal, cowardice, and an avowed allegiance to both the Confederacy and the institution of slavery. Also a prodigious landowner, Pillow was considered at one time to be the wealthiest man in Tennessee.

Pillow found himself in General Scott's crosshairs because he had brazenly taken credit for Scott's victories at the battles of Churubusco and Contreras during the Mexican-American War. Pillow, known for making mistakes on the battlefield, even saw his efforts in previous skirmishes like Cerro Gordo deemed as actually *unhelpful.* Yet he attempted to cover up his shortcomings by asserting he had actually *led* Scott's men to victory in the later battles—an unconscionable lie but not unique as we still see the vain boldly eschewing facts pointing to their uselessness.

What makes Pillow's dishonesty familiar is that he had the temerity to tether insult *to* this injury, sending an anonymous letter to the *New Orleans Delta* inflating his own importance. It is almost as if Donald Trump's own tabloid behavior, his posing for *Forbes Magazine,* his fraudulent grandeur, takes a page right out of the Gideon Pillow playbook.

Confronted about taking credit for the American victory, his dishonor exposed, Pillow was promptly arrested and held for court-martial by General Scott. And here matters get even more interesting.

Facing this unfortunate setback and forced detainment, Pillow, a true trickster, a dastard through and through, reached out to President James K. Polk by letter. Given Polk did not much care for Scott anyway, Pillow set about using *this* leverage to his advantage and concocted one *hell* of a ruse. Long before email or private servers, the knave knew that the more you feed a falsehood, the less chance the truth has to thrive. Then, much like now, a lie could spread long before the truth got its boots on—especially when someone knew how to exploit the right channels. And Pillow, an old Tennessee compadre of Polk's, bent the president's ear to a fable that though highly improbable likely grew arms and legs due to his coercive efforts. According to *Winfield Scott: The Quest for Military Glory*, Pillow implored Polk to question *Scott's* character, convincing the president that the general was embroiled in a bribery scheme with the Mexican leader Antonio López Santa Anna to bring a premature end to the Mexican-American War.

Considering that Pillow was in big trouble, he needed this even *bigger* lie to get out of it. So, as a man of great turpitude, his back against the wall, he soiled his spotless contemporary to cover his own blemish. Just as current leaders drum up scandal to sully their rivals, while taking credit for their good works, men like Pillow would use duplicity for publicity. By projecting their failings onto their nemeses, while inflating their own bravery, these reprobates distract from their *own* weaknesses.

Sadly, such efforts, then as now, can succeed. Polk relieved General Scott of *his* command—and reduced Pillow's charges from a court martial to a far-less-severe court of inquiry. Oh, and because Pillow was a *true* motherfucker, he had already had a toady, Major Archibald W. Burns, take credit for writing the *New Orleans Delta* newspaper article. This invidious forerunner to "fake news" forced Scott to drop *all* charges against Pillow, leading to the latter's complete exoneration. Almost presaging the indecorous behavior exhibited upon the release of Roger Stone from prison, President Polk remarked that Pillow is a "highly meritorious officer, and has been greatly persecuted by General Scott, for no other reason than that he is a Democrat in his politics and was supposed to be my personal and political friend."

After unsuccessful bids for the vice-presidential nomination in 1852 and the U.S. Senate in 1857, Pillow greeted the election of Abraham Lincoln in 1860 by supporting secession and enlisting in the Confederate Army. Appointed as a senior major general in the Tennessee militia, Pillow's first major action put him up against Ulysses S. Grant in the Battle of Belmont. Though Grant initially pushed the Confederates back, the Union ended up retreating under fire, with the two armies suffering comparable losses. However, when the two generals next met, at the Battle of Fort Donelson, Pillow's hubris and all-around ineptness got the better of him, resulting in a staggering blow to the rebel forces and his reputation. That firefight finally exposed Pillow's incompetence. Here, his plan to escape a Union advance by pulling his men back jeopardized the Confederate garrison and, in the process, *erased* much of the rebel soldiers' advances.

As the Confederate commander withdrew into the trenches, his blundering retreat enraged his fellow generals, setting the stage for what can only be regarded as Pillow's most ignoble hour. Facing imminent surrender, he placed his men under the command of cavalry commander Nathan Bedford Forrest, ceded *all* command to Simon Bolivar Buckner, and fled under cover of darkness across the Cumberland River, leaving Buckner to surrender to U.S. Grant. In *The Battle of Fort Donelson*, James Hamilton writes that, upon surrender, Buckner informed Grant of Pillow's escape, remarking: "He thought you'd rather get hold of him than any other man in the Southern Confederacy." To which Grant, well aware of Pillow's reputation from their time in the Mexican-American War, famously replied, "Oh, if I had got him, I'd let him go again. He will do us more good commanding you fellows."

Pillow's shame followed him for the rest of the war, leading Confederate President Jefferson Davis to suspend his command for "grave errors in judgement." Though his command was eventually restored, he could never fully live down his disgrace at Fort Donelson. The death knell to his reputation rang at the Battle of Stones River, where his almost superlative cowardice in many ways sealed his fate. In *Who Was Who in the Civil War*, Stewart Sifakis describes in detail the third day of fighting, when General John C. Breckinridge arrived to find that Pillow had "hid behind a tree rather than lead his men forward."

Union forces captured Pillow at the end of the war, but he eventually received a presidential pardon. Postwar, though forced into bankruptcy, he resumed his law career in Memphis before dying in 1878 at the age of 72.

Though we can hope for the poetic justice of a comparable comeuppance in the present day, I cite Pillow not simply for his obvious parallels to the current president. No, I recently discovered a fact far more relevant to me and actually *far* worse: I am descended from Gideon Johnson Pillow.

My maternal great-grandmother Gladys Pillow and my family can trace our lineage directly to Gideon and the Pillow family in Columbia, Tennessee, her father Henry "Papa" Pillow having been born and sharecropped on that family's land for most of his life. As family legend has it, *our* fateful move to St. Louis during the Great Migration was fillliped when a member of the white branch, spying my then 12-year-old great-grandmother and her father walking along a fence dividing the property, remarked, "Gee Hank, that daughter of yours is growing up mighty fast!" According to my grandmother, this thinly veiled minatory divined, "It's time to go."

In a time of great debate around the removal of Confederate monuments, I find the greater discussion surrounding the systemic genocide of Black lives and the Black family imbued with my disturbing discovery. Here, the ungodly veneration of men like my slave-owning ancestor and my own troubling roots give me both pause and an opportunity to dig deeper, helping me unearth this organic contradiction embedded in American soil. The wealth and identity of our nation were sowed with rape, hate, and torture. Because exclusion and exploitation continue to prevail, we become aware that both the country and who we are today testify to this tempestuous legacy. And, because we continue repeating the *same* mistakes with regard to racial discrimination, and given the unbreakable hold of our unresolved past, we can easily surmise that these statues are less a symbol of where we were then than where we are *now*.

One reason we invariably get stuck is that the Confederacy has not been rightfully scrutinized. Those pig-ignorant motherfuckers flourish outside the context of ignominy. Even within the narrative of film, while Nazis sizzle in infamy, no project dares to portray them in any way that contradicts the truth of their barbarousness; thus, their American counterparts enjoy a counter-narrative that muddies the waters of hero and villain. The blistering, unsparing portrait of a *Schindler's List*, evil clearly delineated in black and white, starkly contrasts to the sprawling technicolor hagiography of a *Gone With the Wind*. Beyond celluloid, we need look no further than cops and customs enforcement for evidence of the mainstreaming of Nazism and the contrast between our continents: Europe destroyed it; America *employs* it.

We have witnessed those on whom power is habitually bestowed customarily squander this American endowment. As the dishonor of my own predecessor led to needless death, history's brutal echo sees our current president, a man in Pillow's making, facilitating the sort of routine death America has not suffered *since* the Civil War. What is truly uncanny is that during a time of inconceivable loss, both men focused on their own self-importance. With their unbelievable vanity and similar efforts to steal the spotlight, it is important to note how both also retreated ingloriously into the shadows when the moment proved too big for them.

Men of ill repute, both past and present, much like the immutable systems producing them, reinvigorate this undeviating design on inequality generation after generation. With hate resuscitated and reconstituted and cowards reborn, can we really argue that the hearts of our fellow man are fundamentally different now from what they were then?

I arrived on this earth exactly one hundred years after Gideon Pillow left it, yet the trenches he dug have all but ensured that members of my outfit would still be climbing to this day, still clawing our way out of an interminable ditch, still catching fire—race an American ambush, a warlike construct whose approximations in no way abated at Appomattox. These outstanding deficits, redressed neither through reparations nor police reform, make inequality my American patrimony. The one-time wealthiest man in Tennessee has bequeathed me only *this* exorbitant moral debt.

This is why, while the matter of Reparations is crucial, and I sure *would* accept my forty acres of Tennessee topsoil, I am chary of computing the outstanding bill. How can one quantify a pain that is incalculable? Tally the torment, centuries of perpetual rape, murder, and social stratification? Total the physical and psychic toll that compounded our corporeal pain with an ethereal one? Assess the gross of a society programmed to hate us, this war waged first in our Constitution then in our courts, morphing into a subtle tool, as popular and corporate culture too adopt this end, our exclusion coming at the expense of Eurocentric inclusion, it igniting a proxy war *so* successful we even hate ourselves?

Our attempts at answering such questions only reinforce the sad fact that we have already been used to facilitate wealth; reducing this blight on humanity to a monetary figure may very well communicate to white power brokers that we can be bought again. If that magical day comes when the descendants of slaves receive paltry restitution, will it absolve America of its crime? Will "debt paid" provide a convenient out, just as many raced to declare a post-racial society upon the election of Obama?

The DNA of America mirrors my own; these abnormal cells have tainted both our history and my very own bloodline. Having now stared at Gideon Pillow's picture to the point that it is burned into my retina, floating spectrally in my periphery, I cannot help but notice certain resemblances. My mind involuntarily spasms, images of my great Uncle Thomas Pillow flickering behind my eyes, alternating with Gideon's like a torturing slideshow. I cannot *unsee* the haunting family resemblance between my great-grandmother's brother and the ignoble general. We have inherited our names and our complexions, our stigma, and, yes, our pain.

The question becomes: how do we reconcile it all? Well, the short answer is, we cannot, not completely.

The immediate answer is to be angry.

Cyrus McQueen @CyrusMMcQueen · Apr 26, 2020
I'm not risking my life around a buncha people in the park... I'm not risking it at a beach, restaurant or the movies... But best believe I will risk it all on November 3rd to vote this motherfucker out... I'll wear a damn hazmat suit if I have to...

9019 46909

We *must* remain irate at the unconscionableness of this social construct—for the pain most will never fathom, for the past that is in many ways unreconcilable despite our best efforts to grapple with such an unwieldy albatross. My own fury is likely endemic—it perhaps a reflection of certain warring entities within. Given that the electrifying legacy of my ancestry is part of my algorithm, maybe victims and victimizers are conspiring to raise my blood pressure—those conflicting branches of my family tree, its very roots like *lightning*, this problematic past, this rage, powering me forward.

And so, I walk angry.

In a COVID world, I find myself marching a hell of a lot. These power walks, propelling me through a weakened borough, are my earnest attempts at breaking the fettering monotony, trying my best to outpace the ever-encroaching melancholy of lockdown. As I slice through avenues, rounding the corners bracketing my Brooklyn neighborhood to the next, I find myself greeted by moving imagery. I am not referring to those declamatory displays, those large banners barely flapping in the summer wind. A new message enters into my traverse. Solemn and subtle, it cannot compete with the louder, tactical spectacles that are ubiquitous in the aftermath of our national uprising. No, as I make the jump from Park Slope to Crown Heights, though Black Lives Matter still bombards me from apartment windows, it is steadily supplanted by an immediate and literal contrast, one that is mournful and nearly missed. A darker reality I cannot outrun catches up with me. Its shadow cast, I am soon blanketed by this somber shroud, my brisk movement encumbered until it stops me dead in my tracks.

As I pass a makeshift memorial, it reaches out and grabs me. I soon find myself poring over the improvised shrine: the candles and liquor bottles bestrewing the corner, the poster boards stuck precariously to the front of the building, the empty baggies and splattered wax evidence of both a recent vigil and a palpable reverence for the newly departed. As I crawl past these penned remembrances of another fallen brotha, yet another victim of gun violence, I see not just signs of collective grief but compelling proof of a people in crisis. Seeing RIP scribbled over cardboard in marker is uniquely dispiriting. Hollowness replaces the full breath and beating heart I am still blessed with. This momentary emptiness evinces an unconscious connection. Though this feeling of loss is familiar, it is forged with a kid I will never know. As the stagnant air beneath my mask corroborates, the taste has been knocked completely out of my mouth. I swallow hard while doing the simple math, ingesting the dates and calculating that I have lived twice as long as he did. A young brotha, born *this* century, has been uprooted before he has even had a chance to blossom.

The flowers splayed across the pavement have begun to wilt in the summer heat, burning an image into me. As the cigar guts and gum stains festoon the rest of the scene, I tread through a forlornness thicker than the humid August air. Eventually passing the brothas perched nearby, sitting *shiva* as we do, I clock a blunt proffered and a bottle shared, a timeless visual and a sobering subtext to this national moratorium. And it is that we have *been* dying.

Our outpouring will mandate we pour a little out, yet this all presents an unmissable contradiction, yet another thing to ponder about Black America's concomitant pandemics. As I receive these contrasting impressions, I know the eyes of my brothas, too, are beholding all of this conflicting stimuli—our shared reality reflecting this outstanding nullification. A COVID world and a cruel summer see shootings up 80 percent in my metropolis. The streets are *hot* right now, hotter than ever, we again forced to endure a season of heightened loss.

As I now push off, picking up my stride, the requisite nod I impart to the brothas soon bounces right back. It evidence of yet another truth: we will always recognize one another. A knowing look, an almost imperceptible tilt of the head that says "I see you" even when the world does not. A lifetime can be contained in a single glance, a bevy of words expressed but ultimately unspoken. A sort of confidentiality agreement is spirited. Aware a grave outcome awaits some, by acknowledging one another, we concede this fate—it the only thing separating any one of us from one day having our epitaph scribbled on the side of a ripped-up box.

Early on, I stumbled upon one of the many truths I was fortunate enough to trip over during the course of this writing, a truth that twisted me up like a hyperextended ankle, the shooting pain producing a throb in my fuckin' head. As I posited that I had not been set up to live, but, in all likelihood, the converse, as I journeyed every which way through my inner-city grid, past the indelible residue of conflict, violent scenes, and the vigils they triggered, this fact burrowed deeper. While lost in thought, thinking these very pages through, I found myself stumbling upon one ghastly scene after another. A penetrating certainty smacked me upside the head, it now *demanding* I take it all in: Leaving my apartment a few fateful minutes earlier for a trip to the bodega—the words having landed on the page a little faster, the hunger hitting moments sooner—I would not have arrived just as the cops cordoned off the area in front. No, I would not have been here to pick my head up just as I was about to walk through the police tape. The brutal crossfire minutes prior, the Black cadaver inside, suggests I could very well have crossed my own finish line.

Within the period of one week, I evaded two shootings by mere minutes. These scattered thunderstorms, that conflict I have eluded to, produced lightning strikes, leaving a twist of limbs and two brown trunks felled. My good fortune attributable to God or just dumb fuckin' luck, I escaped one tempest moments before it picked up and arrived at yet another in the fresh chaotic aftermath. Death always showing up a few moments before doing its business, and lingering ever so briefly after its completion, I noticed its slight tickle along the back of my neck—it herein making its presence felt.

As I breathe it all in, these close brushes soon elicit a concomitant sigh of relief. However, it will never imbue me with any false sense of confidence. Although brothas have no option *but* to walk boldly in a world that humbles us, our telling glances never betray any notion of reprieve.

For some, our terror will eventually escape the unconscious. No longer impalpable, this torment may even take up residence right down the street from us, our recurring nightmare inevitably *proving* tangible. Shit, I have had the same horror interrupt my slumber for years now. Running for my life, my legs have been rendered useless. The blasts keep coming in my direction, but I cannot dodge them. Sometimes, just as the fire hits me, I rocket awake, shirt drenched, heart racing. Other times, the atrocity is drawn out. I move through invisible quicksand, trying to run up a hill, but my damn feet will not move. Try as I might, I cannot escape my fate; my assailant gains on me, unleashing a slew of bullets that chew me to pieces.

I never presume I will be delivered from this hellish epitome. Anyone of us rues the day the macabre will be manifested, that day we find ourselves trapped in permanent darkness, the moment we arrive too soon to see the smoke and just feel the fire.

Cyrus McQueen @CyrusMMcQueen · Sep 11, 2019
6 white kids die from vaping and they look to ban it. How many black kids have died from gun violence and they don't do shit... #WednesdayWisdom

⟲ 2263   ♡ 8239

For Black folk, perhaps the most poignant day of your life is the morning you make the eye-opening discovery your nightmares are more tangible than your dreams. This sobering injunction finds some of us self-medicating, propping up street pharmacists and the warring tycoons of an underground economy. We find it is easier to open a bag and locate a feeling that has been blowing past us our entire lives. Diligently delaying a reconciliation with ourselves, we identify this fleeting sensation and chase it until the equally despairing day when it inevitably chases *us*.

For some, these are themes introduced to us, early and often, when adult behavior first invades our childhoods. The abuse doled out on us, the abuse we witness them doling out on themselves, breeds a sort of sick familiarity. Before long, we resurrect the agony—it *reborn* in our adult lives. This pain becomes the most reliable aspect of our world, so we carry it everywhere, like a cross we dare not bare. Eventually, we allow the past to spoil the present, along with the future, because we *choose* to nurture it. It now thoroughly preserved, our emotional pain heals over into a gnarl, these scars becoming badges we will never showcase. Since no one really *wants* to bring attention to such deep wounds, we assiduously work to distract from them. And though it ultimately hinders healing, the attitudes and dishonest accoutrements we adopt often do the trick, helping impede the inevitable. These sybaritic replacements we struggle to attain bely behavior that screams" look at me"—but not *really*.

However, it is often through acquiring our cover that we court disaster, tempting the fate of an unforgiving universe. Here, the rapacious and equally empty often look to subtract our value from their debt, some willing to abscond with *literally* all we have. Which means, in the end, for many of us, we are actually *dying* to be seen.

Sadly, some are assured they can achieve their much-needed release only *through* violence. Our palpable anger, though endemic and necessary to clarifying the contradictions of a brutal country, can, and often will, *backfire*. In our efforts to stifle a torturing inner life, to muffle this inner narrative, we train our ire on something we can actually see and hear. The living embodiment of what is within sees us *kill* the corroboration, poaching the life around, shattering those who reflect our unvoiced agony. Our breaking the mirror is an ostensible attempt to silence our disquietude, to erase *any* impinging incarnations. Because this American malware has programmed us to self-hate, and given what little we have, those who look as if they have more, those who look like they can take from us, those who simply *look* like us, can trigger this sudden crash. But unlike our white contemporaries, whose violent displays are cries that they deserve more from this country, ours are sadly because that same country has us convinced that we deserve *less*.

With a low price attached to us as Black folk, all of us, each and every one of us, tries to negotiate more. Yet our circumstances are worsened by the pressure of being pushed *and* pulled into oblivion concurrently. As such, our own unwitting contribution to this voiding calls for redressing. Often our self-hate begets self-inflicted wounds, which weakens our vessel further, the downward spiral roiled *because* we no longer consider ourselves worthy. Since conflict predates our arrival, it defining our rocky passage and its four-hundred-year aftermath, both it and its unhealthy byproducts are a steady part of our diet. Just as we have ingested white ideations of power, so, too, have we internalized those that reinforce our own sense of powerlessness. The resultant strife is all *but* inescapable. When no evidence disabuses us of our impending fall, some of us paddle vigorously toward it. At some point, we tire of battling America's exhausting current and getting absolutely nowhere so, we *allow* it to carry us, embracing the impending precipice. For some, accepting that plummet with no reservation, no fear, becomes the loudest, most defiant "fuck you" to this world that does not want us.

When our success rests with parties indifferent to a Black incarnation, our future hinging on a threshold to which our flesh *is* the barrier, we eventually work out that it is incumbent upon us to reverse course. We discover the most defiant thing we can do is to undercut the forces trying to rend our souls as well as our journeys. In this dynamic instant, we divine that survival actually *depends* on our rejecting any premise our country will come to our rescue. Although America's survival *is* tangential to our own, when our survival has never been America's priority, our Black asses realize it better become *ours*. Although our circumstances are indescribable, although racism is ineradicable, our very essence, like that of our ancestors, is *ineffable*. And so, given this vitalizing force, we determine it to be *highly* misguided, and debasing to their legacy, to continue extracting our self-worth through America's brutal sieve.

24

Amerriccaaah Will Nevvah Be De Same

I have certainly alluded to many of the more poignant aspects of Black life, yet I am compelled to share one more—one that is actually defining, of mammoth significance. For an African American, the most momentous day in your life is the day you discover *you* are the only one who is gonna set you free. To experience this clarity, to summon this quieting resolve, is in and of itself *freeing*. Seeking America's acceptance becomes a wholly worthless endeavor the instant you accept that your existence is of consequence. Allowing this most profound and empowering rumble to rock your core, you catch that elusive wind—this the stir that finally *will* carry you forward.

As Black Americans, we live in a world that was not designed to validate us. Reconciling this *is* part of our life work. Yet seeking such endorsement, as if it were a magic stitch capable of patching an existence made threadbare by design, is antithetical. No fulsome threads of approval strung together can repair the torn seams of an identity constructed around such profound irregularities. We should never expect that the forces trying to break us will suddenly reverse course and commit to righting our situation. It would be like expecting a leviathan to release you from its powerful jaws, dress your gaping wounds, and begin the delicate process of nursing you back to health. Given our raw deal and our continual triumph over a system that facilitates our

413

collective despair, we should place this repair job in the right hands. Continuing to think any differently is, again, to empower the oppressor, *overestimating* our detractors while undermining our intrinsic skill and majesty.

To be Black in the 21st century in an America that consciously elected an impotent bigot to spite us, and considering how quickly our waking moments became a nightmare, we accept that some dreams are immaterial. Whether we are hit with "nigger," a knee, or simply a repeated "no," if the last four (hundred) years have taught us anything, it is that continuing to tether our aspirations to our countrymen's improvement is imprudent. Like the great artisans, we must do our damnedest to create the life we deserve independent of them—molding our reality with our hands. Not to get too candid but perhaps we need only heed Voltaire's advice and commit to cultivating our own garden. The very product we now hold in our hands embodies this very edict. Though these words are nowhere nearly divine enough for this book to be regarded as any sort of immaculate conception, this literary baby was forced into being through the artificial insemination of self-publishing. If great art possesses the power to edify, taking cues from the 18th century philosopher, or even a 19th century titan like Walt Whitman, it is undeniable that one's own authority is ample to begin harvesting truths. A lifetime of "nigger" and "no" implies that America's allotment will remain scant, at best. If my expatiation has satiated, if I have imparted anything meaningful, it is that a man or woman of color need not always bank on such parlous entities. The greatest "fuck you" any of us can deliver during this most precarious passage is to steer clear of those perils, sail on home, and start sowing.

Like my intrepid grandmother, who watched from the Colored Section as Nazi POWs enjoyed privileges she could not, who managed to swallow these inexhaustible indignities without letting the poison erode her, she *knew* she possessed all the tools to mend America's damage. She repeatedly sat herself at a machine, and though inundated with discarded and discounted fabrics and patterns, she would piece together something resplendent and remarkable. We must *never* wait for permission to make an impact. If you are angry, then you already *have* your machine. The task is using it to create something smashing and singular.

Anyone who dares minimize or stigmatize Black anger certainly lacks a commitment to replacing it with love, respect, or any semblance of parity. Those who presume they can engender chagrin with the bromide of "Angry Black Man" or "Angry Black Woman" clearly ain't been paying attention. Their projected weakness belies the fact that *this* very engine has always powered us through America's front, ushering in progress while scorching complacency in the very process. Our rage rattles the stasis sustained on our discomfort. Frederick was *angry;* W.E.B., Malcolm, Martin, *and* Rosa were angry. The late great John Lewis instructed us all to "make some noise and get in good trouble." What do we imagine was the source of this profound impetus? To mistake the answer for one fuckin' second is to misrepresent the surge critical to our ascension. Anger *is* our power. The great lesson here is that America should not wait for things to go nuclear before respecting the innate potential *of* all that harnessed energy. It should not take a fallout for folks to grow a second pair of eyes, for finally probing their own debilitating intransigence.

Until parity supplants diversity, until we are not just seen but *wanted,* not merely visible but *valued,* until we can walk into a school or office and not be frozen out by that biting indifference, we shall *burn.* May our fire melt, or singe if necessary, for the worst thing any of us can be is *numb.* The moment we are numb to the pain, it signals the worst can go do down and we will no longer even *feel* it.

Undeniably, America *is* having a moment. But I have been an American for forty years—my people, for four *hundred*—and I was Black long before the hashtags. I realize hope carried us but only so far. Hope can become a garrison protecting us from the reality closing in on us. Its pacifying reassurance can convince us we are actually free from threat. However, hope divorced from action will eventually jeopardize all we gain. Before long, it will leave us sitting ducks. America resembles a netherworld now more than ever, and its unmasked troops are on the move to erode any lingering semblance of progress. If our hellish past and present are any indication, the future can easily mirror either. Because America has never *not* been at war with us, we must continue advancing even if it kills us. The immediate stakes demand we snatch victory from the iguana-like jowls of this ignominious, dangerous president—history's latest yellow-belly general—because we are gonna be dead either way.

There comes a point when you realize you *better* get fuckin' angry. *Especially* on Election Day! You know damn well I *will* be marching to the polls *angry.*

Though we stand on one side of this determining outcome, steadily approaching the election, our staggering regression both trails my every step and greets me at every turn. One could say I rehearse November 3rd as I trek, this an exacting walkthrough *through* Brooklyn. Noticeable vestiges of our great setback greet me. I pass the very cafe I sat in to compile most of these pages, but it is permanently shuttered, one of the many casualties of COVID. I happen upon more businesses now closed for good and others on noticeable life support. Valiant efforts to make lemonade out of a bitter and sour outcome find several setting up tables outside, these makeshift patios a sign they hope the sidewalk can help them squeeze out even a small amount of promise—just enough to keep going. Though I saunter, the scene jogs my memory, as I recall an impression from the woeful aftermath of Trump's election—one providing the smallest glimmer of hope on that dark portentous day.

I walked these very same streets then. That day in question, after he had won, when I was otherwise numb, my body moving without a compass, a vibrant yellow beckoned me. As I was out to sea, the tumult from that great emotional swell had found me rollicking past a school, my trudging signaling that I was in desperate need of help. And then I heard her concern, voiced from a few paces in front of me, her sweet lilt forcing me to slowly raise my head. "Oh no! Not you too baby?"

I looked up to bask in the glow of the most ebullient Black woman. A clear beacon appearing before me, her vivacity parting the clouds, her infectious spirit reeling me in. Although momentarily taken aback, I soon melted in her syrupy grin. This school crossing guard, this most effervescent sista clad in her fluorescent vest, resembled a lighthouse carrying me across this rough fairway. "All day it's been the same thing," my sybil rhapsodized. "I keep tellin' folks, don't let it take your joy!" Now, admittedly inconsolable, I attempted to brush off her sage encouragement. I went, "Yeah, I know, sis, but this Trump shit is *bad*." The words had barely left my mouth before she waved 'em off, her head and arms moving vigorously in opposing directions. "Listen to me!" she commanded. Her eyes locked into mine, her index finger extended to make her point. Arrested by her reassurance, I was hit by the glint from her gold tooth, she now emitting a palpable radiance. Through a disarming grin, she repeated herself, emphatically punching her lesson out in a monosyllabic flurry to bring it all home. "Don't. Let. It. Take. Your. *Joy!* Hear me?"

I will not lie: hers is a righteous lesson, a salient lesson, but a lesson I have nonetheless struggled with for years. At times, it calls to me, piercing the sonorous clatter of despondency. Yet even though I would take to the performing stage, attempting to embody this very tutorial, as the laughs subsided, and the showroom cleared, I inevitably found myself re-engulfed in this miasma. The oppressiveness, the *seriousness*, was just too conspicuous to ignore. Smokey Robinson could not have penned it any better—"The tears of a clown, when no one's around." The second I *stopped* clowning and stepped off stage, I became joyless. There is no *real* levity when it comes to Donald Trump and this unpleasant American moment. And, ironically, there is no such thing as hyperbole when it comes to his diabolical imprint either. Hell, after hundreds of pages, the word-traffic of these chapters, I fear I may have misled you, dear reader, by grossly *understating* his superlative repugnance.

In our singular time of record unemployment and food insecurity, Trump and the Republicans are mainly concerned with gutting Obamacare and Social Security, and repealing *Roe v Wade*. They are addressing neither the seriousness nor the economic and epidemiological wallop of COVID. I need not even touch on their deleterious impact on race relations in America to highlight the almost *delusional* disconnect. As of this writing, over 200,000 Americans who were here on New Year's Day are gone forever. At least 100,000 more will likely never see 2021, and to this, our remorseless president has responded, "It is what it is." As it currently stands, Trump and Republicans in both Congress and in the courts, in state capitols and in communities across the country, have neither enforced nor even sought to popularize protocols that would reduce the bloated crisis. U.S. infection rates continue to dwarf most other countries, with our nightmare taking on a new pulsating tenor as many parents resign themselves to sending America's children back to school—leveraging the most precious canary imaginable, thrusting them down into mines that have already proven caustic.

I hope that Donald Trump will be gone when you read this. Hope again being the optimal word, I invest less in it than in the collective anger we can depend on to emit a powerful light—one that can force this spectral entity back into the shadows from whence it emerged. And perhaps this will stand as an account, for eyes yet to open, of the kind of nightmare that *can* emerge from the illogical mind of American madness. Our nation's tribal politics, the most dangerous output of a warped brain, are a place in which many *willingly* fortify caste and barter their race and status for Black death. Even now, as their corpulent champion promises to not go gently into that great night, with his threats to mail-in voting and forecasted malfeasance, it is anyone's guess what resentments he and his henchman *will* tap into to prevent Joe Biden and his brilliant Black running mate from taking office in the West Wing.

A storm is brewing on the horizon, but today the sun peeks between the branches of my tree-lined block. These rays land softly on my tense forehead, my countenance slowly relaxing as they swathe me in a rejuvenating warmth. The notifications from my phone vibrate my thigh, but I dare not allow the virtual world to supplant the real one and the peerless beauty that abounds. Right now, real birds are chirping. Besides, whatever it is can wait. Taking cues from the calming atmosphere, my stroll slows to a meander. Now a mere heartbeat from home, I find my fears begin to gently dissipate. Soon, the signs of life all around me completely deaden them. I notice I am experiencing the infectious kind of joy that is in ready supply . . . *if* you do not allow anyone to take it. Diverse Brooklyn bastions having taken up permanent residence inside me, I see reflections of their didactic admonishment all around. I peek between the jumble of trees to see a group of West Indian men playing soccer. It is a standing match that I have happened upon on Sundays past. Their writhing energy emanates from the trodden pitch, their patois cutting through the air like the ball itself every time they strike at the goal. And as I watch their beautiful locks dancing in the bright sun, an indefatigable spirit revisits me. Amid this mishmash of uncertainty and visceral determination, one man's canorous dictum reverberates in my inner ear. Before long, the furrows in my brow recede completely and I even smuggle in a smile under my mask.

"Amerriccaaah will NEVVAH be de same!"

"Yeah," I chuckle. "Let's all hope so."

Cyrus McQueen @CyrusMMcQueen · Nov 7

For a President who evicted Black people from their homes, how truly ironic that Black people evicted him from his... #Atlanta #Philly #Detroit #Election2020results #BidenHarris2020

💬 116   ↻ 684   ♡ 3.1K   ↑   ⫯⫯⫯

Acknowledgments

As my dedication implies, I could not have arrived at this point without the love, support, and encouragement of several women. I firstly must express a deep and profound gratitude for my incredible wife Leanne. With all the words I have used, none capture the level of love and respect I hold for her. Writing a book is an all-encompassing endeavor, and be it the moods, the panic, or the middle-of-the-night moments when I'd light up the room to type a thought in my phone, her enduring belief enabled me to compile these pages. I simply cannot overstate her importance to the process or the finished product. She is my champion and my shepherd. Her spirit, her sacrifice, her wisdom—they are invaluable. I truly cherish her!

I must acknowledge the phenomenal woman who raised and inspired me: my mother Candelaria. The woman who taught me to read and write, and who turned our home into a library, has long fostered in me a sense of pride and purpose. In writing this book, I honor her and the myriad sacrifices she made to raise my sister and me, mostly on her own. I am the product of a strong Black woman who, in her selflessness and brilliance, cultivated a home where learning was the highest priority. If I am anything, it is a testament to her edifying example. I love her *mostest*.

I must thank my late father Tommie. His strength and spirit still fill me. His absence haunts me till this day, but I hope I have made him proud. Ditto for my dear brother Douglas, the Duke, losing you so young is indescribable. Your beautiful spirit remains with me.

Having been blessed many times over, I attribute my song to the chorus of strong women who have lifted me up: My late great-grandmother Gladys; my indefatigable and peerless grandmother Norma Jean; my mighty sisters Amber and Evelyn; and my fierce aunts Nina, Jewel, Sharon, and Deborah. I am only who I am because so many loved me, including those fabulous men in my life; my stepfather Tessil, Uncle Glenn, and big brother David.

The book itself reflects the indelible imprint of Delanda Coleman, my project manager. Seeing something in me, she helped bring this project to fruition, her advice and expertise proving critical. This book would never have been designed, printed, and sold without her tutelage. She is one of the most incredible and inspiring people I have had the privilege of knowing. I also must give a heartfelt and impassioned shout out to Marc S. Miller, my fantastic editor. This book reflects my good fortune in finding him. In his brilliance and patience, he sliced through a forest of prose, nearly seven hundred pages at one point, to refine what you now hold in your hands. I am indebted to him for taking a chance on a verbose unknown. His grace and taste helped me craft the best version of this book possible. I have profound appreciation for him. I must take a moment to thank my high school English teacher, and now friend, Barry. His proofreading skills were a boon to this project. The man who gave dreaded vocabulary quizzes every Monday, who undeniably expanded my literary palate, took the time to help an old student. I will never forget that. I love that man so damn much. I must also thank Susan Ely, a good friend who wore many hats during this project, her photography, marketing, and web design skills indispensable to getting this project off the ground. She is a true gem!

I would be remiss in not mentioning the profound impact of those mentors who helped guide me as a youth, including Earl Stafford, the incredible man who's molded many young Black Bostonians and who first put the thought in my head that I should consider writing a book. I recall scoffing at the time and will humbly take all the "I told you so's" I have coming to me the next time I see him. Nancy Murray who expanded my knowledge and understanding of socio-political movements while shepherding me through the South. I've never forgotten her sage and generous tutelage. And Larry Oni who's brilliance and patience helped me identify the antidote to societies ills are best found through rich discussion and interdependence. His kindness and wisdom has remained with me all these years.

Lastly, I wish to express my deepest, fondest appreciation for my Twitter family. We have been in the social media trenches together, and their support and corroboration compelled me to write more. That my thoughts resonated with so many motivated me to break out of the character limit and endeavor to impart something more lasting. Their generous spirit carried me. Words cannot encapsulate the profound undercurrent roiled by those within the Resistance. I love each and every one of you. *We* did it!

Cyrus McQueen is a comedian, cultural critic, and writer whose mirthful and insightful analysis of race and politics has resonated throughout the Twitterverse. His tweets pertaining to politics, pop culture, and race have routinely landed in Variety, TIME magazine, HuffPost, and BuzzFeed. A Top 20 Finalist on Season 9 of NBC's Last Comic Standing, McQueen has also been featured in the A24 film Obvious Child and on AXS TV's Gotham Comedy Live. Tweeting Truth to Power: Chronicling Our Caustic Politics, Crazed Times, & the Great Black & White Divide is McQueen's first book.

Cover and author photograph by Susan Ely

Cover design by Alfred Obare (Behance)

Made in the USA
Las Vegas, NV
29 August 2021